Syntax

Introducing Linguistics

This outstanding series is an indispensable resource for students and teachers – a concise and engaging introduction to the central subjects of contemporary linguistics. Presupposing no prior knowledge on the part of the reader, each volume sets out the fundamental skills and knowledge of the field, and so provides the ideal educational platform for further study in linguistics.

1   Andrew Spencer   *Phonology*
2   John Saeed   *Semantics*, Second Edition
3   Barbara Johnstone   *Discourse Analysis*
4   Andrew Carnie   *Syntax*, Second Edition

Syntax

A Generative Introduction
Second Edition

Andrew Carnie

BLACKWELL PUBLISHING
350 Main Street, Malden, MA 02148-5020, USA
9600 Garsington Road, Oxford OX4 2DQ, UK
550 Swanston Street, Carlton, Victoria 3053, Australia

First edition published 2002 by Blackwell Publishers Ltd
Second edition published 2007 by Blackwell Publishing Ltd

3   2007

Library of Congress Cataloging-in-Publication Data

Carnie, Andrew, 1969–
    Syntax : a generative introduction / Andrew Carnie. — 2nd ed.
      p. cm.
    Includes bibliographical references and index.
    ISBN 978-1-4051-3384-5 (alk. paper)
    1. Grammar, Comparative and general—Syntax. 2. Generative
grammar.   I. Title.
    P295.C37 2006
    415—dc22
                                        2006008835

A catalogue record for this title is available from the British Library.

Layout by Andrew Carnie. Typeset in 10 pt Palatino using ReadSmart® from Language Technologies Inc.
Printed and bound in Singapore by COS Printers Pte Ltd

The publisher's policy is to use permanent paper from mills that operate a sustainable forestry policy, and which has been manufactured from pulp processed using acid-free and elementary chlorine-free practices. Furthermore, the publisher ensures that the text paper and cover board used have met acceptable environmental accreditation standards.

For further information on Blackwell Publishing, visit our website:
www.blackwellpublishing.com

Dedicated with love to my parents, Robert and Jean
and in memory of my teacher and mentor, Ken Hale

Contents

4 Structural Relations   103

5 Binding Theory   135

A Glossary and other supplementary materials can be found on the book's website at www.blackwellpublishing.com

Preface and Acknowledgments

Almost every preface to every syntax textbook out there starts out by telling the reader how different this book is from every other syntax textbook. On one hand, this is often the truth: each author shows their own particular spin or emphasis. This is certainly true of this textbook. For example, you'll be hard pressed to find another textbook on Principles and Parameters syntax that uses as many Irish examples as this one does. Nor will you find another P&P textbook with a supplementary discussion of alternative theoretical approaches like LFG or HPSG. On the other hand, let's face facts. The basic material to be covered in an introductory textbook doesn't really vary much. One linguist may prefer a little more on binding theory, and a little less on control, etc. In this text, I've attempted to provide a relatively balanced presentation of most of the major issues and I've tried to do this in a student-friendly way. I've occasionally abstracted away from some of the thornier controversies, where I felt they weren't crucial to a student understanding the basics. This may, to a certain extent, make the professional syntactician feel that I've cut corners or laid out too rosy a picture. I did this on purpose, however, to give students a chance to absorb the fundamentals before challenging the issues. This is a textbook, not a scholarly tome, so its aim is to reach as many students as possible. The style is deliberately low key and friendly. This doesn't mean I don't want the students to challenge the material I've presented here. Throughout the book, you'll find gray "textboxes" that contain issues for further discussion, or interesting tidbits. Many of the problem sets also invite the student to challenge the black and white presentation I've given in the text. I encourage instructors to assign these, and students to do them, as they form an important part of the textbook. Instructors may note that if a favorite topic is not dealt with in the body of the text, a problem set may very well treat the question.

A quick word on the level of this textbook: This book is intended as an introduction to syntactic theory. It takes the student through most of the major issues in Principles and Parameters, from tree drawing to constraints on movement. While this book is written as an introduction, some students have reported it to be challenging. I use this text in my upper division undergraduate introduction to syntax with success, but I can certainly see it being used in more advanced classes. I hope instructors will flesh out the book, and walk their students through some of the thornier issues.

This textbook has grown out of my lecture notes for my own classes. Needless to say, the form and shape of these notes have been influenced in terms of choice of material and presentation by the textbooks my own students have used. While the book you are reading is entirely my fault, it does owe a particular intellectual debt to the following three textbooks, which I have used in teaching at various times:

Cowper, Elizabeth (1992) *A Concise Introduction to Syntactic Theory: The Government and Binding Approach*. Chicago: Chicago University Press.

Haegeman, Liliane (1994) *Introduction to Government and Binding Theory* (2nd edition). Oxford: Blackwell.

Radford, Andrew (1988) *Transformational Grammar: A First Course*. Cambridge: Cambridge University Press.

I'd like to thank the authors of these books for breaking ground in presenting a complicated and integrated theory to the beginner. Writing this book has given me new appreciation for the difficulty of this task and their presentation of the material has undoubtedly influenced mine.

Sadly, during the final stages of putting the first edition of this text together, my dissertation director, teacher, mentor, and academic hero, Ken Hale passed away after a long illness. Ken always pushed the idea that theoretical syntax is best informed by cross-linguistic research; while at the same time, the accurate documentation of languages requires a sophisticated understanding of grammatical theory. These were important lessons that I learned from Ken and I hope students will glean the significance of both by reading this text. While I was writing this book (and much other work) Ken gave me many comments and his unfettered support. He was a great man and I will miss him terribly.

This, the second edition of this book, is considerably different from the first edition. Here is a brief list of the major differences between the two editions. This list is not comprehensive, many more minor differences can be found.

- The exercise sections of the chapters are now organized differently and are greatly expanded. Exercises are presented in the order that the material appears in the chapter. I have attempted to categorize each exercise for level and type.
- There are two types of problem sets: General and Challenge. These two types roughly correspond to the exercises that I assign to my regular students and my honors students respectively. Challenge Problem Sets often challenge the straightforward presentation of the material in the main body of the text.
- The former chapter 2 on structure and parts of speech has been split into two chapters. The new chapter 2 contains new information on subcategorization

that some instructors requested to better inform students about the role of part of speech in phrase structure processes. Also Adjectives are now distinguished from Adverbs.

- The phrase structure rules in the new chapter 3 have been completely revised. In particular, I'm using non-X-bar versions of TP and CP here, and have added embedded clauses to all the relevant rules.
- The definitions of precedence, exhaustive domination and c-command have all been significantly revised in the chapter on structural relations. A limited version of government is given for those instructors who wish to teach it to their students.
- The chapters on X-bar theory have many more trees and examples.
- DPs are used consistently from chapter 7 forward.
- I have added categories to the theta grids in the chapter on the Lexicon in order to tie them to the subcategories introduced in chapter 2.
- A new section on stacked VPs and affix-hopping has been added to the chapter on head movement
- VP-internal subjects are used consistently from chapter 9 forward
- The treatment of passives in chapter 10 is completely different from the previous edition. I have moved towards a Baker, Johnson and Roberts style approach where the *-en* morphology is directly assigned the internal theta role and accusative case by the verb in the syntax rather than in the lexicon.
- The treatment of locality conditions in the chapter on *wh*-movement is entirely new. I've dropped subjacency in favor of an MLC based approach. The chapter now includes an inventory of the major island types; but theoretical coverage is only given to *wh*-islands. (Although the chapter also contains a brief discussion of the Head-Movement Constraint and Super-raising in the context of the MLC).
- Chapter 12 now contains a more accurate discussion of *wh*-in situ and develops the ideas of feature checking, covert movement, and SPELLOUT.
- There is a brand new chapter on split VPs in a brand new section on "advanced topics," including sections on object shift, ditransitives, a Lasnik style analysis of Pseudogapping and a Hornstein style analysis of ACD.
- The chapter on Raising and Control has been moved to the new part of the book on advanced topics, and uses a split VP (vP-AgrOP-VP) structure to avoid ternary branching.
- There is a new chapter on advanced topics in binding theory. This looks at issues on level of representation, chains and the copy theory of movement. It also takes a relativized view of binding domain consistent with Chomsky (1986).
- I've taken some of the more controversial "comparing theories" language out of the chapters on LFG and HPSG.

I hope that instructors and students will find these revisions helpful. I have attempted where possible to take into account all the many comments and suggestions I received from people using the first edition. Although of course in order to maintain consistency, I was unable to do them all.

Acknowledgements:

I'd like to thank the many people who taught me syntax through the years: Barb Brunson, Noam Chomsky, Elizabeth Cowper, Ken Hale, Alec Marantz, Diane Massam, Jim McCloskey, Shigeru Miyagawa, and David Pesetsky. A number of people have read through this book or the previous edition and have given me extensive and helpful comments: William Alexander, Ash Asudeh, Brett Baker, Andy Barss, Mark Baltin, Luis Barragan, Emily Bender, Abbas Benmamoun, Joan Bresnan, Dirk Bury, Roy Chan, Danny Chen, Deborah Chen Pichler, Barbara Citko, Peter Cole, Lorenzo Demery, Sheila Dooley, Yehuda Falk, Leslie Ford, Alexandra Galani, Jila Ghomeshi, Erin Good, Paul Hagstrom, Ken Hale, Heidi Harley, Josh Harrison, Rachel Hayes, Bernhard Heigl, One-Soon Her, Stephan Hurtubise, Alana Johns, Mark Johnson, Simin Karimi, Andreas Kathol, Péter Lazar, Anne Lobeck, Leila Lomashivili, Sarah Longstaff, Ahmad Reza Lotfi, Ricardo Mairal, Joan Maling, Jack Martin, Diane Massam, Nathan McWhorter, Dave Medeiros, Martha McGinnis, Mirjana Miskovic-Lukovic, Jon Nissenbaum, Peter Norquest, Kazutoshi Ohno, Heidi Orcutt, Hyeson Park, David Pesetsky, Colin Phillips, Carl Pollard, Janet Randall, Norvin Richards, Frank Richter, Betsy Ritter, Ed Rubin, Ivan Sag, Theresa Satterfield, Leslie Saxon, Leah Shocket, Dan Siddiqi, Nick Sobin, Peggy Speas, Tania Strahan, Joshua Strauss, Lisa deMena Travis, Robert Van Valin, Enwei Wang, Dainon Woudstra, Susi Wurmbrand, Kim Youngroung, and several anonymous Blackwell reviewers. I'm absolutely convinced I've left someone off this large list, if it's you many apologies, I really did appreciate the help you gave me. The students in my *Introduction to Syntax* classes in Michigan in 1997, and in Arizona in 1998-2006 have used all or parts of this textbook as their reading. Thanks to them for their patience and suggestions. A special thanks to Dave Medeiros who has been my TA during the writing of this edition, his contributions and suggestions have been invaluable. A number of problem sets in this book were graciously contributed by Sheila Dooley, Jila Ghomeshi, Erin Good, Heidi Harley, Simin Karimi, Chris Kennedy, Amy LaCross, Betsy Ritter and Leslie Saxon. Tom Bever, Chris Nicholas, and Roeland Hancock at Language Technologies, Inc. have been incredibly helpful and responsive in their implementation of the ReadSmart technology on this text. Chris Nicholas is to be particularly thanked for his last-minute late-night help in formatting. I also owe a great debt to all my colleagues here at the University of Arizona for their help and support. In particular, Diana Archangeli, Andy Barss, Sheila Dooley, Sandiway Fong, Mike Hammond, Heidi Harley, Eloise Jelinek, Simin Karimi, Diane Ohala, Adam Ussishkin, and Andy Wedel deserve special mention. Ada Brunstein, Sarah Coleman, Lisa Eaton, Simon Eckley, Tami Kaplan, Becky Kennison, Anna Oxbury, Rhonda Pearce, Beth Remmes, and Steve Smith of Blackwell all deserve many thanks for encouraging me to write this and the previous edition up, and then smoothing its way towards production. My family (Jean, Bob, Morag, Fiona, Pangur and Calvin) were all incredible in their support and love. Go raibh maith agaibh!

The clip art in chapters 1 and 6 is taken from the Microsoft Clip Art Gallery and is used with permission. This usage does not imply Microsoft's endorsement of this book.

Part 1

Preliminaries

chapter 1

Generative Grammar

0. PRELIMINARIES

Although we use it every day, and although we all have strong opinions about its proper form and appropriate use, we rarely stop to think about the wonder of language. So-called language "experts" like William Safire tell us about the misuse of *hopefully* or lecture us about the origins of the word *boondoggle*, but surprisingly, they never get at the true wonder of language: how it actually works. Think about it for a minute; you are reading this and understanding it but you have no conscious knowledge of how you are doing it. The study of this mystery is the science of linguistics. This book is about one aspect of how language works – how sentences are structured: *syntax*.

Language is a psychological or cognitive property of humans. That is, there is some set of neurons in my head firing madly away that allows me to sit here and produce this set of letters, and there is some other set of neurons in your head firing away that allows you to translate these squiggles into coherent ideas and thoughts. There are several subsystems at work here. If you were listening to me speak, I would be producing sound waves with my vocal cords and articulating particular speech sounds with my tongue, lips, and vocal cords. On the other end of things you'd be hearing those sound waves and translating them into speech sounds using your auditory apparatus. The study of the acoustics and articulation of speech is called *phonetics*. Once you've translated the waves of sound into mental representations of speech sounds, you analyze them into syllables and pattern them appropriately. For example, speakers of English know that the made-up word *bluve* is a possible word of English, but the word *bnuck* is not. This is part of the science called **phonology**. Then you take these groups of sounds and organize them into meaningful units (called morphemes) and words. For example, the word *dancer* is made up of two meaningful bits: *dance* and the suffix *-er*. The study of this level of Language is called **morphology**. Next you organize the words into phrases and sentences. **Syntax** is the cover term for studies of this level of Language. Finally, you take the sentences and phrases you hear and translate them into thoughts and ideas. This last step is what we refer to as the **semantic** level of Language.

Syntax, then, studies the level of Language that lies between words and the meaning of utterances: sentences. It is the level that mediates between sounds that someone produces (organized into words) and what they intended to say.

Perhaps one of the truly amazing aspects of the study of Language is not the origins of the word *demerit*, or how to properly punctuate a quote inside parentheses, or how kids have, like, destroyed the English language, eh? Instead it's the question of how we subconsciously get from sounds to meaning. This is the study of syntax.

Language vs. language

When I utter the term *language*, most people immediately think of some particular language such as English, French, or KiSwahili. But this is not the way linguists use the term; when linguists talk about **Language** (or i-language), they are generally talking about the *ability* of humans to speak any (particular) language. Some people (most notably Noam Chomsky) also call this the **Human Language Capacity**. Language (written with a capital L) is the part of the mind or brain that allows you to speak, whereas *language* (with a lower case l) (also known as e-language) is an instantiation of this ability (like French or English). In this book we'll be using language as our primary data, but we'll be trying to come up with a model of Language.

---

1. SYNTAX AS A COGNITIVE SCIENCE

Cognitive science is a cover term for a group of disciplines that all aim for the same goal: describing and explaining human beings' ability to think (or more particularly, to think about abstract notions like subatomic particles, the possibility of life on other planets or even how many angels can fit on the head of a pin, etc.). One thing that distinguishes us from other animals, even relatively smart ones like chimps and elephants, is our ability to use productive, combinatory Language. Language plays an important role in how we think about abstract notions, or, at the very least, Language appears to be structured in such a way that it allows us to express abstract notions.[1] The discipline of linguistics, along with psychology, philosophy, and computer science, thus forms an important subdiscipline within cognitive science. Sentences are how we get at expressing abstract thought processes, so the study of syntax is an important foundation stone for understanding how we communicate and interact with each other as humans.

2. MODELING SYNTAX

The dominant theory of syntax is due to Noam Chomsky and his colleagues, starting in the mid 1950s and continuing to this day. This theory, which has had many different names through its development (Transformational Grammar (TG), Transformational Generative Grammar, Standard Theory, Extended Standard Theory, Government and Binding Theory (GB), Principles and Parameters approach (P&P) and Minimalism (MP)), is often given the blanket name *Generative Grammar*. A number of alternate theories of syntax have also branched off of this research program; these include Lexical-Functional Grammar (LFG) and Head-Driven Phrase Structure Grammar (HPSG). These are also considered part of generative grammar; but we won't cover them extensively in this book, except in chapters 16 and 17. The particular version of generative grammar that we will mostly look at here is roughly the *Principles and Parameters* approach, although we will occasional stray from this into the more recent version called *Minimalism*.

The underlying thesis of generative grammar is that sentences are generated by a subconscious set of procedures (like computer programs). These procedures are part of our minds (or of our cognitive abilities if you prefer). The goal of syntactic theory is to model these procedures. In other words, we are trying to figure out what we subconsciously know about the syntax of our language.

In generative grammar, the means for modeling these procedures is through a set of formal grammatical *rules*. Note that these rules are nothing

---

[1] Whether language constrains what abstract things we can think about (this idea is called the Sapir-Whorf hypothesis) is a matter of great debate and one that lies outside the domain of syntax per se.

like the rules of grammar you might have learned in school. These rules don't tell you how to properly punctuate a sentence or not to split an infinitive. Instead, they tell you the order in which to put your words (in English, for example, we put the subject of a sentence before its verb; this is the kind of information encoded in generative rules). These rules are thought to generate the sentences of a language, hence the name *generative* grammar. You can think of these rules as being like the command lines in a computer program. They tell you step by step how to put together words into a sentence. We'll look at precise examples of these rules in the next chapter. But before we can get into the nitty-gritty of sentence structure, let's look at some of the underlying assumptions of generative grammar.

Noam Chomsky

Avram Noam Chomsky was born on the 7th of December 1928, in Philadelphia. His father was a Hebrew grammarian and his mother a teacher. Chomsky got his Ph.D. from the University of Pennsylvania, where he studied linguistics under Zellig Harris. He took a position in machine translation and language teaching at the Massachusetts Institute of Technology. Eventually his ideas about the structure of language transformed the field of linguistics. Reviled by some and admired by others, Chomsky's ideas have laid the groundwork for the discipline of linguistics, and have been very influential in computer science, and philosophy.

　　Chomsky is also one of the leading intellectuals in the anarchist socialist movement. His political writings about the media and political injustice have profoundly influenced many. Chomsky is among the most quoted authors in the world (among the top ten and the only living person on the list).

---

3. SYNTAX AS SCIENCE – THE SCIENTIFIC METHOD

To many people the study of language properly belongs in the domain of the humanities. That is, the study of language is all about the beauty of its usage in fine (and not so fine) literature. However, there is no particular reason, other than our biases, that the study of language should be confined to a humanistic approach. It is also possible to approach the study of language from a scientific perspective; this is the domain of linguistics. People who study literature often accuse linguists of abstracting away from the richness of good prose and obscuring the beauty of language. Nothing could be further from the truth. Most linguists, including the present author, enjoy nothing more than reading a finely crafted piece of fiction, and many linguists often study, as a sideline, the more humanistic aspects of language. This doesn't mean, however, that one can't appreciate and study the formal properties (or rules) of language and do it from a scientific perspective. The two approaches to language study are both valid; they complement each other; and neither takes away from the other.

Science is perhaps one of the most poorly defined words of the English language. We regularly talk of scientists as people who study bacteria, particle physics, and the formation of chemical compounds, but ask your average Joe or Jill on the street what science means, and you'll be hard pressed to get a decent definition. Science refers to a particular methodology for study: the scientific method. The scientific method dates backs to the ancient Greeks, such as Aristotle, Euclid, and Archimedes. The method involves observing some data, making some generalizations about patterns in the data, developing hypotheses that account for these generalizations, and testing the hypotheses against more data. Finally, the hypotheses are revised to account for any new data and then tested again. A flow chart showing the method is given in (1):

1)

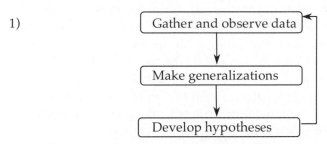

In syntax, we apply this methodology to sentence structure. Syntacticians start[2] by observing data about the language they are studying, then they make generalizations about patterns in the data (e.g., in simple English declarative sentences, the subject precedes the verb). They then generate a hypothesis – preferably one that makes predictions – and test the hypothesis against more syntactic data, and if necessary go back and re-evaluate their hypotheses.

---

[2] This is a bit of an oversimplification. We really have a "chicken and the egg" problem here. You can't know what data to study unless you have a hypothesis about what is important, and you can't have a hypothesis unless you have some basic understanding of the data. Fortunately, as working syntacticians this philosophical conundrum is often irrelevant, as we can just jump feet-first into both the hypothesis-forming and data-analysis at the same time.

Hypotheses are only useful to the extent that they make *predictions*. A hypothesis that makes no predictions (or worse yet, predicts everything) is useless from a scientific perspective. In particular, the hypothesis must be *falsifiable*. That is we must, in principle, be able to look for some data, which if true, show that the hypothesis is wrong. This means that we are often looking for the cases where our hypotheses predict that a sentence will be grammatical (and it is not), or the cases where they predict that the sentence will be ungrammatical (but it is).

In syntax, hypotheses are called *rules,* and the group of hypotheses that describe a language's syntax is called a *grammar*.

Do Rules Really Exist?

Generative grammar claims to be a theory of cognitive psychology, so the natural question to ask at this point is whether formal rules really exist in the brain/minds of speakers. After all, a brain is a mass of neurons firing away, how can formal mathematical rules exist up there? Remember, however, that we are attempting to *model* Language, we aren't trying to describe Language exactly. This question confuses two disciplines: psychology and neurology. Psychology is concerned with the mind, which represents the output and the abstract organization of the brain. Neurology is concerned with the actual firing of the neurons and the physiology of the brain. Generative grammar doesn't try to be a theory of neurology. Instead it is a model of the psychology of Language. Obviously, the rules don't exist, per se in our brains, but they do represent the external behavior of the mind. For more discussion of this issue, look at the readings in the further reading section of this chapter.

The term *grammar* strikes terror into the hearts of many people. But you should note that there are two ways to go about writing grammatical rules. One is to tell people how they should speak (this is of course the domain of English teachers and copy-editors); we call these kinds of rule *prescriptive rules* (as they prescribe how people should speak according to some standard). Some examples of prescriptive rules include "never end a sentence with a preposition," "use *whom* not *who*," "don't split infinitives." These rules tell us how we are supposed to use our language. The other approach is to write rules that describe how people *actually* speak, whether or not they are speaking "correctly." These are called *descriptive rules*. Consider for a moment the approach we're taking in this book; which of the two types (descriptive or prescriptive) is more scientific? Which kind of rule is more likely to give us insight into how the mind uses Language? For these reasons, we focus on descriptive rules. This doesn't mean that prescriptive rules aren't important (in fact, in the problem sets section of this chapter you are asked to critically examine the question of descriptive vs. prescriptive rules), but for our purposes descriptive rules are more important. For an interesting discussion of the prescriptive/descriptive debate, see Pinker's 1995 book: *The Language Instinct*.

You now have enough information to answer General Problem Set 1

3.1 An Example of the Scientific Method as Applied to Syntax

Let's turn now to a real world application of the scientific method to some language data. The following data concern the form of a specific kind of noun, called an ***anaphor*** (plural: ***anaphors***, the phenomenon is called ***anaphora***). These are the nouns that end with *-self* (e.g., *himself, herself, itself,* etc.). In chapter 5, we look at the distribution of anaphora in detail; here we'll only consider one superficial aspect of them. In the following sentences, as is standard in the syntactic literature, a sentence that isn't well-formed is marked with an ***asterisk*** (*) before it. For these sentences assume that *Bill* is male and *Sally* is female.

2) a) Bill kissed himself.
   b) *Bill kissed herself.
   c) Sally kissed herself.
   d) *Sally kissed himself.
   e) *Kiss himself.

To the unskilled eye, the ill-formed sentences in (2b and d) just look silly. It is obvious that Bill can't kiss herself, because Bill is male. However, no matter how matter-of-factly obvious this is, it is part of a bigger generalization about the distribution of anaphors. In particular, the generalization we can draw about the sentences in (2) is that an anaphor must agree in ***gender*** with the noun it refers to (its ***antecedent***). So in (2a and b) we see that the anaphor must agree in gender with *Bill*, its antecedent. The anaphor must take the masculine form *himself*. The situation in (2c and d) is the same; the anaphor must take the form *herself* so that it agrees in gender with the feminine *Sally*. Note further that a sentence like (2e) shows us that anaphors must have an antecedent. An anaphor without an antecedent is unacceptable. A plausible hypothesis (or rule) given the data in (2), then, is stated in (3):

3) An anaphor must (i) have an antecedent and (ii) agree in gender (masculine, feminine, or neuter) with that antecedent.

The next step in the scientific method is to test this hypothesis against more data. Consider the additional data in (4):

4)   a)   The robot kissed itself.
     b)   She knocked herself on the head with a zucchini.
     c)   *She knocked himself on the head with a zucchini.
     d)   The snake flattened itself against the rock.
     e)   ?The snake flattened himself/herself against the rock.
     f)   The Joneses think themselves the best family on the block.
     g)   *The Joneses think himself the most wealthy guy on the block.
     h)   Gary and Kevin ran themselves into exhaustion.
     i)   *Gary and Kevin ran himself into exhaustion.

Sentences (4a, b, and c) are all consistent with our hypothesis that anaphors must agree in gender with their antecedents, which at least confirms that the hypothesis is on the right track. What about the data in (4d and e)? It appears as if any gender is compatible with the antecedent *the snake*. This appears, on the surface, to be a contradiction to our hypothesis. Think about these examples a little more closely, however. Whether sentence (4e) is well-formed or not depends upon your assumptions about the gender of the snake. If you assume (or know) the snake to be male, then *The snake flattened himself against the rock* is perfectly well-formed. But under the same assumption, the sentence *The snake flattened herself against the rock* seems very odd indeed, although it is fine if you assume the snake is female. So it appears as if this example also meets the generalization in (3); the vagueness about its well-formedness has to do with the fact that we are rarely sure what gender a snake is and not with the actual structure of the sentence.

Now, look at the sentences in (4f–i); note that the ill-formedness of (g) and (i) is not predicted by our generalization. In fact, our generalization predicts that sentence (4i) should be perfectly grammatical, since *himself* agrees in gender (masculine) with its antecedents *Gary* and *Kevin*. Yet there is clearly something wrong with this sentence. The hypothesis needs revision. It appears as if the anaphor must agree in gender and **number** with the antecedent. Number refers to the quantity of individuals involved in the sentence; English primarily distinguishes singular number from plural number. (5) reflects our revised hypothesis.

5)   An anaphor must agree in gender and number with its antecedent.

If there is more than one person or object mentioned in the antecedent, then the anaphor must be plural (i.e., *themselves*).

Testing this against more data, we can see that this partially makes the right predictions (6a), but it doesn't properly predict the grammaticality of sentences (6b–e):

6) a) People from Tucson think very highly of themselves.
   b) *I gave yourself the bucket of ice cream.
   c) I gave myself the bucket of ice cream.
   d) *She hit myself with a hammer.
   e) She hit herself with a hammer.

Even more revision is in order. The phenomenon seen in (6b–e) revolves around a grammatical distinction called **person**. Person refers to the perspective of the speaker with respect to the other participants in the speech act. First person refers to the speaker. Second person refers to the listener. Third person refers to people being discussed that aren't participating in the conversation. Here are the English pronouns associated with each person: (**Nominative** refers to the **case** form the pronouns take when in subject position like *I* in "*I* love peanut butter;" *accusative* refers to the form they take when in object positions like *me* in "John loves *me*." We will look at case in much more detail in chapter 9, so don't worry if you don't understand it right now.)

7)	Nominative		Accusative		Anaphoric	
	Singular	Plural	Singular	Plural	Singular	Plural
1	I	we	me	us	myself	ourselves
2	you	you	you	you	yourself	yourselves
3 masc	he		him		himself	
3 fem	she	they	her	them	herself	themselves
3 neut	it		it		itself	

As you can see from this chart, the form of the anaphor seems also to agree in person with its antecedent. So once again we revise our hypothesis (rule):

8) An anaphor must agree in person, gender and number with its antecedent.

With this hypothesis, we have a straightforward statement of the distribution of this noun type, derived using the scientific method. In the problem sets below, and in chapter 5, you'll have an opportunity to revise the rule in (8) with even more data.

You now have enough information to try Challenge Problem Sets 1 & 2

3.2 Sources of Data

If we are going to apply the scientific method to syntax, it is important to consider the sources of data. One obvious source is in collections of either spoken or written texts. Such data are called *corpora* (singular: *corpus*). There are many corpora available, including some searchable through the World Wide Web. For languages without a literary tradition or ones spoken by a small minority, it is often necessary for the linguist to go and gather data and compile a corpus in the field. In the early part of this century, this was the primary occupation of linguists, and it is proudly carried on today by many researchers.

While corpora are unquestionably invaluable sources of data, they are only a partial representation of what goes on in the mind. More particularly, corpora often contain instances of only grammatical (or more precisely well-formed) sentences (sentences that sound "OK" to a native speaker). For example, the online New York Times contains very few ungrammatical sentences. Even corpora of naturalistic speech complete with the errors every speaker makes don't necessarily contain the data we need to test the falsifiable predictions of our hypotheses.

You might think that what's in a corpus would be enough for a linguist to do her job. But corpora are just not enough: there is no way of knowing whether a corpus has *all* possible forms of grammatical sentences. In fact, as we will see in the next chapter, due to the productive nature of language, a corpus could *never* contain all the grammatical forms of a language, nor could it even contain a representative sample. To really get at what we know about our languages (remember syntax is a cognitive science), we have to know what sentences are *not* well-formed. That is, in order to know the range of what are acceptable sentences of English, Italian or Igbo, we *first* have to know what are *not* acceptable sentences in English, Italian or Igbo. This kind of negative information is very rarely available in corpora, which mostly provide grammatical, or well-formed, sentences.

Consider the following sentence:

9)   *Who do you wonder what bought?

For most speakers of English, this sentence borders on word salad – it is not a good sentence of English. How do you know that? Were you ever taught in school that you can't say sentences like (9)? Has anyone ever uttered this sentence in your presence before? I seriously doubt it. The fact that a sentence like (9) sounds strange, but similar sentences like (10a and b) *do* sound OK is not reflected anywhere in a corpus:

10) a)   Who do you think bought the bread machine?
    b)   I wonder what Fiona bought.

Instead we have to rely on our knowledge of our native language (or on the knowledge of a native speaker consultant for languages that we don't speak natively). Notice that this is *not* conscious knowledge. I doubt there are many native speakers of English that could tell you why sentence (9) is terrible, but most can tell you that it is. This is subconscious knowledge. The trick is to get at and describe this subconscious knowledge.

The psychological experiment used to get this subconscious kind of knowledge is called the ***grammaticality judgment task***. The judgment task involves asking a native speaker to read a sentence, and judge whether it is well-formed (grammatical), marginally well-formed, or ill-formed (unacceptable or ungrammatical).

> **Judgments as Science?**
> Many linguists refer to the grammaticality judgment task as "drawing upon our native speaker intuitions." The word "intuition" here is slightly misleading. The last thing that pops into our heads when we hear the term "intuition" is science. Generative grammar has been severely criticized by many for relying on "unscientific" intuitions. But this is based primarily on a misunderstanding of the term. To the lay person, the term "intuition" brings to mind guesses and luck. This usage of the term is certainly standard. When a generative grammarian refers to "intuition" however, she is using the term to mean "tapping into our subconscious knowledge." The term "intuition" may have been badly chosen, but in this circumstance it refers to a real psychological effect. Intuition (as a grammaticality judgment) has an entirely scientific basis. It is replicable under strictly controlled experimental conditions (these conditions are rarely applied, but the validity of the task is well established). Other disciplines also use intuitions or judgment tasks. For example, within the study of vision, it has been determined that people can accurately judge differences in light intensity, drawing upon their subconscious knowledge (Bard et al. 1996). To avoid the negative associations with the term intuition, we will use the term *judgment* instead.

There are actually several different kinds of grammaticality judgments. Both of the following sentences are ill-formed, but for different reasons:

11) a)   #The toothbrush is pregnant.
    b)   *Toothbrush the is blue.

Sentence (11a) sounds bizarre (cf. *the toothbrush is blue*) because we know
that toothbrushes (except in the world of fantasy / science fiction or poetry)
cannot be pregnant. The meaning of the sentence is strange, but the form is
OK. We call this ***semantic ill-formedness*** and mark the sentence with a #. By
contrast, we can glean the meaning of sentence (11b); it seems semantically
reasonable (toothbrushes can be blue), but it is ill-formed from a structural
point of view. That is, the determiner *the* is in the wrong place
in the sentence. This is a ***syntactically ill-formed*** sentence. A native speaker
of English will judge both these sentences as ill-formed, but for very different
reasons. In this text, we will be concerned primarily with syntactic
well-formedness.

You now have enough information to answer General Problem Set 2

---

4. WHERE DO THE RULES COME FROM?

In this chapter we've been talking about our subconscious knowledge of
syntactic rules, but we haven't dealt with how we get this knowledge. This
is sort of a side issue, but it may affect the shape of our theory. If we know
how children acquire their rules, then we are in a better position for a proper
formalization of them. The way by which children develop knowledge is an
important question in cognitive science. The theory of generative grammar
makes some very specific (and very surprising) claims about this.

4.1 Learning vs. Acquisition

One of the most common misconceptions about Language is the idea
that children and adults "learn" languages. Recall that the basic kind
of knowledge we are talking about here is subconscious knowledge. When
producing a sentence you don't consciously think about where to put the
subject, where to put the verb, etc. Your subconscious language faculty does
that for you. Cognitive scientists make a distinction in how we get conscious
and subconscious knowledge. Conscious knowledge (like the rules
of algebra, syntactic theory, principles of organic chemistry, or how to take
apart a carburetor) is ***learned***. Subconscious knowledge, like how to speak
or the ability to visually identify discrete objects, is ***acquired***. In part,
this explains why classes in the formal grammar of a foreign language
often fail abysmally to train people to speak those languages. By contrast,
being immersed in an environment where you can subconsciously acquire
a language is much more effective. In this text we'll be primarily interested

in how people acquire the rules of their language. Not all rules of grammar are acquired, however. Some facts about Language seem to be built into our brains, or *innate*.

You now have enough information to answer General Problem Set 3

4.2 Innateness: Language as an Instinct

If you think about the other types of knowledge that are subconscious, you'll see that many[3] of them (for example, the ability to walk) are built directly into our brains – they are instincts. No one had to teach you to walk (despite what your parents might think!). Kids start walking on their own. Walking is an instinct. Probably the most controversial claim of Noam Chomsky's is that Language is also an instinct. Many parts of Language are built in, or *innate*. Much of Language is an ability hard-wired into our brains by our genes.

Obviously, particular languages are not innate. It isn't the case that a child of Slovak parents growing up in North America who is never spoken to in Slovak, grows up speaking Slovak. They'll speak English (or whatever other language is spoken around them). So on the surface it seems crazy to claim that Language is an instinct. There are very good reasons to believe, however, that a human facility for Language (perhaps in the form of a "Language organ" in the brain) is innate. We call this facility *Universal Grammar* (or *UG*).

4.3 The Logical Problem of Language Acquisition

What follows is a fairly technical proof of the idea that Language is at least plausibly construed as an innate, in-built system. If you aren't interested in this proof (and the problems with it), then you can reasonably skip ahead to section 4.4.

The argument in this section is that a productive system like the rules of Language probably have not been learned or acquired. Infinite systems are in principle, given certain assumptions, both unlearnable and unacquirable. Since we all have such an infinite system in our heads, and we shouldn't have been able to aquire it. So it follows that it is built in. The argument presented here is based on an unpublished paper by Alec Marantz, but is based on an argument dating back to at least Chomsky (1965).

First here's a sketch of the proof, which takes the classical form of an argument by modus ponens:

---

[3] but not all!

Premise (i): Syntax is a productive, recursive and infinite system
Premise (ii): <u>Rule governed infinite systems are unlearnable.</u>
Conclusion: Therefore syntax is an unlearnable system. Since we have it, it follows that at least parts of syntax are innate.

There are parts of this argument that are very controversial. In the challenge problem sets at the end of this chapter you are invited to think very critically about the form of this proof. Challenge Problem Set 3 considers the possibility that premise (i) is false (but hopefully, you will conclude that despite the argument given in the problem set, that the idea Language is productive and infinite is correct). Premise (ii) is more dubious, and is the topic of Challenge Problem Set 4. Here, in the main body of the text, I will give you the classic versions of the support for these premises, without criticizing them. You are invited to be skeptical and critical of them when you do the Challenge Problem sets.

Let's start with premise (i). Language is a productive system. That is, you can produce and understand sentences you have never heard before. For example, I can practically guarantee that you have never heard the following sentence:

12) The dancing chorus-line of elephants broke my television set.

The magic of syntax is that it can generate forms that have never been produced before. Another example of the productive quality lies in what is called **recursion**. It is possible to utter a sentence like (13):

13) Rosie loves magazine ads.

It is also possible to put this sentence inside another sentence, like (14):

14) I think [Rosie loves magazine ads].

Similarly you can put this larger sentence inside of another one:

15) Drew believes [I think [Rosie loves magazine ads]].

and of course you can put this bigger sentence inside of another one:

16) Dana doubts that [Drew believes [I think [Rosie loves magazine ads]]].

and so on, and so on ad infinitum. It is always possible to embed a sentence inside of a larger one. This means that Language is a productive (probably infinite) system. There are no limits on what we can talk about. Other examples of the productivity of syntax can be seen in the fact that you can infinitely repeat adjectives (17) and you can infinitely add coordinated nouns to a noun phrase (18):

17) a) a very big peanut
    b) a very very big peanut
    c) a very very very big peanut
    d) a very very very very big peanut
        etc.

18) a) Dave left
    b) Dave and Alina left
    c) Dave, Dan and Alina left
    d) Dave, Dan, Erin and Alina left
    e) Dave, Dan, Erin, Jaime and Alina left
        etc.

It follows that for every grammatical sentence of English, you can find a longer one (based on one of the rules of recursion, adjective repetition, or coordination) that is longer. This means that language is at least countably infinite. This premise is relatively uncontroversial (however, see the discussion in Challenge Problem Set 3).

Let's now turn to premise (ii): The idea that infinite systems are unlearnable. In order to make this more concrete, let's consider an algebraic treatment of a linguistic example. Imagine that the task of a child is to determine the rules by which her language is constructed. Further, let's simplify the task, and say a child simply has to match up situations in the real world with utterances she hears.[4] So upon hearing the utterance *the cat spots the kissing fishes*, she identifies it with an appropriate situation in the context around her (as represented by the picture).

19) "the cat spots the kissing fishes" =

---

[4] The task is actually several magnitudes more difficult than this, as the child has to work out the phonology, etc., too, but for argument's sake, let's stick with this simplified example.

Her job, then, is to correctly match up the sentences with the situation.[5] More crucially she has to make sure that she does *not* match it up with all the other possible alternatives, such as the things going on around her (like her older brother kicking the furniture, or her mother making her breakfast, etc.). This matching of situations with expressions is a kind of mathematical relation (or function) that *maps* sentences onto a particular situation. Another way of putting it is that she has to figure out the rule(s) that decode(s) the meaning of the sentences. It turns out that this task is, at least very difficult if not impossible.

Let's make this even more abstract to get at the mathematics of the situation. Assign each sentence some number. This number will represent the input to the rule. Similarly we will assign each situation a number. The function (or rule) modeling language acquisition maps from the set of sentence numbers to the set of situation numbers. Now let's assume that the child has the following set of inputs and correctly matched situations (perhaps explicitly pointed out to her by her parents). The x value represents the sentences she hears. The y is the number correctly associated with the situation.

20) *Sentence* (input)   *Situation* (output)

x	y
1	1
2	2
3	3
4	4
5	5

Given this input, what do you suppose that the output where $x = 6$ will be?

6   ?

Most people will jump to the conclusion that the output will be 6 as well. That is, they assume that the function (the rule) mapping between inputs and outputs is $x = y$. But what if I were to tell you that in the hypothetical situation I envision here, the correct answer is situation number 126. The rule that generated the table in (20) is actually:

21) $[(x-5)^*(x-4)^*(x-3)^*(x-2)^*(x-1)] + x = y$

With this rule, all inputs equal to or less than 5 will give an output equal to the input, but for all inputs greater than 5, will give some large number.

---

[5] Note that this is the job of the child who is using universal grammar, not the job of UG itself.

When you hypothesized the rule was $x = y$, you didn't have all the crucial information; you only had part of the data. This seems to mean that if you hear only the first five pieces of data in our table then you won't get the rule, but if you learn the sixth you will figure it out. Is this necessarily the case? Unfortunately not: Even if you add a sixth line, you have no way of being sure that you have the right function until you have heard *all* the possible inputs. The important information might be in the sixth line, but it might also be in the 7,902,821,123,765th sentence that you hear. You have no way of knowing for sure if you have heard all the relevant data until you have heard them all. In an infinite system you can't hear them all, even if you were to hear 1 sentence every 10 seconds for your entire life. If we assume the average person lives to be about 75 years old, if they heard one new sentence every ten seconds, ignoring leap years and assuming they never sleep, they'd have only heard about 39,420,000 sentences over their lifetime. This is a much smaller number than infinity. Despite this poverty of input, by the age of 5 most children are fairly confident with their use of complicated syntax. Productive systems are (possibly) unlearnable, because you never have enough input to be sure you have all the relevant facts. This is called *the logical problem of language acquisition*.

Generative grammar gets around this logical puzzle by claiming that the child acquiring English, Irish, or Yoruba has some help: a flexible blueprint to use in constructing her knowledge of language called Universal Grammar. Universal Grammar restricts the number of possible functions that map between situations and utterances, thus making language learnable.

You now have enough information to try Challenge Problem Sets 3 & 4

4.4 Other Arguments for UG

The evidence for UG doesn't rely on the logical problem alone, however. There are many other arguments that support the hypothesis that at least a certain amount of language is built in.

An argument that is directly related to the logical problem of language acquisition discussed above has to do with the fact that we know things about the grammar of our language that we couldn't possibly have learned. Start with the data in (20). A child might plausibly have heard sentences of these types (the underline represents the place where the question word *who* plausibly starts out – that is either as the object or subject of the verb *will question*):

22) a) Who do you think that Ciaran   will question _____ first?
    b) Who do you think   Ciaran   will question _____ first?
    c) Who do you think   _____   will question Seamus first?

The child has to draw a hypothesis about the distribution of the word *that* in English sentences. One conclusion consistent with this observed data is that the word *that* in English is optional. You can either have it or not. Unfortunately this conclusion is not accurate. Consider the fourth sentence in the paradigm in (22). This sentence is the same as (22c) but with a *that*:

    d) *Who do you think that _____ will question Seamus first?

It appears as if *that* is only optional when the question word (*who* in this case) starts in object position (as in 22a and b) It is obligatorily absent when the question word starts in subject position (as in 22c and d) (don't worry about the details of this generalization). What is important to note is that *no one* has ever taught you that (22d) is ungrammatical. Nor could you have come to that conclusion on the basis of the data you've heard. The logical hypothesis on the basis of the data in (220a–c) predicts sentence (22d) to be grammatical. There is nothing in the input a child hears that would lead them to the conclusion that (22d) is ungrammatical, yet every English-speaking child knows it is. One solution to this conundrum is that we are born with the knowledge that sentences like (22d) are ungrammatical.[6] This kind of argument is often called the **underdetermination of the data** argument for UG.

Most parents raising a toddler will swear up and down that they are teaching their children to speak; that they actively engage in instructing their child in the proper form of the language. That overt instruction by parents plays any role in language development is easily falsified. The evidence from the experimental language acquisition literature is very clear: parents, despite their best intentions, do not, for the most part, correct ungrammatical utterances by their children. More generally, they correct the content rather

---

[6] The phenomenon in (22) is sometimes called the **that-trace effect**. There is no disputing the fact that this phenomenon is not learnable. However, it is also a fact that it is not a universal property of all languages. For example, French and Irish don't seem to have the *that*-trace effect. Here is a challenge for those of you who like to do logic puzzles: If the *that*-trace effect is not learnable and thus must be biologically built in, how is it possible for a speaker of French or Irish to violate it? Think carefully about what kind of input a child might have to have in order to learn an "exception" to a built-in principle. This is a hard problem, but there is a solution. It may become clearer below when we discuss parameters.

than the form of their child's utterance (see for example the extensive discussion in Holzman 1997).

23) (from Marcus et al. 1992)
  Adult: Where is that big piece of paper I gave you yesterday?
  Child: Remember? I writed on it.
  Adult: Oh that's right, don't you have any paper down here, buddy?

When a parent does try to correct a child's sentence structure, it is more often than not ignored by the child:

24) (from Pinker 1995: 281 – attributed to Martin Braine)
  Child: Want other one spoon, Daddy
  Adult: You mean, you want the other spoon.
  Child: Yes, I want other one spoon, please Daddy.
  Adult: Can you say "the other spoon"?
  Child: Other … one … spoon
  Adult: Say "other".
  Child: other
  Adult: "spoon"
  Child: spoon
  Adult: "other … spoon"
  Child: other … spoon. Now give me other one spoon.

This humorous example is typical of parental attempts to "instruct" their children in language. When they do occur, they fail. However, children still acquire language in the face of a complete lack of instruction. Perhaps one of the most convincing explanations for this is UG. In the problem set part of this chapter, you are asked to consider other possible explanations and evaluate which are the most convincing.

There are also typological arguments for the existence of an innate language faculty. All the languages of the world share certain properties (for example they *all* have subjects and predicates – other examples will be seen throughout the rest of this book). These properties are called **universals** of Language. If we assume UG, then the explanation for these language universals is straightforward – they exist because all speakers of human languages share the same basic innate materials for building their language's grammar. In addition to sharing many similar characteristics, recent research into Language acquisition has begun to show that there is a certain amount of consistency cross-linguistically in the way children acquire Language. For example, children seem to go through the same stages and make the same kinds of mistakes when acquiring their language, no matter what their cultural background.

Statistical Probability or UG?

In looking at the logical problem of language acquisition you might be asking yourself "Ok, so maybe kids don't get all the data, but maybe they get enough to draw conclusions about what is the most likely structure of their grammar?" For example, we might conclude that a child learning English would observe the total absence of any sentences that have *that* followed by a trace (e.g., 22d), so after hearing some threshold of sentences they conclude that this sentence type is ungrammatical. This is a common objection to the hypothesis of UG. Unfortunately, this hypothesis can't explain why many sentence types that are extremely rare (to the point that they are probably never heard by children) are still judged as grammatical by the children. For example, English speakers rarely (if ever) produce sentences with seven embeddings (*John said that Mary thinks that Susan believes that Matt exclaimed that Marian claimed that Art said that Andrew wondered if Gwen had lost her pen*); yet speakers of English routinely agree these are acceptable. The actual speech of adult speakers is riddled with errors (due to all sorts of external factors: memory, slips of the tongue, tiredness, distraction, etc.). But children do not seem to assume that any of these errors, which they hear frequently, are part of the data that determines their grammars.

Finally, there are a number of biological arguments in favor of UG. As noted above, Language seems to be both human-specific and pervasive across the species. All humans, unless they have some kind of physical impairment, seem to have Language as we know it. This points towards it being a genetically endowed instinct. Additionally, research from neurolinguistics seems to point towards certain parts of the brain being linked to specific linguistic functions.

With very few exceptions, most linguists believe that some Language is innate. What is of controversy is how much is innate and whether the innateness is specific to Language, or follows from more general innate cognitive functions. We leave these questions unanswered here.

You now have enough information to try General Problem Set 4

4.5 Explaining Language Variation

The evidence for UG seems to be very strong. However, we are still left with the annoying problem that languages differ from one another. This problem is what makes the study of syntax so interesting. It is also not an unsolvable one. One way in which languages differ is in terms of the words used in the language. These clearly have to be learned or memorized. Other differences between languages (such as the fact that basic English word order is subject-verb-object (SVO), but the order of an Irish sentence is verb-subject-object (VSO) and the order of a Turkish sentence is subject-object-verb (SOV)) must also be acquired. The explanation for this kind of fact will be explored in chapter 6. Foreshadowing slightly, we'll claim there that differences in the grammars of languages can be boiled down to the setting of certain innate *parameters* (or switches) that select among possible variants. Language variation thus reduces to learning the correct set of words and selecting from a predetermined set of options.

Oversimplifying slightly, most languages put the order of elements in a sentence in one of the following word orders:

25) a) Subject Verb Object (SVO)   (e.g., English)
    b) Subject Object Verb (SOV)   (e.g., Turkish)
    c) Verb Subject Object (VSO)   (e.g., Irish)

A few languages use:

    d) Verb Object Subject (VOS)   (e.g., Malagasy)

No (or almost no)[7] languages use

    e) Object Subject Verb (OSV)
    f) Object Verb Subject (OVS)

Let us imagine that part of UG is a parameter that determines the basic word order. Four of the options (SVO, SOV, VSO, and VOS) are innately available as possible settings. Two of the possible word orders are not part of UG. The child who is acquiring English is innately biased towards one of the common orders, when she hears a sentence like "Mommy loves Kirsten," if the child knows the meaning of each of the words, then she might hypothesize two possible word orders for English: SVO and OVS. None of the others are consistent with the data. The child thus rejects all the other hypotheses. OVS is not allowed, since it isn't one of the innately available forms. This leaves SVO, which is the correct order for English. So children acquiring English will choose to set the word order parameter at the innately available SVO setting.

In his excellent book *The Atoms of Language*, Mark Baker inventories a set of possible parameters of a language variation within the UG hypothesis.

---

[7] This is a matter of some debate. Derbyshire (1985) has claimed that the language Hixkaryana has object initial order.

This is an excellent and highly accessible treatment of parameters. I strongly recommend this book.

You now have enough information to try General Problem Set 5 and Challenge Set 5

---

5. CHOOSING AMONG THEORIES ABOUT SYNTAX

There is one last preliminary we have to touch on before actually doing some real syntax. In this book we are going to posit many hypotheses. Some of these we'll keep, others we'll revise, and still others we'll reject. How do we know what is a good hypothesis and what is a bad? Chomsky (1965) proposed that we can evaluate how good theories of syntax are, using what are called the *levels of adequacy*. Chomsky claimed that there are three stages that a grammar (the collection of descriptive rules that constitute your theory) can attain in terms of adequacy.

If your theory only accounts for the data in a corpus (say a series of printed texts) and nothing more it is said to be an *observationally adequate grammar*. Needless to say, this isn't much use if we are trying to account for the cognition of Language. As we discussed above, it doesn't tell us the whole picture. We also need to know what kinds of sentences are unacceptable, or ill-formed. A theory that accounts for both corpora and native speaker judgments about well-formedness is called a *descriptively adequate grammar*. On the surface this may seem to be all we need. Chomsky, however, has claimed that we can go one step better. He points out that a theory that also accounts for how children acquire their language is the best. He calls this an *explanatorily adequate grammar*. The simple theory of parameters might get this label. Generative grammar strives towards explanatorily adequate grammars.

You now have enough information to try General Problem Set 6

---

6. THE SCIENTIFIC METHOD AND THE STRUCTURE OF THIS TEXTBOOK

Throughout this chapter I've emphasized the importance of the scientific method to the study of syntax. It's worth noting that we're not only going to apply this principle to small problems or specific rules, but we'll also apply it in a more global way. This principle is in part a guide to the way in which the rest of this book is structured.

In chapters 2–5 (the remainder of Part I of the book) we're going to develop an initial hypothesis about the way in which syntactic rules are formed. These are the Phrase Structure Rules (PSRs). Chapters 2 and 3 examine the words these rules use, the form of the rules, and they structures they generate. Chapters 4 and 5 look at ways we can detail the structure of the trees formed by the PSRs.

In chapters 6–8 (Part 2 of the book), we examine some data that presents problems for the simple grammar presented in Part 1. When faced with more complicated data, we revise our hypotheses, and this is precisely what we do. We develop a special refined kind of PSR known as an X-bar rule. X-bar rules are still phrase structure rules, but they offer a more sophisticated way of looking at trees. This more sophisticated version also needs an additional constraint known as the "theta criterion" which is the focus of chapter 8.

In chapters 9–12 (Part 3) we consider even more data, and refine our hypothesis again. This time adding a new rule type: the transformation (we retain X-bar, but enrich it with transformations). Part 4 of the book (chapters 13–16) refines these proposals even further.

With each step we build upon our initial hypothesis, just as the scientific method tells us to. I've been teaching with this proposal-revision method theory construction for a couple of years now, and every now and then I hear the complaint from a student that we should just start with the final answer (i.e. the revised hypothesis found in the later chapters in the book). Why bother learning all this "other" "wrong" stuff? Why should we bother learning Phrase Structure Rules? Why don't we just jump straight into X-bar theory? Well, in principle, I could have constructed a book like that, but then you, the student, wouldn't understand *why* things are the way they are in the latter chapters. The theory would appear to be unmotivated, and you wouldn't understand what the technology actually does. By proposing a simple hypothesis early on in the initial chapters, and then refining and revising it, building new ideas onto old ones, you not only get an understanding of the motivations for and inner workings of our theoretical premises, but you get practice in working like a real linguist. Professional linguists, like all scientists, work from a set of simple hypotheses and revise them in light of predictions made by the hypotheses. The earlier versions of the theory aren't "wrong" so much as they need refinement and revision. These early versions represent the foundations out of which the rest of the theory has been built This is how science works.

7. SUMMARY

In this chapter, we've done very little syntax but talked a lot about the assumptions underlying the approach we're going to take to the study of sentence structure. The basic approach to syntax that we'll be using here is generative grammar; we've seen that this approach is scientific in that it uses the scientific method. It is descriptive and rule based. Further, it assumes that a certain amount of grammar is built in and the rest is acquired.

IDEAS, RULES, AND CONSTRAINTS INTRODUCED IN THIS CHAPTER

i)   *Syntax*: The level of linguistic organization that mediates between sounds and meaning, where words are organized into phrases and sentences.

ii)   *Language* *(capital L)*: The psychological ability of humans to produce and understand a particular language. Also called the *Human Language Capacity* or *i-Language*. This is the object of study in this book.

iii)   *language* *(lower-case l)*: A language like English or French. These are the particular instances of the human Language. The data source we use to examine Language is language. Also called *e-language*.

iv)   *Generative Grammar*: A theory of linguistics in which grammar is viewed as a cognitive faculty. Language is generated by a set of rules or procedures. The version of generative grammar we are looking at here is primarily the *Principles and Parameters approach* (P&P) touching occasionally on *Minimalism.*

v)   *The Scientific Method*: Observe some data, make generalizations about that data, draw a hypothesis, test the hypothesis against more data.

vi)   *Falsifiable Prediction*: To prove that a hypothesis correct you have to look for the data that would prove it *wrong*. The prediction that might prove a hypothesis wrong is said to be falsifiable.

vii)   *Grammar*: Not what you learned in school. This is the set of rules that generate a language.

viii)   *Prescriptive Grammar*: The grammar rules as taught by so called "language experts." These rules, often inaccurate descriptively, prescribe how people should talk/write, rather than describe what they actually do.

ix)   *Descriptive Grammar*: A scientific grammar that describes, rather than prescribes, how people talk/write.

x)   *Anaphor*: A word that ends in *-self* or *-selves* (a better definition will be given in chapter 5).

xi)   *Antecedent*: The noun an anaphor refers to.

xii)   *Asterisk*: * used to mark syntactically ill-formed (unacceptable or ungrammatical) sentences. The hash mark, pound, or number sign (#) is used to mark semantically strange, but syntactically well-formed, sentences.

xiii)   *Gender (Grammatical)*: Masculine vs. Feminine vs. Neuter. Does not have to be identical to the actual sex of the referent. For example, a dog might be female, but we can refer to it with the neuter pronoun *it*. Similarly, boats don't have a sex, but are grammatically feminine.

xiv)   *Number*: The quantity of individuals or things described by a noun. English distinguishes singular (e.g., *a cat*) from plural (e.g., *the cats*). Other languages have more or less complicated number systems.

xv)   *Person*: The perspective of the participants in the conversation. The speaker or speakers (*I, me, we, us*) are called first person. The listener(s) (*you*), are called the second person. Anyone else (those not involved in the conversation) (*he, him, she, her, it, they, them*) is referred to as the third person.

xvi)   *Case*: The form a noun takes depending upon its position in the sentence. We discuss this more in chapter 10.

xvii)   *Nominative*: The form of a noun in subject position (*I, you, he, she, it, we, they*).

xviii)   *Accusative*: The form of a noun in object position (*me, you, him, her, it, us, them*).

xix)   *Corpus (pl. Corpora)*: A collection of real-world language data.

xx)   *Native Speaker Judgments (intuitions)*: Information about the subconscious knowledge of a language. This information is tapped by means of the grammaticality judgment task.

xxi)   *Semantic Judgment*: A judgment about the meaning of a sentence, often relying on our knowledge of the context in which the sentence was uttered.

xxii)   *Syntactic Judgment*: A judgment about the form or structure of a sentence.

xxiii)   *Learning*: The gathering of conscious knowledge (like linguistics or chemistry).

xxiv)   *Acquisition*: The gathering of subconscious information (like language).

xxv)   *Innate*: Hard-wired or built in, an instinct.

xxvi)   *Recursion*: The ability to embed structures iteratively inside one another. Allows us to produce sentences we've never heard before.

xxvii)   *Universal Grammar (UG)*: The innate (or instinctual) part of each language's grammar.

xxviii)   *The Logical Problem of Language Acquisition*: The proof that an infinite system like human language cannot be learned on the basis of observed data – an argument for UG.

xxix)   *Underdetermination of the Data*: The idea that we know things about our language that we could not have possibly learned – an argument for UG.

xxx)   *Universal*: A property found in all the languages of the world.

xxxi)   *Observationally Adequate Grammar*: A grammar that accounts for observed real-world data (such as corpora).

xxxii)   *Descriptively Adequate Grammar*: A grammar that accounts for observed real-world data and native speaker judgments.

xxxiii)   *Explanatorily Adequate Grammar*: A grammar that accounts for observed real-world data and native speaker judgments and offers an explanation for the facts of language acquisition.

FURTHER READING

Baker, Mark (2001) *The Atoms of Language: The Mind's Hidden Rules of Grammar*. New York: Basic Books.

Barsky, Robert (1997) *Noam Chomsky: A Life of Dissent*. Cambridge: MIT Press.

Chomsky, Noam (1965) *Aspects of the Theory of Syntax*. Cambridge: MIT Press.

Jackendoff, Ray (1993) *Patterns in the Mind*. London: Harvester-Wheatsheaf.

Pinker, Steven (1995) *The Language Instinct*. New York: Harper Perennial.

Sampson, Geoffrey (1997) *Educating Eve: The Language Instinct Debate*. London: Cassell.

Uriagereka, Juan (1998) *Rhyme and Reason: An Introduction to Minimalist Syntax*. Cambridge: MIT Press.

GENERAL PROBLEM SETS

1. PRESCRIPTIVE RULES
[Creative and Critical Thinking; Basic]

In the text above, we argued that descriptive rules are the primary focus of syntactic theory. This doesn't mean that prescriptive rules don't have their uses. What are these uses? Why do we maintain prescriptive rules in our society?

2. JUDGMENTS
[Application of Skills; Intermediate]
All of the following sentences have been claimed to be ungrammatical or unacceptable by someone at some time. For each sentence, indicate whether this unacceptability is

i)   a prescriptive or a descriptive judgment, and
ii) for all descriptive judgments indicate whether the ungrammaticality has to do with syntax or semantics (or both).

One- or two-word answers are appropriate. If you are not a native speaker of English, enlist the help of someone who is. If you are not familiar with the *prescriptive* rules of English grammar, you may want to consult a writing guide or English grammar or look at Pinker's *The Language Instinct*.

a)   Who did you see in Las Vegas?
b)   You are taller than me.
c)   My red is refrigerator.
d)   Who do you think that saw Bill?
e)   Hopefully, we'll make it through the winter without snow.
f)   My friends wanted to quickly leave the party.
g)   Bunnies carrots eat.
h)   John's sister is not his sibling.

3. Learning vs. Acquisition
[Creative and Critical Thinking; Basic]
We have distinguished between learning and acquiring knowledge. Learning is conscious, acquisition is automatic and subconscious. (Note that acquired things are *not* necessarily innate. They are just subconsciously obtained.) Other than language are there other things we acquire? What other things do we learn? What about walking? Or reading? Or sexual identity? An important point in answering this question is to talk about what kind of evidence is necessary to distinguish between learning and acquisition.

4. Universals
[Creative and Critical Thinking; Intermediate]
Pretend for a moment that you don't believe Chomsky and that you don't believe in the innateness of syntax (but only *pretend*!). How might you account for the existence of universals (see definition above) across languages?

5. Innateness
[Creative and Critical Thinking; Intermediate]
We argued that some amount of syntax is innate (inborn). Can you think of an argument that might be raised against innateness? (It doesn't have to be an argument that works, just a plausible one.) Alternately, could you come up with a hypothetical experiment that could *disprove* innateness? What would such an experiment have to show? Remember that cross-linguistic variation (differences between languages) is *not* an argument against innateness or UG, because UG contains parameters that allow minute variations.

6. Levels of Adequacy
[Application of Skills; Basic]
Below, you'll find the description of several different linguists' work. Attribute a level of adequacy to them (state whether the grammars they developed are observationally adequate, descriptively adequate, or explanatorily adequate). Explain *why* you assigned the level of adequacy that you did.

a) Juan Martínez has been working with speakers of Chicano English in the barrios of Los Angeles. He has been looking both at corpora (rap music, recorded snatches of speech) and working with adult native speakers.
b) Fredrike Schwarz has been looking at the structure of sentences in eleventh-century Welsh poems. She has been working at the national archives of Wales in Cardiff.
c) Boris Dimitrov has been working with adults and corpora on the formation of questions in Rhodopian Bulgarian. He is also conducting a longitudinal study of some two-year-old children learning the language to test his hypotheses.

CHALLENGE PROBLEM SETS

Challenge Problem Sets are special exercises that either challenge the presentation of the main text or offer significant enrichment. Students are encouraged to complete the other problem sets before trying the Challenge Sets. Challenge Sets can vary in level from interesting puzzles to downright impossible conundrums. Try your best!

CHALLENGE PROBLEM SET 1: ANAPHORA
[Creative and Critical Thinking and Data Analysis; Challenge]
In this chapter, as an example of the scientific method, we looked at the distribution of anaphora (nouns like *himself*, *herself*, etc.). We came to the following conclusion about their distribution:

> An anaphor must agree in person, gender, and number with its antecedent.

However, there is much more to say about the distribution of these nouns (in fact, chapter 5 of this book is entirely devoted to the question).

Part 1: Consider the data below. Can you make an addition to the above statement that explains the distribution of anaphors and antecedents in the very limited data below?

a)   Geordi sang to himself.
b)   *Himself sang to Geordi.
c)   Betsy loves herself in blue leather.
d)   *Blue leather shows herself that Betsy is pretty.

Part 2: Now consider the following sentences:[8]

e)   Everyone should be able to defend himself/herself/themselves.
f)   I hope nobody will hurt themselves/himself/?herself.

Do these sentences obey your revised generalization? Why or why not? Is there something special about the antecedents that forces an exception here, or can you modify your generalization to fit these cases?

CHALLENGE PROBLEM SET 2: YOURSELF
[Creative and Critical Thinking; Challenge]
In the main body of the text we claimed that all anaphors need an antecedent. Consider the following acceptable sentence. This kind of sentence is called an "imperative" and is used to give orders.

a)   Don't hit yourself!

---

[8] Thanks to Ahmad Lotfi for suggesting this part of the question.

Part 1: Are all anaphors allowed in sentences like (a)? Which ones are allowed there, and which ones aren't.

Part 2: Where is the antecedent for yourself? Is this a counter-example to our rule? Why is this rule an exception? It is easy to add a stipulation to our rule; but we'd rather have an explanatory rule. What is special about the sentence in (a)?

CHALLENGE PROBLEM SET 3: IS LANGUAGE REALLY INFINITE?
[Creative and Critical Thinking; Extra Challenge]
> [**Note to instructors**: this question requires some background either
> in formal logic or mathematical proofs.]

In the text, it was claimed that because language is recursive, it follows that it is infinite. (This was premise (i) of the discussion in section 4.3). The idea is straightforward and at least intuitively correct: if you have some well-formed sentence, and you have a rule that can embed it inside another structure; then you can also take this new structure and embed it inside another and so on and so on. Intuitively this leads to an infinitely large number of possible sentences. Pullum and Scholz (2005) have shown that one formal version of this intuitive idea is either circular or a contradiction.

Here is the structure of the traditional argument (paraphrased and simplified from the version in Pullum and Scholz). This proof is cast in such a way that the way we count the number of sentences is by comparing the number of words in the sentence. If for *any* (extremely high) number of words, we can find a longer sentence, then we know the set is infinite. First some terminology:

> ➤ *Terminology:* call the set of well-formed sentences E. If a sentence x is an element of this set we write $E(x)$.
> ➤ *Terminology:* let us refer to the length of a sentence by counting the number of words in it. The number of words in a sentence is expressed by the variable n. There is a special measurement operation (function) which counts the number of words, this is called μ. If the sentence called x has 4 words in it then we say $\mu(x) = 4$.

Next the formal argument:

Premise 1: There is at least one well-formed sentence that has more than zero words in it.
$$\exists x[E(x)\ \&\ \mu(x) > 0]$$

Premise 2: There is an operation in the PSRs such that any sentence may be embedded in another with more words in it. That means for any sentence in the language, there is another longer sentence. (If some expression has the length n, then some other well-formed sentence has a size greater than n).
$$\forall n\ [\exists x[E(x)\ \&\ \mu(x) = n]] \rightarrow [\exists y[E(y)\ \&\ \mu(y) > n]]$$

Conclusion: Therefore for every positive integer *n*, there are well-formed sentences with a length longer than *n* (i.e., the set of well-formed English expressions is at least countably infinite):

$$\therefore \forall n \ [\exists y[E(y) \ \& \ \mu(y) > n]]$$

Pullum and Scholz claim that the problem with this argument lies with the nature of the set E. Sets come of two kinds: there are finite sets which have a fixed number of elements (e.g. the set {a, b, c, d} has 4 and exactly 4 members). There are also infinite sets, which have an endless possible number of members (e.g., the set {a, b, c, ... } has an infinite number of elements).

Question 1: Assume that E, the set of well-formed sentences, is finite. This is a contradiction of one of the two premises given above. Which one? Why is it a contradiction?

Question 2: Assume that E, the set of well-formed sentences, is infinite. This leads to a circularity in the argument. What is the circularity (i.e., why is the proof circular)?

Question 3: If the logical argument is either contradictory or circular what does that make of our claim that the number of sentences possible in a language is infinite? Is it totally wrong? What does the proof given immediately above really prove?

Question 4: Given that E can be neither a finite nor an infinite set, is there any way we might recast the premises, terminology, or conclusion in order not to have a circular argument and capture the intuitive insight of the claim? Explain how we might do this or why it's impossible. Try to be creative. There is no "right" answer to this question. Hint: one might try a proof that proves that a subset of the sentences of English is infinite (and by definition the entire set of sentences in English is infinite) or one might try a proof by contradiction.

Important notes:
1) Your answers can be given in English prose, you do not need to give a formal mathematical answer.
2) Do not try to look up the answer in the papers cited above. That's just cheating! Try to work out the answers for yourself.

CHALLENGE PROBLEM SET 4: ARE INFINITE SYSTEMS REALLY UNLEARNABLE?
[Creative and Critical Thinking; Challenge]
In section 4.3, you saw the claim that if language is an infinite system then it must be unlearnable. In this problem set, you should aim a critical eye at the premise that infinite systems can't be learned on the basis of the data you hear.

While given the extreme view in section 4.3 is logically true, consider the following alternative possibilities:

a) We as humans have some kind of "cut off mechanism" that stops considering new data after we've heard some threshold number of examples. If we don't hear the crucial example after some period of time we simply assume it doesn't exist. Rules simply can't exist that require access to sentence types so rare that you don't hear them before the cut off point.

b) We are purely statistical engines. Rare sentences types are simply ignored as "statistical noise." We consider only those sentences that are frequent in the input when constructing our rules.

c) Child-directed speech (motherese) is specially designed to give you precisely the kinds of data you need to construct your rule system. The child listens for very specific "triggers" or "cues" in the parental input in order to determine the rules.

Question 1: To what extent are (a), (b) or (c) compatible with the hypothesis of Universal Grammar. If (a), (b) or (c) turned out to be true, would this mean that there was no innate grammar? Explain your answer.

Question 2: How might you experimentally or observationally distinguish between (a), (b), (c) and the infinite input hypothesis of 4.3? What kinds of evidence would you need to tell them apart?

Question 3: When people speak, they make errors. (They switch words around, they mispronounce things, they use the wrong word, they stop mid-sentence without completing what they are saying etc.) Nevertheless children seem to be able to ignore these errors and still come up with the right set of rules. Is this fact compatible with any of the infinite hypothesis, (a), (b), or (c)?

CHALLENGE PROBLEM SET 5: LEARNING PARAMETERS: PRO DROP
[Critical Thinking, Data Analysis; Challenge]
Background: Among the Indo-European languages there are two large groups of languages that pattern differently with respect to whether they require a pronoun (like he, she, it) in the subject position, or whether such pronouns can be "dropped". For example, in both English and French, pronouns are required. Sentences without them are usually ungrammatical:

a) He left
b) *Left
c) Il est parti   (French)
     he is gone
     "he left"
d) *est parti   (French)

In languages, such as Spanish and Italian, however, such pronouns are routinely omitted (1s = first person, singular):

e) Io telephono   (Italian)
    I   called.1s
    "I called (phoned)"
f) telephono
    called.1s
    "Called"

Question 1: Now imagine that you are a small child learning a language. What kind of data would you need to know in order to tell if your language was "pro drop" or not? (Hint. Does the English child hear sentences both with and without subjects? Does the Italian child? Are they listening for sentences with subjects or without them?

Question 2: Assume that one of the two possible settings for this parameter (either your language is pro-drop or it is not) is the "default" setting. This default setting is the version of the parameter one gets if one doesn't hear the right kind of input. Which of the two possibilities is the default?

Question 3: English has imperative constructions such as:

g) Leave now!

Why doesn't the English child assume on the basis of such sentences that English is pro-drop?

chapter 2

Parts of Speech

0. WORDS AND WHY THEY MATTER TO SYNTAX

It goes without saying that sentences are made up of words, so before we get into the meat of this book, it's worth looking carefully at different kinds of words.

What is most important to us here is the word's *part of speech* (also known as *syntactic category*). The most common parts of speech are *nouns*, *verbs*, *adjectives*, *adverbs*, and *prepositions* (we will also look at some other less familiar parts of speech below). Parts of speech tell us how a word is going to function in the sentence. Consider the sentences in (1). Notice that we can substitute various words that are of the type *noun* for the second word in the sentence:

1) a) The *man* loved peanut butter cookies.
   b) The *puppy* loved peanut butter cookies.
   c) The *king* loved peanut butter cookies.

However, we cannot substitute words that aren't nouns:[1]

2) a) *The *green* loved peanut butter cookies.
   b) *The *in* loved peanut butter cookies.
   c) *The *sing* loved peanut butter cookies.

---

[1] Remember, the * symbol means that a sentence is syntactically ill-formed.

The same holds true for larger groups of words (the square brackets [...] mark off the relevant groups of words).

3) a) *[John]* went to the store.
   b) *[The man]* went to the store.
   c) **[Quickly walks]* went to the store.

4) a) *[Norvel]* kissed the blarney stone.
   b) **[To the washroom]* kissed the blarney stone.

If we have categories for words that can appear in certain positions and categories for those that don't we can make generalizations (scientific ones) about the behavior of different word types. This is why we need parts of speech in syntactic theory.

1. DETERMINING PART OF SPEECH

1.1 The Problem of Traditional Definitions

If you were taught any grammar in school, you may have been told that a noun is a "person, place, or thing," or that a verb is "an action, state, or state of being." Alas, this is a very over-simplistic way to characterize various parts of speech. It also isn't terribly scientific or accurate. The first thing to notice about definitions like this is that they are based on semantic criteria. It doesn't take much effort to find counterexamples to these semantic definitions. Consider the following:

5) The *destruction* of the city bothered the Mongols.

The meaning of *destruction* is *not* a "person, place, or thing." It is an action. By semantic criteria, this word should be a verb. But in fact, native speakers unanimously identify it as a noun. Similar cases are seen in (6):

6) a) *Sincerity* is an important quality.
   b) The *assassination* of the president.
   c) *Tucson* is a great place to live.

Sincerity is an attribute, a property normally associated with adjectives. Yet in (6a), *sincerity* is a noun. Similarly in (6b) *assassination*, an action, is functioning as a noun. (6c) is more subtle. The semantic property of identifying a location is usually attributed to a preposition; in (6c) however, the noun *Tucson* refers to a location, but isn't itself a preposition. It thus seems difficult (if not impossible) to rigorously define the parts of speech based solely on semantic criteria. This is made even clearer when we see that a word can change its part of speech depending upon where it appears in a sentence:

7) a) Gabrielle's *mother* is an axe-murderer.   (N)
    b) Anteaters *mother* attractive offspring.   (V)
    c) Wendy's *mother* country is Iceland.   (Adj)

The situation gets even muddier when we consider languages other than English. Consider the following data from Warlpiri:

8) Wita-ngku ka   maliki wajilipinyi.
    small-SUBJ AUX dog   chase.PRES
    "The small (one) is chasing the dog."

In this sentence, we have a thing we'd normally call an adjective (the word *wita* "small") functioning like a noun (e.g., taking subject marking). Is this a noun or an adjective?

It's worth noting that some parts of speech don't lend themselves to semantic definitions at all. Consider the sentence in (9). What is the meaning of the word *that*?

9) Mikaela said that parts of speech intrigued her.

If parts of speech are based on the meaning of the word, how can we assign a part of speech to word for which the meaning isn't clear.[2]

Perhaps the most striking evidence that we can't use semantic definitions for parts of speech comes from the fact that you can know the part of speech of a word without even knowing what it means:

10) The yinkish dripner blorked quastofically into the nindin with the pidibs.

Every native speaker of English will tell you that *yinkish* is an adjective, *dripner* a noun, *blorked* a verb, *quastofically* an adverb, and *nindin* and *pidibs* both nouns, but they'd be very hard pressed to tell you what these words actually mean. How then can you know the part of speech of a word without knowing its meaning? The answer is simple: The definitions for the various parts of speech are not semantically defined. Instead they depend on where the words appear in the sentence and what kinds of affixes they take. Nouns are things that that appear in "noun positions" and take "noun suffixes"

---

[2] Be careful here: the *function* of the word is clear (it is used to subordinate clauses inside of sentences) but it doesn't have an obvious *meaning* with respect to the real world.

(endings). The same is true for verbs, adjectives, etc. Here are the criteria that we used to determine the parts of speech in sentence (10):

11) a)   yinkish   between *the* and a noun
                          takes *-ish* adjective ending
    b)   dripner   after an adjective (and *the*)
                          takes *-er* noun ending
                          subject of the sentence
    c)   blorked   after subject noun
                          takes *-ed* verb ending
    d)   quastofically   after a verb
                          takes *-ly* adverb ending
    e)   nindin   after *the* and after a preposition
    f)   pidibs   after *the* and after a preposition
                          takes *-s* noun plural ending

The part of speech of a word is determined by its place in the sentence and by its morphology, *not* by its meaning. In the next section, there is a list of rules and distributional criteria that you can use to determine the part of speech of a word.

1.2 Distributional Criteria

The criteria we use for determining part of speech then aren't based on the meanings of the word, but on its **distribution**. We will use two kinds of distributional tests for determining part of speech: morphological distribution and syntactic distribution.

First we look at **morphological distribution**; this refers to the kinds of affixes (prefixes and suffixes) and other morphology that appear on a word. Let's consider two different types of affixes. First, we have affixes that make words out of other words. We call these affixes **derivational morphemes**. These suffixes usually result in a particular part of speech. For example, if we take the word *distribute* we can add the derivational suffix *-(t)ion* and we get the noun *distribution*. The *-(t)ion* affix thus creates nouns. Any word ending in *-(t)ion* is a noun. This is an example of a morphological distribution. A similar example is found with the affix *-al*, which creates adjectives. If we take *distribution*, and add *-al* to it, we get the adjective *distributional*. The *-al* ending is a test for being an adjective. Derivational affixes make a word a particular category; by contrast **inflectional morphemes** don't *make* a word into a particular category, but instead only *attach* to certain categories. Take for example the superlative suffix *-est*. This affix only attaches to words that are already adjectives: *big, biggest,* (cf. *dog, *doggest*). Because they are sensitive to what category they attach to, inflectional suffixes can also serve as a test for determining part of speech category.

> **A Warning: Homophony in English Affixes**
>
> Compared to other languages with much richer morphological systems, English morphology is rather poor. In many cases, the same affix can be used in very different ways. For example, the inflectional suffix *-s* is found both as a marker of present tense in the third person, *he walks* and as the plural marker, *peanuts*. In fact, leaving aside the difference in punctuation (the apostrophe), it is also used to mark possessors: *John's backpack; its cover*. A similar effect is seen with many other suffixes. For example -er is used both derivationally to form nouns: *dancer*, and as a comparative inflectional marker on adjectives: *bigger*. Because so many suffixes in English are homophonous (sound the same, but have different usages), be very careful when using them for morphological distribution tests.

The other kind of test we use for determining part of speech uses *syntactic distribution*. Syntactic distribution refers to what other words appear near the word. For example, in nouns typically appear after determiners (articles) such as *the*, although they need not do so to be nouns. We can thus take appearance after *the* to be a test for noun-hood.

> **Something to Think about: Circularity**
>
> In section 1 of this chapter, it was claimed that we needed parts of speech to help us determine where in the sentence a word appeared. So for example, we know that verbs and adjectives in English don't function as the subjects of sentences. Above we have given one test for part of speech category in terms of the words distribution in the sentence. Here's something to think about. Have we created a circular argument: category determines position in the sentence and the position in the sentence determines category? Is this really circular? Does it matter?

2. THE MAJOR PARTS OF SPEECH: N, V, ADJ, AND ADV

Having determined that we are going to use distributional criteria for determining the part of speech of a word, we'll now turn to some tests for particular lexical items. We'll limit ourselves to the major classes of noun

(N), verb (V), adjective (Adj), and adverb (Adv). We'll look at other parts of speech in later sections.

One thing that you'll notice is that these are specific to English. Every language will have its own distributional criteria. For each language linguists have to develop lists like the ones below.[3]

A final word of qualification is in order, not every test will work in every situation, so it is usually best to use multiple morphological and syntactic tests for any given word if you can.

2.1 Nouns

Derivational Suffixes: In English, nouns often end in derivational endings such as *-ment (basement)*, *-ness (friendliness)*, *-ity (sincerity)*, *-ty (certainty)*, *-(t)ion (devotion)*, *-ation (expectation)*, *-ist (specialist)*, *-ant (attendant)*, *-ery (shrubbery)*, *-ee (employee)*, *-ship (hardship)*, *-aire (billionaire)*, *-acy (advocacy)*, *-let (piglet)*, *-ling (underling)*, *-hood (neighborhood)*, *-ism (socialism)*, *-ing (fencing)*.

Inflectional Suffixes: Nouns in English don't show much inflection, but when pluralized can take suffixes such as *-s (cats)*, *-es (glasses)*, *-en (oxen)*, *-ren (children)*, *-i (cacti)*, *-a (addenda)*.

Note that the following endings have homophonous usage with other parts of speech: *-ing, -s, 's, -er, -en*.

Syntactic Distribution: Nouns often appear after determiners such as *the, those, these*, (e.g., *these peanuts*) and can appear after adjectives (*the big peanut*). Nouns can also follow prepositions (*in school*). All of these conditions can happen together: *in the big gymnasium*). Nouns can appear as the subject of the sentence (we will define subject rigorously in a later chapter): *The syntax paper was incomprehensible*; or as the direct object: *I read the syntax paper*. Nouns can be negated by *no* (as opposed to *not* or *un-*): *No apples were eaten*.

One easy way to see if something is a noun is to see if you can replace it with another word that is clearly a noun. So if we want to see if the word *people* is a noun or not, we can substitute another word we know for sure to be a noun, e.g., *John* (*I saw people running all over the place* vs. *I saw John running all over the place*).

---

[3] The lists in this section are based on the discussions of English morphology found in Katamba (2004) and Harley (2006).

2.2 Verbs

Derivational Suffixes: Verbs often end in derivational endings such as *-ate (dissipate)*, and *-ize/-ise (regularize)*.

Inflectional Suffixes: In the past tense, verbs usually take an *-ed* or *-t* ending. In the present tense, third person singular (he, she, it), they take the *-s* ending. Verbs can also take an *-ing* ending in some aspectual constructions, (she was walking) and take either an *-en* or an *-ed* suffix when they are passivized (more on passivization in later chapters): *the ice-cream was eaten*.

 Note that the following endings have homophonous usage with other parts of speech: *ate, -ing, -s, -er, -en, -ed*.

Syntactic Distribution: Verbs can follow auxiliaries and modals such as *will, have, having, had, has, am, be, been, being, is, are, were, was, would, can, could, shall, should,* and the special infinitive marker *to*. Verbs follow subjects, and can follow adverbs such as *often* and *frequently*. Verbs can be negated with *not* (as opposed to *no* and *un-*[4]).

2.3 Adjectives

Derivational Suffixes: Adjectives often end in derivational endings such as *-ing (the dancing cat)*, *-ive (indicative)*, *-able (readable)*, *-al (traditional)*, *-ate (intimate)*, *-ish (childish)*, *-some (tiresome)*, *-(i)an (reptilian)*, *-ful (wishful)*, *-less (selfless)*, *-ly (friendly)*.

Inflectional Suffixes: Adjectives can be inflected into a comparative form using *-er* (alternately they follow the word *more*). They can also be inflected into their superlative form using *-est* (alternately they follow the word *most*). Adjectives are typically negated using the prefix *un-* (in its sense meaning "not," not in its sense meaning "undo").

 Note that the following affixes have homophonous usage with other parts of speech: *-ing, -er, -en, -ed, un-, -ly*.

Syntactic Distribution: Adjectives can appear between determiners such as *the, a, these* etc. and nouns: (*the big peanut*). They also can follow the auxiliary *am/is/are/was/were/be/been/being* (warning: this distribution overlaps with verbs). Frequently, adjectives can be modified by the adverb *very* (warning: this distribution overlaps with adverbs).

---

[4] There are verbs that begin with *un-*, but in these circumstances *un-* usually means "reverse" not negation.

You now have enough information to try Challenge Problem Sets 1 & 2

Adjectives and Adverbs: Part of the Same Category?
Look carefully at the distributions of Adjectives and Adverbs. There is a great deal of overlap between them. Adverbs typically take *-ly*; however, there are also a number of clear adjectives that take this suffix too (e.g., *the friendly cub)*. Both Adj and Adv can be modified by the word *very*, and they both have the same basic function in the grammar – to attribute properties to the items they modify. In fact the only major distinction between them is syntactic: Adjectives appear inside NPs, Adverbs appear elsewhere. This kind of phenomenon is called *Complementary Distribution*. (Where you get an adjective vs. an adverb is entirely predictable.) When two elements are in complementary distribution in linguistics, we normally think of them as variants of the same basic category. For example, when two sounds in phonology are in complementary distribution, we say they are allophones of the same phoneme. We might extend this analysis to parts of speech: there is one "supercategory" labeled "A" that has two subcategories in it (allo-parts-of-speech if you will): Adj and Adv. In this book we'll stick with the traditional Adj and Adv categories, simply because they are familiar to most people. But you should keep in mind that the category A (including both Adjectives and Adverbs) might provide a better analysis and might be better motivated scientifically.

2.4 Adverbs

Derivational Suffixes: Many adverbs end in *-ly*: *quickly, frequently,* etc.

Inflectional Suffixes: Adverbs generally don't take any inflectional suffixes. However, on rare occasions they can be used comparatively and follow the word *more*: *She went more quickly than he did.* Adverbs typically don't take the prefix *un-* unless the adjective they are derived from does first (e.g., *unhelpfully* from *unhelpful*, but **unquickly, *unquick*).

Syntactic Distribution: The syntactic distribution of adverbs is most easily described by stating where they can't appear. Adverbs can't appear between a determiner and a noun (**the quickly fox*) or after the verb *is* and its variants.[5]

---

[5] In some prescriptive variants of English, there are a limited set of adverbs that can appear after *is*. For example, *well* is prescriptively preferred over *good*, in such constructions as *I am well* vs. *I am good* (referring to your state of being rather than the

They can really appear pretty much anywhere else in the sentence, although typically they either appear at the beginning or end of the clause/sentence. Frequently, like adjectives, they can be modified by the adverb *very*.

You now have enough information to answer General Problem Sets 1 & 2

3. OPEN VS. CLOSED; LEXICAL VS. FUNCTIONAL

3.1 Open vs. Closed Parts of Speech

Some parts of speech allow you to add neologisms (new words). For example, imagine I invented a new tool especially for the purpose of removing spines from cacti, and I called this tool a *pulfice*. This kind of word is easily learned and adopted by speakers of English. In fact, we might even predict that speakers would take *pulfice* and develop a verb *pulficize*, which means to remove cacti spines using a *pulfice*. New words may be coined at any time, if they are open class (e.g., *fax, internet, grody*). By contrast there are some parts of speech that don't allow new forms. Suppose I wanted to describe a situation where one arm is under the table and another is over the table, and I called this new preposition *uvder*: *My arms are uvder the table.* It's fairly unlikely that my new preposition, no matter how useful it is, will be adopted into the language. Parts of speech that allow new members are said to be **open class**. Those that don't (or where coinages are very rare) are **closed class**. All of the cases that we've looked at so far have been open class parts of speech.

3.2 Lexical vs. Functional

The open/closed distinction is similar to (but not identical to) another useful distinction in parts of speech. This is the distinction between lexical and functional parts of speech. **Lexical** parts of speech provide the "content" of the sentence. Nouns, verbs, adjectives and adverbs are all lexical parts of speech. **Functional** parts of speech by contrast provide the grammatical information. Functional items are the "glue" that holds a sentence together. One way to tell if a lexical item is functional or lexical is to see if it is left behind in "telegraphic speech" (that is, the way a telegram would be written; e.g., *Brian bring computer! Disaster looms!*). Functional categories include

acceptability of your behavior). Most speakers of American English don't allow any adverbs after *is*.

Determiners, Prepositions, Complementizers, Conjunctions, Negation, Auxiliaries and Modals. We will detail some of these below in section 3.3.

> **A Closed Lexical Subclass**
>
> You may have noticed that the open class and lexical class correspond to exactly the same categories; similarly all of the cases of functional categories I've mentioned are pretty clearly closed class items. So you might be wondering why we have both the notions open and lexical and both the notions closed and functional. There are two cases where we have a mismatch between the terms: Pronouns and Anaphors. These are lexical (they are a subtype of N), but they are closed classes.

You now have enough information to answer Challenge Problem Set 3

3.3 Some Functional (Closed) Categories of English

We'll survey here some of the main functional categories of English. This list is by no means complete. While it is possible to provide distributional definitions for various functional parts of speech, because they are closed, there are relatively few members of each class; so it's possible to simply list most of them.

We'll start our categorization with **Prepositions** (abbreviated P). Prepositions appear before nouns (or more precisely noun phrases). English prepositions include the following:

12) *Prepositions of English* (P): to, from, under, over, with, by, at, above, before, after, through, near, on, off, for, in, into, of, during, across, without, since, until.

The class of **determiners** (D) is a little broader. It contains a number of subcategories including articles, quantifiers, numerals, deictics, and possessive pronouns. Determiners appear at the very beginning of English noun phrases.

13) *Determiners of English* (D)
   a) *Articles:* the, a, an
   b) *Deictic articles:* this, that, these, those, yon

c) *Quantifiers*[6]: every, some, many, most, few, all, each, any, less, fewer, no
d) *(Cardinal) numerals:* one, two, three, four, etc.
e) *Possessive pronouns*[7]: my, your, his, her, its, our, their
f) *Some wh-question words:* which, whose

Conjunctions (Conj) are words that connect two or more phrases together on an equal level:

14) *Conjunctions of English* (Conj): and, or, nor, neither ... nor, either ... or

The class of **complementizers** (C) also connects structures together, but they embed one clause inside of another instead of keeping them on an equal level:

15) *Complementizers of English* (C): that, for, if, whether

One of the most important categories that we'll use is the category of **Tense** (T). For the moment we will *not* include tense suffixes such as *-ed* and *-s* in this class, and treat those as parts of verbs (we will revisit this issue in chapter 8). Instead the category T consists of auxiliaries, modals and the non-finite clause marker. In the older syntactic literature, the category T is sometimes called Infl (inflection) or Aux (Auxiliary). We'll use the more modern T.

16) *Tense categories of English* (T)
    Auxiliaries: have/has/had, am/is/are/was/were, do
    Modals: will, would, shall, should, can, could
    Non-finite Tense marker: to

There is one special category containing only one word: *not* which we'll call **negation** (Neg). There are other categories that express negation (e.g., the determiners *no, any,* and the noun *none*). We'll reserve the category Neg for the word *not*, however.

You now have enough information to answer General Problem Sets 4 & 5 and Challenge Problem Set 4

---

[6] Not all quantifiers can be determiners, for example, the quantifiers *lot* and *least* cannot function in this capacity (and are a noun and adjective respectively).
[7] The possessive forms *mine, yours, hers, theirs,* and *ours* are nouns, as are some uses of *his* and *its* (when there is no other noun in the NP).

3.4 Summary

This concludes our discussion of the major classes of words. We've looked at the distributional criteria for the open/lexical categories of N, V, Adj, and Adv, and we've listed the main functional/closed categories of P, D, Conj, Neg, C, and T.

4. SUBCATEGORIES AND FEATURES

You may have noticed that in sections 2 and 3, I hinted that each major part of speech category may have sub-types. For example, we listed six different kinds of D (articles, deictics, quantifiers, numerals, possessive pronouns, *wh*-pronouns) and three kinds of T (auxiliaries, modals, and the non-finite marker). The technical term for these subtypes is **subcategories**. For the most part, we are going to be interested in the main Parts of Speech Categories (N, V, Adj, Adv, P, D, Conj, C, T, and Neg), but sometimes we will want to refer to the subcategories.

One way to mark subcategories is through the use of *features*. Consider the case of T. To distinguish among the subcategories we can appeal to the features [±modal] and ±non-finite]:

17) Auxiliary $T_{[-modal, -nonfinite]}$
    Modal $T_{[+modal, -nonfinite]}$
    to $T_{[-modal, +nonfinite]}$

There is, of course, one set of possible values of these features which is missing ([+modal, +nonfinite]). We might similarly distinguish among tense forms using features like [±past] etc.

Similarly we can distinguish among the various kinds of determiner using features like [±wh], [±quantifier], [±deictic], etc. The details of this kind of analysis aren't crucial to the grammar fragments you are given in this book, as long as you understand the basic concept behind using features to mark subcategories. In the rest of this section, we look at some of the subcategories of N, V and P that will be of use to us in the rest of the book.

I'm not going to discuss subcategories of Adj and Adv, although they exist. In a grey textbox above, I've suggested that Adj and Adv are themselves subcategories of a larger category A. We also find many subcategories *within* the Adj and Adv categories. These distinctions are explored in problem sets at the end of the chapter.

4.1 Subcategories of Nouns

We can slice the pie of English nouns apart along several dimensions including plural vs. singular, proper vs. common, pronoun vs. lexical noun, and count vs. mass noun.

First let's distinguish along the line of **plurality**. English nouns can be either singular or plural. The distinction between singular and plural is usually morphologically marked with one of the plural endings (although it need not be: *mice, deer*). Singular nouns in English require a D; plural ones do not require a D, although they allow one:

18) a) *Cat ate the spider.
    b) The cat ate the spider.
    c) Cats ate the spider.
    d) The Cats ate the spider.

We mark this distinction with the feature [±plural].

Closely related to the plural/singular distinction is the **count** vs. **mass** noun distinction. Count nouns represent individual, "countable" elements. For example, *apple* is a count noun. "Mass nouns" usually can't be counted in the same way. For example *sincerity* and *air* are mass nouns. There are two easy distributional tests to distinguish between mass and count nouns. Mass nouns take the quantifier *much*, count nouns take the quantifier *many*.

19) a) many apples
    b) *much apples/apple[8]
    c) *many sincerity
    d) *many air
    e) much sincerity
    f) much air

Like plurals mass nouns generally don't require a determiner, but count nouns do:

20) a) *I ate apple.
    b) I ate the apple.
    c) I ate sugar.
    d) I ate the sugar.
    e) He is filled with sincerity.

---

[8] Many native speakers of English will be able to "force" a reading onto *much apple*. But what they are doing is using *apple* as a mass noun (referring to the state of being an apple or the totality of apples in the universe). It is often possible to force a mass reading on count nouns, and a count reading on mass nouns (e.g. the water).

f)   I doubt his sincerity.

We distinguish between count and mass nouns using the feature [±count].

Next, let us distinguish between **proper names** and **common nouns**. Proper names are nouns like *Andrew Carnie*. Common nouns are all other nouns. For the most part proper names resist taking determiners:

21) a)   Andrew Carnie
    b)   *the Andrew Carnie

There are some exceptions to this generalization. For example, when referring to a family it's common to say *the Smiths*. In other languages, proper names can take determiners. For example, in Spanish, it is perfectly acceptable to say *La Rosamaria* "the Rosemary." If necessary, we can distinguish proper names from common nouns using the feature [±common], although this feature is less useful than the others.

Finally let's look at the subcategories of **pronouns** and **anaphors**. These classes differ from the others in that they are closed. They never allow determiners or adjectival modification.

22) a)   he
    b)   himself
    c)   *the he
    d)   *the himself
    e)   *big he
    f)   *big himself

Pronouns belong to the class [+pronoun, –anaphor]. Anaphors are [+pronoun, +anaphor]. All other nouns are [–pronoun, –anaphor]. For the purposes of this book we are treating possessive pronouns as determiners, not as a subcategory of nouns.

You now have enough information to do General Problem Set 6

4.2 Subcategories of Verbs

There are really two major ways in which we can divide up verbs into subcategories. One is along the lines of tense/finiteness (i.e., whether the verb is *left*, *leaves*, *(will) leave* or *(to) leave*. We're going to leave these distinctions aside until chapter 8, although hopefully it is obvious by now how we'd use features to distinguish among them, even if the precise features we'd use aren't defined yet. The other way to divvy up verbs is in terms of the number of Noun Phrases (NPs) and Prepositional Phrases (PPs) or clauses (CPs) they require. This second kind of division is known as *argument structure*.

In order to discuss argument structure, we first need to define some basic terms. If you took grammar in school, you probably learned that "every sentence has a subject and a predicate." Under your schoolroom definitions, the subject is usually the first noun phrase (that is, the first noun and all things that go along with it), and the predicate is everything else. So for example, in (23) the subject is *the dastardly phonologist*, and the predicate would be *stole the syntactician's lunch*.

23) [The dastardly phonologist][stole the syntactician's lunch].
   subject   *predicate*   (traditional definitions)

The definition of subject isn't too bad (we'll refine it later though), but syntacticians use the term "predicate" <u>entirely differently</u>. The syntactician's definition of predicate is based on the mathematical notion of a "relation." The **predicate** defines the relation between the individuals being talked about and the real world – as well as with each other. The entities (which can be abstract) participating in the relation are called **arguments**. To see how this works, look at the following example:

24) Gwen hit the baseball.

There are two arguments in this example, *Gwen* and *the baseball*. These are elements in the world that are participants in the action described by the sentence. The predicate here is *hit*. *Hit* expresses a relation between the two arguments: more precisely, it indicates that the first argument (*Gwen*) is applying some force to the second argument (*the baseball*). This may seem patently self-evident, but it's important to understand what is going on here on an abstract level. This usage of the terms predicate and argument is identical to how they are used in formal logic.

We can speak about any particular predicate's **argument structure**. This refers to the number of arguments that a particular predicate requires. Another name for argument structure is **valency**. Take, for example, predicates that take only one argument (i.e., they have a valency of 1). These are predicates like *smile, arrive, sit, run*, etc. The property of transitivity refers to how many arguments follow the verb. In predicates with a valency of 1, no arguments follow the verb (the single argument *precedes* the verb), so these predicates are said to be **intransitive**. Predicates that take two obligatory arguments have a valency of 2; some examples are *hit, love, see, kiss, admire*, etc. These predicates are said to be **transitive**, because they have a single argument after the noun (the other argument precedes the verb). Finally predicates that take three arguments have a valency of 3. *Put* and *give* are the best examples of this class. These predicates have two arguments after the verb so are said to be ***ditransitive***.

25)

Transitivity	Valency	Example
Intransitive	1 argument	smile, arrive
Transitive	2 arguments	hit, love, kiss
Ditransitive	3 arguments	give, put

In determining how many arguments a predicate has, we only consider the obligatory NPs and PPs. Optional ones are never counted in the list of arguments. Only obligatory elements are considered arguments.

Did You Run the Race?
The claim that only obligatory arguments are found in argument structure is not as straightforward as it sounds. Consider the verb *run*. It has both an intransitive use *(I ran)* and a transitive use *(I ran the race)*. A similar problem is raised by languages that can drop the subject argument (e.g. Spanish and Italian) and by imperative sentences in English (*Go home now!*). The subject is still an argument in these constructions, even though you can't hear it. In situations like the verb *run*, we'll simply claim that there are two verbs *to run*: one that takes an object and one that doesn't.

Predicates impose other restrictions on their arguments too. For example, they also place restrictions on the categories of the things that go with them. A verb like *ask* can take either an NP or a clause (embedded sentence = CP) as a complement:

26) a) I asked [NP the question].
   b) I asked [CP if you knew the answer].

But a verb like *hit* can only take an NP complement:

27) a) I hit [NP the ball].
   b)*I hit [CP that you knew the answer].

With these basics in mind, we can set up a series of features based on how many and what kind of arguments a verb takes.

Let's start with intransitives. These require a single NP subject. We'll mark this with the feature [NP ___] where the underscore represents where the verb would go in the sentence. An example of such a verb would be *leave*.

Most transitive verbs require an NP object, so we can mark these with the feature [NP ___ NP], an example of this is the verb *hit*, seen above in (27).

Verbs like *ask* (see 26 above), *think, say*, etc. allow either an NP object or a CP (embedded clause) object. We can mark this using curly brackets {} and a slash. {NP/CP} means "a choice of NP or CP." So the feature structure for predicates like this is [NP __ {NP/CP}].

Ditransitive verbs come of several major types. Some ditransitives require two NP objects (the first is an indirect object the other a direct object). The verb *spare* is of this category. It does not allow an NP and a PP:

28) a) I spared [NP him] [NP the trouble].
    b) *I spared [NP the trouble] [PP to him].

This category of ditransitive is marked with the feature [NP __ NP NP]. The opposite kind of ditransitive is found with the verb put. Put requires an NP and a PP:

29) a) *I put [NP the box] [NP the book].
    b) I put [NP the book] [PP in the box].

This kind of ditransitive takes the feature [NP __ NP PP]. We also have ditransitives that appear to be a combination of these two types and allow either an NP or a PP in the second position:

30) a) I gave [NP the box] [PP to Leah].
    b) I gave [NP Leah] [NP the box].

These have the feature [NP ___ NP {NP/PP}]. Finally we have ditranstives that take either two NPs, or one NP and one CP, or an NP and a PP:

31) a) I told [NP Daniel] [NP the story].
    b) I told [NP Daniel] [CP that the exam was cancelled].
    c) I told [NP the story] [PP to Daniel].

Verbs like *tell* have the feature [NP __ NP {NP/PP/CP}].

The following chart summarizes all the different subcategories of verb we've discussed here:

32)

Subcategory	Example
$V_{[NP\_]}$ (intransitive)	Leave
$V_{[NP\_\_NP]}$ (transitive type 1)	Hit
$V_{[NP\_\_\{NP/CP\}]}$ (transitive type 2)	Ask
$V_{[NP\_\_NP\,NP]}$ (ditransitive type 1)	Spare
$V_{[NP\_\_NP\,PP]}$ (ditransitive type 2)	Put
$V_{[NP\_\_NP\,\{NP/PP\}]}$ (ditransitive type 3)	Give
$V_{[NP\_\_NP\,\{NP/PP/CP\}]}$ (ditransitive type 4)	Tell

There are other types of verbs that we haven't listed here. We'll introduce the features as we need them.

You can now try General Problem Set 7 and Challenge Problem Sets 5 & 6

---

5. SUMMARY

In this chapter, we've surveyed the parts of speech categories that we will use in this book. We have the Lexical parts of speech N, V, Adj, Adv, and the functional categories D, P, C, Conj, Neg, and T. Determining part of speech is done not by traditional semantic criteria, but by using morphological and syntactic distribution tests. We also looked at distributional evidence for various subcategories of Nouns and Verbs, and represented these distinctions as feature notations on the major categories.

IDEAS, RULES, AND CONSTRAINTS INTRODUCED IN THIS CHAPTER

i)   ***Parts of Speech*** (*a.k.a.* ***word class***, ***syntactic categories***): The labels we give to constituents (N, V, Adj, Adv, D, P, C, T, Neg, Conj). These determine the position of the word in the sentence

ii)   ***Distribution***: Parts of Speech are determined based on their distribution. We have both ***morphological distribution*** (what affixes are found on the word) and ***syntactic distribution*** (what other words are nearby).

iii)   *Complementary Distribution*: When you have two categories and they never appear in the same environment (context), you have complementary distribution. Typically Complementary Distribution means that the two categories are subtypes of a larger class.

iv)   Parts of speech that are *open class* can take new members or coinages: N, V, Adj, Adv.

v)   Parts of speech that are *closed class* don't allow new coinages: D, P, Conj, C, T, Neg, and the pronoun subcategory of N.

vi)   *Lexical Categories* express the content of the sentence. N (including pronouns), V, Adj, Adv.

vii)   *Functional Categories* contain the grammatical information in a sentence: D, P, Conj, T, Neg, C.

viii)   *Subcategories*: The major parts of speech can often be divided up into subtypes, these are called subcategories.

ix)   *Feature notations* on major categories are a mechanism for indicating subcategories.

x)   *Plurality* refers to the number of nouns. It is usually indicated in English with an -*s* suffix. Plural nouns in English do not require a determiner.

xi)   *Count vs. Mass*: Count nouns can appear with determiners and the quantifier *many*. Mass nouns appear with *much* and usually don't have articles.

xii)   The *predicate* defines the relation between the individuals being talked about and some fact about them – as well as relations among the arguments.

xiii)   *Argument Structure*: The number of arguments that a predicate takes.

xiv)   The *arguments* are the entities who are participating in the predicate relation.

xv)   *Intransitive*: A predicate that takes only one argument.

xvi)   *Transitive*: A predicate that takes two arguments.

xvii)   *Ditransitive*: A predicate that takes three arguments.

FURTHER READING

Grimshaw, Jane (1990) *Argument Structure*. Cambridge: MIT Press.

Harley, Heidi (2006) *English Words: A Linguistic Introduction*. Oxford. Blackwell.

Katamba, Francis (2004) *English Words*. New York: Routledge.

Levin, Beth (1993) *English Verb Classes and Alternations: A Preliminary Investigation*. Chicago: University of Chicago Press.

Williams, Edwin (1983) Semantic vs. syntactic categories. *Linguistics and Philosophy* 6, 423–46.

GENERAL PROBLEM SETS

1. PART OF SPEECH 1[9]

[Application of Skills; Basic]

Identify the main parts of speech (i.e., Nouns, Verbs, Adjectives/Adverbs, and Prepositions) in the following sentences. Treat hyphenated words as single words:

a) The old rusty pot-belly stove has been replaced.
b) The red-haired assistant put the vital documents through the new efficient shredder.
c) The large evil leathery alligator complained to his aging keeper about his extremely unattractive description.
d) I've just eaten the last piece of chocolate cake.

2. NOOTKA

[Application of Skills; Intermediate]

Consider the following data from Nootka (data from Sapir and Swadesh 1939), a language spoken in British Columbia, Canada and answer the questions that follow the grey text box.

a) Mamu:k-ma   qu:ʔas-ʔi.
    working-PRES   man-DEF
    "The man is working."

---

[9] Problem set contributed by Sheila Dooley-Collberg.

b) Qu:ʔas-ma   mamu:k-ʔi.
    man-PRES   working-DEF
    "The working one is a man."

(The : mark indicates a long vowel. ʔ is a glottal stop. *PRES* in the second line means "present tense," *DEF* means "definite determiner" (the).)

> **Reading Foreign Language Examples**
>
> There are three parts to most foreign language examples used in syntax. Look at the sentences above. The first line is the sentence or phrase in the language under consideration. The second line, which is the most important for our purposes, contains a word-by-word translation of the sentence. Finally, there is a colloquial English translation. The second line, called the *gloss*, is the most useful if you don't speak the language. It shows you the order of elements in the sentence. *When reading about the syntax of foreign languages, concentrate on the order of elements in this second line.*

Questions about Nootka:
1) In sentence a, is *Qu:ʔas* functioning as a verb or a noun?
2) In sentence a, is *Mamu:k* functioning as a verb or a noun?
3) In sentence b, is *Qu:ʔas* a verb or a noun?
4) In sentence b, is *Mamu:k* a verb or a noun?
5) What criteria did you use to tell what is a noun in Nootka and what is a verb?
6) How does this data support the idea that there are no semantic criteria involved in determining the part of speech?

3. GENDER NEUTRAL PRONOUNS
[Creative and Critical Thinking; Basic]
Most standard varieties of English don't have a gender-neutral singular pronoun that can refer to humans (other than the very awkward "one"). There have been numerous attempts to introduce gender-neutral singular human pronouns into English. The following list is a subset of the ones found on John Chao's gender neutral pronoun FAQ[10]:

ae, ar, co, e, em, ems, en, es, et, ey, fm, ha, hann, he'er, heesh, heir, hem, her'n, herim, herm, hes, hesh, heshe, hey, hez, hi, himer, hir, hirem, hires, hirm, his'er, his'n, hisher, hizer, ho, hom, hse, hymer, im, ip, ir, iro, jhe, le, lem, na, ne, ner, nim,

---

[10] http://www.aetherlumina.com/gnp/index.html

on, per, po, rim, s/he, sap, se, sem, ser, sheehy, shem, shey, shim, sie, sim, ta, tem, term, tey, thim, thon, uh, ve, vim, vir, vis, xe, z, ze, zie, zim, zir.

None of these have caught on. Instead, the otherwise plural *they/them/their/themselves* is usually felt to be more natural by native speakers. Why have the above forms not caught on, but instead we have co-opted a plural pronoun for this usage?

4. Functional Categories
[Application of Skills; Basic]
The following is an extract from the preface to Captain Grose's *Dictionary of the Vulgar Tongue* (1811) (from the open source Gutenberg project):

> The propriety of introducing the university slang will be readily admitted; it is not less curious than that of the College in the Old Bailey, and is less generally understood. When the number and accuracy of our additions are compared with the price of the volume, we have no doubt that its editors will meet with the encouragement that is due to learning, modesty, and virtue.

For every word in this paragraph identify its part of speech, and mark whether part of speech is a lexical or functional part of speech and whether the part of speech is open or closed.

5. Part of Speech 2
[Application of Skills; Intermediate]
Consider the following selection from *Jabberwocky*, a poem by Lewis Carroll (From *Through the Looking-Glass and What Alice Found There*, 1872):

> Twas brillig and the slithy toves
> Did gyre and gimble in the <u>wabe</u>;
> All mimsy <u>were</u> the borogoves,
> And the <u>mome</u> raths <u>outgrabe</u>.

> "Beware the Jabberwock, my son!
> The jaws that bite, the claws that catch!
> Beware the <u>Jubjub</u> bird, and shun
> The <u>frumious</u> <u>bandersnatch</u>!"

> He took his <u>vorpal</u> sword in hand:
> Long time the <u>manxome</u> foe he sought –
> So rested he by the <u>tumtum</u> tree
> <u>And</u> stood a while <u>in</u> <u>thought</u>.

And as in <u>uffish</u> thought <u>he</u> stood
The <u>Jabberwock</u> with eyes of flame,
Came <u>whiffling</u> through <u>the</u> <u>tulgey</u> wood,
and <u>burbled</u> as it came.

For each underlined word, indicate its part of speech (word class), and for
Ns, Vs, Adjs, Advs, explain the *distributional* criteria by which you came up
with that classification. If the item is a closed class part of speech, indicate
that. Do not try to use a dictionary. Most of these words are nonsense words.
You will need to figure out what part of speech they are based upon what
suffixes and prefixes they take, along with where they appear relative
to other words. Capitalization and punctuation should *not* be used as a guide
to part of speech.

6. SUBCATEGORIES OF NOUNS
[Application of Knowledge; Basic]
For each of the nouns below put a + sign in the box under the features
that they have. Note that some nouns might have a plus value for more than
one feature. The first one is done for you. Do not mark the minus (−) values,
or the values for which the word is not specified; mark <u>only</u> the plus values!

Noun	Plural	Count	Proper	Pronoun	Anaphor
Cats	+	+			
Milk					
New York					
They					
People					
Language					
Printer					
Himself					
Wind					
Lightbulb					

7. SUBCATEGORIES OF VERBS
[Application of Knowledge; intermediate]
For each of the verbs below, list whether they are intransitive, transitive
or ditransitive <u>and</u> list which features they take (see the list in (32) as
an example). In some cases they may allow more than one feature. E.g., the
verb *eat* is both [NP __ NP] and [NP ___]. Give an example for each feature:

spray, sleep, escape, throw, wipe, say, think, grudge, thank, pour, send, promise, kiss, arrive

---

CHALLENGE PROBLEM SETS

CHALLENGE PROBLEM SET 1: *-IAN AND -ISH*
[Critical and Creative Thinking; Challenge]
In the text we claimed that the suffixes *-ian* and *-ish* mark adjectives. Consider the following sentences:

a) The Canadian government uses a parliamentary system of democracy.
b) The Canadian bought himself a barbeque.
c) The prudish linguist didn't enjoy looking at the internet.
d) We keep those censored copies of the book available to protect the sensibilities of the prudish.

What should we make the words ending in *-ish* and *-ian* in sentences (b) and (d)? Are they adjectives? If not, how can we account for the fact that these words end in *-ish* and *-ian*? There are many possible answers to this question.

CHALLENGE PROBLEM SET 2: NOMINAL PRENOMINAL MODIFIERS[11]
[Critical and Creative Thinking; Challenge]
Part 1: By the syntactic criteria given to you in section, what part of speech should the underlined words in the following examples be?

a) the <u>leather</u> couch
b) the <u>water</u> spout

Part 2: By contrast what do the following facts tell us about the parts of speech of *leather* and *water*:

a) the leather
b) the water
c) ?the very leather couch (cf. the very red couch)
d) ?the very water spout (cf. the very big spout)
e) *The more leather couch / *The leatherer couch (cf. the bigger couch)
f) *The more water spout

---

[11] Thanks to Jack Martin for suggesting this problem set.

CHALLENGE PROBLEM SET 3: INTENSIFIERS
[Application of Knowledge; Challenge]
English has a subcategory of Adverbs called **intensifiers**. This class includes *very, rather, too* (when used before an adjective), *quite, less, nearly, partly, fully, mostly,* and *sometimes*.

Question 1: Is this subcategory an open class part of speech or a closed class part of speech? Explain your answer.
Question 2: Describe the distribution of this subcategory. In particular describe where it can appear relative to other adverbs (and adjectives). Can other adverbs appear in this environment?

CHALLENGE PROBLEM SET 4: COMPLEMENTARY DISTRIBUTION
[Critical Thinking; Challenge]
In a grey textbox in section 2.4, it's argued that Adjectives and Adverbs are in complementary distribution and thus might be part of the same super-category A. Are N and V in complementary distribution? What about Adv and V? What about N and Adj? Create examples to show whether these categories are in complementary distribution. If any are in complementary distribution with the others what does this tell us about the parts of speech? Next consider whether any functional categories are in complementary distribution with lexical categories.

CHALLENGE PROBLEM SET 5: SUBCATEGORIES OF ADVERBS
[Application of Skills and Knowledge; Challenge]
Your goal in this problem set is to set up a set of subcategories for Adverbs. Consider the following adverbs:

> *luckily, earnestly, intently, hopefully, probably, certainly, frequently, patiently, always, completely, almost, again, evidently, frankly, demandingly, yesterday, necessarily*

Part 1: For each adverb determine:
1) Can it appear before the subject? (e.g., <u>Unbelievably</u>, I don't know any pixies.)
2) Can it appear between the T (e.g., *will, have, is, can,* etc.) and the verb? (e.g., *I have <u>often</u> wondered about the existence of pixies.*)
3) Can it appear after the object? Or at the end of the sentence? (e.g., *Pixies eat mushrooms <u>vigorously</u>.*)
4) Can it appear between an object and a PP in a ditransitive (e.g., I put the book *carefully* on the table.)
(Note, these adverbs may appear in several of these positions.)

Part 2: Group the adverbs together into subcategories based on your answers to part 1.

Part 3: Within each group you may find more subtle orderings. For example, within the subcategory of adverbs that can appear between auxiliaries and verbs there may be an ordering of adverbs. Try putting multiple adverbs in each position. What are the orderings you find?

CHALLENGE PROBLEM SET 6: SUBCATEGORIES OF ADJECTIVES
[Application of Knowledge; Challenge]

Just as there are positional differences among adverbs (see Challenge set 3), we find an ordering of adjectives with respect to each other. Below is a list of adjectives. Pair each adjective with every other adjective and see which must come first in a noun phrase. Try to come up with a general ordering among these adjectives. (Although in the text I've told you to include numerals with the class of determiners, I've listed them here as adjectives, for the rest of the book treat them as determiners.)

> *deep, big, young, blue, desperate, two, scaly, thick*

One word of caution: it is sometimes possible to put some adjectives in any order. However, many of these orders are only possible if you are using the adjective contrastively or emphatically. For example, you can say *the old rubber sneaker* with a normal non-contrastive meaning, but *the rubber old sneaker* is only possible when it has a contrastive emphatic meaning (*the <u>RUBBER</u> old sneaker as opposed to the leather one*). Don't let these contrastive readings interfere with your subcategorization.

chapter 3

Constituency, Trees, and Rules

0. INTRODUCTION

Syntax is about the study of sentence *structure*. So let's start by defining what we mean by "structure." Consider the sentence in (1):

1) The students loved their syntax assignments.

One way to describe this sentence is as a simple linear string of words. Certainly this is how it is represented on the page. We could describe the sentence as consisting of the words *the, students, loved, their, syntax, assignments* in that order. As you can probably figure out, if that were all there was to syntax, you could put down this book here and not bother with the next fourteen chapters. But that isn't all there is to syntax. The statement that sentence (1) consists of a linear string of words misses several important generalizations about the internal structure of sentences and how these structures are represented in our minds. In point of fact we are going to claim that the words in sentence (1) are grouped into units (called constituents) and that these constituents are grouped into larger constituents, and so on until you get a sentence.

Notice that on a purely intuitive level there is some notion that certain words are more closely related to one another. For example, the word *the* seems to be tied more to the meaning of *students* than it is to *loved* or *syntax*. A related intuition can be seen by looking at the sentences in (2).

2) a)   The student loved his phonology readings.
    b)   The student hated his morphology professor.

Compare these sentences to (1). You'll see right away that the relationship between *the student* and *his syntax assignments* in (1) and *the student* and *his phonology readings* in (2a) is the same. Similarly, the relation between *the student* and *his morphology professor* in (2b), while of a different kind (hating instead of loving), is of a similar type: There is one entity (*the student*) who are either hating or loving another entity (*his syntax assignments*, *his phonology readings* or *his morphology professor*). In order to capture these intuitions (the intuition that certain words are more closely connected than others, and the intuitions about relationships between words in the sentence), we need a more complex notion. The notions we use to capture these intuitions are **constituency** and **hierarchical structure**. The notion that *the* and *student* are closely related to one another is captured by the fact that we treat them as part of a bigger unit that contains them, but not other words. We have two different ways to represent this bigger unit. One of them is to put square brackets around units:

3) [the student]

The other is to represent the units with a group of lines called a tree structure:

4)
       the student

These bigger units are called **constituents**. An informal definition for a constituent is given in (5):

5) *Constituent*: A group of words that functions together as a unit.

Constituency is the most important and basic notion in syntactic theory. Constituents form the backbone of the rest of this book. They capture the intuitions mentioned above. The "relatedness" is captured by membership in a constituent. As we will see it also allows us to capture the relationships between constituents exemplified in (1).

    Constituents don't float out in space. Instead they are embedded one inside another to form larger and larger constituents. This is **hierarchical structure**. Foreshadowing the discussion below a bit, here is the structure we'll develop for (1):

6)

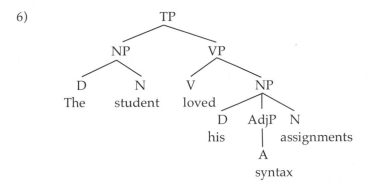

This is a typical hierarchical *tree structure*. The sentence constituent (represented by the symbol TP) consists of two constituents: a subject *noun phrase* (NP) *[the student]* and a predicate or *verb phrase* (VP) *[love his syntax assignments]*. The subject NP in turn contains a *noun* (N) *student* and a *determiner* (or article) (D) *the*. Similarly the VP contains a *verb* (V), and an object NP *[his syntax assignments]*. The object NP is further broken down into three bits: a determiner *his*, an adjective *syntax*, and a noun *assignments*. As you can see this tree has constituents (each represented by the point where lines come together) which are inside other constituents. This is hierarchical structure. Hierarchical constituent structure can also be represented with brackets. Each pair of brackets ([ ]) represents a constituent. We normally put the label of the constituent on the left member of the pair. The *bracketed diagram* for (6) is given in (7):

The Psychological Reality of Constituency

In the 1960s, Merrill Garrett and his colleagues showed that constituency has some reality in the minds of speakers. The researchers developed a series of experiments that involved placing a click in a neutral place in the stream of sounds. People tend to perceive these clicks not in the place where they actually occur, but at the edges of constituents. The italicized strings of words in the following sentences differ only in how the constituents are arranged.

i)   [In her *hope of marrying*]   *An/na was impractical.*
                                ↑
ii) [Harry's *hope of marrying An/na]   was impractical.*
                                ↑

Syntactic constituency is marked with square brackets [ ]; the placement of the click is marked with a slash /. People perceive the click in different places (marked with a ↑) in the two sentences, corresponding to the constituent boundaries – even though the click actually appears in the same place in each sentence (in the middle of the word *Anna*).

7) [$_{TP}$[$_{NP}$[$_D$The][$_N$student]][$_{VP}$[$_V$loved][$_{NP}$[$_D$his][$_{AdjP}$[$_{Adj}$syntax]][$_N$assignments]]]].

As you can see, bracketed diagrams are much harder to read, so for the most part we will use tree diagrams in this book. However, sometimes bracketed diagrams have their uses, so you should be able to translate back and forth between trees and bracketed diagrams.

1. RULES AND TREES

Now we have the tools necessary to develop a simple theory of sentence structure. We have a notion of constituent, which is a group of words that functions as a unit, and we have labels (parts of speech) that we can use to describe the parts of those units. Let's put the two of these together and try to develop a description of a possible English sentence. In generative grammar, generalizations about structure are represented by rules. These rules are said to "generate" the tree. So if we draw a tree a particular way, we need a rule to generate that tree. The rules we are going to consider in this chapter are called *phrase structure rules* (PSRs) because they generate the phrase structure tree of a sentence.

1.1 Noun Phrases (NPs)

Let's start with the constituents we call noun phrases (or NPs) and explore the range of material that can appear in them. The simplest NPs contain only a noun (usually a proper noun [+proper], pronoun [+pron], mass noun [−count] or a plural noun [+plural]):

8) a) John   b) water   c) cats

Our rule must minimally generate NPs then that contain only an N. The format for PSRs is shown in (9a), we use X, Y, and Z here as variables to stand for any category. (9b) shows our first pass at an NP rule:

9) a)   XP   →   X Y Z
              ↑   ↑   ↑
        the label   *"consists of"*   *the elements that make up*
        for the constituent   *the constituent*

    b) NP → N

This rule says that an NP is composed of (written as →) an N. This rule would generate a tree like (10):

10)   NP
        |
        N

There are many NPs (e.g., those that are [+count]) that are more complex than this of course:

11) a)   the box
    b)   his binder
    c)   that pink fluffy cushion

We must revise our rule to account for the presence of determiners:

12) a)   NP → D N

This generates a tree like:

b)   NP
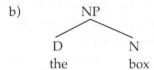
         D   N
        the   box

Compare the NPs in (8) and (11): You'll see that determiners are optional. As such we must indicate their optionality in the rule. We do this with parentheses ( ) around the optional elements:

13) NP → (D) N

Nouns can also be optionally modified by adjectives, so we will need to revise our rule as in (14) (don't worry about the "P" in AdjP yet, we'll explain that below).

14) a)   the big box   b)   his yellow binder

15) NP → (D) (AdjP) N

Nouns can also take prepositional phrase (PP) modifiers (see below where we discuss the structure of these constituents), so once again we'll have to revise our rule:

16) a)   the big box of crayons
    b)   his yellow binder with the red stripe

17) NP → (D) (AdjP) N (PP)

For concreteness, let's apply the rule in (17):

18)

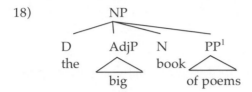

The NP constituent in (18) consists of four subconstituents: D, AdjP, N and PP.

For the moment, we need to make one more major revision to our NP rule. It turns out that you can have more than one adjective and more than one PP in an English NP:

19) The [$_{AdjP}$ big] [$_{AdjP}$ yellow] box [$_{PP}$ of cookies] [$_{PP}$ with the pink lid].

In this NP, the noun *box* is modified by *big, yellow, of cookies*, and *with the pink lid*. The rule must be changed then to account for this. It must allow more than one adjective and more than one PP modifier. We indicate this with a +, which means "repeat this category as many times as needed":

20) NP → (D) (AdjP+) N (PP+)

We will have cause to slightly revise this rule in later sections of this chapter and later chapters, but for now we can use this rule as a working hypothesis.

You now have enough information to try Challenge Problem Set 1

1.2 Adjective Phrases (AdjPs) and Adverb Phrases (AdvPs)

Consider the following two NPs:

21) a)   the big yellow book
    b)   the very yellow book

On the surface, these two NPs look very similar. They both consist of a determiner, followed by two modifiers and then a noun. But consider what modifies what in these NPs. In (21a) *big* modifies *book*, as does *yellow*. In (21b) on the other hand only *yellow* modifies book; *very* does not modify *book* (**very book*) – it modifies *yellow*. On an intuitive level then, the structures of these two phrases are actually quite different. (21a) has two adjective constituents that modify the N, whereas (21b) has only one *[very yellow]*. This constituent

---

[1] We use a triangle here to obscure the details of the PP and AdjP. Students should avoid using triangles when drawing trees, as you want to be as explicit as possible. I use it here only to draw attention to other aspects of the structure.

is called an adjective phrase (AdjP). The rule for the adjective phrase is given in (22a):

22) a) AdjP → (AdvP) Adj

b)

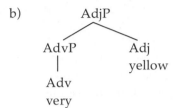

This will give us the following structures for the two NPs in (21):

23) a)

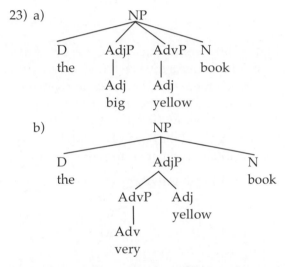

b)

So despite their surface similarity, these two NPs have radically different structures. In (23a) the N is modified by two AdjPs, in (23b) by only one. This leads us to an important observation about tree structures:

24) *Principle of Modification (informal):* Modifiers are always attached within the phrase they modify.

The adverb *very* modifies *yellow*, so it is part of the *yellow* AdjP in (23b). In (23a) by contrast, *big* doesn't modify *yellow*, it modifies *book*, so it is attached directly to the NP containing *book*.

A very similar rule is used to introduce AdvPs:

25) AdvP → (AdvP) Adv

26) very quickly

27)   AdvP

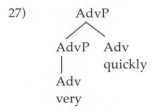

AdvP   Adv
  | quickly
Adv
very

Here is a common mistake to avoid: Notice that the AdvP rule specifies that its modifier is another AdvP: AdvP → (AdvP) Adv. The rule does NOT say *AdvP → (Adv) Adv, so you will never get trees of the form shown in (28):

28)

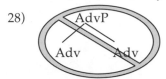

You might find the tree in (27) a little confusing. There are two Advs and two AdvPs. In order to understand that tree a little better, let's introduce a new concept: **heads**. We'll spend much more time on heads in chapters 6 and 7, but here's a first pass: The head of a phrase is the word that gives the phrase its category. For example, the head of the NP is the N, the head of a PP is the P, the head of the AdjP is Adj and the head of an AdvP is Adv. Let's look first at an adjective phrase (29a) and compare it to a complex AdvP:

29) a)

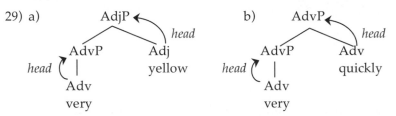

In (29a), the heads should be clear. The adverb *very* is the head of the adverb phrase and the adjective *yellow* is the head of AdjP. In (29b) we have the same kind of headedness, except both elements are adverbs. *Very* is the head of the lower AdvP, and *quickly* is the head of the higher one. We have two adverbs, so we have two AdvPs – each has their own head.

With this in mind, we can explain why the "very" AdvP is embedded in the AdjP. Above we gave a very informal description of the principle of modification. Let's try for a more precise version here:

30) **Principle of Modification** (revised): If an XP (that is, a phrase with some category X) modifies some head Y, then XP must be a sister to Y (i.e., a daughter of YP).

31)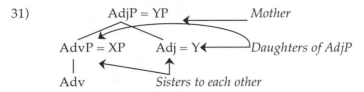

The diagram in (31) shows you the relations mentioned in the definition in (30). If we take the AdjP to be the *mother* then its *daughters* are the AdvP and the head Adj. Since AdvP and Adj are both daughters of the same mother then we say they are *sisters*. In (30) X and Y are variables that stand for any category. If one phrase, XP (AdvP) modifies some head Y (Adj), then the XP must be a sister to Y (i.e., the AdvP must be a sister to the head Adj), meaning they must share a mother. You'll notice that this relationship is asymmetric: AdvP modifies Adj, but Adj does _not_ modify AdvP.

You now have enough information to try General Problem Set 1

1.3 Prepositional Phrases (PPs)

The next major kind of constituent we consider is the prepositional phrase (PP). Most PPs take the form of a preposition (the head) followed by an NP:

32) a)   [$_{PP}$ to [$_{NP}$ the store]]
    b)   [$_{PP}$ with [$_{NP}$ an axe]]
    c)   [$_{PP}$ behind [$_{NP}$ the rubber tree]]

The PP rule appears to be:

33) a)   PP → P NP

    b)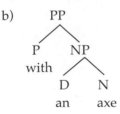

In the rule we've given the NP in the PP is obligatory. There may actually be some evidence for treating the NP in PPs as optional. There is a class of prepositions, traditionally called particles, that don't require a following NP:

34) a)   I haven't seen him *before*.
    b)   I blew it *up*.
    c)   I threw the garbage *out*.

If these are prepositions, then it appears as if the NP in the PP rule is optional:

35) PP → P (NP)

Even though all these particles look similar to prepositions (or are at least homophonous with them), there is some debate about whether they are or not. As an exercise you might try to think about the kinds of phenomena that would distinguish particles from prepositions without NPs.

> *You now have enough information to try General Problem Set 2*
> *If you read the Appendix, you should be able to do General Problem Set 3*

1.4 Verb Phrases (VPs)

Next we have the category headed by the verb: the verb phrase (VP). Minimally a VP consists of a single verb. This is the case of intransitives ($V_{[NP\_]}$):

36) a)   VP → V
    b)   Ignacious [$_{VP}$ left].

    c)   VP
                    |
                    V
                   left

Verbs may be modified by adverbs (AdvPs), which are, of course, optional:

37) a)   Ignacious [$_{VP}$ left quickly].
    b)   VP → V (AdvP)

    c)   VP

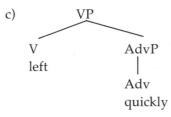

         V   AdvP
        left |
                        Adv
                      quickly

Interestingly, many of these adverbs can appear on either side of the V, and you can have as many AdvPs as you like:

38) a)   Ignacious [$_{VP}$ quickly left].
    b)   Ignacious [$_{VP}$ [$_{AdvP}$ deliberately] [$_{AdvP}$ always] left [$_{AdvP}$ quietly] [$_{AdvP}$ early]].
    c)   VP → (AdvP+) V (AdvP+)

39)

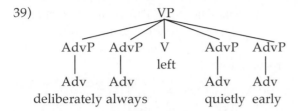

You'll recall from chapter 2 that there is a subcategory of verbs that can take an NP object (the transitive V$_{[NP\_NP]}$); these NPs appear immediately after the V and before any AdvPs:

40) a) VP → (AP+) V (NP) (AP+)

b) Bill [$_{VP}$ frequently kissed *his mother-in-law*].

c) Bill [$_{VP}$ kissed *his mother-in-law* quietly]. (cf. *Bill [$_{VP}$ kissed quietly *his mother-in-law*].)

41)

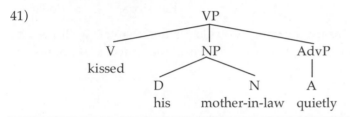

You now have enough information to try Challenge Problem Set 2

It is also possible to have two NPs in a sentence, for example with a double object verb like *spare* (V$_{[NP\_NP\,NP]}$). Both these NPs must come between the verb and any AdvPs:

42) I spared [$_{NP}$ the student] [$_{NP}$ any embarrassment] [$_{AdvP}$ yesterday].

Note, you are allowed to have a maximum of only two argument NPs. For this reason, we are not going to use the kleene plus (+) which entails that you can have as many as you like. Instead we are going to simply list both NPs in the rule:

43) a) VP → (AP+) V (NP) (NP) (AP+)

b)

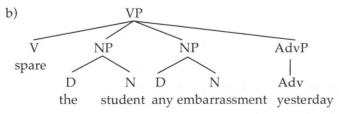

Verbs can be modified by PPs as well. These PPs can be arguments as in ditransitive verbs of the type V[NP _ NP PP] (e.g., the PP argument of the verb *put*) or they can be simple modifiers PP like *for a dollar* below. These PPs can appear either after an adverb or before it.

44) a) Bill [VPfrequently got his buckets [PP *from the store*] [PP *for a dollar*]].
    b) VP → (AdvP+) V (NP) (NP) (AdvP+) (PP+) (AdvP+)

    c)

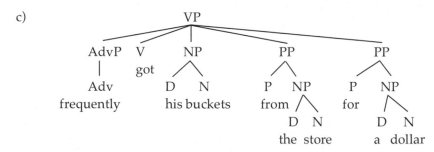

The rule in (44b) is nearly our final VP rule for this chapter; we'll need to make one further adjustment to it once we look at the structure of clauses.

1.5 Clauses

Thus far, we have NPs, VPs, APs, and PPs, and we've seen how they can be hierarchically organized with respect to one another. One thing that we have not accounted for is the structure of the sentence (or more accurately *clause*).[2] A clause consists of a subject NP and a VP. The label we use for clause is TP.[3]

45) [TP[NP Bill] [VP frequently got his buckets from the store for a dollar]].

This can be represented by the rule in (46):

46) TP → NP VP

A tree for (45) is given in (47):

---

[2] We'll give a proper definition for clause in a later chapter.
[3] In other books you might find sentences labeled as S or IP. S and IP are essentially the same thing as TP. We'll use TP here since it will make the transition to X-bar theory (in chapter 6) a little easier.

47)
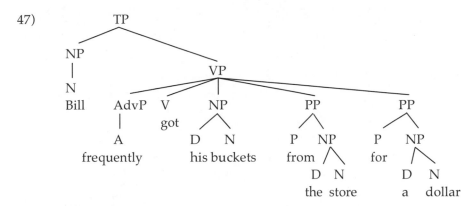

TPs can also include other items, including unsurprisingly elements of the category T (such as modal verbs and auxiliary verbs) like those in (48):

48) a) Cedric *might* crash the longboat.
    b) Gustaf *has* crashed the semi-truck.

It may surprise you that we won't treat these as verbs, the reason for this will become clear in later chapters. Note that the T in the TP is optional.

49) TP → NP (T) VP

A tree showing the application of this rule is given in (50):

50)
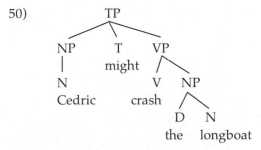

Clauses don't always have to stand on their own. There are times when one clause is embedded inside another:

51) [TP Shawn said [TP he decked the janitor]].

In sentence (51) the clause *he decked the janitor* lies inside the larger main clause. Often embedded clauses are introduced by a complementizer like *that* or *if*:

52) [TP Shawn said [CP [C that] [TP he decked the janitor]]].

We need a special rule to introduce complementizers (C):

53) a)   CP → (C) TP

b)

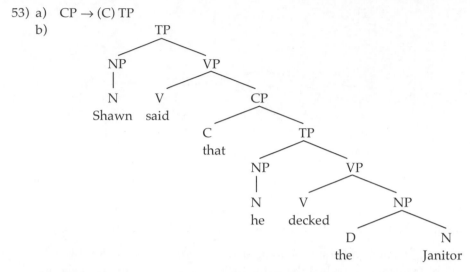

For the moment we will assume that *all* embedded clauses are CPs, whether or not they have a complementizer. We'll show evidence for this in chapter 7. This means that a sentence like *Shawn said he decked the janitor* will have a CP in it even though there is no complementizer *that*.

54)

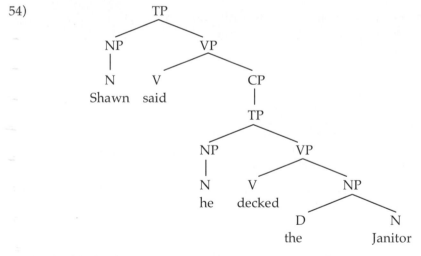

Embedded clauses appear in a variety of positions. In (54), the embedded clause appears in essentially the same slot as the direct object. Embedded clauses can also appear in subject position:

55) [$_{TP}$ [$_{CP}$ That he decked the janitor] worried Jeff].

Because of this we are going to have to modify our TP and VP rules to allow embedded clauses. Syntacticians use curly brackets { } to indicate a choice.

So {NP/CP} means that you are allowed *either* an NP or an CP but not both. The Modification to the TP rule is relatively straightforward. We simply allow the choice between an NP and a CP in the initial NP:

56) a)   TP → {NP/CP} (T) VP
    b)

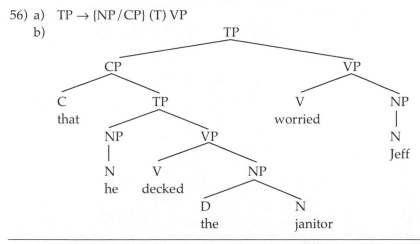

You now have enough information to try Challenge Problem Set 3

The revised VP rule requires a little more finesse. First observe that in verbs that allow both an NP and a CP (V$_{[NP\_\ \{NP/CP\}]}$ such as *ask*), the CP follows the NP but precedes the PP (in the following sentence *yesterday* and *over the phone* should be interpreted as modifying *ask*, not *ate*), essentially in the position of the second NP in the rule:

57) Naomi asked [$_{NP}$ Erin] [$_{CP}$ if [$_{TP}$ Dan ate her Kung-Pao chicken]] yesterday over the phone.

This gives us the rule :

58) a)   VP → (AdvP+) V (NP) ({NP/CP}) (AdvP+) (PP+) (AdvP+)

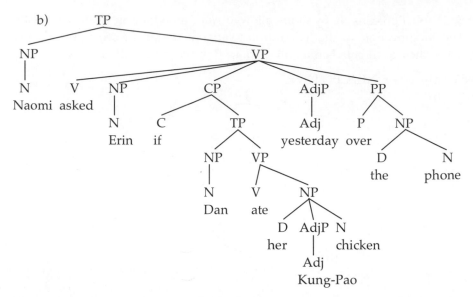

This rule is by no means perfect. There is no way to draw the tree for sentences where an AdvP can appear before the CP (*Naomi asked Erin quietly if Dan ate her KungPao Chicken*). We don't want to add an optional AdjP before the ({CP/NP}) in the rule because AdvPs cannot appear before the NP. For the moment, we'll go with the VP rule as it is written, and return to questions like this later, although we return to the issue in chapter 6.

The last revision we have to make to our PSRs is to add the CP as a modifier to NPs to account for cases like:

59) a) [NP The fact about Bill [CP that he likes icecream]] bothers Natasha.
   b) NP → (D) (AdjP+) N (PP+) (CP)
   c)

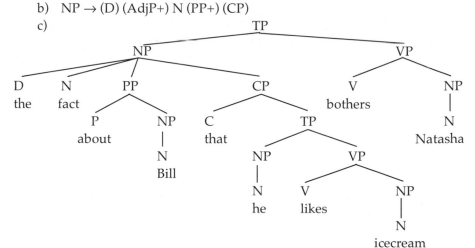

You now have enough information to try General Problem Set 4.
If you read the Appendix you will have enough information to do
General Problem Sets 5, 6 & 7.

Relative Clauses

In addition to the CPs that modify Ns as in the above cases, there is another kind of CP modifier to an N. These are called ***relative clauses***. We aren't going to include relative clauses in our rules yet. This is because they often contain what is called a "gap" or a place where some part of the clause is missing. For example:

i) The man [whose car I hit ____ last week] sued me.

The underscore in the sentence indicates where the gap is – the object of the verb *hit* is in the wrong place, it should be where the underscore is. Corresponding to the gap we also have the *wh*-word *whose* and the noun *car*. These are appearing at the beginning of the clause. Because of these gaps and fronted *wh*-elements, we aren't going to worry about the internal structure of these clauses.

   Here's a challenge: relative clauses actually appear in a different position than the CPs that follow nouns like *the fact*. Can you figure out what the difference is? (Hint: it has to do with the relative position of the CP and the PP in the NP rule.)

1.6 Summary

In this section we've been looking at the PSRs needed to generate trees that account for English sentences. As we'll see in later chapters, this is nothing but a first pass at a very complex set of data. It is probably worth repeating the final form of each of the rules here:

60) a) CP → (C) TP
   b) TP → {NP/CP} (T) VP
   c) VP → (AdvP+) V (NP)({NP/CP}) (AdvP+) (PP+) (AdvP+)
   d) NP → (D) (AdjP+) N (PP+) (CP)
   e) PP → P (NP)
   f) AdjP → (AdvP) Adj
   g) AdvP → (AdvP) Adv

Recursion

The rules we have written here have a very important property. Notice the following thing: The TP rule has a VP under it. Similarly, the VP rule can take a CP under it, and the CP takes a TP. This means that the three rules can form a loop and repeat endlessly:

i)   Fred said that Mary believes that Susan wants that Peter desires that … etc.

This property, called *recursion*, accounts partially for the infinite nature of human language. Because you get these endless loops, it is possible to generate sentences that have never been heard before. This simple property of these rules thus at least partly explains the creativity of human language, which in itself is a remarkable result.

These rules account for a wide variety of English sentences. A sentence using each of these rules is shown in (61):

61) The big man from NY has often said that he gave peanuts to elephants.

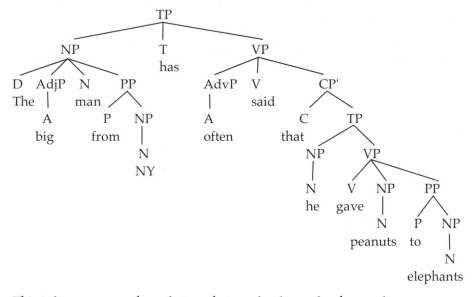

This is by no means the only tree that can be drawn by these rules.

2. HOW TO DRAW A TREE

You now have the tools you need to start drawing trees. You have the rules, and you have the parts of speech. I suspect that you'll find drawing trees much more difficult than you expect. It takes a lot of practice to know which rules to apply and apply them consistently and accurately to a sentence. You won't be able to draw trees easily until you literally do dozens of them. Drawing syntactic trees is a learned skill that needs lots of practice, just like learning to play the piano.

There are actually two ways to go about drawing a tree. You can start at the bottom and work your way up to the TP, or you can start with the TP and work your way down. Which technique you use depends upon your individual style. For most people who are just starting out, starting at the bottom of the tree with the words works best. When you become more practiced and experienced you may find starting at the top quicker. Below, I give step-by-step instructions for both of these techniques.

2.1 Bottom-up Trees

This method for tree drawing often works best for beginners. Here are some (hopefully helpful) steps to go through when drawing trees.

1. Write out the sentence and identify the parts of speech:

    D Adv Adj N   V   D   N
    The very small boy kissed the platypus.

2. Identify what modifies what. Remember the modification relations. If the word modifies something then it is contained in the same constituent as that thing.

    Very modifies *small*.   *Very small* modifies *boy*.
    The modifies *boy*.   *The* modifies *platypus*.
    The platypus modifies *kissed*.

3. Start linking together items that modify one another. It often helps to start at the right edge. Always start with adjacent words. If the modifier is modifying a noun, then the rule you must apply is the NP rule:

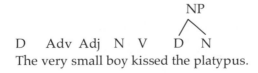

    D   Adv Adj N   V   D   N
    The very small boy kissed the platypus.

Similarly if the word that is being modified is an adjective, then you must apply the AdjP rule:

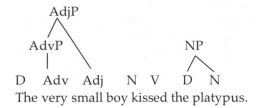

The very small boy kissed the platypus.

4. Make sure you apply the rule *exactly* as it is written. For example the AdjP rule reads AdjP → (AdvP) Adj. This means that the Adv must have an AdvP on top of it before it can combine with the Adj.

5. Keep applying the rules until you have attached all the modifiers to the modified constituents. Apply one rule at a time. Work from right to left (from the end of the sentence to the beginning.) Try doing the rules in the following order:

a) AdjPs & AdvPs   b) NPs & PPs
c) VPs   d) TP
e) If your sentence has more than one clause in it, start with the most embedded clause.

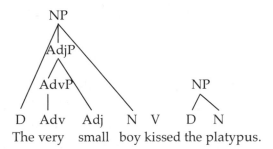

The very small boy kissed the platypus.

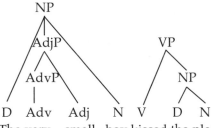

The very small boy kissed the platypus.

6. When you've built up the subject NP and the VP, apply the TP (and if appropriate the CP) rule:

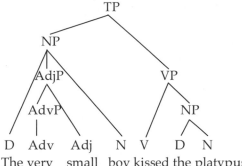

The very small boy kissed the platypus.

7. *This is the most important step of all*: Now go back and make sure that your tree is really generated by the rules. Check each level in the tree and make sure your rules will generate it. If they don't, apply the rule correctly and fix the structure.

8. Some important considerations:
    a) Make sure that everything is attached to the tree.
    b) Make sure that every category has only *one* line immediately on top of it (it can have more than one under it, but only one immediately on top of it).
    c) Don't cross lines.
    d) Make sure all branches in the tree have a part of speech label.
    e) Avoid triangles.

To Line or Not?

In many works on syntax you will find trees that have the word connected to the category with a line, rather than writing the word immediately under its category as we have been doing. This is a historical artifact of the way trees used to be constructed in the 1950s. The lines that connect elements in trees mean "created by a phrase structure rule." There are no phrase structure rules that connect words with their categories (i.e., there is no rule V→ *kissed*), so technically speaking any line between the word's category and the word is incorrect.

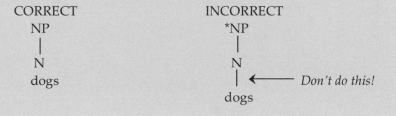

Skill at tree drawing comes only with practice. At the end of this chapter are a number of sentences that you can practice on. Use the suggestions above if you find them helpful. Another helpful idea is to model your trees on ones that you can find in this chapter. Look carefully at them, and use them as a starting point. Finally, don't forget: Always check your trees against the rules that generate them.

2.2 The Top-down Method of Drawing Trees

Most professional syntacticians use a slightly quicker means of drawing trees. Once you are practiced at identifying the structure of trees, you will probably want to use this technique. But be warned, sometimes this technique can lead you astray if you are not careful.

1. This method starts out the same way as the other: write out the sentence and identify the parts of speech.

    D   Adv Adj N   V   D   N
    The very small boy kissed the platypus.

2. Next draw the TP node at the top of the tree, with the subject NP and VP underneath:

    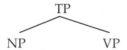

    D   Adv Adj N   V   D   N
    The very small boy kissed the platypus.

3. Using the NP rule, flesh out the subject NP. You will have to look ahead here. If there is a P, you will probably need a PP. Similarly, if there is an Adj, you'll need at least one AdjP, maybe more. Remember the principle of modification: elements that modify one another are part of the same constituent.

    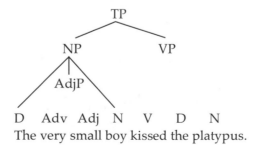

    D   Adv Adj N   V   D   N
    The very small boy kissed the platypus.

4. Fill in the AdvPs, AdjPs and PPs as necessary. You may need to do other NPs inside PPs

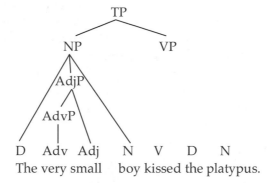

5. Next do constituents inside the VP, including object NPs, and any APs and PPs inside them.

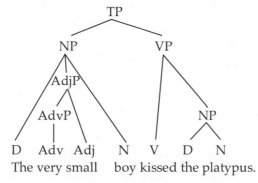

6. Again, the most important step is to go back and make sure that your tree obeys all the rules, as well as the golden rule of tree structures.

7. Some important considerations:
    a) Make sure that everything is attached.
    b) Make sure that every category has only *one* line immediately on top of it. (It can have more than one under it, but only one immediately on top of it.)
    c) Don't cross lines.
    d) Make sure all branches in the tree have a part of speech label.
    e) Avoid triangles.

Again, I strongly recommend that you start your tree drawing using the bottom-up method, but after some practice, you may find this latter method quicker.

2.3 Bracketed Diagrams

Sometimes it is preferable to use the bracketed notation instead of the tree notation. This is especially true when there are large parts of the sentence that are irrelevant to the discussion at hand. Drawing bracketed diagrams essentially follows the same principles for tree drawing (see 2.1 or 2.2 above). The exception is that instead of drawing to lines connecting at the top, you put square brackets on either side of the constituent. A label is usually put on the left member of the bracket pair as a subscript.

62)

$= [_{NP}[_D \text{ the}] [_N \text{ man}]]$

Both words and phrases are bracketed this way. For each point where you have a bunch of lines connecting, you have a pair of brackets.

To see how this works, let's take our sentence from sections 2.1 and 2.2 above and do it again in brackets:

1.   First we mark the parts of speech. This time with labeled brackets:

$[_D \text{ The}] [_{Adv} \text{ very}] [_{Adj} \text{ small}] [_N \text{ boy}] [_V \text{ kissed}] [_D \text{ the}] [_N \text{ platypus}]$.

2.   Next we apply the AP rule, NP and PP rules:

   AP:
$[_D \text{ The}] [_{AdvP}[_{Adv} \text{ very}]] [_{Adj} \text{ small}] [_N \text{ boy}] [_V \text{ kissed}] [_D \text{ the}] [_N \text{ platypus}]$.
$[_D \text{ The}] [_{AdjP}[_{AdvP}[_{Adv} \text{ very}]] [_{Adj} \text{ small}]] [_N \text{ boy}] [_V \text{ kissed}] [_D \text{ the}] [_N \text{ platypus}]$.

   NP:
$[_{NP}[_D \text{ The}][_{AdjP}[_{AdvP}[_{Adv} \text{ very}]][_{Adj} \text{ small}]][_N \text{ boy}]] [_V \text{ kissed}] [_D \text{ the}] [_N \text{ platypus}]$.
$[_{NP}[_D \text{ The}][_{AdjP}[_{AdvP}[_{Adv} \text{ very}]][_{Adj} \text{ small}]][_N \text{ boy}]][_V \text{ kissed}][_{NP}[_D \text{the}][_N \text{platypus}]]$.

3.   Now the VP and TP rules:

   VP:
$[_{NP}[_D \text{The}][_{AdjP}[_{AdvP}[_{Adv} \text{very}]][_{Adj} \text{small}]][_N \text{boy}]][_{VP}[_V \text{kissed}][_{NP}[_D \text{the}][_N \text{platypus}]]]$.

   TP:
$[_{TP}[_{NP}[_D \text{The}][_{AdjP}[_{AdvP}[_{Adv} \text{very}]][_{Adj} \text{small}]][_N \text{boy}]][_{VP}[_V \text{kissed}][_{NP}[_D \text{the}][_N \text{platypus}]]]]$.

4.   Finally, go back and check that the structure can be generated by the rules.

3. MODIFICATION AND AMBIGUITY

Syntactic trees allow us to capture another remarkable fact about language. Let's start with the following sentence:

63) The man killed the king with a knife.

This sentences turns out to have more than one meaning, but for the moment consider only the least difficult reading for it (the phrase in quotes in (64) is called a *paraphrase*, which is the technical term for "another way of saying the same thing"):

64) (63) meaning "the man used a knife to kill the king."

Remember the Principle of modification:

65) *Principle of Modification* (revised): If an XP (that is, a phrase with some category X) modifies some head Y, then XP must be a sister to Y (i.e., a daughter of YP).

In (63) the PP *with a knife* modifies *killed*, so the structure will look like (66):

66)

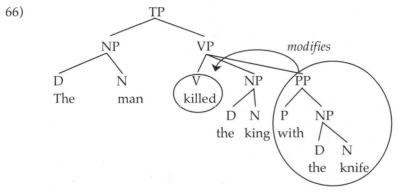

[*With a knife*] describes how the man killed the king. It modifies the verb *killed*, so it is attached under the VP. Now consider the other meaning of (63).

67) (63a) meaning "the king with the knife was killed by the man (who used a gun)."

The meaning in (67) has the PP *with the knife* modifying *king*, and thus attached to the NP:

68)

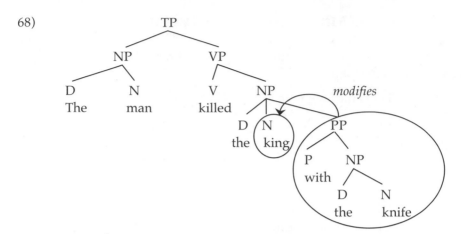

These examples illustrate an important property of syntactic trees. Trees allow us to capture the differences between ambiguous readings of the same surface sentence.

You now have enough information to try General Problem Set 8

4. CONSTITUENCY TESTS

In chapter 1, we held linguistics in general (and syntax specifically) up to the light of the scientific method. That is, if we make a hypothesis about something, we must be able to test that hypothesis. In this chapter, we have proposed the hypothesis that sentences are composed of higher-level groupings called constituents. Constituents are represented in tree structures and are generated by rules. If the hypothesis of constituency is correct, we should be able to test it in general (as well as test the specific instances of the rules).

In order to figure out what kinds of tests we need, it is helpful to reconsider the specifics of the hypothesis. The definition of constituents states that they are groups of words that function as a unit. If this is the case, then we should find instances where groups of words behave as single units. These instances can serve as tests for the hypothesis. In other words, they are *tests for constituency*. There are a lot of constituency tests listed in the syntactic literature. We are going to look at only four here: replacement, stand alone, movement, and coordination.

First, the smallest constituent is a single word, so it follows that if you can replace a group of words with a single word then we know that group forms a constituent. Consider the italicized NP in (69), it can be replaced with a single word (in this case a pronoun). This is the *replacement* test.

69) a)   *The man from NY* flew only ultra-light planes.
   b)   *He* flew only ultra-light planes.

There is one important caveat to the test of replacement: There are many cases in our rules of optional items (those things marked in parentheses like the AP in NP → (D) (AdjP+) N.) When we replace a string of words with a single word, how do we know that we aren't just leaving off the optional items? To avoid this problem, we have to keep the meaning as closely related to the original as possible. This requires some judgment on your part. None of these tests is absolute or foolproof.

   The second test we will use is the **stand alone** test (sometimes also called the **sentence fragment** test). If the words can stand alone in response to a question, then they probably constitute a constituent. Consider the sentence in (70a) and repeated in (70b). We are going to test for the constituency of the italicized phrases.

70) a)   Paul *ate at a really fancy restaurant*.
   b)   Paul *ate at* a really fancy restaurant.

If we ask the question "What did Paul do yesterday afternoon?" we can answer with the italicized group of words in (70a), but not in (70b):

71) a)   Ate at a really fancy restaurant.
   b)   *Ate at.

Neither of these responses is proper English in prescriptive terms, but you can easily tell that (71a) is better than (71b).

   Movement is our third test of constituency. If you can move a group of words around in the sentence, then they are a constituent because you can move them as a unit. Some typical examples are shown in (72). **Clefting** (72a) involves putting a string of words between *It was* (or *It is*) and a *that* at the beginning of the sentence. **Preposing** (72b) (also called *pseudoclefting*) involves putting the string of words before a *is/are what* or *is/are who* at the front of the sentence. We discuss the **passive** (72c) at length in chapter 10. Briefly, it involves putting the object in the subject position, the subject in a "by phrase" (after the word *by*) and changing the verb form (for example from *kiss* to *was kissed*).

72) a) Clefting: It was [a brand new car] that he bought.
                           (from *He bought a brand new car*)

    b) Preposing: [Big bowls of beans] are what I like.
                           (from *I like big bowls of beans*)

    c) Passive: [The big boy] was kissed by [the slobbering dog].
                           (from *The slobbering dog kissed the big boy*)

Again, the movement test is only reliable when you keep the meaning

---

PSRs for Conjunction

In order to draw trees with conjunction in them, we need two more rules.
These rules are slightly different than the ones we have looked at up to
now. These rules are not category specific. Instead they use a variable (X).
This X can stand for N or V or A or P etc. Just like in algebra, it is a
variable that can stand for different categories. We need two rules, one to
conjoin phrases (*[The Flintstones] and [the Rubbles]*) and one to conjoin
words (*the [dancer] and [singer]*):

i)   XP → XP conj XP
ii) X → X conj X

These result in trees like:

iii)

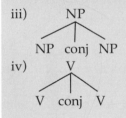

iv)

---

roughly the same as the original sentence.

Finally, we have the test of **coordination** (also called **conjunction**).
Coordinate structures are constituents linked by a conjunction like *and* or *or*.
Only constituents of the same syntactic category can be conjoined:

73) a) [John] and [the man] went to the store.
    b) *John and very blue went to the store.

If you can coordinate a group of words with a similar group of words, then
they form a constituent.

You now have enough information to try General Problem Sets 9 & 10 and
Challenge Problem Set 4

When Constituency Tests Fail

Unfortunately, sometimes it is the case that constituency tests give false results (which is one of the reasons we haven't spent much time on them in this text). Consider the case of the subject of a sentence and its verb. These do not form a constituent:

i)

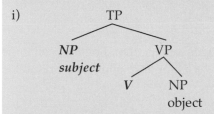

However, under certain circumstances you can conjoin a subject and verb to the exclusion of the object:

ii)   Bruce loved and Kelly hated phonology class.

Sentence (ii) seems to indicate that the verb and subject form a constituent, which they don't according to the tree in (i). As you will see in later chapters, it turns out that things can move around in sentences or be deleted. This means that sometimes the constituency is obscured by other factors. For this reason, to be sure that a test is working correctly you have to apply more than one test to a given structure. Always perform at least two different tests to check constituency; as one alone may give you a false result.

5. SUMMARY AND CONCLUSION

We've done a lot in this chapter. We looked at the idea that sentences are hierarchically organized into constituent structures. We represented these constituent structures in trees and bracketed diagrams. We also developed a set of rules to generate those structures, and finally we looked at constituency tests that can be used to test the structures. Parts of speech are the labeling system for constituent structure. We showed that parts of speech can't be determined by meaning alone. In the appendix to this chapter, we sketch out some distributional tests for part of speech class.

APPENDIX: HOW TO DO FOREIGN LANGUAGE PSR PROBLEMS

There are two kinds of non-English language problems found in syntax:
those that provide a word-by-word gloss and those that don't.

A1. Doing problems with word-by-word glosses

Often, linguistic examples from languages other than English will take
the following form (example from Sinhala – a language spoken in Sri Lanka;
data from Lehmann 1978):

74) Jōn   ballavə däkka ◄——————————— *Actual language data*
    John   dog   saw   ◄——————————— *Word-by-word gloss*
    "John saw the dog."   ◄——————————— *Idiomatic translation*

There are three lines: the actual data, a word-by-word gloss and an idiomatic
translation into English. Of these the most important for doing the problem
set is the second line – the word-by-word gloss. The glosses are lined up
word for word (and sometimes morpheme for morpheme) with the foreign
language on the line above. This line tells you (1) what each word
in the foreign language example means, and more importantly, (2) the order
of the words in the foreign language. When trying to determine the phrase
structure of a foreign language or the behavior of a word or phrase, this
is the line to look at! (However, when drawing trees and citing examples
in your answer it is considered more respectful of the language to use
the actual foreign language words.) Remember: <u>don't</u> do an analysis
of the idiomatic translation of the sentence, because then you are only doing
an analysis of English!

Here's a more complete paradigm of Sinhala, along with a series of
typical questions:

i)   Jōn   ballavə däkka
     John   dog   saw
     "John saw the dog."

ii) Jōn   janēle iñdəla ballavə däkka
     John   window from   dog   saw
     "John saw the dog from the window."

iii) Jōn   eyāge   taḍi   ballavə däkka
     John   his   big   dog   saw
     "John saw his big dog."

a) Assume there is an AdjP rule: AdjP → Adj. What is the NP rule of
    Sinhala?
b) What is the PP rule of Sinhala?
c) What is the VP rule of Sinhala? (Assume all non-head material is
    optional.)
d) What is the TP rule of Sinhala?
e) Draw the tree for sentences (ii) and (iii).

The first step in analyzing a language like this is to determine the parts
of speech of each of the words. Be very careful here, do not assume
that because English has certain categories that the language you are looking
at has the same categories; however, all other things being equal
you can assume that there will be some parallels (unless we have evidence
to the contrary):

i)   Jōn   ballavə däkka
     John   dog   saw
     N   N   V

ii) Jōn   janēle   iñdəla   ballavə däkka
     John   window   from   dog   saw
     N   N   P   N   V

iii) Jōn   eyāge   taḍi   ballavə däkka
     John   his   big   dog   saw
     N   D   Adj   N   V

Next let's answer question (a). We can observe from sentence (i) that an NP
in Sinhala (just like in English) can be an N by itself (e.g., *Jōn*). This means
that anything other than the noun has to be optional. Consider now the
sentence in (iii); from the literal English translation we can tell that the words
meaning "big" and "his" modify the word "dog," and are thus part of the
NP headed by "dog." We're told in (a) to assume that there is an AdjP rule
(AdjP → Adj), and we are treating the word for "his" as a determiner. Thus it
follows that the Sinhala NP rule is at least NP → (D) (AdjP) N. You'll notice
that the order of elements in this rule is the same as the order of elements
in the Sinhala sentence. You should also note that the PP meaning "from the
window" does not modify the N, so is not part of the NP rule at this point.
Since it modifies the V, it will be part of the VP rule.

   Question (b) asks us about the PP rule. We have one P in the data –
the word meaning "from" in sentence (ii). Pay careful attention here.
This P appears between two nouns; but the noun associated with the P is
the one meaning "window." This means that the P in Sinhala *follows* the NP;
so the rule is PP → NP P. We have no evidence if the NP here is optional.
   The VP rule is next in (c). Sentence (ii) is the most informative here.
Looking at what would be in the VP in English, we have the PP meaning
"from the window" and the NP meaning "dog." These both precede the V.
This is true in sentences (i) and (iii) too. The PP is clearly optional, but there
is no evidence in the data about whether the NP is or not. However,
you are told to assume that "all non-head material is optional." So the rule
is VP → (PP) (NP) V.
   Finally we have the TP rule. Like English, the subject NP precedes
the VP. So the rule is TP → NP VP. We have no evidence for a T node so we
have not posited one.
   Here are the trees for (ii) and (iii).

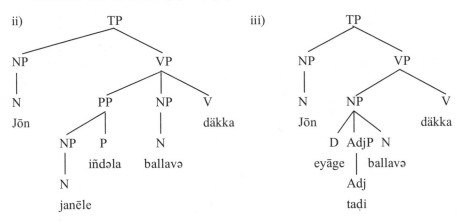

A2. Doing problems without word-by-word glosses

Sometimes you will be given data without word-by-word glosses, and only
an idiomatic sentence translation. Take the following example from Welsh:

i)   Agorodd y dyn y drws.   "The man opened the door."
ii) Collodd y dyn ddwy bunt.   "The man lost two pounds (money)."
iii) Gyrhaeddodd y dyn.   "The man arrived."
iv) Gaeth y dyn ddwy bunt.   "The man got two pounds."
v)   Agorodd Fred ddwy ddrws.   "Fred opened two doors."

Since word-by-word glosses are the most important part of a foreign
language problem (see section A1), the first thing you have to do is develop

a word-by-word gloss (or morphological analysis). To do this you compare and contrast the sentences in the data set, using the translation as a guide.

Let us do the above sentences as an example. First, look at the first four of the sentences, what words in the English gloss is common to them all? "The man". Now, look at the Welsh in the left column. What words are found in all of these sentences? *Y dyn*. There is a high probability that the Welsh words *y dyn* means "the man." We can deduce that *y* means "the" by looking at the other instance of *y* in sentence (i). Sentence (i) has two "the"s in it, and the Welsh has two *y*s. This means that *dyn* probably means man. We might even venture that *drws* means door. This appears to be consistent with the fact that sentence (v) has *ddrws* in it. Although *ddrws* and *drws* aren't identical, neither are their glosses: sentence (i) has the singular "door" in it, and sentence (v) has the plural "doors."[4]

Similarly by looking at sentences (ii) and (v) we can see that the only two words they have in common in both the English and the Welsh is *ddwy* "two." Hopefully the meaning of *Fred* is self-evident, but even if it weren't we could deduce it by process of elimination. The same is true of each of the verbs. Sentences (i) and (v) have in common the word *agorodd* and the gloss "open." We might suppose that initial position is where verbs like "open" go. This means that the first word in each of the other sentences is the verb. Alternately we could have deduced that these were the various verbs, based on the fact that we had meanings for all the nouns and determiners, so by process of elimination all that is left in each sentence is the verb.

Once you've done this morphological analysis, you are ready to tackle the rest of the problem as we did in section A1.

IDEAS, RULES, AND CONSTRAINTS INTRODUCED IN THIS CHAPTER

i)   **Constituent**: A group of words that functions together as a unit.

ii)   **Hierarchical Structure**: Constituents in a sentence are embedded inside of other constituents.

iii)   **Syntactic Trees and Bracketed Diagrams**: These are means of representing constituency. They are generated by rules.

---

[4] You might be tempted to think that the *dd* is a plural marker. While consistent with the facts above, the *dd* is actually a result of a special morphophonological process triggered by *dwy* (*ddwy*) called a consonant mutation. Knowing this isn't necessary to solving the problem set.

iv)   ***Phrase Structure Rules***
         a)   CP → (C) TP
         b)   TP → {NP/CP} (T) VP
         c)   VP → (AdvP+) V (NP) ({NP/CP}) (AdvP+) (PP+) (AdvP+)
         d)   NP → (D) (AdjP+) N (PP+) (CP)
         e)   PP → P (NP)
         f)   AdjP → (AdvP) Adj
         g)   AdvP → (AdvP) Adv
         h)   XP → XP conj XP
         i)   X → X conj X

v)   ***Head***: The word that gives its category to the phrase.

vi)   ***Recursion***: The possibility of loops in the phrase structure rules
         that allow infinitely long sentences, and explain the creativity
         of language.

vii)   ***The Principle of Modification***: If an XP (that is, a phrase with some
         category X) modifies some head Y, then XP must be a sister to Y (i.e.,
         a daughter of YP).

viii)   ***Constituency Tests***: Tests that show that a group of words function
         as a unit. There are four major constituency tests given here:
         movement, coordination, stand alone, and ***replacement***.

FURTHER READING

Chomsky, Noam (1957) *Syntactic Structures*. The Hague: Janua Linguarum 4.
Chomsky, Noam (1965) *Aspects of the Theory of Syntax*: Cambridge: MIT
         Press.

GENERAL PROBLEM SETS

1. TREES: NPS, ADJPS AND ADVPS
[Application of Skills; Basic]
Draw the trees for the following AdjPs, AdvPs, and NPs:
a)   very smelly   b)   too quickly
c)   much too quickly   d)   very much too quickly
e)   the old shoelace
f)   the soggy limp spaghetti noodle *[assume* spaghetti = *Adj]*
g)   these very finicky children

2. TREES II: ENGLISH PPS
[Application of Skills; Basic]
Draw the trees for the following English NPs and PPs:
a)   The desk with the wobbly drawer
b)   In my black rubber boots *[assume* rubber *is an Adj]*
c)   That notebook with the scribbles in the margin
d)   The pen at the back of the drawer in the desk near the bright yellow
     painting

3. SWEDISH NPS
[Application of Skills and Knowledge; Basic]
Consider the following data from Swedish. (If you speak Swedish, please
confine yourself to this data, do *not* try to include definite forms, e.g.,
the umbrella.) You may wish to review Appendix A before attempting
this problem. (Data courtesy of Sheila Dooley.)

a)   folk   "people"
b)   ett paraply   "an umbrella"
c)   tre paraplyer   "three umbrellas"
d)   ett äpple   "an apple"
e)   ett rött paraply   "a red umbrella"
f)   ett gult äpple   "a yellow apple"
g)   ett mycket fint paraply   "a very fine umbrella"
h)   ett gammalt fint paraply   "a fine old umbrella"
i)   ett rött paraply med ett gult handtag "a red umbrella with a yellow handle"

1)   Assume the Adv rule of Swedish is AdvP → Adv. What is the AdjP rule?
2)   Are determiners obligatory in Swedish NPs?
3)   Are AdjPs obligatory in Swedish NPs?
4)   What is the PP rule for Swedish?
5)   Are PPs obligatory in Swedish NPs?
6)   What is the NP rule for Swedish?
7)   Draw the trees for (g), (h), and (i).
8)   Give the bracketed diagram for (f) and (i).

4. ENGLISH
[Application of Skills and Knowledge; Basic to Advanced]
Draw phrase structure trees *and* bracketed diagrams for each of the
following sentences, indicate all the categories (phrase (e.g., NP) and word
level (e.g., N)) on the tree. Use the rules given above in the "Ideas" summary
of this chapter. Be careful that items that modify one another are part of the
same constituent. Treat words like *can, should, might, was,* as instances
of the category T (tense). (Sentences d–h are from Sheila Dooley.)

a)   The kangaroo hopped over the truck.
b)   I haven't seen this sentence before.   *[before is a P,* haven't *is a T]*
c)   Susan will never sing at weddings.   *[never is an Adv]*
d)   The officer carefully inspected the license.

e)   Every cat always knows the location of her favorite catnip toy.
f)   The cat put her catnip toy on the plastic mat.
g)   The very young child walked from school to the store.
h)   John paid a dollar for a head of lettuce.
i)   Teenagers drive rather quickly.
j)   A clever magician with the right equipment can fool the audience easily.
k)   The police might plant the drugs in the apartment.
l)   Those Olympic hopefuls should practice diligently daily.
m)   The latest research on dieting always warns people about the dangers of too much cholesterol.
n)   That annoying faucet was dripping constantly for months.
o)   Marian wonders if the package from Boston will ever arrive.
p)   I said that Bonny should do some dances from the Middle East.
q)   That Dan smokes in the office really bothers Alina.
r)   The belief that syntactic theory reveals the inner structure of sentences emboldened the already much too cocky professor.

5. BAMBARA
[Application of Skills; Basic]
Consider the following data from Bambara, a Mande language spoken in Mali. (The glosses have been slightly simplified.) Pay careful attention to the second line, where the word order of Bambara is shown. (Data from Koopman 1992.)

a)   A   kasira.
     he   cried
      "He cried."

b)   Den   ye   ji   min.
     child   PAST   water   drink
     "The child drank water."

c)   N sonna a ma.
     I agreed it to
     "I agreed to it."

Answer the following questions about Bambara. Do not break apart words in your analysis.

1)   Do you need a T category in Bambara?
2)   Do you need a D category in Bambara?
3)   What is the NP rule for Bambara? (You do not need any AdjP or PPs in the rule.)
4)   What is the PP rule for Bambara?
5)   What is the VP rule for Bambara?
6)   What is the TP rule for Bambara? (Keep in mind your answers to the above questions; be consistent.)
7)   Draw trees for (a), (b), and (c) using your rules.
8)   Draw bracketed diagrams for (b) and (c).

6. HIXKARYANA

[Application of Skills; Basic/Intermediate]
Look carefully at the following data from a Carib language from Brazil (the glosses have been slightly simplified from the original). In your analysis do not break apart words. (Data from Derbyshire 1985.)

a) Kuraha   yonyhoryeno   bɨyekomo.
   bow   made   boy
   "The boy made a bow."

b) Newehyatxhe   woriskomo komo.
   take-bath   women   all
   "All the women take a bath."

c) Toto   heno komo   yonoye kamara.
   person   dead all   ate   jaguar
   "The jaguar ate all the dead people."

Now answer the following questions about Hixkaryana:

1) Is there any evidence for a determiner category in Hixkaryana? Be sure to consider quantifier words as possible determiners (like *some* and *all*).
2) Posit an NP rule to account for Hixkaryana. (Be careful to do it for the second line, the word-by-word gloss, in these examples not the third line.) Assume there is an AdjP rule: AdjP → Adj.
3) Posit a VP rule for Hixkaryana.
4) Posit a TP rule for Hixkaryana.
5) What is the part of speech of *newehyatxhe*? How do you know?
6) Draw the trees for (a) and (c) using the rules you posited above. (Hint: if your trees don't work, then you have probably made a mistake in the rules.)
7) Give bracketed diagrams for the same sentences.

7. DUTCH

[Application of Skills: Intermediate]
Consider the following sentences of Dutch. (Data from Ferdinand de Haan.)

a) De man in de regenjas is naar Amsterdam gegaan.
   the man in the raincoat is to   Amsterdam going
   "The man in the raincoat is going to Amsterdam."

b) De man heeft een gele   auto met een aanhanger gekocht.
   the man has   a   yellow car with a   trailer   bought
   "The man has bought a yellow car with a trailer."

c) De vrouw   heeft een auto gekocht.
   the woman has   a   car bought
   "The woman has bought a car."

d)   Jan is vertrokken.
     John is gone
     "John left."

(If you speak Dutch, please confine your answer to the data given above and do not add any other examples.)

1)   Assume an AdjP rule, AdjP → Adj; What is the NP rule of Dutch?
2)   What is the PP rule of Dutch?
3)   What is the VP rule of Dutch? (Assume that *is* and *heeft* are of the category T and are not part of the VP.)
4)   What is the TP rule for Dutch?
5)   Draw the trees for (a) and (b).

8. AMBIGUITY
[Application of Knowledge and Skills; Basic to Intermediate]
The following English sentences are all ambiguous. Provide a paraphrase (a sentence with roughly the same meaning) for each of the possible meanings, and then draw (two) trees of the <u>original</u> sentence that distinguish the two meanings. Be careful not to draw the tree of the paraphrase. Your two trees should be different from one another, where the difference reflects which elements modify what. (For sentence (b) ignore the issue of capitalization.) You may need to assume that *old* and *seven* can function as adverbs. Sentences (c), (d), (e), and (f) are ambiguous newspaper headlines taken from http://www.fun-with-words.com/ambiguous_headlines.html.

a)   John said Mary went to the store quickly.
b)   I discovered an old English poem.
c)   Two sisters reunited after 18 years in checkout counter
d)   Enraged cow injures farmer with ax
e)   Hospitals are sued by seven foot doctors
f)   Dealers will hear car talk after noon

9. STRUCTURE
[Application of Knowledge; Intermediate]
In the following sentences a sequence of words is marked as a constituent with square brackets. State whether or not it is a real constituent, and what criteria (that is constituency tests) you applied to determine that result.

a)   Susanne gave [the minivan to Petunia].
b)   Clyde got [a passionate love letter from Stacy].

10. ENGLISH PREPOSITIONS
[Critical Thinking; Intermediate]
In the text, we claimed that perhaps the NP in PPs was optional, explaining why we can say *He passed out*, where the preposition *out* has no object. Consider an alternative: the expression *[passed out]* is really a "complex"

verb. Using constituency tests, provide arguments that the structure of expressions like (a–d) is really [[V P] NP] rather than: [V [P NP]].

a)   He blew out the candle.
b)   He turned off the light.
c)   He blew up the building.
d)   He rode out the storm.

CHALLENGE PROBLEM SETS

CHALLENGE PROBLEM SET 1: QUANTIFIERS
[Critical Thinking; Challenge]
Our NP rule only allows one determiner. How can we deal with NPs like (a) and (b), but still rule out NPs like (c):

a)   the two CDs
b)   the many reasons
c)   *the those books

CHALLENGE PROBLEM SET 2: NOMINAL ADVERBIALS
[Critical Thinking; Data Analysis; Challenge]
In the text we observed that NPs must appear adjacent to the Verb in VPs, they cannot come after a post-verbal AdvP:

a)   *Shannon kissed quietly the kitten.
b)   Shannon kissed the kitten quietly

However, there appears to be a class of nouns that can appear in this position. These are nouns expressing quantities of time:

c)   Shannon left quietly *every day*

Other example include *last year, every day, each week* etc.

Part 1: How do we know that these constituents are NPs and not AdvPs? (Pay attention to what can modify the N.)

Part 2: Is there a way to incorporate such NPs into our PSR system? Explain your answer.

CHALLENGE PROBLEM SET 3: POSSESSIVE NPS
[Critical Thinking; Challenge]
Part 1: Our NP rule reads NP → (D) (AdjP+) N (PP+) (CP). Consider the following NPs. What problem do these NPs cause our rule:

a)   Patrick's box
b)   the man's box

Part 2: Consider the following data:

c)   *Patrick's the box
d)   *the man's the box

How might you revise the NP rule to account for NPs like (a) and (b), keeping in mind that a possessive NP (like *Patrick's*) cannot appear in the same NP as a determiner. Given the rule you develop draw the tree for (b).

CHALLENGE PROBLEM SET 4: CONSTITUENCY TESTS[5]
[Application of Knowledge; Challenge]
Do the words in boldface in the following sentence form a *single* constituent? That is, is there a *[Barbie and Ken kissing]* constituent? How do you know? Use all the tests available to you.

Barbie and Ken were seen by everyone at the party **kissing**.

A couple of things may help you in this problem. (1) Remember that constituents can be inside other constituents. (2) This sentence is a passive, which means that some movement has happened, so don't let the fact that there is other stuff in between the two bits throw you off.

---

[5] Sheila Dooley is the source of this problem set.

chapter 4

Structural Relations

0. INTRODUCTION

In chapter 3, we developed the notion of constituency. Constituents are groups of words that function as single units. In order to systematically identify these, we proposed a set of rules. These rules generate trees, which in turn represent constituency. Take a careful look at any tree in the last chapter and you'll notice that it is a collection of labels and lines; within this collection of labels there is an organization. In particular, various parts of the tree are organized hierarchically with respect to one another. A collection of lines and labels with an internal organization like syntactic trees is a geometric object. It isn't a geometric object like a circle or a square, but nonetheless it has bits that are spatially organized with respect to one another. If syntactic trees are geometric objects, they can be studied and described mathematically – the focus of this chapter. This chapter differs from all the others in this book. You won't see many sentences or phrases here, and there is very little data. This chapter is about the purely formal properties of trees. But don't think you can skip it. The terminology we develop here is a fundamental part of syntactic theory and will play an important role in subsequent chapters.

Why Study the Geometry of Trees?

It is worth considering whether it is necessary to concern ourselves with the mathematics of tree diagrams. There are actually two very good reasons why we should do this. First, by considering the geometry of trees, we can assign names to the various parts and describe how the parts relate to one another. For example, in the last chapter we were only able to give a vague definition of the term *constituent*. In this chapter, we'll be able to give a precise description. Second, it turns out that there are many syntactic phenomena that make explicit reference to the geometry of trees. One of the most obvious of these refers to anaphors. Anaphors can only appear in certain positions in the geometry of the tree. The distribution of anaphors and other types of nouns is the focus of the next chapter.

1. THE PARTS OF A TREE

Let's start with a very abstract tree drawing:

1)

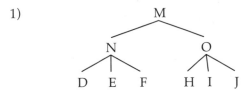

This tree would be generated by the rules in (2):

2) $M \rightarrow N\,O$
    $N \rightarrow D\,E\,F$
    $O \rightarrow H\,I\,J$

You can check this by applying each of the rules to the tree in (1). I'm using an abstract tree here because I don't want the content of each of the nodes to interfere with the underlying abstract mathematics. (But if you find this confusing, you can substitute TP for M, NP for N, VP for O, etc., and you'll see that this is just a normal tree.) Now we can describe the various parts of this tree. The lines in the tree are called **branches**. A formal definition of branch is given in (3), and the branches are marked in (4):

3) *Branch:* A line connecting two parts of a tree.

4)

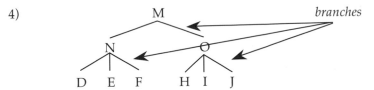

The end of any branch is called a *node*. Both ends are called nodes. For example, N and F are both called nodes of a branch. Any time two or more branches come together, this is also called a node:

5)   *Node*: The end of a branch.

A node with two or more branches below it is said to be **branching**; a node that has a single branch below it is said to be **non-branching**.

Nodes in a tree are labeled. In the tree above, M, N, O, D, E, F, H, I, J are the *labels* for the nodes that make up the tree. This is very abstract of course. In the last chapter, we looked at the various parts of speech (N, V, A, P, etc.) and the phrasal categories associated with them (NP, VP, AP, PP, etc.). These are the labels in a real syntactic tree.

6)   *Label*: The name given to a node.

There are actually different kinds of nodes that we'll want to make reference to. The first of these is called the **root node**. The root node doesn't have any branch on top of it. There is only ever one root node in a sentence. (The term root is a little confusing, but try turning the trees upside down and you'll see that they actually do look like a tree (or a bush at least). In most trees we looked at in the last chapter, the root node is almost always the TP (sentence) node.

7)   *Root node (preliminary)*: The node with no line on top of it.

At the opposite end of the tree are the nodes that don't have any lines underneath them. If the tree analogy were to really hold up, we should call these "leaves." More commonly, however, these are called **terminal nodes**.

8)   *Terminal node (preliminary):* Any node with no branch underneath it.

Any node that isn't a terminal node is called a **non-terminal node**:

9)   *Non-terminal node (preliminary):* Any node with a branch underneath it.

Notice that the root node is also a non-terminal node by this definition. After we add some definitions in the next chapter, we'll have reason to reformulate the definitions of root, terminal and non-terminal nodes, but for now these should give you the basic idea. In (10), we have a tree where the root node, the terminal nodes, and the non-terminal nodes are all marked.

10)

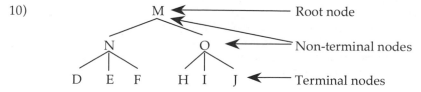

In this tree, M is the root node. M, N, and O are non-terminals, and D, E, F, H, I, and J are terminal nodes.

We now have all the terms we need to describe the various parts of a tree. The lines are called branches. The ends of the lines are called nodes, and each of the nodes has a label. Depending upon where the node is in the tree, it can be a root node (the top), a terminal (the bottom), or a non-terminal (any node except the bottom). Next we turn to a set of terms and descriptions that will allow us to describe the relations that hold between these parts. Because we are talking about a tree structure here, these relations are often called *structural relations*.

2. DOMINATION

2.1 Domination

Some nodes are higher in the tree than others. This reflects the fact that trees show a hierarchy of constituents. In particular, we want to talk about nodes that are higher than one another *and* are connected by a branch. The relation that describes two nodes that stand in this configuration is called *domination*. A node that sits atop another and is connected to it by a branch is said to dominate that node.

11) *Domination*[1]: Node A dominates node B if and only if A is higher up in the tree than B and if you can trace a line from A to B going only downwards.

In (12), M dominates all the other nodes (N, O, D, E, F, H, I, J). N dominates D, E, and F, and O dominates H, I, J. O does not dominate F, as you can see by virtue of the fact that there is no branch connecting them.

12)

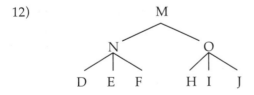

---

[1] The definition given here is actually for proper domination (an irreflexive relation). Simple domination is usually reflexive (nodes dominate themselves). For the most part linguists are interested in proper domination rather than simple domination, and they use the term "domination" to mean "proper domination" as we do here. Domination is sometimes also called *dominance*.

Domination is essentially a containment relation. The phrasal category N contains the terminal nodes D, E, and F. Containment is seen more clearly when the tree is converted into a bracketed diagram:

13) [$_M$ [$_N$ D E F] [$_O$ H I J]]

In (13) the brackets associated with N ([$_N$ D E F]) contains the nodes D, E, and F. The same holds true for O which contains H, I, and J. M contains both N and O and all the nodes that they contain. So domination is a technical way of expressing which categories belong to larger categories.

You now have enough information to try General Problem Sets 1 & 2

2.2 Exhaustive Domination

In the last chapter, we developed an intuitive notion of constituent. The relation of domination actually allows us to be a little more rigorous and develop a formal notion of constituency. In order to do this, we need another definition, **exhaustive domination**:

14) *Exhaustive domination*: Node A exhaustively dominates a *set* of terminal nodes {B, C, ..., D}, provided it dominates all the members of the set (so that there is no member of the set that is not dominated by A) *and* there is no terminal node G dominated by A that is not a member of the set.

This is a rather laborious definition. Let's tease it apart by considering an example.

15)

What we are concerned with here is a *set* of nodes and whether or not a given node dominates the entire set. Sets are indicated with curly brackets {}. Start with the set of terminal {B, C, D}. In (15) all members of the set {B, C, D} are dominated by A; there is no member of the set that isn't dominated by A. This satisfies the first part of the definition in (15). Turning to the second part, A *only* dominates these terminal nodes and no other terminals. There is no node G dominated by A that is not a member of the set. This being the case we can say of the tree in (15) that A exhaustively dominates the set {B, C, D}. Let's turn to a different tree now.

16)

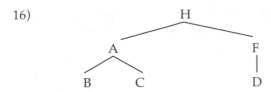

Again let's consider whether A exhaustively dominates the set {B, C, D}. In (16), one member of the set, D, is not immediately dominated by A. As such the set {B, C, D} is *not* exhaustively dominated by A. The reverse situation is seen in (17):

17)

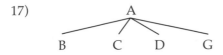

While it is the case that in (17), B, C, and D are all immediately dominated by A, there is also the node G, which is not a member of the set {B, C, D}, so the set {B, C, D} is not exhaustively dominated by A (although the set {B, C, D, G} is). On a more intuitive level, exhaustive domination holds between a set of nodes and their mother. Only when the entire set (and only that set) are immediately dominated by their mother can we say that the mother exhaustively dominates the set.

Look carefully at the structures in (15), (16), and (17). In (15) you'll see that the set {B, C, D} forms a constituent (labeled A). In (16), that set does not form a constituent, nor does it form a constituent in (17) (although the set is part of a larger constituent in that tree). In (17), there is no sense in which B, C, D form a unit that excludes G. It seems then that the notion of constituency is closely related to the relation of exhaustive domination. This is reflected in the following formal definition of a constituent.

18) *Constituent*: A set of terminal nodes exhaustively dominated by a particular node.

If we look at the tree in (16) again, you can see that each constituent meets this definition. The set of nodes exhaustively dominated by A is {B, C} which is the set of terminals that make up the A constituent. Similarly, The constituent F is made up of the set {D} which is exhaustively dominated by F; finally, H exhaustively dominates {B, C, D} (remember the definition is defined over *terminals*, so A and F don't count) which is the constituent that H represents.

Before turning to some other structural relations, it is important to look at one confusing piece of terminology. This is the distinction between *constituent* and *constituent of*. A constituent, as defined in (18), is a set of nodes exhaustively dominated by a single node. A **constituent of**, by contrast, is a *member* of the constituent set. Consider the tree in (19):

19)

Here we have the constituent A, which exhaustively dominates the set {B, C, D}. Each member of this set is called a "constituent of A." So B is a constituent of A. "Constituent of" boils down to domination. A dominates B therefore B is a constituent of A:

20) *Constituent of*: B is a constituent of A if and only if A dominates B.

You now have enough information to try General Problem Set 3

2.3 Immediate Domination

Domination is actually quite a general notion: In (21), M dominates all of the nodes under it.

21)

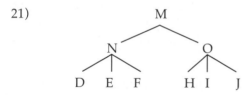

In certain circumstances we might want to talk about relationships that are smaller and more local. This is the relationship of **immediate domination**. A node immediately dominates another if there is only one branch between them.

22) *Immediately dominate*: Node A immediately dominates node B if there is no intervening node G that is dominated by A, but dominates B. (In other words, A is the first node that dominates B.)

In (21), M dominates all the other nodes in the tree, but it only immediately dominates N and O. It does not immediately dominate any of the other nodes because N and O intervene.

There is an informal set of terms that we frequently use to refer to immediate domination. This set of terms is based on the fact that syntactic trees look a bit like family trees. If one node immediately dominates another, it is said to be the **mother**; the node that is immediately dominated is called the **daughter**. In the tree above in (21), N is D's mother and D is

N's daughter. We can even extend the analogy (although this is pushing things a bit) and call M D's grandmother.

23) *Mother*: A is the mother of B if A immediately dominates B.

24) *Daughter:* B is the daughter of A if B is immediately dominated by A.

Closely related to these definitions is the definition of **sister**:

25) *Sisters:* Two nodes that share the same mother.

With this set of terms in place we can now redefine our definitions of root nodes, terminal nodes, and non-terminals a little more rigorously:

26) *Root node (revised)*: The node that dominates everything, but is dominated by nothing. (The node that is no node's daughter.)

27) *Terminal node (revised)*: A node that dominates nothing. (A node that is not a mother.)

28) *Non-terminal node (revised)* A node that dominates something. (A node that is a mother.)

We defined "constituent" in terms of domination, and from that we derived the "constituent of" relation (essentially the opposite of domination). We can also define a local variety of the "constituent of" relation that is the opposite of immediate domination:

29) *Immediate constituent of*: B is an immediate constituent of A if and only if A immediately dominates B.

This ends our discussion of the vertical axis of syntactic trees. Next we consider horizontal relations.

You now have enough information to try General Problem Set 4

---

3. PRECEDENCE

Syntactic trees don't only encode the hierarchical organization of sentences, they also encode the linear order of the constituents. Linear order refers to the order in which words are spoken or written (left to right if you are writing in English). Consider the following rule:

30) M → A B

This rule not only says that M dominates A and B and is composed of A and B. It also says that A must precede B in linear order. A must be said before B, because it appears to the left of B in the rule. The relation of "what is said first" is called *precedence*.[2] In order to define this rigorously we have to first appeal to a notion known as *sister precedence*:

31) *Sister precedence*: Node A sister-precedes node B if and only if both are immediately dominated by the same node, and A appears to the left of B.

The ordering in this definition follows from the order of elements within a phrase structure rule. If A is to the left of B in a phrase structure rule M → A B, then A and B are immediately dominated by M, and are in the relevant order by virtue of the ordering within that rule. With this basic definition in mind we can define the more general precedence relation:

32) *Precedence*: Node A precedes node B if and only if neither A dominates B nor B dominates A *and* A or some node dominating A sister-precedes B or some node dominating B.

This definition is pretty complex, so let's break it apart. The first bit of the definition says "neither A dominates B nor B dominates A." The reason for this should be obvious on an intuitive level. Remember, domination is a containment relation. If A contains B, there is no obvious way in which A could be to the left of B. Think of it this way. If you have a box, and the box has a ball in it, you can't say that the box is to the left of the ball. That is physically impossible. The box surrounds the ball. The same holds true for domination. You can't both dominate and precede/follow.

The second part of the definition says "A or some node dominating A sister-precedes B or some node dominating B" This may seems like an overly complex way to say "to the left," but there is a good reason we phrase it this. This has to do with the fact that the terminals of a tree don't float out in space, they are dominated by other nodes that might precede or follow themselves and other nodes. Consider the following tree drawn by a sloppy tree-drawer:

---

[2] Thanks to Dave Medieros for helpful discussion of these notions.

33)

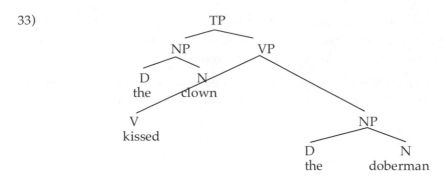

In this sloppily drawn tree, the verb *kissed* actually appears to the *left* of the noun *clown*. However, we wouldn't want to say that *kissed* precedes *clown*; this is clearly wrong. The sentence is said "The clown kissed the doberman," where *kissed* follows *clown*. We guarantee this ordering by making reference to the material that dominates the nodes we are looking at. Let A = *clown* and B = *kissed*. Let's substitute those into the definition:

34) $[_N$ *clown]* or some node dominating $[_N$ *clown]* (in this case NP) sister-precedes $[_V$ *kissed]* or some node dominating $[_V$ *kissed]* (in this case VP).

This means that $[_N$ *clown]* precedes $[_V$ *kissed]*, because NP precedes VP. Note that precedence holds over <u>all</u> nodes not just terminals. So $[_N$ *clown]* also precedes $[_{NP}$ *the doberman]*.

The second clause of the definition also allows us to explain an important restriction on syntactic trees: ***You cannot allow branches to cross***. Trees like (35) are completely unacceptable (they are also impossible to generate with phrase structure rules – try to write one and you'll see):

35)

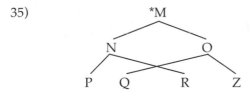

In this tree, Q is written to the left of R, apparently preceding R, but by the definition of precedence given above, this tree is ruled out. Q is to the left of R, but O *which dominates Q* is not. In other words, you can't cross branches. Another way of phrasing this is given below in (36):

36) *No crossing branches constraint*: If one node X precedes another node Y then X and all nodes dominated by X must precede Y and all nodes dominated by Y.

You now have enough information to try General Problem Set 5 and Challenge Problem Set 1

Just as in the domination relation, where there is the special local definition called "immediate domination," there is a special local form of precedence called ***immediate precedence***:

37) *Immediate precedence:* A immediately precedes B if there is no node G that follows A but precedes B.

Consider the string given in (38) (assume that the nodes dominating this string meet all the criteria set out in (32)):

38)   A   B   G

In this linear string, A immediately precedes B, because A precedes B and there is nothing in between them. Contrast this with (39):

39)   A   G   B

In this string, A does ***not*** immediately precede B. It does precede B, but G intervenes between them, so the relation is not immediate.

You now have enough information to try General Problem Set 6

4. C-COMMAND

Perhaps the most important of the structural relations is the one we call ***c-command***. Although c-command takes a little getting used to, it is actually the most useful of all the relations. In the next chapter, we'll look at the phenomenon of ***binding***, which makes explicit reference to the c-command relation. C-command is defined intuitively in (40) and more formally in (41):

40) *C-command (informal):* A node c-commands its sisters and all the daughters (and granddaughters and great-granddaughters, etc.) of its sisters.

41) *C-command (formal):* Node A c-commands node B if every[3] node dominating A also dominates B, and neither A nor B dominate the other.

Look at the tree in (42). The node A c-commands all the nodes in the circle. It doesn't c-command any others:

---

[3] The usual requirement on c-command is that every ***branching*** node dominating A also dominate B. This additional branching requirement isn't necessary given the irreflexive definition of domination (i.e. proper domination) that we've given above. However, students may run into the branching definition in other works if other definitions of domination are used.

42)

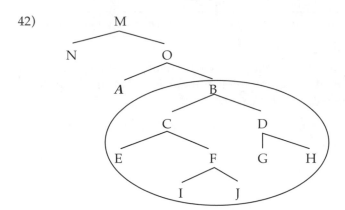

That is, A c-commands its sister (B) and all the nodes dominated by its sister (C, D, E, F, G, H, I, J). Consider now the same tree without the circle, and look at the nodes c-commanded by G:

43)

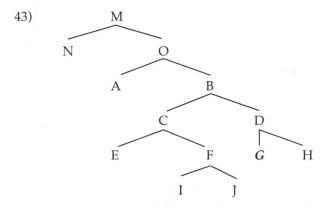

G c-commands *only* H (its sister). Notice that it does not c-command C, E, F, I, or J. C-command is a relation that holds between sisters and aunts and nieces. It *never* holds between cousins or between a mother and daughter.

You now have enough information to try General Problem Set 7 and Challenge Problem Set 2

There are various kinds of c-command. The first of these is when two nodes c-command one another. This is called **symmetric c-command** and is defined in (44):

44) *Symmetric c-command*: A symmetrically c-commands B, if A c-commands B *and* B c-commands A.

This relation holds only between sisters. The other kind of c-command is the kind that holds between an aunt and her nieces. This is called (unsurprisingly) *asymmetric c-command*:

45) *Asymmetric c-command:* A asymmetrically c-commands B if A c-commands B but B does *not* c-command A.

Consider again the tree in (42); N and O symmetrically c-command each other (as do all other pairs of sisters). However, N asymmetrically c-commands A, B, C, D, E, F, G, H, I, and J, since none of these c-command N.

You now have enough information to try General Problem Set 8

   Just as we had local (immediate) versions of domination and precedence, there is a local version of c-command. This is typically called *government*[4] (rather than immediate c-command). There are a number of different definitions for government. If you look back at our definitions for immediate precedence and immediate domination, you'll see that in both cases the locality (i.e., the closeness) of the relationship was defined by making reference to a potential intervening category. So for domination, some node A immediately dominates B another provided there is no intermediate node G that A dominates and that dominates B. In (46a) there is no node between A and B, so A immediately dominates B. In (46b) by contrast G is in between them, so A does not immediately dominate B.

46)   a)      b)

The same idea played a role in precedence. In (47a), A immediately precedes B because there is nothing between them; in (47b) A precedes B, but it doesn't immediately precede B, because G intervenes.

47)   a)      b)

Government is similarly defined:

---

[4] Technically speaking, government isn't just immediate c-command, it also expresses a licensing relationship (that is it has or had the special status of a constraint on the grammar). In this book, this licensing function isn't going to be used, so we're going to concentrate on the structural relationship part of the definition only.

48) *Government (first version)*: Node A governs node B if A c-commands B, and there is no node G, such that G is c-commanded by A and G c-commands B.

To see this at work, look at the tree in (49):

49)

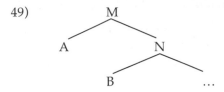

In this tree, A governs B. It c-commands B, and there is no node that c-commands B that A also c-commands. (You should note that A also governs N under this definition, A c-commands N, and there is no node that N c-commands that also c-commands A. The reverse is also true N governs A because the relationship between A and N is symmetric c-command. B does not govern A, because B does not c-command A.) Contrast this with the tree in (50):

50)

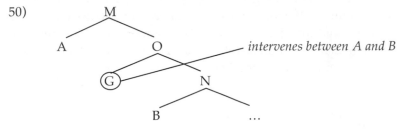

intervenes between A and B

Here A does not govern B, because the node G intervenes (or more precisely, A c-commands G and G c-command B, thus violating the definition).

Government is often "relativized" to the particular kind of element that's doing the government. For example, if the governor (the element doing the governing is a phrase (an NP, a VP, etc.), then what counts as an intervener are only other phrases, not heads like N, V, etc.

51)

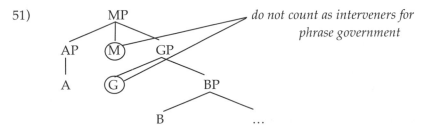

do not count as interveners for phrase government

In (51) the AP *phrase-governs*[5] B. G and M don't count as interveners, even though they both are c-commanded by AP and they both c-command B. This is because they are not phrases – they are heads. GP and BP don't count as interveners either, because they don't command B; they dominate it.

Similarly, if the governor is a head (*head-government*), then phrasal interveners don't count:

52)

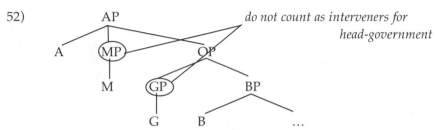

In (52), MP and GP do not count as interveners for A head-governing B because they are phrases. M and G don't count because they don't c-command B.[6] With this in mind we can revise the definition:

53) *Government*

Node A governs node B if A c-commands B, and there is no node G, such that G is c-commanded by A and G c-commands B.
- *Phrase-government*: If A is a phrase, then the categories that count for G in the above definition must also be phrases
- *Head-government*: If A is a head (word), then the categories that count for G in the above definition must also be heads.

In recent years, government has to a greater or lesser degree fallen out of fashion. Instead local relations previously linked to government are often determined by what is called the specifier-head relation. However, it is important to know what government is, because if you read many influential papers in syntax they will refer to this relation.

You now have enough information to try General Problem Set 9

---

[5] In the syntactic literature, this is more usually called *antecedent government* (which has an additional constraint called coindexing on it and is defined over particular categories – so NP antecedent governs another coindexed NP, provided there is no intervening c-commanding NP that also is c-commanded by the first). This is a refinement that we won't pursue here because it is rarely used anymore.

[6] These don't c-command B only if the branching requirement on c-command does not hold.

5. GRAMMATICAL RELATIONS

In addition to the structural relations that hold between items in a tree, there are also some traditional grammatical terms that can be defined structurally. These are useful terms, and we will frequently make reference to them. We call these **grammatical relations**. Technically speaking, grammatical relations are not structural relations. Some theories of grammar (for example Lexical Functional Grammar and Relational Grammar) posit primitive grammatical relations (meaning they are not structurally defined). In the approach we are developing here, however, grammatical relations are defined structurally; that is, they are defined in terms of the tree.

In English the subject is always the NP or CP that appears before the verb or auxiliary:

54) a) *The puppy* licked the kitten's face.
    b) *It* is raining.
    c) *Fred* feels fine.
    d) *The kitten* was licked.
    e) *That Bill's breath smells of onions* bothers Erin.

Notice that the definition of subject is not a semantic one. It is not necessarily the doer of the action. In (54c) for example, Fred is not deliberately feeling fine. In sentence (54d), the kitten is the one being licked, not the licker. Different semantic types[7] of noun phrases appear to be allowed to function as the subject. There is a straightforward structural definition of the **subject**:

55) *Subject (preliminary)*: NP or CP daughter of TP

In later chapters, we will have cause to refine this definition somewhat, but for now, this will do.

Next we have the **direct object** of the verb and the **object of a preposition**. Examples of these are seen in (56) and (57) respectively:

56) *Direct object*
    a) Susan kissed *the clown's nose.*
    b) Cedric danced *a jolly jig.*
    c) Dale said *that the lawn was overgrown.*

57) *Object of a preposition*
    a) Gilgamesh cut the steak with *a knife.*
    b) We drove all the way to *Buenos Aires.*

---

[7] In chapter 8, we will look at different semantic types of noun phrases. These types are called **thematic relations**.

Preliminary definitions of these are given in (58) and (59), again we will have reason to revise these in later chapters.

58) *(Direct) object (preliminary)*: NP or CP daughter of a VP headed by a transitive verb

59) *Object of preposition*: NP daughter of PP

To see these definitions at work consider the following tree. The NP *Les* is the daughter of TP, and is thus the subject. The NP *Paula* is a daughter of the VP headed by the transitive verb *kissed*, so *Paula* is the direct object. *Tuesday* is the NP daughter of a PP, thus the object of a preposition.

60)

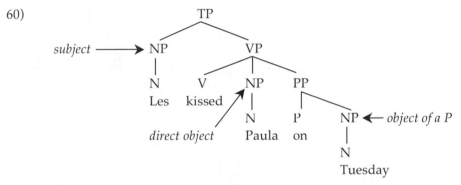

In addition to direct objects, when you have a ditransitive verb like give or put, you also have an indirect object. Indirect objects in English come of several types in terms of the types of arguments they take. The two most common types are the direct object which we preliminarily defined above and indirect object. The **indirect object** in English shows up in two places. It can be the PP that follows the direct object:

61)

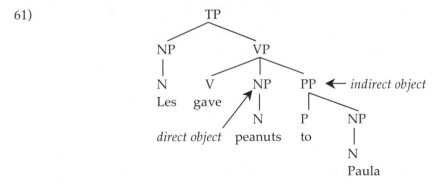

It can also be the *first* NP after the verb when the verb takes two NPs:

62)

```
                              TP
                       ┌──────┴──────┐
                      NP             VP
                      │        ┌──────┴──────┐
                      N     V       NP      NP  ← direct object
                     Les   gave   ↗  │       │
                                     N       N
                   indirect object  Paula   peanuts
```

Notice that the direct object is the second of the two NPs, roughly the reverse of the tree in (61). This means complicating our definitions somewhat:

63) *Direct Object (second pass):*
   a) With verbs of type $V_{[NP\_NP]}$, $V_{[NP\_CP]}$ and $V_{[NP\_NP\ PP]}$, the NP or CP daughter of VP
   b) With verbs of type $V_{[NP\_NP\ \{NP/CP\}]}$, An NP or CP daughter of VP that is preceded by another NP daughter of VP. (i.e., the second NP daughter of VP)

64) *Indirect Object (preliminary):*
   a) With verbs of type $V_{[NP\_NP\ PP]}$, the PP daughter of VP immediately preceded by an NP daughter of VP.
   b) With verbs of type $V_{[NP\_NP\ \{NP/CP\}]}$, the NP daughter of VP immediately preceded by V (i.e., the first NP daughter of VP).

In addition to subjects, objects, and indirect objects, you may also occasionally see reference made to **obliques**. In English, obliques are almost always marked with a preposition. The PPs in the following sentence are obliques:

65) John tagged Lewis [PP *with a regulation baseball*][PP *on Tuesday*].

In many languages, such as Finnish, obliques aren't marked with prepositions, instead they get special suffixes that mark them as oblique; so obliqueness is not necessarily defined by being a preposition, that is just a convenient definition for now. Notice that obliques can structurally show up in the same position as indirect objects (compare (66a) to (66b)). The difference between the two is in whether the PP is part of the argument structure of the verb or not. If verb is of type $V_{[NP\_NP\ PP]}$ like *give*, then the PP is an indirect object, but if the verb is of type $V_{[NP\_NP]}$ (where the PP isn't specified by the feature), like *eat*, then the PP is an oblique.

66) a)

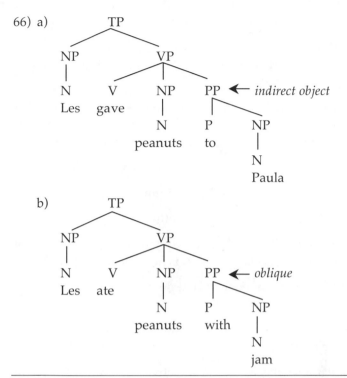

b)

---

*You now have enough information to try General Problem Sets 10–16 and
Challenge Problem Set 3*

---

6. SUMMARY AND CONCLUSIONS

This chapter has been a bit different from the rest of this book. It hasn't
been about Language per se, but rather about the mathematical properties
of the system we use to describe language. We looked at the various parts
of a syntactic tree and then at the three relations that can hold between
these parts: domination, precedence, and c-command. In all the subsequent
chapters of this book, you'll find much utility for the terms and the relations
described here.

IDEAS, RULES, AND CONSTRAINTS INTRODUCED IN THIS CHAPTER

i)   *Branch*: A line connecting two parts of a tree.

ii)   *Node*: The end of a branch.

iii)   *Label*: The name given to a node (e.g., N, NP, TP, etc.).

iv)   *(Proper) Domination*: Node A dominates node B if and only if A is higher up in the tree than B and if you can trace a branch from A to B going only downwards.

v)   *Immediately Dominate*: Node A immediately dominates node B if there is no intervening node G that is dominated by A, but dominates B. (In other words, A is the first node that dominates B.)

vi)   A is the *mother* of B if A immediately dominates B.

vii)   B is the *daughter* of A if B is immediately dominated by A.

viii)   *Sisters*: Two nodes that share the same mother.

ix)   *Root Node* (*revised*): The node that dominates everything, but is dominated by nothing. (The node that is no node's daughter.)

x)   *Terminal Node* (*revised*): A node that dominates nothing. (A node that is not a mother.)

xi)   *Non-terminal Node* (*revised*): A node that dominates something. (A node that is a mother.)

xii)   *Exhaustive Domination*: Node A exhaustively dominates a *set* of terminal nodes {B, C, ... , D}, provided it dominates all the members of the set (so that there is no member of the set that is not dominated by A) *and* there is no terminal node G dominated by A that is not a member of the set.

xiii)   *Constituent*: A set of terminal nodes exhaustively dominated by a particular node.

xiv)   *Constituent of*: A is a constituent of B if and only if B dominates A.

xv)   *Immediate Constituent of*: A is an immediate constituent of B if and only if B immediately dominates A.

xvi)   *Sister Precedence*: Node A sister-precedes node B if and only if both are immediately dominated by the same node, and A appears to the left of B.

xvii)   *Precedence*: Node A precedes node B if and only if neither A dominates B nor B dominates A *and* A or some node dominating A sister-precedes B or some node dominating B.

xviii) **No Crossing Branches Constraint**: If node X precedes another node Y then X and all nodes dominated by X must precede Y and all nodes dominated by Y.

xix) **Immediate Precedence**: A immediately precedes B if there is no node G that follows A but precedes B.

xx) **C-command** *(informal)*: A node c-commands its sisters and all the daughters (and granddaughters, and great-granddaughters, etc.) of its sisters.

xxi) **C-command** *(formal)*: Node A c-commands node B if every node dominating A also dominates B *and* neither A nor B dominates the other.

xxii) **Symmetric C-command**: A symmetrically c-commands B if A c-commands B *and* B c-commands A.

xxiii) **Asymmetric C-command**: A asymmetrically c-commands B if A c-commands B but B does *not* c-command A.

xxiv) **Government**: Node A governs node B if A c-commands B, and there is no node G, where G is c-commanded by A and G c-commands B.
   - *Phrase-government*: If A is a phrase, then the categories that count for G in the above definition must also be phrases
   - *Head-government*: If A is a head (word), then the categories that count for G in the above definition must also be heads.

xxv) **Subject** *(preliminary)*: NP or CP daughter of TP.

xxvi) **Object of Preposition** *(preliminary)*: NP daughter of PP.

xxvii) **Direct Object**:
   a) With verbs of type $V_{[NP\_NP]}$, $V_{[NP\_CP]}$ and $V_{[NP\_NP\ PP]}$, the NP or CP daughter of VP.
   b) With verbs of type $V_{[NP\_NP\ (NP/CP)]}$, an NP or CP daughter of VP that is preceded by another NP daughter of VP (i.e., the second NP daughter of VP).

xxviii) **Indirect Object** *(preliminary)*:
   a) With verbs of type $V_{[NP\_NP\ PP]}$, the PP daughter of VP immediately preceded by an NP daughter of VP.
   b) With verbs of type $V_{[NP\_NP\ (NP/CP)]}$, the NP daughter of VP immediately preceded by V (i.e., the first NP daughter of VP).

xxix) **Oblique**: any NP/PP in the sentence that is not a subject, object of a preposition, or indirect object.

FURTHER READING

Barker, Chris and Geoffrey Pullum (1990) A theory of command relations. *Linguistics and Philosophy* 13, 1–34.

Chomsky, Noam (1975) *The Logical Structure of Linguistic Theory.* New York: Plenum.

Higginbotham, James (1985) A note on phrase markers. *MIT Working Papers in Linguistics* 6, 87–101.

Reinhart, Tanya (1976) The Syntactic Domain of Anaphora. Ph.D. dissertation, MIT.

Reinhart, Tanya (1983) *Anaphora and Semantic Interpretation.* London: Croom Helm.

GENERAL PROBLEM SETS

1. TREES
[Application of Skills; Basic to Intermediate]
Using the rules we developed in chapter 3, draw the trees for the following sentences. Many of the sentences are ambiguous. For those sentences draw *one* possible tree, indicating the meaning by providing a paraphrase.

a) The big man from New York loves bagels with cream cheese.
b) Susan rode a bright blue train from New York.
c) The plucky platypus kicked a can of soup from New York to Tucson.
d) John said Martha sang the aria with gusto.
e) Martha said John sang the aria from *La Bohème*.
f) The book of poems with the bright red cover stinks.
g) Louis hinted Mary stole the purse deftly.
h) The extremely tired students hated syntactic trees with a passion.
i) Many soldiers have claimed bottled water quenches thirst best.
j) Networking helps you grow your business.

2. DOMINATION
[Application of Skills; Basic]
Study the following tree carefully and then answer the questions about it that follow:

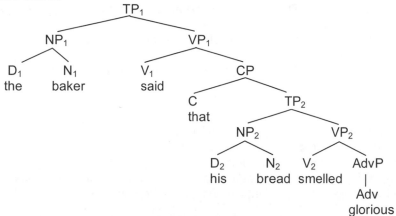

1) List all the nodes that dominate D_1 *the*.
2) List all the nodes that dominate D_2 *his*.
3) List all the nodes that dominate N_1 *baker*.
4) List all the nodes that dominate N_2 *bread*.
5) List all the nodes that dominate V_1 *said*.
6) List all the nodes that dominate V_2 *smelled*.
7) List all the nodes that dominate Adv *glorious*.
8) List all the nodes that dominate C *that*.
9) List all the nodes that dominate TP_1 (if there are any).
10) List all the nodes that dominate TP_2.
11) List all the nodes that dominate NP_1.
12) List all the nodes that dominate NP_2.
13) List all the nodes that dominate VP_1.
14) List all the nodes that dominate VP_2.
15) List all the nodes that dominate CP.
16) List all the nodes that dominate AdvP.
17) What is the root node?
18) List all the terminal nodes.
19) List all the non-terminal nodes.
20) List all the nodes that VP_2 dominates.
21) List all the nodes that CP dominates.
22) List all the nodes that NP_1 dominates.

3. EXHAUSTIVE DOMINATION
[Application of Skills; Intermediate]
Refer back to the tree for problem set 2 to answer this question.

1) In the tree, is the set of terminals {N_1, N_2} exhaustively dominated by a single node? If so, which one?

2) In the tree, is the set $\{D_1, N_1\}$ exhaustively dominated by a single node? If so, which one?
3) In the tree, is the set $\{V_2, Adv\}$ exhaustively dominated by a single node? If so, which one?
4) In the tree, is the set $\{D_2, N_2, V_2, Adv\}$ exhaustively dominated by a single node? If so, which one?
5) In the tree, is the set $\{D_1, N_1, V_1\}$ exhaustively dominated by a single node? If so, which one?
6) In the tree, is the set $\{D_1\}$ exhaustively dominated by a single node? If so, which one?
7) In the tree, is the set $\{C, D_2, N_2, V_2, Adv\}$ exhaustively dominated by a single node? If so, which one?
8) What is the set of terminal nodes exhaustively dominated by VP_1?
9) Is the string *that his bread* a constituent? Explain your answer using the terminology of exhaustive domination.
10) Is the string *The baker said that his bread smelled glorious* a constituent? Explain your answer using the terminology of exhaustive domination.
11) Is NP_1 a constituent of TP_1?
12) Is NP_2 a constituent of TP_1?
13) Is NP_1 a constituent of TP_2?
14) Is NP_2 a constituent of TP_2?
15) Is V_2 a constituent of CP?
16) Is VP_2 a constituent of CP?
17) Are both Adv and AdvP constituents of VP_2?

4. IMMEDIATE DOMINATION
[Application of Skills; Basic]
Go back to problem set 2, study the tree again and answer the questions (1–16) as in problem set 2, **except** limiting your answer to immediate domination instead of domination.

5. PRECEDENCE
[Application of Skills; Basic]
Go back to problem set 2, study the tree again and answer the questions (1–16) **except** changing domination to precedence (i.e., list all the nodes that precede D_1 etc.). For some elements there may be nothing that precedes them.

6. IMMEDIATE PRECEDENCE
[Application of Skills; Basic]
Go back to problem set 2, study the tree again and answer the questions (1–16) **except** changing domination to immediate precedence (i.e. list all the nodes that immediately precede D_1, etc.). For some elements there may be nothing that immediately precedes them.

7. C-COMMAND
[Application of Skills; Basic]
Go back to problem set 2, study the tree again and answer the following questions:

1) List all the nodes that D_1 *the* c-commands (note NOT the nodes that c-command D_1, but the ones that D_1 c-commands).
2) List all the nodes that D_2 *his* c-commands.
3) List all the nodes that N_1 *baker* c-commands.
4) List all the nodes that N_2 *bread* c-commands.
5) List all the nodes that V_1 *said* c-commands.
6) List all the nodes that V_2 *smelled* c-commands.
7) List all the nodes that Adv *glorious* c-commands.
8) List all the nodes that C *that* c-commands.
9) List all the nodes that TP_1 c-commands (if there are any).
10) List all the nodes that TP_2 c-commands.
11) List all the nodes that NP_1 c-commands.
12) List all the nodes that NP_2 c-commands.
13) List all the nodes that VP_1 c-commands.
14) List all the nodes that VP_2 c-commands.
15) List all the nodes that CP c-commands.
16) List all the nodes that AdvP c-commands.
17) What nodes c-command TP_2?
18) What nodes c-command NP_1?
19) What nodes c-command C?

8. SYMMETRIC AND ASYMMETRIC C-COMMAND
[Application of Skills; Basic/Intermediate]
Go back to problem set 2, study the tree again and answer the following questions. For some questions the answer may be "none":

1) List all the nodes that D_1 *the* symmetrically c-commands.
2) List all the nodes that D_2 *his* symmetrically c-commands.
3) List all the nodes that N_1 *baker* symmetrically c-commands.
4) List all the nodes that N_2 *bread* symmetrically c-commands.
5) List all the nodes that V_1 *said* symmetrically c-commands.
6) List all the nodes that V_2 *smelled* symmetrically c-commands.
7) List all the nodes that Adv *glorious* symmetrically c-commands.
8) List all the nodes that C *that* symmetrically c-commands.
9) List all the nodes that TP_1 symmetrically c-commands (if there are any).
10) List all the nodes that TP_2 symmetrically c-commands.
11) List all the nodes that NP_1 symmetrically c-commands.
12) List all the nodes that NP_2 symmetrically c-commands.
13) List all the nodes that VP_1 symmetrically c-commands.
14) List all the nodes that VP_2 symmetrically c-commands.
15) List all the nodes that CP symmetrically c-commands.
16) List all the nodes that AdvP symmetrically c-commands.

17) List all the nodes that D_1 *the* asymmetrically c-commands.
18) List all the nodes that D_2 *his* asymmetrically c-commands.
19) List all the nodes that N_1 *baker* asymmetrically c-commands.
20) List all the nodes that N_2 *bread* asymmetrically c-commands.
21) List all the nodes that V_1 *said* asymmetrically c-commands.
22) List all the nodes that V_2 *smelled* asymmetrically c-commands.
23) List all the nodes that Adv *glorious* asymmetrically c-commands.
24) List all the nodes that C *that* asymmetrically c-commands.
25) List all the nodes that TP_1 asymmetrically c-commands (if there are any).
26) List all the nodes that TP_2 asymmetrically c-commands.
27) List all the nodes that NP_1 asymmetrically c-commands.
28) List all the nodes that NP_2 asymmetrically c-commands.
29) List all the nodes that VP_1 asymmetrically c-commands.
30) List all the nodes that VP_2 asymmetrically c-commands.
31) List all the nodes that CP asymmetrically c-commands.
32) List all the nodes that AdvP asymmetrically c-commands.
33) What nodes asymmetrically c-command V_2?
34) What nodes symmetrically c-command NP_1?
35) What nodes asymmetrically c-command C?
36) What nodes symmetrically c-command C?

9. GOVERNMENT

[Application of Skills; Intermediate/Advanced]
Go back to problem set 2, study the tree again and answer the following
questions:

1) Does NP_1 govern VP_2? Why or why not?
2) Does NP_1 govern C *that*? Why or why not?
3) What nodes does N_1 govern?
4) Does V_1 head-govern V_2? Why or why not?
5) What node(s) does C *that* head-govern?
6) Does NP_1 phrase-govern AdvP? Why or why not?
7) Does VP_2 phrase-govern N_2? Why or why not?

10. GRAMMATICAL RELATIONS I

[Application of Skills; Intermediate]
Go back to problem set 2, study the tree again and answer the following
questions:

1) What is the subject of TP1?
2) What is the subject of TP2?
3) What is the object of VP1?
4) Does VP2 have an object? Why or why not?

11. GRAMMATICAL RELATIONS II

[Application of Skills; Intermediate]
Examine the following tree and then answer the questions that follow:

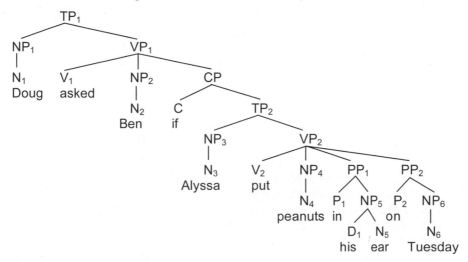

1) What is the subject of TP_1?
2) What is the subject of TP_2?
3) What is the object of P_1?
4) What is the object of P_2?
5) What is the direct object of VP_1?
6) What is the direct object of VP_2?
7) What is the indirect object of VP_1?
8) What is the indirect object of VP_2?
9) Is PP_2 an indirect object or an oblique. How can you tell?

12. GRAMMATICAL RELATIONS III[8]

[Application of Skills and Data Analysis; Basic]
For each of the following sentences, identify the subject, the object (if there is one), the indirect object (if there is one), any objects of prepositions, the verb, and any obliques. Draw the tree for each sentence.

a) It never rains violently in southern California.
b) Soon we should give the family dog another bath.
c) The quiz show contestant bravely made a wild guess about the answer.

---

[8] Problem set contributed by Sheila Dooley.

13. STRUCTURAL RELATIONS I[9]
[Application of Skills; Advanced]
Consider the following tree:

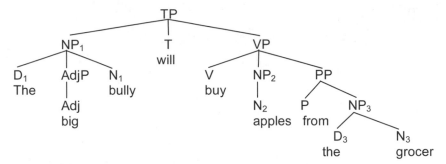

1) What node(s) dominate N₃ *grocer*?
2) What node(s) immediately dominate D₃ *the*?
3) Do T *will* and V *buy* form a constituent?
4) What nodes does N₁ *bully* c-command?
5) What nodes does NP₁ *the big bully* c-command?
6) What is V *buy*'s mother?
7) What nodes does T *will* precede?
8) List all the sets of sisters in the tree.
9) What is the PP's mother?
10) Do NP₁ and VP asymmetrically or symmetrically c-command one another?
11) List all the nodes c-commanded by V.
12) What is the subject of the sentence?
13) What is the object of the sentence?
14) What is the object of the preposition?
15) Is NP₃ a constituent of VP?
16) What node(s) is NP₃ an immediate constituent of?
17) What node(s) does VP exhaustively dominate?
18) What is the root node?
19) List all the terminal nodes.
20) What immediately precedes N₃ *grocer*?

14. STRUCTURAL RELATIONS II
[Application of Skills; Advanced]
Look at your tree for sentence (a) of problem set 1. Number the nodes the way I did for problem set 13.

1) List all the nodes that the subject NP c-commands.
2) List all the nodes that the subject NP asymmetrically c-commands.
3) List all the nodes that the subject NP dominates.

---

⁹ The idea for this problem set is borrowed from Radford (1988).

4) List all the nodes that the subject NP immediately dominates.
5) List all the nodes that the subject NP precedes.
6) List all the nodes that the VP node c-commands.
7) List all the nodes that the VP asymmetrically c-commands.
8) List all the nodes that the VP dominates.
9) List all the nodes that the VP immediately dominates.
10) List all the nodes that the VP precedes.
11) List all the nodes that the VP follows (i.e., is preceded by).

15. Tzotzil
[Data Analysis; Basic]
Tzotzil is a Mayan language spoken in Mexico. Consider the following sentences, then answer the questions that follow. Glosses have been simplified and the orthography altered from the original source. (Data from Aissen 1987.)

a) 'ispet lok'el 'antz   ti   t'ule.
    carry away woman the rabbit
    "The rabbit carried away (the) woman."

b) 'ibat xchi'uk smalal   li Maruche.
    go   with   her-husband the Maruche
    "(the) Maruch went with her husband." (Maruche is a proper name.)

c) Pas ti   'eklixa'une.
    built the church
    "The church was built."

1) What is the NP rule for Tzotzil?
2) What is the PP rule for Tzotzil?
3) What is the VP rule for Tzotzil?
4) What is the TP rule for Tzotzil?
5) What is the subject of sentence (b)?
6) Is [*the church*] a subject or an object of sentence (c)?
7) Does the verb precede the subject in Tzotzil?
8) Does the object precede the subject in Tzotzil?
9) Does the verb precede the object in Tzotzil?
10) Using the rules you developed in (1–4) above, draw the trees for (b) and (c).

16. Hiaki
[Data Analysis; Intermediate]
Consider the data from the following sentences of Hiaki (also known as Yaqui), an Uto-Aztecan language from Arizona and Mexico. Data have been simplified. (Data from Dedrick and Casad 1999.)

a) Tékil   né-u   'aáyu-k.
    work   me-for is
    "There is work for me." (literally: "Work is for me.")

b) Hunáa'a yá'uraa hunáka'a hámutta nokriak.
   that   chief   that   woman defend
   "That chief defended that woman."

c) Taáwe tótoi'asó'olam káamomólim híba-tu'ure.
   Hawk   chickens   young   like
   "(The) hawk likes young chickens."

d) Tá'abwikasu   'áma   yépsak.
   different-person   there   arrived
   "A different person arrived there." (assume *there* is an adverb not a N)

Assume the rules AdjP → Adj and AdvP → Adj and answer the following questions.

1) What is the NP rule for Hiaki?
2) Do you need a PP rule for Hiaki? Why or why not?
3) What is the VP rule for Hiaki?
4) What is the TP rule for Hiaki?
5) Using the rules you developed in questions 1–4, draw the tree for sentences (b, c, d).
6) What is the subject of sentence (b)?
7) Is there an object in (d)? If so, what is it?
8) What node(s) does *hunáa'a* c-command in (b)?
9) What node(s) does *hunáa'a yá'uraa* c-command in (b)?
10) What does *'áma* precede in (d)?
11) What node immediately dominates *káamomólim* in (c)?
12) What nodes dominate *káamomólim* in (c)?
13) What node immediately precedes *káamomólim* in (c)?
14) What nodes precede *káamomólim* in (c)?
15) Does *káamomólim* c-command *táawe* in (c)?
16) Do *hunáka'a* and *hámutta* symmetrically c-command one another in (b)?

CHALLENGE PROBLEM SETS

CHALLENGE PROBLEM SET 1: DISCONTINUOUS CONSTITUENTS
[Critical Thinking; Challenge]
Consider the following data:

a) A woman entered who was eating a chocolate enchiladas.
b) The man that Bill said that Mary disliked loves beef waffles.

With sentence (a) assume that the relative clause *[who was wearing a hat]* is a modifier of *man*. Assume that *the man* is both the direct object of the verb *disliked* and the subject of the verb *loves*. Is it possible to draw trees for these sentences without crossing lines? Explain why or why not.

CHALLENGE PROBLEM SET 2: NEGATIVE POLARITY ITEMS
[Critical Thinking; Challenge]
There is a class of phrase, such as [a red cent] and [a single thing], that are called Negative Polarity Items (NPI). These are only allowed in sentences with a negative word like *not*. So for example, in sentences (a) and (c) the NPI is fine, in the (b) and (d) sentences, however, the sentence is at best strange.

a)   I didn't have a red cent.
b)   *I had a red cent.   *(ungrammatical with idiomatic reading)*
c)   I didn't read a single book the whole time I was in the library.
d)   *I read a single book the whole time I was in the library.

It turns out that sentences with NPIs not only must have a word like *not*, they also have to be in a particular structural relationship with that *not* word. On the basis of the following sentences figure out what that relationship is. There are two possible answers consistent with this data. Assume that *not* and *n't* are dominated by the VP node.

e)   I did not have a red cent.
f)   *A red cent was not found in the box.

What kind of data would you need to decide between the two possible answers to this question?

CHALLENGE PROBLEM SET 3: IRISH
[Data Analysis and Critical Thinking: Challenge]
Consider the following data from Modern Irish Gaelic:

a)   Phóg Liam   Seán.
     kissed William John
     "William kissed John."

b)   Phóg   Seán Liam.
     Kissed John William
     "John kissed William."

c)   Phóg an fear   an mhuc.
     kissed the man the pig
     "The man kissed the pig."

d)   Chonaic mé an mhuc mhór.
     Saw   I   the pig   big
     "I saw the big pig."

e)   Rince   an bhean.
     Danced   the woman
     "The woman danced."

On the basis of this data answer the following questions:

1) What is the AdjP rule in Irish (if there is one)? Constrain your answer to the data here.
2) Write the NP rule for Irish, be sure to mark optional things in parentheses.
3) Can you write a VP rule for Irish? Assume that if you have a VP then object NPs (like *William* in (b) and *the big pig* in (d)) *must* be part of the VP, and that subject NPs (like *John* in (b) and *I* in (d)) are *never* part of VPs. Is it possible to keep those assumptions and not cross lines? *If you can't, then don't posit a VP*.
4) If you don't have a VP rule for Irish, then how do we define direct object in this language?
5) What is the TP rule for Irish? (Be careful that your TP rule is consistent with your answer in (3).)
6) Using the rules you developed, draw trees for sentences (c), (d) and (e).

chapter 5

Binding Theory

0. INTRODUCTION

Let's leave syntax for a moment and consider some facts about the meaning of NPs in English. There are some NPs that get their meaning from the context and discourse around them. For example, in the sentence in (1), the meaning of the word *Felicia* comes from the situation in which the sentence is uttered:

1) Felicia wrote a fine paper on Zapotec.[1]

If you heard this sentence said in the real world, the speaker is assuming that you know who Felicia is and that there is somebody called Felicia who is contextually relevant. Although you may not have already known that she wrote a paper on Zapotec, this sentence informs you that there is some paper in the world that Felicia wrote, and it's about Zapotec. It presupposes that there is a paper in the real world and that this paper is the meaning of the phrase *a fine paper on Zapotec*. Both *a fine paper on Zapotec* and *Felicia* get their meaning by referring to objects in the world.[2] This kind of NP is called a ***referring expression*** (or ***R-expression***):

2) *R-expression*: An NP that gets its meaning by referring to an entity in the world.

---

[1] Zapotec is a language spoken in southern Mexico.
[2] This is true whether the world being referred to is the actual world, or some fictional imaginary world created by the speaker/hearer.

The vast majority of NPs are R-expressions. But it is by no means the case that all NPs are R-expressions. Consider the case of the NP *herself* in the following sentence:

3)   Heidi bopped *herself* on the head with a zucchini.

In this sentence, *Heidi* is an R-expression and gets its meaning from the context, but *herself* must refer back to *Heidi*. It cannot refer to Arthur, Miriam, or Andrea. It must get its meaning from a previous word in the sentence (in this case *Heidi*). This kind of NP, one that obligatorily gets its meaning from another NP in the sentence, is called an ***anaphor*** (as we saw in chapter 1).

4)   *Anaphor:* An NP that obligatorily gets its meaning from another NP in the sentence.

Typical anaphors are *himself, herself, themselves, myself, yourself,* and *each other.*

> ### Types of Anaphors
> There are actually (at least) two different kinds of anaphors. One type is the ***reflexive pronouns*** like *herself, himself,* and *themselves*. The other kind are called ***reciprocals***, and include words like *each other*. For our purposes, we'll just treat this group like a single class, although there are minor differences between the distribution of reflexives and reciprocals.

There is yet another kind of NP. These are NPs that can optionally get their meaning from another NP in the sentence, but may also optionally get it from somewhere else (including context or previous sentences in the discourse). These NPs are called ***pronouns***.[3] Look at the sentence in (5):

5)   Art said that he played basketball.

In this sentence, the word *he* can optionally refer to Art (i.e., the sentence can mean "Art said that Art played basketball") or it can refer to someone else (i.e. "Art said that Noam played basketball"). Typical pronouns include: *he, she, it, I, you, me, we, they, us, him, her, them, his, her, your, my, our, their, one.* A definition of pronoun is given in (6):

6)   *Pronoun*: An NP that may (but need not) get its meaning from another word in the sentence.

---

[3] There is some discrepancy among linguists in the use of this term. Some linguists use the term ***pronominal*** instead of pronoun and use the term pronoun to cover both anaphors and pronominals. This distinction, while more precise, is confusing to the beginner, so for our purposes we'll just contrast pronouns to anaphors, and avoid the term pronominal.

Getting back to syntax, it turns out that these different semantic types of NPs can only appear in certain syntactic positions that are defined using the structural relations we developed in the last chapter. Anaphors, R-expressions, and pronouns can only appear in specific parts of the sentence. For example, an anaphor may not appear in the subject position of sentence:

7) *Herself bopped Heidi on the head with a zucchini.

The theory of the syntactic restrictions on where these different NP types can appear in a sentence is called **Binding Theory** and is the focus of this chapter and makes reference to the structural relations we learned about in the previous chapter. This chapter thus will be your first exposure to why structural relations are so important to linguists.

You now have enough information to try General Problem Set 1

---

1. THE NOTIONS *COINDEX* AND *ANTECEDENT*

We're going to start with the distribution of anaphors. First, we need some terminology to set out the facts. An NP that gives its meaning to another noun in the sentence is called the **antecedent**:

8) *Antecedent*[4]: An NP that gives its meaning to another NP.

For example, in sentence (3) (repeated here as 9), the NP *Heidi* is the source of the meaning for the anaphor *herself*, so *Heidi* is called the antecedent:

9) Heidi bopped herself on the head with a zucchini.
         ↑   ↑
    antecedent   anaphor

We use a special mechanism to indicate that two NPs refer to the same entity. After each NP we write a subscript letter. If the NPs refer to the same entity, then they get the same letter. If they refer to different entities they get different letters. Usually we start (as a matter of tradition) with the letter *i* and work our way down the alphabet. These subscript letters are called **indices** or **indexes** (singular: **index**).

---

[4] In Latin the prefix *ante* means "before." However, in the system we are developing here, antecedents do *not* need to precede the noun they give their meaning to (although they frequently do). In some cases the antecedent may follow the noun that it gives its meaning to: e.g., *Everyone who knows him loves Dan. Him* can get its meaning from *Dan*, even though *Dan* follows *him*.

10) a)   [Colin]ᵢ gave [Andrea]ⱼ [a basketball]ₖ.
     b)   [Art]ᵢ said that [he]ⱼ played [basketball]ₖ in [the dark]ₗ.
     c)   [Art]ᵢ said that [he]ᵢ played [basketball]ₖ in [the dark]ₗ.
     d)   [Heidi]ᵢ bopped [herself]ᵢ on [the head]ⱼ with [a zucchini]ₖ.

In (10a), all the NPs refer to different entities in the world, so they all get
different indexes. The same is true for (10b). Note that with this indexing, the
sentence only has the meaning where *he* is not *Art*, but someone else – the
pronoun *he* and *Art* have different indexes. Sentence (10c), by contrast, has *he*
and *Art* referring to the same person. In this sentence, *Art* is the antecedent
of the pronoun *he*, so they have the same index. Finally in (10d), the anaphor
herself, by definition, refers back to *Heidi* so they get the same index. Two
NPs that get the same index are said to be **coindexed**. NPs that are coindexed
with each other are said to **corefer** (i.e., refer to the same entity in the world).

11) *Coindexed*: Two NPs are said to be coindexed if they have the same
     index.

In (10c) *Art* and *he* are coindexed; in (10b) *Art* and *he* are not coindexed.

2. BINDING

The notions of coindexation, coreference, and antecedence are actually
quite general ones. They hold no matter what structural position an NP is in
the sentence. It turns out, however, that the relations between an antecedent
and a pronoun or anaphor must bear particular structural relations. Contrast
the three sentences in (12).[5]

12) a)   Heidiᵢ bopped herselfᵢ on the head with a zucchini.
     b)   [Heidiᵢ's mother]ⱼ bopped herselfⱼ on the head with a zucchini.
     c)   *[Heidiᵢ's mother]ⱼ bopped herselfᵢ on the head with a zucchini.

In particular notice the pattern of indexes on (12b) and (12c). These sentences
show, that while the word *herself* can refer to the whole subject NP *Heidi's
mother*, it can't refer to an NP embedded inside the subject NP, such as *Heidi*.
Similar facts are seen in (13).

13) a)   [The mother of Heidiᵢ]ⱼ bopped herselfⱼ on the head with a zucchini.
     b)   *[The mother of Heidiᵢ]ⱼ bopped herselfᵢ on the head with a zucchini.

---

[5] In order to account for these sentences we'll have to slightly modify our NP rule:
   NP → ({D/NP's}) (AdjP+) N (PP+)

A Quick Note on Notation

Syntacticians will sometimes abbreviate two sentences that are otherwise identical, but have different indices. The two possible indices are separated by a slash (/) and the index that would make the sentence ungrammatical is marked with an asterisk (*). So the abbreviated form of the two sentences in (13) would be:

13') [The mother of Heidi$_i$]$_j$ bopped herself$_{j/*i}$ on the head with a zucchini.

This means that that the version of this sentence where *herself* is indexed j (i.e., coindexed with *[the mother of Heidi]$_j$*) is grammatical; but when it is indexed i (i.e., coindexed with *[Heidi]$_i$*) it is ungrammatical.

Look at the trees for (12a and b), shown in (14a and b) below, and you will notice a significant difference in terms of the position where the NP immediately dominating *Heidi* is placed.

14) a) (=12a)

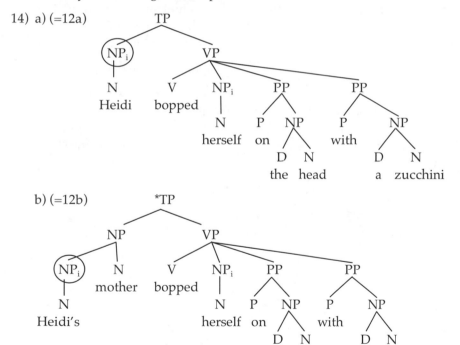

In (14a) the circled NP c-commands the NP dominating *herself*, but in (14b) it does not. It appears that the crucial relationship between an anaphor and its antecedent involves c-command. So in describing the relationship between an anaphor and an antecedent we need a more specific notion than simple coindexation. This is **binding**:

15) *Binds*: A binds B if and only if A c-commands B *and* A and B are coindexed.

Binding is a kind of coindexation. It is coindexation that happens when one of the two NPs c-commands the other. Notice that coindexation alone does not constitute binding. Binding requires *both* coindexation and c-command.

You now have enough information to try General Problem Set 2 and Challenge Problem Set 1

Now we can make the following generalization, which explains the ungrammaticality of sentences (16a) (=7) and (16b) (=12c):

16) a) (=7)   *Herself$_i$ bopped Heidi$_i$ on the head with a zucchini.
    b) (=12c) *[Heidi$_i$'s mother]$_j$ bopped herself$_i$ on the head with a zucchini.

In neither of these sentences is the anaphor bound. In other words, it is not c-commanded by the NP it is coindexed with. This generalization is called **Binding Principle A**. Principle A determines the distribution of anaphors:

17) *Binding Principle A (preliminary)*: An anaphor must be bound.

Remember, bound means coindexed with an NP that c-commands it. If you look at the tree in (14b) you'll see that the anaphor *herself*, and the NP *Heidi* are coindexed. However they are not bound, since [$_{NP}$ *Heidi*] does not c-command [$_{NP}$ *herself*]. The same is true in the tree for (16a) (=7) shown in (18):

18)

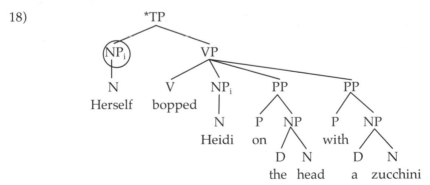

Even though the two NPs are coindexed, they do not form a binding relation, since the antecedent doesn't c-command the anaphor. You might think that *Heidi* binds *herself*, since the anaphor c-commands the antecedent.[6] But notice that this is not the way binding is defined. Binding is *not* a symmetric relationship. The **binder** (or antecedent) must do the c-commanding of the **bindee** (anaphor or pronoun), not the reverse.

3. LOCALITY CONDITIONS ON THE BINDING OF ANAPHORS

Consider now the following fact about anaphors:

19) *Heidi$_i$ said that herself$_i$ discoed with Art.
    (cf. Heidi$_i$ said that she$_i$ discoed with Art.)

A tree for sentence (19) is given below:

20)

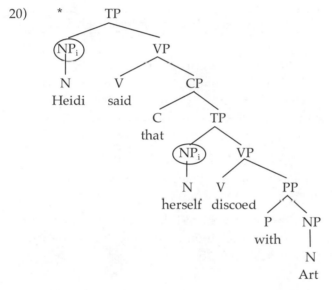

As you can see from this tree, the anaphor is bound by its antecedent: [$_{NP}$*Heidi*] c-commands [$_{NP}$ *herself*] and is coindexed with it. This sentence is predicted to be grammatical by the version of Principle A presented in (17), since it meets the requirement that anaphors be bound. Surprisingly, however, the sentence is ungrammatical. Notice that the difference between a sentence like (19) and a sentence like (12a) is that in the ungrammatical (19), the anaphor is in an embedded clause. The anaphor seems to need to find its antecedent in the same clause. This is called a *locality constraint*.

---

[6] In fact, in this tree *herself* binds *Heidi*, and therein lies the problem; anaphors must be bound, they aren't the binders.

The anaphor's antecedent must be near it or "local" in some way. The syntactic space in which an anaphor must find its antecedent is called a **binding domain**. For the moment let's just assume that the binding domain is the clause (TP).

21) *Binding domain*: The clause containing the NP (anaphor, pronoun, or R-expression).

With this in mind, let's revise Principle A:

22) *Binding Principle A (revised):* An anaphor must be bound in its binding domain.

This constraint says that anaphors must find an antecedent within the clause that immediately contains them.

You now have enough information to try General Problem Set 3

Binding Domain

The definition we've given here for "binding domain" is clearly over-simplistic. For example, when there is an NP that contains an anaphor and an NP marked with *'s*, that NP seems to function as a binding domain:

i)   Heidi$_i$ believes any description of herself$_i$.
ii) *Heidi$_i$ believes Martha$_j$'s description of herself$_i$.
iii) Heidi$_i$ believes Martha$_j$'s description of herself$_j$.

The literature on this is extensive and beyond the scope of this chapter. But you should be aware that the definition given here needs extensive revision, we will return to this in chapter 15.

4. THE DISTRIBUTION OF PRONOUNS

Anaphors are not the only NP type with restrictions on their syntactic position. Pronouns can also be restricted in where they may appear:

23) a) Heidi$_i$ bopped her$_j$ on the head with the zucchini.
    b) *Heidi$_i$ bopped her$_i$ on the head with the zucchini.

Pronouns like *her* in the sentences in (23) may not be bound. (They may not be coindexed by a c-commanding NP.) The sentence in (23) may only have the meaning where the *her* refers to someone other than *Heidi*. Contrast this situation with the one in which the pronoun is in an embedded clause:

24) a)   Heidi$_i$ said [$_{S'}$ that she$_i$ discoed with Art].
    b)   Heidi$_i$ said [$_{S'}$ that she$_k$ discoed with Art].

In this situation, a pronoun may be bound by an antecedent, but it doesn't have to be. It can be bound as in (24a), or not bound as in (24b). Unlike the case of anaphors, (which *must* be bound in a particular configuration), pronouns seem only to have a limitation on where they *cannot* be bound. That is, a pronoun cannot be bound by an antecedent that is a clause-mate (in the same immediate clause). You'll notice that this is exactly the opposite of where anaphors are allowed. This restriction is called **Principle B** of the binding theory. It makes use of the term free. *Free* is the opposite of bound.

25) *Free*: Not bound.
26) *Principle B*: A pronoun must be free in its binding domain.

Given that the binding domain is a clause, the ungrammaticality of (23b) is explained. Both *Heidi* and *her* are in the same clause, so they may not be bound to each other. The pronoun must be free. In (24) both indexings are allowed by Principle B. In (24b) the pronoun isn't bound at all (so is free within its binding domain). In (24a), the situation is a little trickier: The pronoun is bound, but it isn't bound within its binding domain (the embedded clause). Its binder lies outside the binding domain, so the sentence is grammatical.

You now have enough information to try Challenge Problem Sets 2 & 3

5. THE DISTRIBUTION OF R-EXPRESSIONS

R-expressions have yet another distribution. R-expressions don't seem to allow any instances of binding at all, not within the binding domain and not outside it either.

27) a)   *Heidi$_i$ kissed Miriam$_i$.
    b)   *Art$_i$ kissed Geoff$_i$.
    c)   *She$_i$ kissed Heidi$_i$.[7]

---

[7] Note that this sentence is *not* a violation of Principle B. *Heidi* does not bind *she* here, even though they are coindexed. This is because *Heidi* does not c-command *she*. Note that *[Even her$_i$ enemies] love Heidi$_i$* is well-formed, because neither NP c-commands the other, so there is no binding, even if they are coindexed. Remember coindexation is not the same thing as binding.

d)   *She_i said that Heidi_i was a disco queen.

In none of these sentences can the second NP (all R-expressions) be bound by a c-commanding word. This in and of itself isn't terribly surprising, given the fact that R-expressions receive their meaning from outside the sentence (i.e., from the context). That they don't get their meaning from another word in the sentence (via binding) is entirely expected. We do have to rule out situations like (27). The constraint that describes the distribution of R-expressions is called **Principle C**.

28) *Principle C*: An R-expression must be free.

Notice that Principle C says nothing about a binding domain. Essentially R-expressions must be free everywhere. They cannot be bound at all.

You now have enough information to try General Problem Set 4 and Challenge Problem Sets 4–6

A Common Mistake

Consider the sentence *She_i loves Mary_i*. Which of the two NPs in this sentence is the antecedent? Common sense might tell us that *Mary* is. But common sense is wrong. The antecedent here is *she*. This is because *she* c-commands *Mary*, and not vice versa.

One easy way to avoid this mistake is not to think in terms of antecedent and anaphor/pronoun, but in terms of **binder** and **bindee**. The binder here is *she* because it is coindexed with *Mary* and c-commands *Mary*. *Mary* is the thing being bound (the bindee). Note that binding is typically an asymmetric relationship.

6. CONCLUSION

In this chapter, we looked at a very complex set of data concerning the distribution of different kinds of NPs. We saw that these different kinds of NPs can appear in different syntactic positions. A simple set of Binding Principles (A, B, and C) governs the distribution of NPs. This set of binding principles is built upon the structural relations developed in the last chapter.

In the next chapter, we are going to look at how we can develop a similarly simple set of revisions to the phrase structure rules. The constraints developed in this chapter have the shape of locality constraints (in that they require local, or nearness, relations between certain syntactic objects). In later chapters, we'll see a trend towards using locality constraints in other parts of the grammar.

The constraints developed in this chapter account for a wide range of data, but there are many cases that don't work; In particular there is a problem with our definition of binding domain. You can see some of these problems by trying some of the challenge problem sets at the end of this chapter. We return to a more sophisticated version of the binding theory in chapter 15 in the last part of this book.

IDEAS, RULES, AND CONSTRAINTS INTRODUCED IN THIS CHAPTER

i)   ***R-expression***: An NP that gets it meaning by referring to an entity in the world.

ii)   ***Anaphor***: An NP that obligatorily gets its meaning from another NP in the sentence.

iii)   ***Pronoun***: An NP that may (but need not) get its meaning from another NP in the sentence.

iv)   ***Antecedent***: The element that binds a pronoun, anaphor or R-expression. When this element c-commands another coindexed NP, it is a ***binder*** of that NP.

v)   ***Index***: A subscript mark that indicates what an NP refers to.

vi)   ***Coindexed***: Two NPs that have the same index ($_i$, $_j$, $_k$, etc.) are said to be coindexed.

vii)   ***Corefer***: Two NPs that are coindexed are said to corefer (refer to the same entity in the world).

viii)   ***Binding***: A binds B if and only if A c-commands B *and* A and B are coindexed. A is the ***binder***, B is the ***bindee***.

ix)   ***Locality Constraint***: A constraint on the grammar, such that two syntactic entities must be "local" or near to one another.

x)   ***Binding Domain***: The clause (for our purposes).

xi)   ***Free***: Not bound.

xii)   ***The Binding Principles***
        Principle A: An anaphor must be bound in its binding domain.
        Principle B: A pronoun must be free in its binding domain.
        Principle C: An R-expression must be free.

FURTHER READING

Aoun, Joseph (1985) *A Grammar of Anaphora*. Cambridge: MIT Press.

Chomsky, Noam (1980) On Binding. *Linguistic Inquiry* 11, 1–46.

Chomsky, Noam (1981) *Lectures on Government and Binding*. Dordrecht: Foris.

Higginbotham, James (1980) Pronouns and bound variables. *Linguistic Inquiry* 11, 697–708.

Lasnik, Howard (1989) *Essays on Anaphora*. Dordrecht: Kluwer Academic Publishers.

Reinhart, Tanya (1976) The Syntactic Domain of Anaphora. Ph.D. dissertation, MIT.

GENERAL PROBLEM SETS

1. NP TYPES
[Application of Skills; Very Basic]
Identify the type of NP (Anaphor, Pronoun, R-expression) of each of the following:

   their, each cat, folk dancing, oneself, each other, she, her, themselves

2. C-COMMAND AND BINDING
[Application of Skills; Basic]
Draw the trees for each of the following sentences and for the bolded NPs indicate whether (i) there is a binding relationship between the two nouns, and (ii) if there is relationship, which noun is the binder and which is the element that is being bound; if there is no binding relationship explain why (i.e., state which part of the definition of "binding" is not met). Note, this is not a question about the binding conditions (A, B, C) but about the definition of binding itself.

a)   [The book about **[the president]**$_i$]$_k$ didn't bother **him**$_i$.
b)   **[The book about [the president]**$_i$ **]**$_k$ didn't bother **him**$_i$.
c)   **[The book about [the president]**$_i$ **]**$_k$ sold **itself**$_k$.
d)   **[Andy**$_i$'s constant lack of effort]$_k$ dismayed **[his**$_i$ father]$_m$.
e)   **[Andy**$_i$'s constant lack of effort]$_k$ dismayed **[his**$_n$ father]$_m$.

3. BINDING DOMAIN
[Application of Skills; Basic]
Draw the tree for each of the following sentences. In your tree circle the binding domain for the boldfaced noun:

a)   The students told **themselves** that the exam wouldn't be too hard.
b)   The students told their professor that **they** weren't worried about binding theory.
c)   Michael said **the binding judgments** were wrong.

4. BINDING PRINCIPLES
[Application of Skills, Data Analysis; Intermediate]
Explain why the following sentences are ungrammatical. For each sentence, say what the binding domain of the NP causing the problem is, if it is c-commanded by its binder (antecedent), and name the binding condition that is violated.

a)   *Michael$_i$ loves him$_i$.
b)   *He$_i$ loves Michael$_i$.
c)   *Michael$_i$'s father$_j$ loves himself$_i$.
d)   *Michael$_i$'s father$_j$ loves him$_j$.
e)   *Susan$_i$ thinks that John should marry herself$_i$.
f)   *John thinks that Susan$_i$ should kiss her$_i$.

CHALLENGE PROBLEM SETS

CHALLENGE PROBLEM SET 1: WH-QUESTIONS
[Critical Thinking; Challenge]
What problem(s) does the following sentence make for the binding theory as we have sketched it in this chapter? Can you think of a solution? (Hint: consider the non-question form of this sentence *John despises these pictures of himself*.)

Which pictures of himself$_i$ does John$_i$ despise?

Assume the following tree for this sentence:

CHALLENGE PROBLEM SET 2: BINDING DOMAIN
[Critical Thinking; Challenge]
The following sentence with the assigned indexing is predicted by the theory we have given so far to be ungrammatical. But it is actually ok. Explain why our theory says this should be ungrammatical.

   Andy$_i$ dismayed [**his**$_i$ father]$_m$.

CHALLENGE PROBLEM SET 3: PERSIAN[8]
[Critical Thinking; Challenge]
Does the binding theory account for the following data? Explain. (*Râ* means "the" when following object NPs. 3SG means "third person singular.")

a) Jân$_i$ goft [$_{S'}$ ke [$_S$ Mery$_k$ ketâb-â ro be xodesh$_{i/k}$ bargardune]].
    John said that   Mary book-PL râ to himself/herself return
    "John said that Mary (should) return the books to him/herself."

b) Jân$_i$ goft [$_{S'}$ ke [$_S$ Mery$_j$ ketâb-â ro be xodesh$_{i/j}$ barmigardune]].
    John said that   Mary book-PL râ to himself/herself return3SG.FUT
    "John said that Mary will return the books to him/herself."

Now consider (c) and (d): in these examples, *xod* "self" instead of *xodesh* "himself" is used. How do you explain the contrast between (a and b) and (c and d)? Note that (a and b) are taken from the spoken language, whereas (c and d) represent the formal written variant.

c) Jân$_i$ goft [ke [$_S$ Mery$_k$ ketâb râ   barâye   xod$_{*i/k}$ bexânad]].
    John said that   Mary book râ   for   self   read3SG
    "John said that Mary (should) read the book to *himself/herself."

d) Jân$_i$ goft [ke [$_S$ Mery$_k$ ketâb râ   barâye xod$_{*i/k}$ negahdârad]].
    John said that Mary book râ   for   self   keep3SG
    "John said that Mary (should) keep the books for *himself/herself."

CHALLENGE PROBLEM SET 4: JAPANESE
[Data Analysis and Critical Thinking; Challenge]
Japanese has a number of items that can be called pronouns or anaphors. One of these is *zibunzisin*. For the purposes of this assignment assume that any noun that has the suffix *-wa* c-commands any other NP, and assume that any noun that has the suffix *-ga* c-commands any NP with the suffix *-o*. Consider the following data (Data from Aikawa 1994):

a) Johnwa$_i$ [$_{CP}$ [$_{TP}$ Maryga$_k$ zibunzisino$_{k/*i}$ hihansita] [$_C$ to]] itta.
    John   Mary   zibunzisin   criticized   that said
    "John said that Mary$_k$ criticized herself$_k$."
    "*John$_i$ said that Mary criticized himself$_i$."

---

[8] This problem set was contributed by Simin Karimi.

Question 1: On the basis of only the data in (a) is *zibunzisin* an anaphor or a pronoun? How can you tell?

Now consider this sentence:

b) Johnwa$_i$ [$_{CP}$ [$_{TP}$ zibunzisinga$_i$ Maryo korosita] [$_C$ to]] omotteiru.
    John   zibunzisin   Mary killed   that think
    "John thinks that himself killed Mary."
        (*note:* grammatical in Japanese.)

Question 2: Given this additional evidence, do you need to revise your hypothesis from question 1? Is *zibunzisin* an anaphor, a pronoun or something else entirely? How can you tell?

One more piece of data:

c) *Johnwa$_i$ [$_{CP}$[$_{TP}$ zibunzisinga$_k$ Maryo$_k$ korosita] [$_C$ to]] omotteiru.
    John   zibunzisin   Mary killed   that think
    "*John thinks that herself$_k$ killed Mary$_k$."

Question 3: Sentence (c) is a violation of which binding principle? (A, B, or C?) Which NP is binding which other NP in this sentence to cause the ungrammaticality?

CHALLENGE PROBLEM SET 5: COUNTEREXAMPLES?[9]
[Critical Thinking and Data Analysis; Challenge]
Each of the following examples is problematic for the binding theory we formulated above. Briefly explain why. For data from languages other than English, your answer should be based on the facts of the target language, and not the English translations. Use the word-by-word glosses to determine whether the Dogrib and Modern Greek NPs should be analyzed as anaphors, pronouns or R-expressions. Your discussion of Dogrib should be based on consideration of both sentences taken together.

a) I have no money on me.
b) John knew that there would be a picture of himself hanging in the post office.

c) *Modern Greek*

    O Yanis$_i$ ipe stin Katerina   oti   i Maria aghapa ton idhio$_i$.
    John   said to Catherin   that Mary   loves   himself
    "John$_i$ told Catherine that Mary loves him$_{i/*k}$."

---

[9] This problem set was contributed by Betsy Ritter. The Dogrib data come from Saxon (1984).

d) *Dogrib*
    (i) John   ye-hk'è   ha
        John   3SG(=him)-shoot   future
        "John$_i$ is going to shoot him$_{k/*i}$."

    (ii) *ye-zha   shèeti
        3SG(=his)-son   ate
        "His son ate."

CHALLENGE PROBLEM SET 6: C-COMMAND OR PRECEDENCE?

[Critical Thinking and Data Analysis; Challenge]

In the text above, we proposed that binding required both c-command and coindexation. Consider an alternative: binding requires that the binder precedes (rather than c-commands) and is coindexed with the element is bound. Which of these alternatives is right? How can you tell? You might consider data such as the following:

a) [$_{CP}$ [$_{CP}$ Although he$_i$ loves marshmallows] [$_{TP}$ Art$_i$ is not a big fan of Smores[10]]].
b) [$_{TP}$ [$_{NP}$ His$_i$ yearbook picture] gives Tom$_i$ the creeps].

Be very careful about this data. In particular, do <u>not</u> assume that an R-expression is automatically the binder, pronouns can be binders for the purposes of binding theory.

---

[10] For those who may not be familiar with the term, Smores are a typical American camp-fire treat. They involve a marshmallow candy cooked over an open fire, squished between two layers of graham cracker along with a layer of dark chocolate candy.

Part 2

The Base

chapter 6

X-bar Theory

0. INTRODUCTION

As we saw in the last chapter, the theory of sentence structure that we've developed is quite powerful. It correctly predicts constituency and – along with structural relations and the binding theory – it also accounts for the structural restrictions on the interpretation of pronouns, anaphors and R-expressions. This said, if we look a little more closely at sentence structure in many languages, we see that our theory has some empirical inadequacies. (It can't account for all the data.) Consider, for example, the subject NP in the sentence in (1):

1) [The big book of poems with the blue cover] is on the table.

The structure our NP rule NP → (D) (AdjP+) N (PP+) assigns to this is:

2)

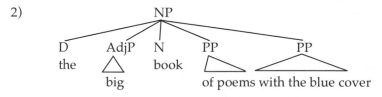

We can call this a *flat structure*. The PP *of poems* and the PP *with the blue cover* are on the same level hierarchically; there is no distinction between them in terms of dominance or c-command. In other words they are "flat" with respect to the head word *book*. From the point of view of constituency, we see that a number of tests point towards a more complicated structure. Consider first the constituency test of *replacement*. There is a particular variety of this process, called **one-*replacement***, that seems to target precisely a group of nodes that don't form a constituent in the tree in (2):

3)   I bought the big [book of poems with the blue cover] not the small [one].

Here, *one*-replacement targets *book of poems with the blue cover*, this group of words does not form a constituent in the tree in (2). Furthermore, *one*-replacement seems to be able to target other subgroups of words that similarly don't form constituents in (2):

4)   I bought the big [book of poems] with the blue cover not the small [one] with the red cover.

These facts seem to point to a more deeply embedded structure for the NP:

5)

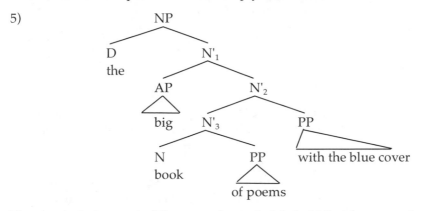

The *one*-replacement in (4) targets the node labeled N'$_3$. The *one*-replacement in (3) targets the node labeled N'$_2$. We have to change the NP slightly to get evidence for N'$_1$. If we change the determiner *the* to the determiner *that*, we can use *one*-replacement to target N'$_1$.

6)   I want [$_{NP}$ this [$_{N'}$ big book of poems with the red cover]] not [$_{NP}$ that [$_{N'}$ one]].

Similar evidence comes from conjunction:

7)   Calvin is [the [dean of humanities] and [director of social sciences]].
8)   Give me [the [blue book] and [red binder]].

We need these "intermediate" N' (pronounced "en-bar") categories to explain the items that are conjoined in these sentences.

The flat structure seen in (2) is clearly inadequate and a more articulated structure is needed. This chapter is about these articulated trees. The theory that accounts for these is called X-bar theory.

Before getting into the content of this chapter, a few bibliographic notes are in order. The first presentation of X-bar theory appeared in Chomsky (1970). Jackendoff's (1977) seminal book *X-bar Syntax* is the source of many of the ideas surrounding X-bar theory. Perhaps the most complete description of X-bar theory comes from an introductory syntax textbook (like this one). This is Radford's (1988) *Transformational Grammar: A First Course*. That textbook presents one of the most comprehensive arguments for X-bar theory. This chapter draws heavily on all three of these sources. If you are interested in reading a more comprehensive (although slightly out-of-date) version of X-bar theory, then you should look at Radford's book.

1. BAR-LEVEL PROJECTIONS

In order to account for the data seen above in the introduction, let us revise our NP rules to add the intermediate structure:

9) NP → (D) N'
10) N' → (AP) N' *or* N' (PP)
11) N' → N (PP)

Equivalent Notations

The name "X-bar theory" comes from the original mechanism for indicating intermediate categories. N' was written N̄ with a bar over the letter. This overbar is the origin of the "bar" in the name of the theory. "X" is a variable that stands for any category (N, Adj, V, P, etc.). The following notations are all equivalent: ⟵ our notations

Phrase level	$\boxed{\text{NP}} = \text{N''} = \text{N''} = \bar{\bar{\text{N}}} = \text{N}^{max}$
Intermediate level	$\boxed{\text{N'}} = \text{N'} = \bar{\text{N}}$
Word/Head level	$\boxed{\text{N}} = \text{N}°$

The same is true of all other categories as well (e.g., PP $= \bar{\bar{\text{P}}} = \text{P''} = \text{P''} =$ P^{max}, etc.). Since overbars are hard to type, even with Unicode fonts, most people use a prime (') or apostrophe (') for the intermediate level and write the phrasal level as NP (or more rarely, N'').

These rules introduce a new character to our cast of nodes, seen briefly above. This is the N' node. It plays the role of the intermediate constituent replaced by *one* above. The tree in (5) is repeated here showing how these rules (9–11) apply.

(12)

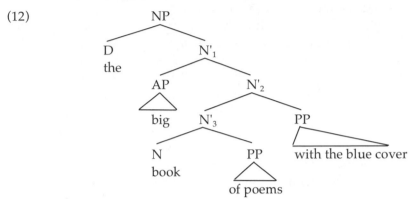

Rule (9) generates the NP node of this tree, with its daughters D and N'. The first version of rule (10) generates N'₁. The second version of rule (10) generates N'₂. Finally the last rule (11) spells out N'₃ as N and its PP sister.

We can now straightforwardly account for the *one*-replacement sentences. *One*-replacement is a process that targets the N' node:

13) One-*replacement:* Replace an N' node with *one*.

Without the intermediate N' node, we would have no way of accounting for *one*-replacement or conjunction facts. With N', explaining these sentences is easy, since there is more structure in each phrase.

The rule system in (9–11) has a number of striking properties (including the facts that it is binary branching and the first N' rule is iterative or self-recursive). We will return to these properties in a later section and show how they account for a number of surprising facts about the internal structure of phrases. First, however, let's see if any other categories also have intermediate structure.

1.1 V-bar

There is a similar process to *one*-replacement found in the syntax of VPs. This is the process of **do-so-**[1] (or **did-so-**) *replacement*. Consider first the VP in the following sentence, which has both an NP and a PP in it.

14) I [eat beans with a fork].

---

[1] Depending upon which dialect of English you speak, you may prefer "did too" over "did so too" or "did so." If the VPs below sound odd, try substituting "did too" for "did so."

The rule we developed for VPs in chapter 3 generates the following flat tree:

15)

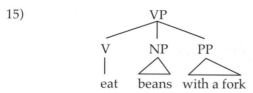

In this tree, there is no constituent that groups together the V and NP and excludes the PP. However, *do-so*-replacement targets exactly this unit:

16) I [eat beans] with a fork but Janet [does (so)] with a spoon.

Let's formalize this rule as:

17) Do-so-*replacement*: Replace a V' with *do so* (or *do* or *do so too* or *do too*).

For this to work we need the following rules[2]:

18) VP → V'
19) V' → V' (PP) or V' (AdvP)
20) V' → V (NP)

The tree structure for the VP in (14) will look like (21).

21)

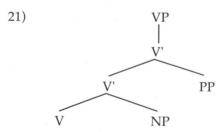

Rule (18) generates the VP and the V' under it; the next rule (19) expands the top V' into another V' and a PP. Finally, the lower V' is expanded into V and NP by rule (20).

    The rule of *do-so*-replacement seen in (17) targets the lower V' and replaces it with *do so*. Evidence for the higher V' comes from sentences like (22):

---

[2] The rule in (18) may appear a little mysterious right now (since it appears to introduce a vacuous structure) but we will have need of it in a later chapter. For the moment, just assume that it is necessary, and we will provide additional justification for it   later. You can note for now that in order to account for sentences like (22) below, we will need to assume that the entire replaced structure is a V', if we assume that *do-so*-replacement only targets V' nodes (and not VP nodes).

22) Kevin [ate spaghetti with a spoon] and Geordi [did so] too.

In this sentence, *did so* replaces the higher V' (which includes the V, the lower V', the NP, and the PP).

Similarly, conjunction seems to show an intermediate V' projection:

23) The chef [eats beans] and [tosses salads] with forks.

The tree for a structure like this requires a V' node (a description of the conjunction rule can be found below in the *additional rules* in the Ideas section at the end of the chapter):

24)

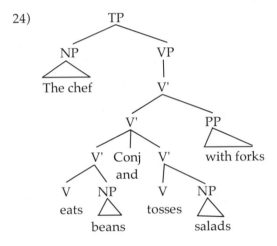

You now have enough information to try Challenge Problem Set 1

1.2 Adj-bar and Adv-bar

The arguments for intermediate structure in AdjPs are a little more tricky, as English seems to limit the amount of material that can appear in an AdjP. However, we do see such structure in phrases like (25):

25) the [very [[bright blue] and [dull green]]] gown

In this NP, *bright* clearly modifies *blue*, and *dull* clearly modifies *green*. One possible interpretation of this phrase (although not the only one) allows *very* to modify both *bright blue* and *dull green*. If this is the case then the structure must minimally look like (26) (note: we will have reason to revise this tree later).

26)

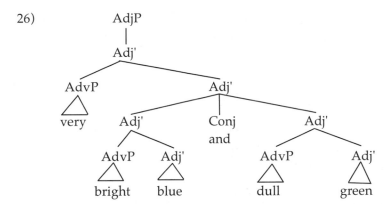

This must be the structure so that the AdvP can modify both *bright blue* and *dull green*.

Under certain circumstances, some adjectives appear to allow prepositional modifiers to follow them:

27) I am afraid / frightened of tigers.
28) I am fond of circus performers.

These post-adjectival PPs parallel the direct object of related verbs:

29) I fear tigers.
30) I like circus performers.

Consider now:

31) I am [[afraid/frightened of tigers] and [fond of clowns] without exception].

Under one reading of this sentence, *without exception* modifies both *afraid of tigers* and *fond of circus performers*. Again this would seem to suggest that the sentence has the constituency represented by the above bracketing, which points towards an intermediate category of Adj'.

There is also a replacement phenomenon that seems to target Adj's. This is *so*-replacement:

32) Bob is [very [serious about Mary]], but [less [so]] than Paul.

The adjective phrase here is *very serious about Mary*, but *so*-replacement only targets *serious about Mary*.

The rules that generate these structures are:

33) AdjP → Adj'
34) Adj' → (AdvP) Adj'
35) Adj' → Adj (PP)

For reasons of parsimony, we might presume that a similar set of rules governs Adverbs as well, although the evidence is very scarce.

1.3 P-bar

Consider the following sentences:

36) Gwen placed it [right [in the middle of the spaghetti sauce]].
37) Maurice was [[in love] with his boss].
38) Susanna was [utterly [in love]].

In these examples, we have what appear to be prepositional phrases (*in the middle of the spaghetti sauce, in love*) that are modified by some other element: *right, with his boss,* and *utterly* respectively. Note, however, that you can target smaller units within these large PPs with constituency tests:

39) Gwen knocked it [right [off the table] and [into the trash]].
40) Maurice was [[in love] and [at odds] with his boss].
41) Susanna was [utterly [in love]], but Louis was only [partly [so]].

Examples (39) and (40) show conjunction of the two smaller constituents. Example (41) is an example of *so*-replacement. Let us call the smaller constituent here P' on a parallel with N', Adj', and V'. The rules that generate PPs are given below:

42) PP → P'
43) P' → P' (PP)
44) P' → P (NP)

With this, we complete our tour of intermediate structure. In developing our phrase structure system, we've managed to complicate it significantly. In the next section we look at ways to simplify the rule system yet capture all the constituency facts we've considered here.

2. GENERALIZING THE RULES: THE X-BAR SCHEMA

For each of the major phrase types (NPs, VPs, AdjPs, AdvPs and PPs) we have come up with three rules, where the first and second rules serve to introduce intermediate structure. Let's repeat all the rules here. (Rules (48), (51), (54), and (57) are admittedly here simply by stipulation, we've seen no evidence for them. We're positing them now for reasons of parsimony with rule (45), but we'll see in the next chapter and the chapter that follows that the structures these rules introduce will be useful to us. Please allow me this one mysterious stipulation for the moment, I promise we'll return to the issue later in the book.)

45) NP → (D) N'
46) N' → (AdjP) N' *or* N' (PP)
47) N' → N (PP)
48) VP → V'
49) V' → V' (PP) or V' (AdvP)
50) V' → V (NP)
51) AdvP → Adv'
52) Adv' → (AdvP) Adv'
53) Adv' → Adv' (PP)
54) AdjP → Adj'
55) Adj' → (AdvP) Adj'
56) Adj' → Adj (PP)
57) PP → P'
58) P' → P' (PP)
59) P' → P (NP)

This is quite a complicated set, but seems to be more empirically motivated than the set of rules we set out in chapter 3. We can now ask, are we missing any generalizations here?

Indeed, we seem to be missing several. First, note that in all the rules above, the category of the rule is the same as the only element that is not optional. For example, in the NP rule, the element that isn't optional is N'. This is the same part of speech. Similarly, the only obligatory element in N' is either another N' or N. This is a very general notion in phrase structure; we call this headedness. All phrases appear to have *heads*. Heads are the most prominent element in a phrasal category and give their part of speech category to the whole phrase. Note that we don't have any rules of the form:

60) NP → V AdjP

This rule not only seems meaningless, it is unattested in the system we've developed here. This property is called *endocentricity*, meaning that every phrase has a head. The only obligatory element in a phrase is the head.

Second, note that with the exception of the determiner in the NP rule, all non-head material in the rules is both phrasal and optional. We never find rules of the form:

61) V' → Adv V

With the exception of the determiner (an exception that we'll resolve in chapter 7), anything in an X-bar rule that isn't a head must be a phrase and optional.

Finally, notice that for each major category, there are three rules, one that introduces the NP, VP, AdvP, AdjP and PP, one that takes a bar level and repeats it (e.g., $\underline{N'} \rightarrow \underline{N'}$ (PP)), and one that takes a bar level and spells out the head (e.g., N' → N (PP)). We seem to be missing the generalization that for each kind of phrase, the *same kinds of rules* appear. X-bar theory is an attempt to capture these similarities between rules.

We can condense the rules we've proposed into a simple set. To do this we are going to make use of variables (like variables in algebra) to stand for particular parts of speech. Let X be a variable that can stand for any category N, V, Adj, Adv, P. An XP is a catch-all term to cover NP, VP, AP, PP, similarly X' stands for N', V', Adj', Adv', P', and X represents N, V, Adj, Adv, and P.

Using this variable notation we can capture the generalizations that we have missed. Let's start with the rules that introduce heads:

62) a)   N' → N (PP)
    b)   V' → V (NP)
    c)   Adj' → Adj (PP)
    d)   Adv' → Adv (PP)
    e)   P' → P (NP)

By using the variable notation we can generalize across these rules with the single general statement:

63) X' → X (WP) (*to be revised*)

Both X and W here are variables for categories. This rule says that some bar level (on the left of the arrow) consists of some head followed by an optional, phrasal[3] element.

Now turn to the recursive N', A', V' and P' rules:

64) a)   N' → (AdjP) N' *or* N' (PP)
    b)   V' → V' (PP) or V' (AdvP)
    c)   Adj' → (AdvP) Adj'
    d)   Adv' → (AdvP) Adv'
    e)   P' → P' (PP)

---

[3] The D in the NP rule is, of course, not phrasal. This is a problem we will return to in the next chapter.

For each of these rules, a category with a single bar level is iterated (repeated), with some optional material either on the right or the left. Again using X as a variable, we can condense these into a single statement:

65) X' → (ZP) X' *or* X' (ZP) (*to be revised*)

Again the Xs here must be consistent in part of speech category. The material that is not the head (i.e., not X) must be phrasal and optional. Note that the categories of these non-head items are also indicated with variables (in this case: ZP).

Finally, let's consider the rules that introduce the last layer of structure:

66) a) NP → (D) N'
    b) VP → V'
    c) AdjP → Adj'
    d) AdvP → Adv'
    e) PP → P'

These rules can also be collapsed into a single rule:

67) XP → (YP) X' (*to be revised*)

We haven't motivated the existence of the YP here, except in the form of determiners. I know you're naturally suspicious of me saying "trust me on this" (and rightly so); but I promise we will resolve this in the next chapter.

The system we've come up with here is simple. We've reduced our phrase structure rules down to three general rules using variables: Because they use variables, these rules can generate the correct constituent of the sentences of English. This analysis isn't without problems, however. Before we turn to resolving these problems and drafting a final version of the X-bar rules, we need to introduce some new terminology.

3. COMPLEMENTS, ADJUNCTS, AND SPECIFIERS

Consider now the two prepositional phrases that are subconstituents of the following NP:

68) the book [PP of poems] [PP with the glossy cover]

Using the X-bar rules,[4] we can generate the following tree for this NP:

---

[4] Specific instructions on drawing trees using the X-bar rules are found at the end of this chapter.

69)

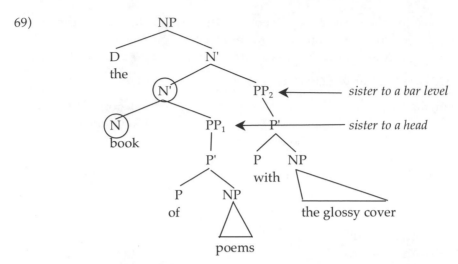

(I've used triangles in this tree to obscure some of the irrelevant details, but you should not do this when you are drawing trees, until you have a confident grasp of how tree notation works.) You'll note that the two PPs in this tree are at different levels in the tree. The lower PP_1 is a sister to the head N (*book*), whereas the higher PP_2 is a sister to the N' dominating the head N and PP_1. You'll also notice that these two PPs were introduced by different rules. PP_1 is introduced by the rule:

70) X' → X (WP)

and PP_2 is introduced by the higher level rule:

71) X' → X' (ZP)

An XP that is a sister to a head (N, V, A, or P) is called a ***complement***. PP_1 is a complement. Complements roughly correspond to the notion "object" in traditional grammar. XPs that are sisters to single bar levels (N', V', A', or P') and are daughters of an N' are called ***adjuncts***. PP_2 is an adjunct. Adjuncts often have the feel of adverbial or obliques.

72) *Adjunct:* An XP that is a sister to a single bar level (N', V', A', or P') and a daughter of a single bar level (N', V', A', or P').

73) *Complement:* An XP that is a sister to a head (N, V, A, P), and a daughter of a single bar level (N', V', A', or P').

The rules that introduce these two kinds of XPs get special names:

74) *Adjunct rule:*   X' → X' (ZP)
75) *Complement rule:*   X' → X (WP)

A tree showing the structural difference between these is given below:

76)

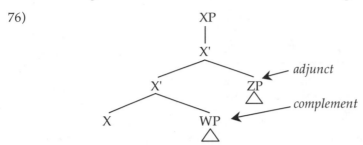

If there really are two different kinds of PP within an NP, then we expect that they will exhibit different kinds of behavior. It turns out that this is true: There are significant differences in behavior between adjuncts and complements.

3.1 Complements and Adjuncts in NPs

Take NPs as a prototypical example. Consider the difference in meaning between the two NPs below:

77) the book of poems
78) the book with a red cover

Although both these examples seem to have, on the surface, parallel structures (a determiner, followed by a noun, followed by a prepositional phrase), in reality, they have quite different structures. The PP in (77) is a complement and has the following tree:

79)

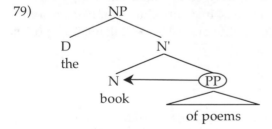

You'll note that the circled PP is a sister to N, so it is a complement. By contrast, the structure of (78) is:

80)

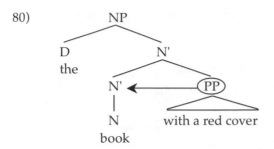

Here the PP *with a red cover* is a sister to N', so it is an adjunct. The differences between these two NPs is not one that you can *hear*. The difference between the two is in terms of the amount of structure in the tree. In (80), there is an extra N'. While this difference may at first seem abstract, it has important implications for the behavior of the two PPs. Consider first the meaning of our two NPs. In (77), the PP seems to complete (or complement) the meaning of the noun. It tells us what kind of book is being referred to. In (78), by contrast, the PP seems more optional and more loosely related to the NP. This is a highly subjective piece of evidence, but it corresponds to more syntactic and structural evidence too.

An easy heuristic (guiding principle) for distinguishing complements from adjunct PPs inside NPs, is by looking at what preposition they take. In English, almost always (although there are some exceptions) complement PPs take the preposition *of*. Adjuncts, by contrast, take other prepositions (such as *from, at, to, with, under, on,* etc.). This test isn't 100 percent reliable, but will allow you to eyeball PPs and tell whether they are complements or adjuncts for the vast majority of cases. With this in mind, let's look at some of the other behavioral distinctions between complements and adjuncts.

Think carefully about the two rules that introduce complements and adjuncts. There are several significant differences between them. These rules are repeated here for your convenience:

81) *Adjunct rule:*   X' → X' (ZP)
82) *Complement rule:*   X' → X (WP)

First observe that because the complement rule introduces the head (X), the complement PP will always be adjacent to the head. Or more particularly, it will always be closer to the head than an adjunct PP will be. This is seen in the following data:

83) the book   [of poems]   [with a red cover]
        head   *complement*   *adjunct*

84) *the book   [with a red cover] [of poems]
        head   *adjunct*   *complement*

You can see how this is true if you look at the tree for sentence (83):

85)

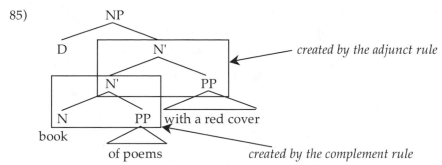

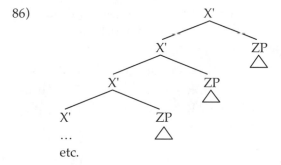

Since the adjunct rule takes an X' level category and generates another X' category, it will always be higher in the tree than the output of the complement rule (which takes an X' and generates an X). Since lines can't cross, this means that complements will always be lower in the tree than adjuncts, and will always be closer to the head than adjuncts.

There is another property of the rules that manifests itself in the difference between adjuncts and complements. The adjunct rule, as passingly observed above, is an iterative rule. That is, within the rule itself, it shows the property of recursion (discussed in chapter 3): On the left-hand side of the rule there is an X' category, and on the right hand side there is another X'. This means that the rule can generate infinite strings of X' nodes, since you can apply the rule over and over again to its own output:

86)

```
                              X'
                        ┌─────┴─────┐
                       X'           ZP
                   ┌────┴────┐       △
                  X'         ZP
              ┌────┴────┐     △
             X'         ZP
          ┌───┴───┐      △
         X'       ZP
         ...       △
       etc.
```

The complement rule does not have this property. On the left side of the rule there is an X', but on the right there is only X. So the rule cannot apply iteratively. That is, it can only apply once within an XP. What this means for complements and adjuncts is that you can have any number of adjuncts (87), but you can only ever have one complement (88):

87) the book [of poems] [with a red cover] [from Blackwell] [by Robert Burns]
       head complement   adjunct   adjunct   adjunct

88) *the book [of poems] [of fiction] [with a red cover]
       head complement complement   adjunct

The tree for (87) is given below; you'll note that since there is only one N, there can only be one complement, but since there are multiple N's, there can be as many adjuncts as desired.

89)

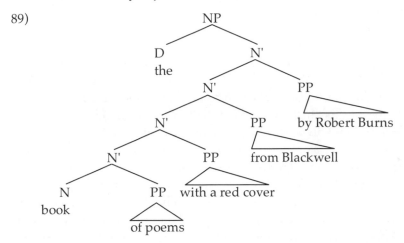

Related to the facts that the number of adjuncts is unlimited, but only one complement is allowed, and complements are always adjacent to the head, observe that you can usually reorder adjuncts with respect to one another, but you can never reorder a complement with the adjuncts:

90) a)   the book of poems with a red cover from Blackwell by Robert Burns
     b)   the book of poems from Blackwell with a red cover by Robert Burns
     c)   the book of poems from Blackwell by Robert Burns with a red cover
     d)   the book of poems by Robert Burns from Blackwell with a red cover
     e)   the book of poems by Robert Burns with a red cover from Blackwell
     f)   the book of poems with a red cover by Robert Burns from Blackwell
     g)   *the book with a red cover of poems from Blackwell by Robert Burns
     h)   *the book with a red cover from Blackwell of poems by Robert Burns
     i)   *the book with a red cover from Blackwell by Robert Burns of poems
             (etc.)

Note that adjuncts and complements are constituents of different types. The definition of adjuncthood holds that adjuncts are sisters to X'. Since conjunction (see under ***additional rules*** at the end of this chapter) requires that you conjoin elements of the same bar level, you could not, for example, conjoin an adjunct with a complement. This would result in a contradiction: Something can't be both a sister to X' and X at the same time. Adjuncts can conjoin with other adjuncts (other sisters to X'), and complements can conjoin with other complements (other sisters to X), but complements cannot conjoin with adjuncts:

91) a)   the book of poems with a red cover and with a blue spine[5]
    b)   the book of poems and of fiction from Blackwell
    c)   *the book of poems and from Blackwell

There is one final difference between adjuncts and complements that we will examine here. Recall the test of *one*-replacement:

92) One-*replacement:* Replace an N' node with *one.*

This operation replaces an N' node with the word *one.* Look at the tree in (93):

93)
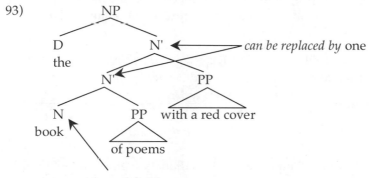

If you look closely at this tree you'll see that two possibilities for *one*-replacement exist. We can either target the highest N', and get:

94) the one

or we can target the lower N' and get:

95) the one with a red cover

But we cannot target the N head; it is not an N'. This means that *one* followed by a complement is ill-formed:

96) *the one of poems with a red cover[6]

---

[5] If this NP sounds odd to you, try putting emphasis on the *and.*
[6] Not everyone finds this NP ill-formed. There is at least one major US dialect that allows sentence (96). One possible explanation for this is that different dialects

Since complements are sisters to X and not X', they cannot stand next to the word *one*. Adjuncts, by definition, can.

So far in this chapter, we've covered a huge range of facts, so a quick summary is probably in order. In section 1, we saw that constituency tests pointed towards a more articulated structure for our trees than the one we developed in chapter 3. In section 2, we introduced the X' notation to account for this more complicated structure. In X-bar structure, there are three levels of categories. There are XPs, X's, and Xs. In this section – focusing exclusively on NPs – we introduced special terms for elements that are sisters to X' and X: *adjuncts* and *complements*. These two different kinds of modifier have different properties. Adjuncts but not complements can be iterated and reordered and can stand next to *one*. Complements, by contrast, must be located next to the head and can't be reordered. We also saw that we could conjoin complements with complements and adjuncts with adjuncts, but that we couldn't mix the two. All of these data provide support for the extra structure proposed in X-bar theory. In the next subsection, we'll briefly consider evidence that the complement/adjunct distinction holds for categories other than NP as well.

You can now try General Problem Sets 1, 2 & 3 and Challenge Problem Set 2.
You may want to read section 6 (on tree drawing) before attempting
General Problem Set 3.

3.2 Complements and Adjuncts in VPs, AdjPs, AdvPs, and PPs

The distinction between complements and adjuncts is not limited to NPs; we find it holds in all the major syntactic categories. The best example is seen in VPs. The direct object of a verb is a complement of the verb. Prepositional and adverbial modifiers of verbs are adjuncts:

97) I loved [the policeman] [intensely] [with all my heart].
    V   direct object   adverbial   PP phrase
           complement   *adjunct*   *adjunct*

---

have different *one*-replacement rules. The dialect that finds this NP well-formed allows either N or N' to be replaced. The dialect that finds this ill-formed (or at least odd), only allows N' to be replaced.

98)

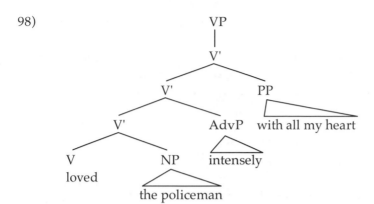

Direct objects must be adjacent to the verb, and there can only be one of them.

99) a)   *I loved intensely the policeman with all my heart.
    b)   *I loved the policeman the baker intensely with all my heart.

Did-so (*did-too*) replacement targets V'. Like one-replacement, this means that it can only apply before an adjunct and not before a complement:

100)   Mika loved the policemen intensely and
    a)   Susan did so half-heartedly.
    b)   *Susan did so the baker.

This is classic adjunct/complement distinction. In general, complements of all categories (N, V, A, P, etc.) are the semantic objects of the head. Consider for example all the complements below.

101) a) John fears dogs.   *(verb)*
    b) John is afraid of dogs.   *(adjective)*
    c) John has a fear of dogs. *(noun)*

In all these sentences, *(of) dogs* is a complement.

You now have enough information to try General Problem Set 4

    The evidence for the adjunct/complement distinction in adjective phrases and prepositional phrases is considerably weaker than that of nouns and verbs. Adverbs that modify adjectives have an adjunct flair – they can be stacked and reordered. Other than this, however, the evidence for the distinction in PPs and AdjPs, comes mainly as a parallel to the NPs and VPs. This may be less than satisfying, but is balanced by the formal simplicity of having the same system apply to all categories.

3.3 The Notion Specifier

In the section 3.1 above, we introduced two structural notions: adjuncts and complements. These correspond to two of the three X-bar rules:

102) a) *Adjunct rule:*   X' → X' (ZP) *or* X' → (ZP) X'
      b) *Complement rule:*   X' → X (WP)

The third rule also introduces a structural position: the **specifier**.

103) *Specifier rule:*   XP → (YP) X'

We have only seen one specifier so far – the determiner in NPs:

104) [the]   [book]   [of poems]   [with a red cover]
      specifier head   complement   adjunct

105)

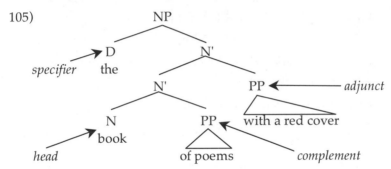

The specifier is defined as the daughter of XP and sister to X':

106) *Specifier:* An XP[7] that is a sister to an X' level, and a daughter of an XP.

We can show that specifiers are different from adjuncts and complements. Since the specifier rule is not recursive, you can only have one specifier:[8]

107) *the these red books

The specifier rule has to apply at the top of the structure, this means that the specifier will always be the left-most element (in English anyway):

---

[7] If you are being observant you'll notice that the single example we have of a specifier is not a phrase, but a word (*the*), so it may seem odd to say XP here. We return to this issue in later chapters.
[8] One possible exception to this is the quantifier *all*, as in *all the books*. In the next chapter, we discuss the idea that determiners head their own phrase (called a DP), which might provide a partial explanation for this exception.

108)   *boring the book

The above example also shows that specifiers can't be reordered with respect to other adjuncts or complements. As the final difference between specifiers and other types of modifier, specifiers can only be conjoined with other specifiers:

109)   a)   two or three books
       b)   *two or boring books

On the surface, the usefulness of this position may seem obscure, since only determiners appear in it. But in later chapters we will have important use for specifiers. (In particular, we will claim that they are the position where subjects are generated in a variety of categories.)

4. SOME DEFINITIONAL HOUSEKEEPING

With the refinements to the grammar we've made by adding X-bar theory to our system, we need to make some minor modifications to the rules and definitions that we introduced in previous chapters.

First, we need some terminology to describe the new parts of the phrase that we have added. We can refer to all the elements in an NP, for example, that are introduced (i.e. appear on the left side of the rule) by the three phrase structure rules as *projections* of the head. In the following tree, all the N's and the NP said to be projections of the head N.

110)

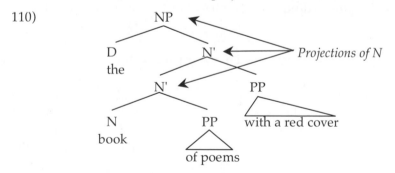

The NP is called the *maximal projection*; the N's are called *intermediate projections*.

Recall our definition of the principle of modification from chapter 3; a modifier must be a sister to the head it modifies:

111) ***Principle of Modification*** (old)
      If a YP (that is, a phrase with some category Y) modifies some head X,
      then YP must be a sister to X.

This definition no longer works for us. If you look at the tree in (110) you'll
see that only the complement is actually a sister to the head. Modifiers
that are adjuncts and specifiers aren't. To fix this we need to again revise
the principle of modification:

111′) ***Principle of Modification*** (revised)
       If a YP modifies some head X, then YP must be a sister to X or
       a projection of X (i.e., X′, XP).

   By adding extra layers of structure we also need to revise our definitions
of object and indirect object. In chapter 4, these relations are defined in terms
of being immediately dominated by VP. But with the new X-bar structures
these NPs aren't immediately dominated by VP anymore, so we need
to change them so they are defined in terms of intermediate structure.
This is easy to do for the direct object of transitive verbs:

112) ***Direct Object*** *(partly revised):*
      With verbs of type $V_{[NP\_NP]}$ and $V_{[NP\_CP]}$, the NP or CP sister to the V.

The definitions of indirect and direct objects in other types (e.g.,
ditransitives) are much harder. This is because our rules as stated only allow
binary branching; only one complement is allowed. Yet for ditransitives
we would ideally like to have two complements. This is a problem for X-bar
theory. We will return to ditransitives and indirect objects in chapter 13.

5. PARAMETERS OF WORD ORDER

In this chapter, and thus far in this book, we've been concentrating primarily
on English. The reason for this is that, since you are reading this book, it is
the language most accessible to you. However, syntacticians aren't interested
only in English. One of the most interesting parts of syntax is comparing the
sentence structure of different languages. The X-bar rules we've developed
so far for English do an acceptable job of accounting for the order of
constituents and hierarchical structure of English:

113) a) *Specifier rule:*   XP → (YP) X′
      b) *Adjunct rule:*   X′ → X′ (ZP) *or* X′ → (ZP) X′
      c) *Complement rule:*   X′ → X (WP)

They don't, however, account well for other languages. Consider the position of direct objects (complements) in Turkish. In Turkish, the complement precedes the head:

114) Hasan   kitab-i   oku-du.
      Hasan-SUBJ   book-OBJ   read-PAST
      "Hasan read the book."

If you look carefully at sentence (114) you notice that the word *kitabi* "book" precedes the word *okudu* "read."

Not all languages put the complement on the right-hand side like English. Not all languages put the specifier before the head either. Our rules, while adequate for English, don't really get at the syntactic structure of languages in general. Remember, syntax is the study of the mental representation of sentence structure, and since we all have the same basic gray matter in our brains, it would be nice if our theory accounted for both the similarities and the differences among languages.

X-bar theory provides us with an avenue for exploring the differences and similarities among languages. Let's start by generalizing our rules a little bit. Let's allow specifiers and adjuncts to appear on either side of the head:

115) a) *Specifier rule:*   XP → (YP) X' *or* XP → X' (YP)
      b) *Adjunct rule:*   X' → X' (ZP) *or* X' → (ZP) X'
      c) *Complement rule:*   X' → X (WP) *or* X' → (WP) X

Each of these rules has two options, the specifier/complement/adjunct can all appear on either side of their head. Obviously, these rules are now too general to account for English. If these rules, as stated, were adopted straight out, they would predict the grammaticality of sentences like:

116) *[$_{NP}$ Policeman the] [$_{VP}$ Mary kissed].
      (meaning *The policeman kissed Mary.*)

It would be a bad thing to do this. At the same time, constituent orders like those of Turkish, in fact, exist, so this clearly is an option. Our theory must capture both facts: The fact that the object-verb (OV) order is an option that languages use, and that it isn't the option used by English.

The way that generative syntacticians accomplish this is by claiming that the rules in (115) are the possibilities universally available to human beings. When you acquire a particular language you select *one* of the options in the rule, based upon the input you hear from your parents. Take, for example, the complement rule. In English, complements of verbs follow the verbal head. In Turkish, they precede the head. There are two options in the rule:

117) a)   X'→ X (WP)
      b)   X' → (WP) X

The child learning English will adopt option (a), the child learning Turkish will adopt option (b). These options are called **parameters**. The proposal that word order is parameterized finds its origins in Travis (1984).

Here is an analogy that might help you understand this concept. Imagine that in your head you have a box of switches, just like the box of master breaker switches which controls the electricity in your house. These switches can be set *on* or *off*. The options in the X-bar rules are like these switches, they can be set in one direction or the other (and in some situations – such as adjuncts in English – allow both settings).

118)   X-bar parameters switch box

Specifier	*Adjunct*	*Complement*
XP → (YP) X'	X' → (ZP) X'	X' → (WP) X
XP → X' (YP)	X' → X' (ZP)	X' → X (WP)

When you are a child acquiring your language, you subconsciously set these switches, to tell you which version of the rules to use.

Notice that this gives us a very simple system for acquiring the word order of our languages. There are a finite set of possibilities, represented by the different settings of the parameters. English sets its complement parameter so that the complement follows the head. Turkish sets it the other way. The child only has to hear a small amount of data (perhaps even as little as one sentence) to know what side of the head complements go in their language. Once children have set the parameter, they can apply the right version of the rule and generate an unlimited number of sentences. In the problem sets at the end of this chapter, you have the opportunity of looking at some data from a variety of languages and determining how their X-bar parameters are set. For your reference, the English settings are given below:

119) a) *Specifier*   specifier on left, head on right (XP → (YP) X')
                            e.g., *the* book

b) *Adjunct*   both options allowed (X'→ (ZP) X' and X' → X' (ZP))
                     e.g.,   *yellow* roses
                                books *from Poland*

c) *Complement*   head on left, complement on right (X' → X (WP))
                     e.g.,   books *of poems*
                                John kissed *his mother*.

You now have enough information to try General Problem Sets 5 & 6 (although you
may want to read section 6 (on tree drawing) before attempting Problem Set 4).
You also have enough information to answer Challenge Problem sets 3 & 4

---

6. DRAWING TREES IN X-BAR NOTATION

6.1 Important Considerations in Tree Drawing

In this section, we'll run through the steps for drawing trees in X-bar notation. The basics of tree drawing that you learned in chapter 3 hold here too. However, some special principles apply to X-bar tree drawing:

i) When identifying what modifies what, it is also important to know whether it is a complement, adjunct, or specifier. This is important because you have to know whether to make it a sister to the head, to an X', etc.

ii) When linking material up, start with the modifiers closest to the head. Because X-bar structure is formulated the way it is, material closest to the head will be the most deeply embedded material – so it will have to attach to the head *first*.
   a) Identify the head.
   b) Attach the complement (must be a phrase!).
   c) Attach any adjuncts (which must be phrases themselves) working progressively away from the head, each adjunct gets its own X' mother. (See points (iv) and (v) below for dealing with cases when you have either no adjuncts or have an adjunct on either side of the head.)
   d) When there are no more adjuncts, attach the specifier, if there is one. This gets an XP on top.
   e) Even if there is no specifier, put an XP on top of the projections. This indicates that there are no more modifiers of the head X.

iii) Keep in mind that none of the X-bar rules are optional. That is, they must all apply. This results in a fair amount of vacuous or non-branching structure. Even if the phrase has only a single word in it you will have *at least* the following structures:

120)   a) NP   b) VP   c) AdjP   d) AdvP   e) PP

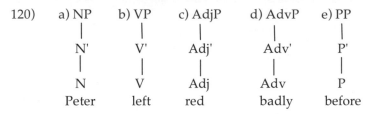

N'	V'	Adj'	Adv'	P'
N	V	Adj	Adv	P
Peter	left	red	badly	before

iv) Perhaps one of the most common errors of new syntacticians is in drawing trees for phrases with an adjunct but no complement. Consider the NP [notebook with a red cover]. *With a red cover* is an adjunct – that means that it has to be a sister to N' and a daughter to N' (by definition). This is seen in the following tree:

121)

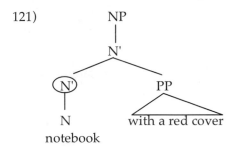

The circled N' here must be present in order to make the PP an adjunct. Be very careful to draw in these vacuous nodes that distinguish adjuncts from complements.

v)   Another common issue that arises for new syntacticians is how to tree a sentence when there is an adjunct on either side of the head. Consider the sentence in (123):

122)   Andy [_{VP} frequently   eats   sushi   with his boss].
            adjunct   head   complement   adjunct

We start by attaching the complement to the head:

123)

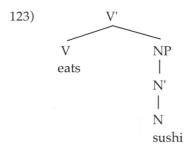

Our next step should be to attach an adjunct. But there are two adjuncts. Which one comes first? Interestingly, the answer is *either*. Two possible trees can come out of this VP:

124)   a)   b)

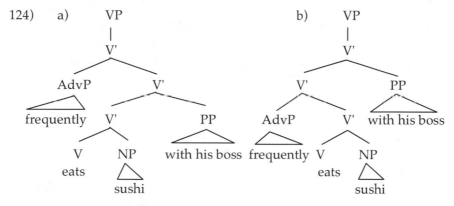

In (124a), the AdvP *frequently* is attached higher than the PP *with his boss*. In (124b), the PP is attached higher than the AdvP. Both of these trees are acceptable, because the adjunct rule iterates. This means that either version of it can appear in either order. Since we have two structures for this sentence you might wonder if there is any semantic ambiguity in this phrase. The distinction is subtle, but it is there. For (124a), we can identify a set of events of sushi-eating with the boss, and then we identify those events as occurring frequently. The meaning of (124b) is very subtly different, there is a set of frequent events of sushi eating, and we are identifying those as occurring with his boss. This distinction is a little easier to see in NPs:

125)   The red dress with the pink stripes

This can be treed two different ways:

126)

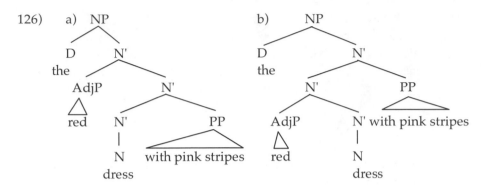

The first tree corresponds to a meaning where we are picking a red member out of the set of dresses with pink stripes. (126b) corresponds to the situation where we are picking a dress with pink stripes out of the set of red dresses. These two trees may pick out the same individuals in the world, but they do so in different contexts (one where we are trying to distinguish among red dresses; and the other where we are distinguishing among pink-striped dresses).

With these additional X-bar theoretic considerations in mind we can now draw a sample tree:

6.2 A Sample Tree

The sentence we'll draw is:

127)   The₁ ugly man from Brazil found books of poems in the₂ puddle.

Our first step, as always, is to identify the parts of speech:

128)   D   Adj   N   P   N   V   N   P N   P D   N
         The₁ ugly man from Brazil found books of poems in the₂ puddle.

Next, and most importantly, we have to identify what modifies or relates to what, and whether that modification is as an adjunct, complement, or specifier. This is perhaps the most difficult and tedious step, but it is also the most important. You will get better at this with practice. You can use the tests we developed above (stacking, coordination, etc.) to determine whether the modifier is a complement, adjunct, or specifier.

129)   [The₁] modifies [man] as a specifier.
         [ugly] modifies [man] as an adjunct.
         [Brazil] modifies [from] as a complement.
         [from Brazil] modifies [man] as an adjunct.
         [Poems] modifies [of] as a complement.

[of Poems] modifies [books] as a complement.
[books of poems] modifies [found] as a complement.
[the₂] modifies [puddle] as a specifier.
[the puddle] modifies [in] as a complement.
[in the puddle] modifies [found] as an adjunct.

Keeping in mind the (revised) principle of modification, and the strict X-bar structure, we next start to build the trees. I suggest you generally start with AdjPs and AdvPs. We have one Adj here. Note that nothing modifies this Adj. As such, it has the minimal structure given above in (120c).

130)

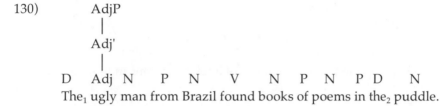

The₁ ugly man from Brazil found books of poems in the₂ puddle.

Next we do NPs and PPs. Again, we'll also start on the right hand side of the sentence. The first NP is *the puddle*, be sure to apply all three of the NP rules here. Don't forget the N' node in the middle. The determiner is the specifier of the NP, so it must be the sister to N' and daughter of NP.

131)

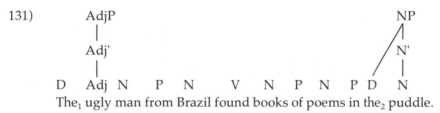

The₁ ugly man from Brazil found books of poems in the₂ puddle.

There are two nouns in this sentence that aren't modified by anything (*Brazil* and *poems*). Let's do these next. Even though they aren't modified by anything they get the full X-bar structure, with NP, N' and N: This is because the rules are *not* optional.

132)

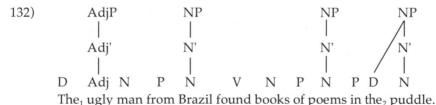

The₁ ugly man from Brazil found books of poems in the₂ puddle.

There are two more nouns in this sentence (*man* and *books*), but if you look carefully at our list of modifications (129), you'll see that they are both modified by PPs. So in order to do them, we have to first build our PPs.

There are three Ps in this sentence (and hence three PPs), each of them takes one of the NPs we've built as a complement. The objects of prepositions are always complements. That means that they are sisters to P, and daughters of P':

133)

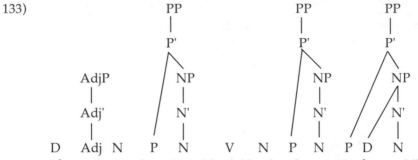

The₁ ugly man from Brazil found books of poems in the₂ puddle.

Now that we've generated our PPs, we'll go back to the two remaining NPs. Let's first observe that the PP *in the puddle* does <u>not</u> modify an N (it modifies the V *found*), so it is <u>not</u> attached at this stage. Now, turn to the N *books*. We start with the complement. *Of poems* is the complement meaning that the PP will be the sister to the N head, and the daughter of N'.

134)

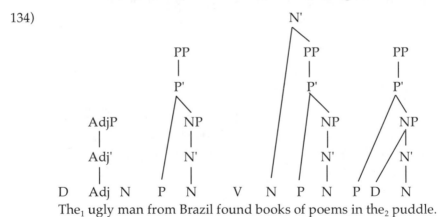

The₁ ugly man from Brazil found books of poems in the₂ puddle.

Nothing else modifies books. When there are no more modifiers we close off the projection with the phrase level:

135)

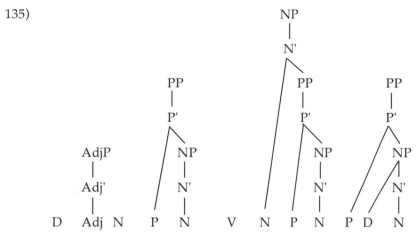

The₁ ugly man from Brazil found books of poems in the₂ puddle.

Finally, we have the NP *the ugly man from Brazil*. There is no complement here, so we project to N' without any branching. Were there a complement in the NP we would attach it first.

136)

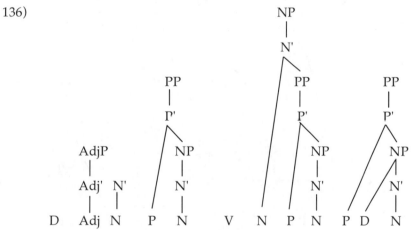

The₁ ugly man from Brazil found books of poems in the₂ puddle.

There are two adjuncts in this NP: *from Brazil* and *ugly*. As per point (v) (and see the trees in (126), this can be treed two different ways. We can attach either adjunct first. I'll arbitrarily pick to attach the PP first here. Because it is an adjunct, it has to be a sister to N' and a daughter of N'. (Note the difference between this NP and *books of poems*.)

137)

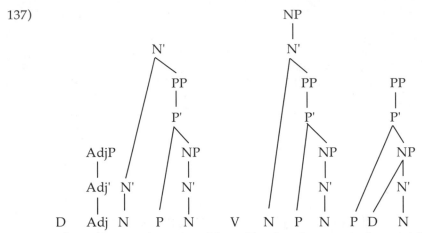

The₁ ugly man from Brazil found books of poems in the₂ puddle.

Next we attach the AdjP. Note that because it is an adjunct, it has to be sister to an N' and daughter of an N'. The N' it is a sister to is already in the tree (having been added in the previous step).

138)

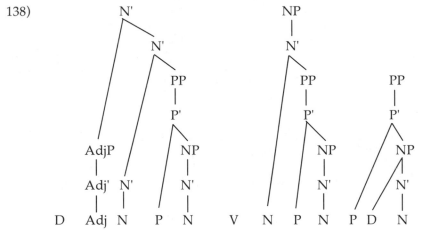

The₁ ugly man from Brazil found books of poems in the₂ puddle.

We're nearly finished with this NP. The determiner is a specifier, which is a daughter of NP and a sister to N'.

139)

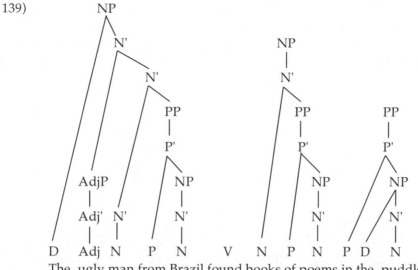

The₁ ugly man from Brazil found books of poems in the₂ puddle.

Now we turn to the VP. The verb *found* has two modifiers. *Books of poems* is a complement, and *in the puddle* is an adjunct. You should always start with the complement, and then follow with the adjuncts, because complements are closer to the head. Remember, complements are sisters to V, and adjuncts are sisters to V'. Notice that the complement NP, which is closer to the head, is attached lower than the adjunct PP, it is the sister to V and daughter of V'.

140)

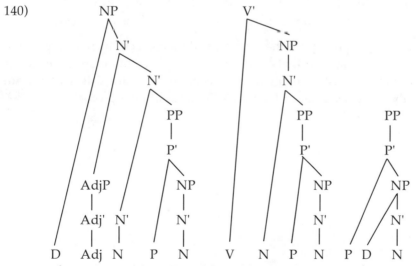

The₁ ugly man from Brazil found books of poems in the₂ puddle.

Now we attach the adjunct PP, it has to be a sister to V' (the one just created by the previous step) and daughter of a V' (which we will add here). Since there are no other modifiers of the V, we will also complete this phrase with the VP:

141)

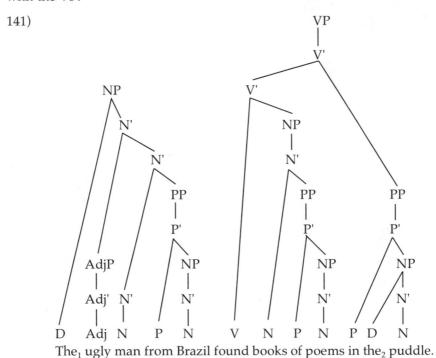

The₁ ugly man from Brazil found books of poems in the₂ puddle.

Last, but not least, we apply the TP rule, and then check the tree against the X-bar rules. Making sure that everything is attached; there are no crossing lines; adjuncts are sisters to a bar level, complements are sisters to a head; and finally every head has at least an X, X', and XP on top of it.

142)

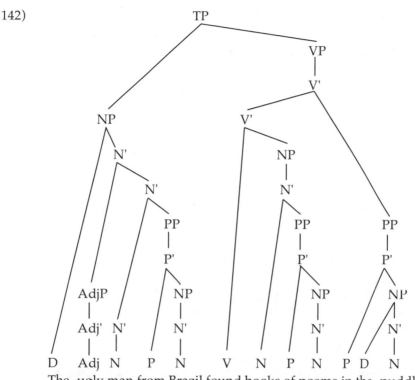

The₁ ugly man from Brazil found books of poems in the₂ puddle.

Each tree will be different, of course, but with practice and patience you will develop the skill quite easily.

You now have enough information to try General Problem Set 7

7. X-BAR THEORY: A SUMMARY

Let's summarize the rather lengthy discussion we've had so far in this chapter. We started off with the observation that there seemed to be more structure to our trees than that given by the basic phrase structure rules we developed in chapter 3. In particular, we introduced the intermediate levels of structure called N', V', Adj', and P'. The evidence for these comes from standard constituency tests like conjunction, and from processes like *one*-replacement, and *do-so*-replacement. We also saw that material on different levels of structure behaved differently. Complements exhibit one set of behaviors and adjuncts a different set. Next we observed that our rules were failing to capture several generalizations about the data. First was the endocentricity generalization: all NPs, have an N head, all AdjPs an Adj head, etc. There is no rule like NP → V Adj. Next, there was the observation that all trees have three levels of structure. They all have specifiers (weak evidence here), adjuncts and complements. In response to this, we proposed the following general X-bar theoretic rules:

143) a) *Specifier rule:*   XP → (YP) X' *or* XP → X' (YP)
      b) *Adjunct rule:*   X' → X' (ZP) *or* X' → (ZP) X'
      c) *Complement rule:*   X' → X (WP) *or* X' → (WP) X

These rules use variables to capture cross-categorial generalizations. In order to limit the power of these rules, and in order to capture differences between languages, we proposed that the options within these rules were parameterized. Speakers of languages select the appropriate option for their language.

　　This is, you'll note, a very simple system. There are, of course, some loose ends, and in the next couple of chapters we'll try to tidy these up. First of all we have the problem of specifiers, we only have one specifier (the determiner). In the next chapter we'll suggest that in fact determiners aren't specifiers at all, instead they are their own heads. Then we'll reserve specifier positions for something else: subjects. We'll also try to integrate our TP and CP rules into the system.

IDEAS, RULES, AND CONSTRAINTS INTRODUCED IN THIS CHAPTER

i)   *Specifier*: Sister to X', daughter of XP.

ii)   *Adjunct*: Sister to X', daughter of X'.

iii)   *Complement*: Sister to X, daughter of X'.

iv)   *Head*: The word that gives its category to the phrase.

v)   *Projection*: The string of elements associated with a head that bear the same category as the head (N, N', N', N', NP etc).

vi)   *Maximal Projection*: The topmost projection in a phrase (XP).

vii)   *Intermediate Projection*: Any projection that is neither the head nor the phrase (i.e. all the X' levels).

viii)   **One-*replacement***: Replace an N' node with *one*.

ix)   **Do-so-*replacement***: Replace a V' with *do so*.

x)   *Specifier Rule*:   XP → (YP) X' or XP →X' (YP)

xi)   ***Adjunct Rule***:   X' → X' (ZP) or X' → (ZP) X'

xii)   ***Complement Rule***:   X' → X (WP) or X' → (WP) X

xiii)   ***Additional Rules***:
         CP → (C) TP
         TP → NP VP
         XP → XP Conj XP
         X' → X' Conj X'
         X → X Conj X

xiv)   ***Parameterization***: The idea that there is a fixed set of possibilities in
         terms of structure (such as the options in the X-bar framework), and
         people acquiring a language choose from among those possibilities.

xv)   ***Principle of Modification*** (revised): If a YP modifies some head X,
         then YP must be a sister to X or a projection of X (i.e., X', XP).

FURTHER READING

Baltin, Mark and Anthony Kroch (1989) *Alternative Conceptions of Phrase Structure*. Chicago: University of Chicago Press.

Borsley, Robert (1996) *Modern Phrase Structure Grammar*. Oxford: Blackwell.

Carnie, Andrew (1995) Head Movement and Non-Verbal Predication. Ph.D. dissertation, MIT.

Chametzky, Robert (1996) *A Theory of Phrase Markers and the Extended Base*. Albany: SUNY Press.

Chomsky, Noam (1970) Remarks on nominalization. In Roderick Jacobs and Peter Rosenbaum (eds.), *Readings in English Transformational Grammar*. Waltham: Ginn. pp. 184–221.

Jackendoff, Ray (1977) *X-bar Syntax: A Theory of Phrase Structure*. Cambridge: MIT Press.

Kayne, Richard (1994) *The Antisymmetry of Syntax*. Cambridge: MIT Press.

Lightfoot, David (1991) *How to Set Parameters: Evidence from Language Change*. Cambridge: MIT Press.

Speas, Margaret (1990) *Phrase Structure in Natural Language*. Dordrecht: Kluwer Academic Publishers.

Stowell, Tim (1981) Origins of Phrase Structure. Ph.D. dissertation, MIT.

Travis, Lisa de Mena (1984) Parameters and Effects of Word Order Derivation. Ph.D. dissertation, MIT.

GENERAL PROBLEM SETS

1. COMPLEMENTS VS. ADJUNCTS in NPs

[Application of Skills; Basic]

Using the tests you have been given (reordering, adjacency, conjunction of likes, *one*-replacement) determine whether the PPs in the following NPs are complements or adjuncts; give the examples that you used in constructing your tests. Some of the NPs have multiple PPs, be sure to answer the question for every PP in the NP.

a)   A container [of flour]
b)   A container [with a glass lid]
c)   The collection [of figurines] [in the window]
d)   The statue [of Napoleon] [on the corner]
e)   Every window [in the building] [with a broken pane]

2. ADJECTIVES

[Critical Thinking; Intermediate]

Are adjectives complements or adjuncts to the N? Use the tests you have been given to determine if adjectives are complements or adjuncts. Do NOT use the reordering test – it will not work because adjectives in English are strictly ordered by other principles. Also confine yourself to the adjectives listed below. (Other adjectives, such as *leather* in *leather shoes* or *Chemistry* in *Chemistry Professor*, behave differently. However, you can use these adjectives as interveners if you need to check adjacency to the head.)

> *hot, big, red, tiny, ugly*

3. GERMAN NOUN PHRASES

[Data Analysis; Intermediate/Advanced]

Consider sentence (a) from German:[9]

a)   Die schlanke Frau aus Frankreich isst   Kuchen mit Sahne.
　　the thin   woman from France   eats cake with cream
　　"The thin woman from France eats cake with cream."

The following sentences are grammatical if they refer to the same woman described in (a):

---

[9] Thanks to Simin Karimi for providing the data for this question, and to Susi Wurmbrand for clarifying the facts.

b)   Die Schlanke aus Frankreich isst Kuchen mit Sahne.
      "The thin one from France eats cake with cream."

c)   Die aus Frankreich isst Kuchen mit Sahne.
      "The one from France eats cake with cream."

d)   Die Schlanke isst Kuchen mit Sahne.
      "The thin one eats cake with cream."

e)   Die isst Kuchen mit Sahne.
      "She eats cake with cream."

Now consider sentences (f–i):

f)   Die junge Koenigin von England liebte die Prinzessin.
      The young queen   of England loved the princess
      "The young queen of England loved the princess."

g)   Die Junge liebte die Prinzessin.
      "The young one loved the princess."

h)   Die liebte die Prinzessin.
      "She loved the princess."

i)   *Die von England liebte die Prinzessin.
      "*The one of England loved the princess."

(*Native speakers of German should assume the judgments given even if they don't agree with them.*)

Assume the following things:

i)   *Der/Die* are always determiners, they are never nouns or pronouns.

ii)   *Schlanke* and *junge* are always adjectives, even in sentences (d) and
      (g) – **assume they never become nouns**. (Ignore the rules of German
      capitalization.)

The questions:

1)   Describe and explain the process seen in (a–e) and (f–i), be sure
      to make explicit reference to X-bar theory. What English phenomenon
      (discussed in this chapter) is this similar to? Make sure you analyze
      the _German_ sentences not the English translations.

2)   Draw the trees for sentences (a) and (f). Sentence (a) requires _two_
      different trees (important hint: the relevant ambiguity in (a) is inside
      the subject NP, _not_ in the position of the PP *mit sahne*).

3) Explain the ungrammaticality of (i) in terms of X-bar theory. In particular explain the difference between it and sentence (c). Draw trees to explicate your answer.

4. COMPLEMENTS AND ADJUNCTS IN VPS
[Application of Skills; Basic]
Using the tests you have been given (reordering, adjacency, conjunction of likes, *do-so*-replacement) determine whether the marked NPs, PPs and AdvPs in the following VPs are complements or adjuncts; give the examples that you used in constructing your tests. Some of the VPs have multiple PPs and AdvPs, be sure to answer the question for every PP, NP, and AdvP in the VP.

a) Erin [VP [AdvP never] keeps [NP her pencils] [PP in the correct drawer]].
b) Dan [VP walked [PP to New Mexico] [PP in the rain] [AdvP last year]].

5. JAPANESE
[Data Analysis; Basic]
Consider the following data from Japanese:

a) Masa-ga kita.   "Masa came."
b) Toru-ga shinda.   "Toru died."
c) Kumiko-ga yonda.   "Kumiko read."
d) Kumiko-ga hon-o yonda.   "Kumiko read the book."
e) Toru-ga Kumiko-o mita.   "Toru saw Kumiko."
f) Kumiko-ga Toru-o mita.   "Kumiko saw Toru."
g) Hon-ga akai desu.   "The book is red."
h) Toru-ga sensei desu.   "Toru is a teacher."
i) Masa-ga ookii desu.   "Masa is big."
j) Sono hon-ga ookii desu.   "That book is big."
k) Toru-ga sono akai hon-o mita.   "Toru saw that red book."

1) What is the function of the suffixes *-o* and *-ga*?
2) What is the word order of Japanese?
3) Does the complement precede or follow the head in Japanese?
4) Do adjuncts precede or follow the head in Japanese?
5) Do specifiers precede or follow the X' node in Japanese?
6) Draw the tree for sentence (k) using X-bar theory. Keep in mind your answers to questions (1–5).

6. PARAMETERS

[Data Analysis; Basic to Intermediate]

Go back to the foreign language problems from chapters 3 and 4, (Hiaki, Irish, Bambara, Hixkaryana, Swedish, Dutch, Tzotzil) and see if you can determine the parameter settings for these languages. You may not be able to determine all the settings for each language. (Suggestion: put your answer in a table like the one below. English is done for you as an example.) Assume the following: Determiners are typical examples of specifiers, Adjectives and many PPs (although not all) are adjuncts. "of" PPs and direct objects are complements. Be sure to check the complement/adjunct relation in all categories (N, Adj, Adv, V, P etc.) if you can.

	Specifier	Adjunct	Complement
English	(YP) X'	Both	X (ZP)

7. TREES

[Application of Skills; Basic to Advanced]

Draw the X-bar theoretic trees for the following sentences. Treat possessive NPs like *Héloïse's* as specifiers. Several of the sentences are ambiguous; draw only one tree, but indicate using a paraphrase (or paraphrases) which meaning you intend by your tree.

a) Abelard wrote a volume of poems in Latin for Héloïse.
b) Armadillos from New York often destroy old pillowcases with their snouts. (NB: assume "their" is a determiner)
c) People with boxes of old clothes lined up behind the door of the building with the leaky roof.
d) That automobile factories abound in Michigan worries me greatly.
e) No-one understands that phrase structure rules explain the little understood phenomenon of the infinite length of sentences.
f) My favorite language is a language with simple morphology and complicated syntax.
g) Ivan got a noogie on Wednesday from the disgruntled students of phonology from Michigan.
h) The collection of syntax articles with the red cover bores students of syntax in Tucson
i) The red volume of obscene verse from Italy shocked the puritan soul of the minister with the beard quite thoroughly yesterday.
j) The biggest man in the room said that John danced an Irish jig from County Kerry to County Tipperary on Thursday.

k) A burlap sack of potatoes with mealy skins fell on the professor of linguistics with the terrible taste in T-shirts from the twelfth story of the Douglass Building last Friday.

l) The bright green filing cabinet was filled to the brim with the most boring articles from a prestigious journal of linguistics with a moderately large readership

CHALLENGE PROBLEM SETS

CHALLENGE PROBLEM SET 1: INTERMEDIATE STRUCTURE
[Application of Knowledge, Critical Thinking; Advanced-Challenge]
The following verb phrase is ambiguous in its structure

Adam [VP frequently buys paintings from Natasha].

The ambiguity has to do with where [AdvP frequently] and [PP from Natasha] are attached in the string of V' categories. Note that the V' rule can be either V' → V' (PP) or V' →V' (AdvP) and these rules can apply in either order. Using the *do-so/did-so/did-too* replacement test, provide some sentences that show that there is an ambiguity in structure here.

CHALLENGE PROBLEM SET 2: COMPLEMENT ADJPS?
[Data Analysis and Critical Thinking; Challenge]
You should do general problem set 2 above before attempting this problem.

Part 1: Consider the following adjectives:

leather (as in *leather shoe*), *Chemistry* (as in *Chemistry student*)

Using your tests for complements and adjuncthood in NPs (adjacency, *one*-replacement, coordination of likes, only one complement – the test of reordering doesn't work since adjectives in English are ordered by other principles), decide whether these adjectives are functioning more like complements or adjuncts. Contrast them explicitly to adverbs such as *red* and *big*. Provide the relevant examples to support your claim.

Part 2: Two analyses of these adjectives have been proposed. One is that they are complements (a); the other, more common, analysis is that these aren't adjectives at all, but are noun-noun compounds (notice that both *leather* and *Chemistry* can function as nouns in their own right) as in (b).

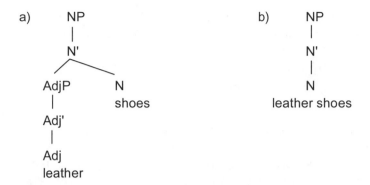

Which of these proposals is right? Try to come up with some arguments to distinguish between them. The following data may be helpful to you. But you should look for arguments beyond this data (i.e., come up with data of your own).

c) plastic and leather shoes
d) ?very leather shoes
e) *very Chemistry professor

CHALLENGE PROBLEM SET 3: AMBIGUOUS ADJPS?
[Data Analysis and Critical Thinking; Challenge]
Before trying this problem set you should try Challenge Problem Set 2 above.

Part 1: No matter what your answer to challenge problem set 2 was above, assume for the moment that some AdjPs can function as adjuncts and others can function as complements. This requires that we modify our parameter settings for English. Propose a revised set of parameters for English to allow for the possibility that *Chemistry* in *Chemistry professor* is a complement. Note: your proposal must explain why in English object NP complements cannot appear before verbs but AdjP complements can appear before nouns (i.e., your proposal must account for why complement-head order is allowed in NPs but not in VPs).

Part 2: Consider the following ambiguous NP:

a) the German teacher

It can mean either a teacher (say of math) who is German, or it can mean someone (of any nationality) who teaches the German language. Using the complement/adjunct distinction and the following data, explain this ambiguity in meaning. Pay attention to the meaning of *German* (whether it refers to the nationality or the subject) in each of the following sentences. Draw trees to explain your answer.

b)   the French German teacher
c)   the math and German teacher
d)   … not the American teacher but the German one

CHALLENGE PROBLEM SET 4: COMPLEMENTS TO ADJ HEADS[10]

[Critical Thinking and Application of Skills; Challenge]

Part 1: Consider the word *sick*. This word seems to have two or more meanings. One meaning corresponds to the meaning "ill," as in *I feel sick*. The other meaning is something like "I've had enough," as in the expression *I am sick of it.* This second meaning seems to take a complement PP. The evidence for this is twofold: (1) To get this meaning of *sick* the complement must be present in the sentence. Otherwise we understand the physical meaning of *sick*. (2) The preposition that we find, *of*, is the most common preposition used with complement PP of adjectives and nouns. Judging from their meanings and other properties, do any of the adjectives below regularly occur with complements?

delightful, familiar, sensitive, adjacent, full

Part 2: Draw the trees for the following two sentences according to the principles of X-bar Theory. Think about the reasons you would use for considering a PP either a complement or an adjunct of an adjective. This is what you need to think about to get each PP attached in the right place.

a)   The director is as aware of the problems as the committee members.
b)   Everyone was curious about it to the *n*th degree.

---

[10] Thanks to Leslie Saxon for contributing this problem set.

chapter 7

Extending X-bar
Theory to Functional
Categories

0. INTRODUCTION

In the last chapter, we looked at a refinement of our phrase structure rules that not only accounted for intermediate structure, but also generalized patterns across categories. This refinement is X-bar theory:

1) a) *Specifier rule:*   XP → (YP) X' *or* XP → X' (YP)
   b) *Adjunct rule:*   X' → X' (ZP) *or* X' → (ZP) X'
   c) *Complement rule:*   X' → X (WP) *or* X' → (WP) X

These rules not only generate most of the trees we need for the sentences of the world's languages, they also capture the additional properties of hierarchical structure found within the major constituents. This said, you may have noticed that this system is far from perfect. First, there is the status of specifiers. In particular, the specifier rule we proposed above requires that the specifier be a phrase (XP) level category. However, the only instances of specifiers we've looked at are determiners, which appear *not* to be phrasal. In this chapter, we will look at determiners, and specifiers, and propose a new category that fits X-bar theory: a ***determiner phrase*** (DP). We will see that determiners are not specifiers. Instead, we'll claim that the specifier position is used to mark a particular grammatical function: that of subjects. You'll see that specifiers (of all categories) are where subjects go.

Another troubling aspect of the X-bar theory is the exceptional CP and TP rules that we have yet to incorporate into the system:

2)   CP → (C) TP
     TP → NP (T) VP

These rules do not fit X-bar theory. In the X-bar rules in (1), you'll note that the only obligatory element is the head. In the sentence rules in (2), the opposite is true: the only optional element is the head itself. In this chapter, we will look at how we can modify these so that they fit into the more general pattern.

1. DETERMINER PHRASES (DPS)

In the last chapter, for lack of a better place to put them, we put determiners, like *the, a, that, this, those, these* in the specifiers of NPs. This however, violates one of the basic principles underlying X-bar theory: All non-head material must be phrasal. Notice that this principle is a theoretical rather than an empirical requirement (i.e., it is motivated by the elegance of the theory and not by any data), but it is a nice idea from a mathematical point of view, and it would be good if we could show that it has some empirical basis.

   One thing to note about determiners is that they are heads. There can only be one of them in an NP (this isn't true cross-linguistically, but for now let us limit ourselves to English):

3)   *the that book

In other words, they don't seem to be phrasal.[1] If our requirement says that the only thing that isn't a phrase in an NP is the N itself, then we have a problem. One solution, perhaps not obvious, to this is to claim that the determiner is not actually inside the NP. Instead, it heads its own phrasal projection. This was first proposed by Abney (1987):

---

[1] In the last chapter we used this exact same piece of evidence to distinguish specifiers from adjuncts. As an exercise, you could try to construct an argument that distinguishes these two accounts of the same data.

4)   *Old view*   *DP hypothesis*

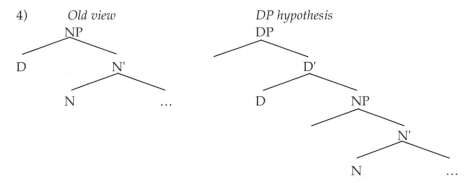

Determiners, in this view, are not part of the NP. Instead the NP is the complement to the determiner head. This solution solves the theoretical problem of the non-phrasality of the D, but we still need empirical evidence in its favor.

One piece of evidence comes from the behavior of genitive (possessive) NPs. There are two kinds of possessive NPs. The first is of less interest to us. This one is often called the *free genitive* or **of-genitive**:

5) a) the coat of the panther
    b) the roof of the building
    c) the hat of the man standing over there

The free genitive uses the preposition *of* to mark the possessive relation between the two NPs. More important in terms of evidence for DP is the behavior of the other kind of possessive: the **construct** or **'s-genitive**.

6) a) the panther's coat
    b) the building's roof
    c) the man standing over there's hat

There are a couple of important things to note about this construction. Notice first that the *'s* marker appears after the *entire* possessor NP. For example, it attaches to the whole phrase *the man standing over there* not just to the head *man*:

7) a) [the man standing over there]'s hat
    b) *the man's standing over there hat

This means that *'s* is not a suffix. Instead it seems to be a small word indicating possession. Next, note that it is in complementary distribution with (i.e., cannot co-occur with) determiners:

8) a) *the building's the roof (cf. the roof of the building)
    b) *the panther's the coat (cf. the coat of the panther)

   c)   *the man standing over there's the hat (cf. the hat of the man
        standing over there)

Unlike the *of*-genitive, the *'s*-genitive does not allow both the nouns to have
a determiner. In other words, *'s* and determiners are in complementary
distribution. As in other domains of linguistics, when two items are in
complementary distribution, they are instances of the same thing. (Take
for example, phonology, where when two phones are found in different
environments – in complementary distribution – then they are allophones
of the same phoneme.) Determiners like *the* and *'s* are different tokens of
the same type. Assuming that *'s* is a determiner, and assuming the DP
hypothesis holds true, we can now account for the positioning of the *'s*
relative to the possessor. The *'s* occupies the head D position, and
the possessor appears in its specifier:

9)

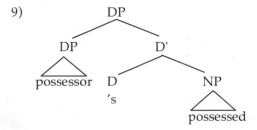

A tree for (8c) shows this:

10)

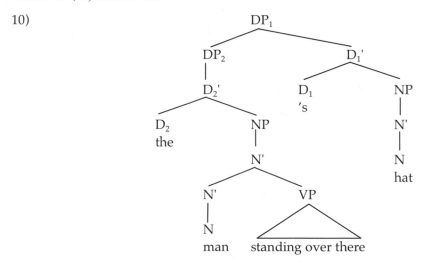

The possessor $[_{DP2}$ *the man standing over there]* sits in the specifier of DP_1, which is headed by *'s*. So *'s* follows the whole thing.[2] Notice that with our old theory, where determiners were specifiers of NP, there is no way at all to generate *'s* as a determiner and to also have the possessor NP preceding it.

11)

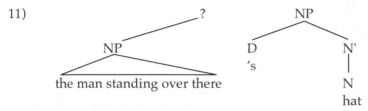

The X-bar rules don't provide any place to attach this pre-determiner NP, if determiners are specifiers.

Notice that in the tree in (10) there is a specifier of DP_1 (filled by DP_2). Note further that this specifier is phrasal (projects to an XP). Which means that it meets with our requirement that all non-head material be phrasal.

You might ask if by moving determiners out of the specifier we have completely destroyed the empirical justification for the specifier rule. Actually, we haven't. Again if you look closely at the tree in (10) we still have a specifier, it just isn't D_1, *instead* it is the DP possessor (DP_2). Further, as we will see below, there are other related uses for the specifier positions. In particular, we will come to associate specifiers with subjects of various kinds of constituents.

You now have enough information to try Challenge Problem Sets 1 & 2

---

2. A DESCRIPTIVE TANGENT INTO CLAUSE TYPES

A *clause* is essentially a *subject* (usually a DP that has the property indicated by the predicate; this is what the clause is about) and a *predicate phrase* (a group of words that assign a property to the subject). The most obvious kind of clause is the simple sentence. In the following examples, the subject is indicated in italics and the predicate phrase is in bold:

12) a)   *The boy* **ran**.
    b)   *Howard* is a **linguistics student**.

---

[2] We might extend this analysis to possessive pronouns. Take the pronoun *his* for example, we could analyze this as *he* occupying the specifier of *'s*, then there is a morphological operation that turns *he+'s* into *his*. (This of course is less plausible with pronouns like *her* or *your*; unless the morphological rule is extremely abstract.)

As we'll see below, there are many other kinds of clauses. But we can use this as a working definition.

A clause that stands on its own is called a *root, matrix,* or *main clause.* Sometimes, however, we can find examples of clauses within clauses. Examples of this are seen below:

13) a)   [Peter said [that Danny danced]].
    b)   [Bill wants [Susan to leave]].

In each of these sentences there are two clauses. In sentence (13a), there is the clause *(that) Danny danced* which is inside the root clause *Peter said that Danny danced*. In (13b), we have the clause *Susan to leave* which has the subject *Susan*, and the predicate phrase *(to) leave*. This is contained within the main clause *Bill wants Susan to leave*.

Both of these clauses within clauses are called *embedded clauses*. Another name for embedded clause is *subordinate clause*. The clause containing the embedded clause is still called the *main* or *root clause*.

> ### Embedded Clauses are Part of Main Clauses
> A very common error among new syntacticians is to forget that embedded clauses are contained *within* main clauses. That is, when faced with identifying what is the main clause in a sentence like
>
> i)   Peter thinks that Cathy loves him.
>
> most students will properly identify the embedded clause, as *(that) Cathy loves him*, but will claim that the main clause is only *Peter thinks*. This is completely incorrect. *Peter thinks* is not a constituent. The main clause is <u>everything</u> under the root TP node. So the main clause is *Peter thinks that Cathy loves him*. Be very careful about this.

Using the TP and CP rules we developed in chapter 3, the structure of a root clause containing an embedded clause is given below (I've obscured the irrelevant details with triangles):

14)

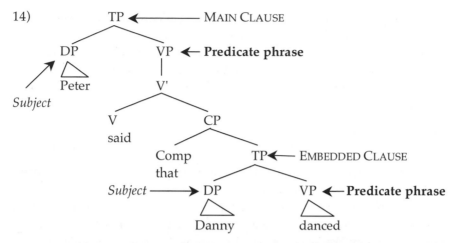

In addition to the distinction between main and embedded clauses, we can also distinguish among specifier, complement, and adjunct clauses. Here are some examples of **complement clauses**:

15) a)   Heidi said [that Art loves peanut butter].
    b)   Colin asked [if they could get a mortgage].

These complement clauses (CPs) are sisters to the verb, and thus complements. Clauses can also appear in adjunct positions. Relative clauses are one example of **adjunct clauses**:

16) [The man [I saw get into the cab]] robbed the bank.

The relative clause in (16) *[I saw get into the cab]* modifies the head *man*. **Specifier clauses** are ones that serve as the subject of a sentence (why these are specifiers will be made clear below):

17) a)   [[People selling their stocks] caused the crash of 1929].
    b)   [[For Mary to love that boor] is a travesty].

To summarize, we have two basic kinds of clauses, main and embedded. Embedded clauses are contained within main clauses. Further, there are three types of embedded clauses: specifier clauses, complement clauses and adjunct clauses. This is summarized in the following table:

18)

Main clauses	Embedded clauses		
	specifier clauses	complement clauses	adjunct clauses

There is another way of dividing up the clause-type pie. We class clauses into two groups depending upon whether they are tensed or not.[3] Clauses with predicates that are tensed are sometimes called (obviously) **tensed clauses**, but you may more frequently find them called **finite clauses**. Clauses without a tensed verb are called **tenseless** or **non-finite clauses** (sometimes also **infinitival clauses**).[4]

19) a)   I said [that Mary signed my yearbook].   *tensed or finite*
    b)   I want [Mary to sign my yearbook].   *tenseless or non-finite*

There are a number of tests for distinguishing finite from non-finite clauses. These tests are taken from Radford (1988). The embedded clause in sentence (20a) is tensed, the one in (20b) is untensed. I have deliberately selected a verb that is ambiguous between tensed and untensed in terms of its morphology (suffixes) here as an illustration:

20) a)   I know [you eat asparagus].   *finite*
    b)   I've never seen [you eat asparagus].   *non-finite*

One way to tell if a clause is finite or not is to look for agreement and tense morphology on the verb. These include the *-s* ending associated with third person nouns (*he eats*) and the past tense suffixes like *-ed*. The above examples don't show any such suffixes. However, if we change the tense to the past a difference emerges:

21) a)   I know you ate asparagus.   *finite*
    b)   *I've never seen you ate asparagus.   *non-finite*

Finite clauses allow past tense morphology (the *ate* form of the verb *eat*), non-finite clauses don't. The same effect is seen if you change the person of the subject in the embedded clause. Third person subjects trigger the *-s* ending. This is allowed only in finite clauses.

---

[3] There is a third kind of clause that we won't discuss here, called "small clauses." Small clauses don't have verbal predicates (that is, a DP, PP, or AP serves as the predicate. These generally don't get tense marking. An example is the embedded string in:

i)   [Maurice considers [Jason a fine upstanding gentleman]].

Small clauses are an important part of syntactic theory, but they are notoriously difficult to spot until you have some practice. For the purposes of this text we'll just ignore small clauses, but if you pursue syntax at a higher level you'll have to learn how to identify them.

[4] In many languages, the form of a verb found in a non-finite clause is called the *infinitive*. In English, infinitives are often marked with the auxiliary *to*, as in *to sign*.

22) a)   I know he eat̲s asparagus.   *finite*
    b)   *I've never seen him eat̲s asparagus.   *non-finite*

The case on the subject of the noun is often a giveaway for determining whether or not a clause is finite. Case refers to the notions **nominative** and **accusative** introduced in chapter 1, repeated here:

23)

	Nominative		Accusative		Anaphoric	
	Singular	Plural	Singular	Plural	Singular	Plural
1	I	we	me	us	myself	ourselves
2	you	you	you	you	yourself	yourselves
3 masc	he		him		himself	
3 fem	she	they	her	them	herself	themselves
3 neut	it		it		itself	

If the clause is finite, then a subject pronoun will take the nominative case form:

24) I know *he* eats asparagus.   *finite*

If the clause is non-finite then the subject will take the accusative form:

25) I've never seen *him* eat asparagus.   *non-finite*

One test that works most of the time, but is not as reliable as the others, is to see if the subject is obligatory. If the subject is obligatory, then the clause is finite. If the subject is optional, or is not allowed at all, then it is non-finite. (Note: this test only works for English; in many languages, such as Spanish, subjects of finite clauses are optional.)

26) a)   I think that he eats asparagus.   *finite*
         (cf. *I think that eats asparagus.)
    b)   I want (him) to eat asparagus.   *non-finite*
         (cf. I want to eat asparagus.)

Another way to tell if a clause is finite or not is by looking at the complementizer. The complementizer *for* is only found with non-finite clauses. By contrast *that* and *if* are only found with tensed clauses:

27) a)   I wonder if he eats asparagus.   *finite*
    b)   I think that he eats asparagus.   *finite*
    c)   [For him to eat asparagus] is a travesty.   *non-finite*
    d)   I asked for him to eat the asparagus.   *non-finite*

As a final test, we can note that finite and non-finite clauses take different kinds of T elements. The T in tensed clauses can contain auxiliaries and modals like *will, can, must, may, should, shall, is, have*. By contrast the only auxiliary allowed in non-finite clauses is *to*.[5]

28) a)   I think [he *will* eat asparagus].
    b)   I want him *to* eat asparagus. (cf. *I want him will eat asparagus.)

This last property gets at the heart of the distinction between finite and non-finite clauses. In structural terms the difference between a finite and a non-finite clause lies in terms of what kind of T the clause has. If a clause is finite it bears some tense feature (like [±past] or [±future]). If it is non-finite, it doesn't have any of these features. The question of how this works for clauses where there is no auxiliary, we'll leave as a bit of a mystery for now, but will return to later in this chapter.

Let's summarize the discussion we've had thus far. We've been looking at a number of terms for describing various kinds of clauses. We defined clauses as a subject and a predicate phrase. We distinguished root or main clauses from embedded clauses. Embedded clauses come in three types: specifier clauses, complement clauses and adjunct clauses. The other dimension along which we can describe clauses is the finite/non-finite distinction.

With this terminology under our belts, we'll now turn to the structure of clauses, and see if we can make them fit better into X-bar theory.

You now have enough information to try General Problem Sets 1, 2 & 3

3. COMPLEMENTIZER PHRASES (CPs)

We've observed that the TP rule and the CP rule stand out, since they don't fit X-bar theory. In X-bar theory, the head is always obligatory. This is not true of these two rules:

29) a)   CP → (C) TP
    b)   TP → DP (T) VP

In fact, it is a fairly trivial matter to change these rules into X-bar theoretic format. Let us deal with the CP rule first. If we take X-bar theory to extend to CPs, we can assimilate the rule in (29a) to get a tree like that in (30):

---

[5] English has two words *to*. One is a preposition, the other is non-finite T.

30)

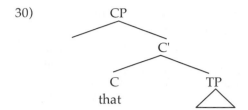

This CP structure has C as the head, a TP complement and an empty specifier position (this empty specifier position will become very important later for us when we do *wh*-movement in chapter 11).

We might ask how pervasive this rule is in our mental grammars. That is, do all clauses have CPs, or do only embedded clauses have CPs? On the surface, the answer to this question seems obvious: Only embedded clauses have CPs, since only embedded clauses appear to allow complementizers:

31) a)   John thinks that asparagus is yummy.
    b)   *That asparagus is yummy. (cf. Asparagus is yummy.)

However, there is evidence that all clauses, even root clauses like (31), require some kind of complementizer.

32) Asparagus grows in California.

In particular, we'll claim that some sentences have null complementizers. Don't assume that I'm crazy. No matter how strange this proposal sounds, there is actually some good evidence that this is correct. The tree in (33) shows one of these null complementizers.

33)

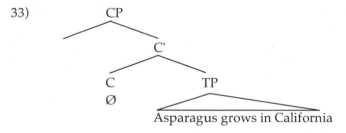

The evidence for this claim comes from cross-linguistic comparison of questions among languages. In particular, we'll focus on **yes/no questions** (see chapter 9 for more discussion on these). These are questions that can be answered with either *yes*, *no* or *maybe*. Examples of yes/no questions in English are given below:

34) a)   Did John leave?
    b)   Have you seen Louis?

In English, to form a yes/no question you either insert some form of the verb *do* (*do, does, did*) before the subject, or you invert the subject and the auxiliary (*You have seen Louis.* → *Have you seen Louis?*). This operation is called **subject-aux inversion** (more on this in chapter 9). In many other languages, however, yes/no questions are formed with a complementizer particle that precedes the verb. Take for example, Irish, which indicates yes/no questions with a special particle *Ar* (or its allomorph *An*):

35) Ar thit Seán?
     Q fall John
     "Did John fall?"

Languages like English that use subject-aux inversion don't have special complementizer question particles. The opposite also holds true. If a language has complementizer question particles, then it won't have subject-aux inversion. The phenomena are in complementary distribution. It seems reasonable to claim then, that question complementizers and subject-aux inversion are part of the same basic phenomenon. In order to make this concrete, let's make the following proposal: There is a question complementizer particle in English, just like there is in Irish. The difference is that in English this complementizer particle is null (has no phonological content). We will represent this **null complementizer** with the symbol $\emptyset_{[+Q]}$. It has no phonological content, but it must be realized or pronounced someway. The way English satisfies this requirement is by moving T into the C head:

36)

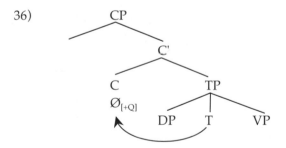

This results in the correct order, where the auxiliary (in T) now appears before the subject. By contrast, languages like Irish don't utilize this mechanism. Instead they have a particle that fills their [+Q] complementizer (like *Ar/An* in Irish).

English does, in fact, have an overt [+Q] complementizer, but it is only found in embedded questions. This complementizer is *if*. Unsurprisingly, subject-aux inversion is completely disallowed when *if* is present:

37) a) Fabio asked if Claus had run a marathon.

b) *Fabio asked if had Claus run a marathon.
c) *Fabio asked had if Claus run a marathon.
d) ?Fabio asked had Claus run a marathon.

If occupies the [+Q] complementizer, so no subject-aux inversion is required (or allowed).

Given the existence of overt root complementizers in other languages and the evidence that subject-aux inversion patterns like these overt root complementizers, we can conclude that, for questions at least, there are complementizers (and CPs) present, even in main clauses.

Of course, we haven't yet shown that non-question sentences have a root complementizer. For this, we need to add an extra step in the argument. You can only conjoin identical categories. If sentences showing subject-aux inversion use a null complementizer and if you can conjoin that question with a non-question (such as a statement), then that statement must also include a (null) complementizer and CP. It is indeed possible to conjoin a statement with a question:

38) [You can lead a horse to water] but [will it drink]?

Since the second clause here shows subject-aux inversion, we know there is a Ø[+Q] question complementizer present. By extension, we know that the clause it is conjoined with must *also* have a complementizer – this time, a non-question Ø[–Q]. A CP can only be conjoined with another CP.

39)

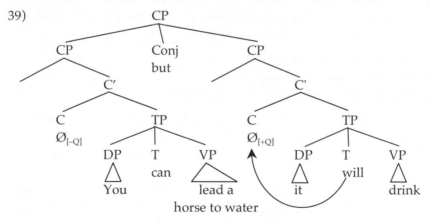

This is an argument for null complementizers attached to root clauses, even in simple statements. From this point forward, we will assume that there is a CP on top of every clause. For brevity's sake, I may occasionally leave this CP off my trees, but the underlying assumption is that it is always there. You should always draw it in when you are drawing your trees.

4. TENSE PHRASES (TPS)

The other rule that doesn't fit the X-bar pattern is our S rule:

40) TP → DP (T) VP

Assimilating this rule to X-bar theory results in a structure like the following:

41)

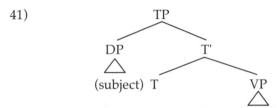

In this tree, S is replaced by TP; the subject DP sits in the specifier of TP, and the VP is the complement. (This is our first clear instance where the notion of specifier corresponds to the notion of subject. We will consider some other cases below.) Again the problem here is that the element that we have designated as the head of the phrase (T) is apparently optional. In X-bar theory, heads are the only obligatory element.

In chapter 2, we equated T with auxiliary verbs. But we might ask what happens in clauses where there is no auxiliary: Is there a TP? Is there a T? Can we make the same claim we did for CPs that the C is obligatory? In order to answer this question, let's make the following observation: Tense inflection on a verb is in complementary distribution with auxiliaries (you never get both of them at the same time):

42) a)   The roadrunner walks funny.
    b)   The roadrunner is walking funny.
    c)   *The roadrunner is walks/walkings funny.

Recall that when two elements are in complementary distribution then they are instances of the same category. This means that T is both auxiliaries and inflectional endings on verbs. Similar evidence comes from coordination. Recall that you can only coordinate two items that are of the same category and bar level. In the following sentence, we are conjoining a T' that has an auxiliary with a T' that has a tensed verb. The tense inflection and auxiliary are italicized.

43) [$_{TP}$ I [$_T$[$_T$ kiss*ed* the toad] and [$_T$ *must* go wash my mouth now]]].

This evidence suggests that the two T's are identical in some deep sense: that is they both involve a T node: one an auxiliary, the other a tense inflectional ending.

If you think about the basic order of the elements we seem to have argued ourselves into a corner. Auxiliaries appear on the left of verbs, and inflectional suffixes (like -*ed*, and -*s*) appear on the right:

44) a)   He *will* go.
    b)   He   go*es*.

There are other differences between auxiliaries and inflectional suffixes. For example, auxiliaries, but not suffixes undergo subject-aux inversion. If we are to claim that inflectional suffixes and auxiliaries are both instances of T we have to account for these differences.

One possibility is to claim that both inflectional suffixes and auxiliaries are indeed generated under T. They differ, however, in terms of whether they can stand alone or not. Auxiliaries are independent words and can stand alone. By contrast, suffixes like -*s* and -*ed* have to be attached to a verb. Much like the case of moving T to C in order to pronounce $\emptyset_{[+Q]}$, we might hypothesize that endings like -*s* and -*ed* can't be pronounced in isolation, so they move to attach to the verb. In particular they seem to lower onto the verb: The following tree shows how this would work for the simple sentence *He walked*. This sentence starts out as *[he -ed walk]* then the -*ed* ending lowers to attach to the end of the verb:

45)

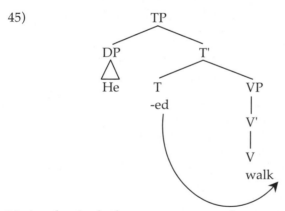

Notice that both the movements we have proposed (***T-affix lowering***, and T → C) have morphophonological motivations. Auxiliaries move to $\emptyset_{[+Q]}$ to pronounce it, inflectional endings lower to V since they are verbal suffixes.

There is much more to the study of T and C and movement of these elements. (For example, the issue of what happens when you have both a $\emptyset_{[+Q]}$ and an inflectional suffix that need to be pronounced leaps to mind.) We will return to these issues in chapter 9.

You can now try General Problem Sets 4 & 5 and Challenge Problem Set 3

5. CP, TP, DP Tree

Here is the tree drawn in section 6.2 of chapter 6, but with CP, TP, and DP:

46)

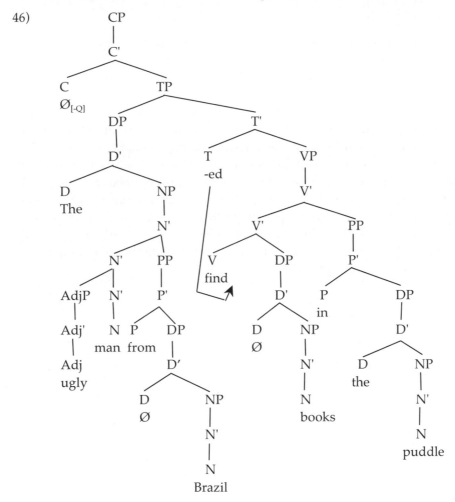

This tree has the subject DP in the specifier of TP. The past tense ending is in T, and lowers to the verb (we of course have to assume that there is some morphological readjustment process that turns *finded* into *found*). You will also notice that we have a null $\emptyset_{[-Q]}$ complementizer. In addition you'll note that all NPs are complements to DPs. In a move parallel to having null Cs, I have drawn in null Ø D heads as well, although this is a matter of some controversy.

IDEAS, RULES, AND CONSTRAINTS INTRODUCED IN THIS CHAPTER

i)   *Determiner Phrase (DP)*: D is not in the specifier of NP. D heads its own phrase: [$_{DP}$ [$_{D'}$ D NP]].

ii)   *Complementizer Phrase (CP)*: C is the head of CP and is obligatory in all clauses, although sometimes phonologically null:
[$_{CP}$ [$_{C'}$ C TP]].

iii)   *Tense Phrase (TP)*: T is the head of TP and is obligatory in all clauses, sometimes it involves lowering of the affix to the V. The subject DP occupies the specifier position: [$_{TP}$ DP$_{subject}$ [$_{T'}$ T VP]].

iv)   *Free Genitive/**of**-Genitive*: Possessed of the possessor.

v)   *Construct Genitive/**'s**-Genitive*: Possessor 's possessed.

vi)   *Subject*: A DP which has the property indicated by the predicate phrase. What the sentence is about. In most sentences, this surfaces in the specifier of TP.

vii)   *Predicate Phrase*: A group of words that attributes a property to the subject. (In most sentences this is the VP, although not necessarily so.)

viii)   *Clause*: A subject and a predicate phrase. Always a CP in our system

ix)   *Root, Matrix,* or *Main Clause*: A clause (CP) that isn't dominated by anything.

x)   *Embedded Clause/Subordinate Clause*: A clause inside of another.

xi)   *Specifier Clause*: An embedded clause in a specifier position.

xii)   *Adjunct Clause*: An embedded clause in an adjunct position.

xiii)   *Complement Clause*: An embedded clause in a complement position.

xiv)   *Tenseless* or *Non-finite Clause*: A clause that isn't tensed (e.g., I want *[Mary to leave]*).

xv)   *Tensed* or *Finite Clause*: A clause that is tensed.

xvi)   *Yes/No Question*: A question that can be answered with a *yes*, a *no* or *maybe*.

xvii)   *Subject-Aux Inversion*: A means of indicating a *yes/no* question. Involves movement of T to $\emptyset_{[+Q]}$ complementizer for morpho-phonological reasons.

xviii)   *Affix Lowering*: The lowering of inflectional suffixes to attach to their verb.

FURTHER READING

Abney, Steven (1987) The English Noun Phrase in its Sentential Aspect. Ph.D. dissertation, MIT.
Chomsky, Noam (1991) Some notes on economy of derivation and representation. In Robert Freidin (ed.), *Principles and Parameters in Comparative Grammar*. Cambridge: MIT Press. pp. 417–54.
Emonds, Joseph (1980) Word order in Generative Grammar. *Journal of Linguistic Research* 1, 33–54.
Pollock, Jean-Yves (1989) Verb-movement, Universal Grammar, and the structure of IP. Linguistic Inquiry 20, 365–424.

GENERAL PROBLEM SETS

1. SUBJECTS AND PREDICATE PHRASES
[Data Analysis; Basic]
In each of the following clauses identify the subject and the predicate phrase. Some sentences contain multiple clauses, be sure to identify the subjects and predicate phrases of *all* clauses.

a)   The peanut butter has got[6] moldy.
b)   The duffer's swing blasted the golf ball across the green.
c)   That Harry loves dancing is evidenced by his shiny tap shoes.
d)   The Brazilians pumped the oil across the river.

2. CLAUSE TYPES
[Data Analysis; Basic]
The following sentences are "complex" in that they contain more than one clause. For each sentence, identify each clause. Remember main clauses include embedded clauses. Identify the complementizer, the T, and the

---

[6] You may prefer *gotten* to *got* here. The choice is dialect-dependent.

subject of the clause; be sure to identify even *null* (Ø) complementizers and Ts with suffixes in them. State whether each clause is a finite clause or a non-finite clause.

a) Stalin may think that Roosevelt is a fool.
b) Lenin believes the Tsar to be a power-hungry dictator.
c) Brezhnev had said for Andropov to leave.
d) Yeltsin saw Chernyenko holding the bag.

3. ENGLISH *THAT* [7]
[Critical Thinking; Basic]
Discuss the status of the word *that* in each of the following two sentences. Explain the differences between the two sentences. If you assign a different category status to *that* in each sentence, explain why. Draw the tree (use X-bar theory) for each of the sentences.

a) Robert thinks <u>that</u> students should eat asparagus.
b) Robert thinks <u>that</u> student should eat asparagus.

4. TREES
[Application of Skills; Basic to Intermediate]
Draw the trees for the following sentences. Use X-bar theory, show all CPs, DPs, and TPs.

a) The very young child walked from school to the store.
b) Linguistics students like phonetics tutorials.
c) John paid a dollar for a head of lettuce.
d) Teenagers drive rather quickly.
e) Martha said that Bill loved his Cheerios in the morning.
f) Eloise wants you to study a new language. [assume *to* = T]
g) For Maurice to quarrel with Joel frightened Maggie.
h) John's drum will always bother me.

5. TREES II
[Application of Skills; Basic to Intermediate]
1) Go back to chapter 3, general problem set 1, and draw the trees using X-bar theory, including DPs.
2) Go back to chapter 3, general problem set 4, and draw the trees using X-bar theory, including DPs, TPs, and CPs.

---

[7] Thanks to Eithne Guilfoyle for contributing this problem set.

3) Go back to chapter 4, general problem set 1, and draw the trees using X-bar theory, including DPs, TPs, and CPs.

CHALLENGE PROBLEM SETS

CHALLENGE PROBLEM SET 1: HUNGARIAN DPS
[Data Analysis; Challenge]

In the text above, we argued that the structure of genitive constructions in English looks like:

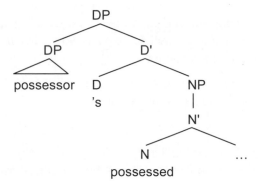

Consider the follow data from Hungarian. Does the possessor DP appear in the same place as the English ones? Assume the determiners *az* and *a* modify the *possessed* noun, not the possessor. The ending on the word hat varies depending upon the possessor, this does not affect the answer to this question. (Data from Szabolcsi 1994.)

a) az én kalapom
   the I   hat-1SG
   "my hat"

b) a   te   kalapod
   the you hat-2SG
   "your hat"

Hungarian has another possessive construction, seen in (c).

c) Marinak a   kalapja
   Mary   the hat-3SG
   "Mary's hat"

Where is the possessor DP in (c)? Explain your answer.

CHALLENGE PROBLEM SET 2: NPI LICENSERS

[Data Analysis and Critical Thinking; Challenge]

The adverb *ever* is a negative polarity item. Negative polarity items must stand in a c-command relationship with a negative licenser. Assume that the properties of the head uniquely determine the properties of a phrase. Explain how the following sentences are an argument for the subject being a DP rather than an NP:

a)   No man has ever beaten the centaur.
b)   *Some man has ever beaten the centaur.
c)   *Every man has ever beaten the centaur.

CHALLENGE PROBLEM SET 3: ENGLISH MODALS AND AUXILIARIES

[Data Analysis and Critical Thinking; Challenge]

In traditional grammar, two different kinds of T are found: modals and auxiliaries. Modals include words like *can, must, should, would, could, may, will* and in some dialects *shall*. Auxiliary verbs, by contrast, include such words as *have* and *be*. In this book, we've treated both modals and auxiliaries as T. An alternative is that only modals are really of category T, and that auxiliaries are real verbs. Auxiliary and verb combinations are actually a stacked set of VPs:

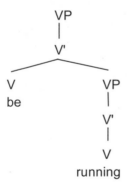

Construct an argument in favor of the idea that modals are of category T, but auxiliaries are really verbs. Assume the following: You may have as many V categories as you like, but there is only one T in any tensed clause's tree.

chapter 8

Constraining X-bar Theory: The Lexicon

0. INTRODUCTION

In chapters 6 and 7, we developed a very simple and general theory of phrase structure: X-bar theory. Using only three rules, this theory accounts for the distinction between adjuncts, complements, and specifiers. It incorporates the more articulated view of sentence hierarchy required by constituency tests, and it captures cross-categorial generalizations (i.e., the fact that all kinds of phrases – NPs, VPs, APs, PPs, CPs, DPs, and TPs – have the same basic properties). Most importantly, it allows us to draw trees for most of the sentences of any language.

This said, there is a significant problem with X-bar theory: it also generates sentences that are not acceptable or grammatical. Take for example the following pairs of grammatical and ungrammatical sentences:

1) a) Rosemary hates New York.
   b) *Rosemary hates.

2) a) Jennie smiled.
   b) *Jennie smiled the breadbox.

3) a) Traci gave the whale a jawbreaker.
   b) *Traci gave the whale.
   c) *Traci gave a jawbreaker.

Sentence (1b) should be perfectly acceptable (compare it to *Rosemary ran*). X-bar theory says that complements are optional. Therefore, direct objects, which are complements, should always be optional. The opposite type of fact is seen in the pair in (2). X-bar theory optionally allows a complement. So having a direct object here should be fine too. The same kind of effect is seen in (3), where both the direct object and indirect object are obligatory – contra X-bar theory.

What seems to be at work here is that certain verbs require objects and others don't. It appears to be a property of the *particular* verb. Information about the peculiar or particular properties of verbs is contained in our mental dictionary or **lexicon**. In this chapter, we'll look at how we can use the lexicon to constrain X-bar theory, so that it doesn't predict the existence of ungrammatical sentences.

1. SOME BASIC TERMINOLOGY

In chapter 2, we discussed how different verb types take a different number of arguments. For example, an intransitive verb like *leave* takes a single DP, which is the subject. A transitive verb such as *hit* takes a DP subject and a DP object. Below are the subcategories we came up with in chapter 2 (substituting DP for NP):

4)

Subcategory	Example
$V_{[DP\_\_]}$ (intransitive)	Leave
$V_{[DP\_\_\_DP]}$ (transitive type 1)	Hit
$V_{[DP\_\_\_\{DP/CP\}]}$ (transitive type 2)	Ask
$V_{[DP\_\_\_DP\ DP]}$ (ditransitive type 1)	Spare
$V_{[DP\_\_\_DP\ PP]}$ (ditransitive type 2)	Put
$V_{[DP\_\_\_DP\ \{DP/PP\}]}$ (ditransitive type 3)	Give
$V_{[DP\_\_\_DP\ \{DP/PP/CP\}]}$ (ditransitive type 4)	Tell

In addition to these restrictions, we also find semantic restrictions on what can appear in particular positions:

5) a) #My comb hates raisonettes.
    b) #A bolt of lightning killed the rock.

There is something decidedly strange about these sentences. Combs can't hate anything and rocks can't be killed. These semantic criteria are called **selectional restrictions**.

In the next section, we'll look at the theory of thematic relations, which is a particular way of representing selectional and subcategorizational restrictions.

2. THEMATIC RELATIONS AND THETA ROLES

One way of encoding selectional restrictions is through the use of what are called **thematic relations**. These are particular semantic terms that are used to describe the role that the argument plays with respect to the predicate. This section describes some common thematic relations (this list is by no means exhaustive, and the particular definitions are not universally accepted).

The initiator or doer of an action is called the **agent**. In the following sentences, *Ryan* and *Michael* are agents.

6) a) *Ryan* hit Andrew.
    b) *Michael* accidentally broke the glass.

Agents are most frequently subjects, but they can also appear in other positions.

Arguments that feel or perceive events are called **experiencers**. Experiencers can appear in a number of argument positions including subject and object:

7) a) *Leah* likes cookies.
    b) *Lorenzo* saw the eclipse.
    c) Syntax frightens *Kenna*.

Entities that undergo actions, are moved, experienced or perceived are called **themes**.

8) a) Alyssa kept *her syntax book*.
    b) The arrow hit *Ben*.
    c) The syntactician hates *phonology*.

The entity towards which motion takes place is called a **goal**. Goals may involve abstract motion:

9) a) Doug went *to Chicago*.
    b) *Dave* was given the piña colada mix.

There is a special kind of goal called **recipient**. Recipients only occur with verbs that denote a change of possession:

10) a) Mikaela gave *Jessica* the book.

   b) *Daniel* received a scolding from Hanna.

The opposite of a goal is the **source**. This is the entity from which a motion takes place:

11) a) *Bob* gave Steve the syntax assignment.
    b) Stacy came directly *from sociolinguistics class*.

The place where the action occurs is called the **location**:

12) a) Andrew is *in Tucson's finest apartment*.
    b) We're all *at school*.

The object with which an action is performed is called the **instrument**:

13) a) Chris hacked the computer apart *with an axe*.
    b) *This key* will open the door to the linguistics building.

Finally, the one for whose benefit an event took place is called the **beneficiary**:

14) a) He bought these flowers for *Aaron*.
    b) She cooked *Matt* dinner.

You now have enough information to try General Problem Sets 1 & 2

    Notice that any given DP can have more than one thematic relation. In the following sentence, the DP *Jason* bears the thematic relations of agent and source (at the very least).

15) *Jason* gave the books to Anna.

There is not a one-to-one relationship between thematic relations and arguments. However, linguists have a special construct called a **theta role** (or **θ role**) that does map one-to-one with arguments. Theta roles are bundles of thematic relations that cluster on one argument. In (15) above, *Jason* gets two thematic relations (agent and source), but only one theta role (the one that contains the agent and source thematic relations). Somewhat confusingly, syntacticians often refer to particular theta roles by the most prominent thematic relation that they contain. So you might hear a syntactician refer to the "agent theta role" of [$_{DP}$ *Jason*]. Strictly speaking, this is incorrect: Agent refers to a thematic relation, whereas the theta role is a bundle of thematic relations. But the practice is common, so we'll do it here. Remember, thematic relations are things like agent, theme, goal, etc., but theta roles are bundles of thematic relations assigned to a particular argument.

    Let's now see how we can use these theta roles to represent the argument structure of a verb. Take a ditransitive verb like *place*.

Place requires three arguments, a subject that must be an agent (the placer), a direct object, which represents the theme (the thing being placed), and an indirect object, which represents a location or goal (the the thing on which the theme is being placed). Any variation from this results in ungrammaticality:

16) a) John placed the flute on the table.
   b) *placed the flute on the table.
   c) *John placed on the table.
   d) *John placed the flute.
   e) *John placed the flute the violin on the table.[1]
   f) *The rock placed the sky with the fork.
   g) *John placed the flute the table.

Examples (16a–e) show that either having too many or too few arguments results in ungrammaticality. Example (16f) shows that using DPs with the wrong theta roles does the same (*the rock* can't be an agent; *the sky* can't be a theme – it can't be given to anyone; and *with the fork* is an instrument, not a goal). (16g) shows us that the category of the argument is important (this we already knew from chapter 2), the goal argument of the verb *place* must be a PP. It appears as if the verb *place* requires three arguments, which bear precisely the theta roles of agent (DP), theme (DP), and goal (PP). We represent this formally in terms of what is called a ***theta grid***.[2]

17)

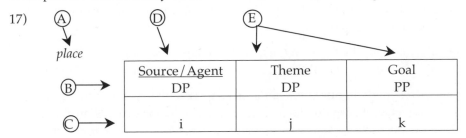

This grid consists of several parts. First of all, we have the name of the predicate (A). Next, for each argument that the predicate requires, there is a column (with two rows). Each of these columns represents a theta role. Notice that a column can have more than one thematic relation in it (but only one theta role). The number of columns corresponds exactly to the number of arguments the predicate requires. The first row (B) tells you the thematic

---

[1] This sentence would be OK if there were a conjunction between *the flute* and *the violin*. What does this tell us about what conjunction does to theta roles?

[2] There are many ways to formalize theta grids, but I adopt here the indexing box method that Haegeman (1994) uses, since it seems to be the most transparent.

relations and the categories associated with each of these theta roles. The second row (C), gives you what are called indices (singular: index) for each theta role. These are not the same as the indices in binding theory. When a predicate appears in an actual sentence, we mark the DP bearing the particular theta role with that index. Applying our grid to sentence (18), we get the following indexed sentence:

18) John$_i$ placed [the flute]$_j$ [on the table]$_k$.

The $_i$ index maps the agent theta role to *John*. The $_j$ index maps the theme theta role to *the book*, etc.

Theta roles actually come in two types. The first is the **external theta role** (D). This is the one assigned to the subject. External theta roles are usually indicated by underlining the name of the theta role in the theta grid. The other kind are **internal theta roles** (E). These are the theta roles assigned to the object and indirect object. There is a semantic reason for the distinction between internal and external theta roles (see Marantz 1984 for extensive discussion), but we will leave that issue aside here. We will have use for the external/internal distinction in chapter 10, when we do DP movement. For now, however, you should simply indicate which argument is the subject by underlining its name.

If you look carefully at the theta grid in (17) you'll notice that it only contains a specifier (subject) and complements (direct object and indirect object). There are no adjuncts listed in the theta grid. Adjuncts seem to be entirely optional:

19) a)   John put the book on the table (with a pair of tongs).   *instrument*
    b)   (In the classroom) John put the book on the table.   *location*

This corresponds to our observation in chapter 6, that you can have as many or as few adjuncts as you like, but the number of complements and specifiers are more restricted. *Adjuncts are never arguments, and they never appear in theta grids.*

You can now try General Problem Sets 3 & 4 (you may wish to review section 4 below before trying these)

Up until now, we have been representing our grammar solely through the mechanism of rules (phrase structure, then X-bar rules). In order to stop X-bar rules from overgenerating, we need a constraint. Constraints are like filters. They take the output of rules, and throw away any that don't meet the constraint's requirements. In essence, we are going to allow the X-bar rules to wildly overgenerate, and produce ungrammatical sentences. Those sentences, however, will be thrown out by our constraint. The constraint we are going to use is called the **Theta Criterion**. The theta criterion ensures that there is a strict match between the number and types of arguments in a sentence and the theta grid.

20) *The Theta Criterion*
   a)   Each argument is assigned one and only one theta role.
   b)   Each theta role is assigned to one and only one argument.

This constraint requires that there is a strict one-to-one match between argument DPs and theta roles. You can't have more arguments than you have theta roles, and you can't have more theta roles than you have DPs. Furthermore, since theta roles express particular thematic relations, the arguments will have to be of appropriate semantic types for the sentence to pass the constraint.

Let's look at some examples to see how this works. Consider the verb *love*. It has the theta grid given in (21). I haven't written in the indices here, because we'll add them when we compare the grid to a particular sentence.

21) *love*

Experiencer	Theme
DP	DP

When a sentence containing the predicate *love* is produced, we apply indices to each of the arguments, and match those arguments to theta roles in the grid. The sentence in (22) is grammatical with the correct number of arguments. It is matched to the theta grid in (23). There is a one-to-one matching between arguments and theta roles. So the theta criterion is satisfied, and the sentence is allowed to pass through the filter and surface.

22) Megan$_i$ loves Kevin$_j$.

23) *love*

Experiencer	Theme
DP	DP
i	j

Contrast this with the ungrammatical sentence in (24):

24) *Megan$_i$ loves.

This sentence lacks a theme argument, as seen in the following theta grid:

25) *love*

Experiencer	Theme
DP	DP
i	

The theme theta role is not assigned to an argument (there is no index in its lower box). This violates the second condition of the theta criterion: Every theta role is assigned to an argument. There is not a one-to-one matching of the theta roles to the arguments in this sentence. Since the theta criterion is violated, the sentence is filtered out (marked as ungrammatical). Notice, our X-bar rules *can* generate this sentence; it is ruled as ungrammatical by our constraint.

The next sentence shows the opposite problem: A sentence with too many arguments.

26) *Megan$_i$ loves Jason$_j$ Kevin$_k$.

27) *love*

Experiencer	Theme	
DP	DP	
i	j	k

Here, the argument *Kevin* doesn't get a theta role. There are only two theta roles to be assigned, but there are three arguments. This violates the first part of the theta criterion: the requirement that every argument have a theta role. Again, the theta criterion filters out this sentence as ungrammatical.

To summarize, we can constrain the output of the X-bar rules using a semantic tool: theta roles. The theta criterion is a constraint or filter that rules out otherwise well-formed sentences. The theta criterion requires that there is a strict one-to-one matching between the number and kind of theta roles and the number and kind of arguments.

You now have enough information to try General Problem Set 5 and Challenge Problem Set 1

---

3. THE LEXICON

Let's take a step back from these details and look at the big picture. We have developed a model of grammar where we have three simple rules (the X-bar rules) that can generate a hierarchical constituent structure. These rules are constrained by the theta criterion, which uses the semantic notion of theta roles. Recall that our theory of syntax is meant to be a cognitive theory, so let's consider the question of where these rules and these theta roles are stored in the mind. Chomsky proposes that the part of the mind devoted to language is essentially divided into two parts. One part, which he calls the **computational component**, contains all the rules and constraints. This part of the mind does the work of building sentences and filtering out any ill-formed ones. The computational component can't work in a vacuum, however. It needs access to information about theta roles and the like. Chomsky claims that this information is stored in the **lexicon**, the other part of the human language faculty. The lexicon is your mental dictionary or list of words (and their properties). If you think about it, this is the obvious place for theta grids to be stored. Which theta role is assigned to which argument is a property of each predicate. It is information that must be associated with that predicate and that predicate only. The obvious place to store information about particular words (or more properly **lexical items**) is in the lexicon.

The lexicon contains all the irregular and memorized parts of language. Each lexical entry (dictionary entry) must contain at least the following information):

- the meaning of the word
- the syntactic category of the word (N, V, A, P, T, C, etc.)
- the pronunciation of the word
- exceptional information of all kinds (such as morphological irregularities)
- the theta grid (argument structure).

When you learn a new word, you memorize all this information.

On an abstract level we can diagram the grammatical system as looking something like:

28)

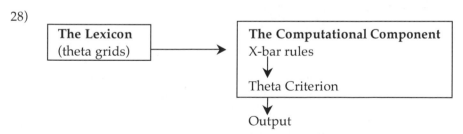

The lexicon feeds into the computational component, which then combines words and generates sentences. The fact that lexical information affects the form of the sentence is formalized in what we call the **Projection Principle**:

29) *The Projection Principle*
   Lexical information (such as theta roles) is syntactically represented at
   all levels.

4. EXPLETIVES AND THE EXTENDED PROJECTION PRINCIPLE

Before leaving the topic of the lexicon, I'd like to point out two special classes
of predicates. Consider first the following "weather" verbs. These predicates
don't seem to assign any theta roles:

30) a)   It rained.
    b)   It snowed.
    c)   It hailed.

What theta role does the pronoun *it* get in these sentences? If you are having
a problem figuring this out, ask yourself what *it* refers to in the above
sentences. It appears as if *it* doesn't refer to anything. In syntax, we refer to
pronouns like this as *expletive* or *pleonastic pronouns*. These pronouns don't
get a theta role (which of course is a violation of the theta criterion – a point
we will return to below). The theta grid for weather verbs is empty.
They don't assign any theta roles.
       There is another class of predicates that take expletive pronouns. These
are predicates that optionally take a CP subject:

31) [CP That Bill loves chocolate] is likely.

The predicate *is likely* assigns one theta role. It takes one argument (the
clause). (We will notate clausal arguments with the theta role *proposition*.)

32) *is likely*

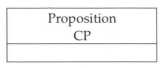

| Proposition |
| CP |
| |

You'll note that in (32) the theta role is not underlined. This is because the
clause bearing the theta role of proposition is a complement. This can be seen
in the following example:

33) It is likely that Bill likes chocolate.

In this sentence, we again have an expletive *it*, which gets no theta role.
       In order to maintain the theta criterion, we need to account for these
expletive DPs without theta roles. Expletive pronouns usually appear

in subject position. When *it* appears in other positions, it usually bears a theta role:

34) a) I love *it*.   (*it* is a theme)
    b) I put a book on *it*.   (*it* is a goal or location)

Expletives seem to appear where there is no theta marked DP (or CP) that fills the subject position. This is encoded in a revised version of the Projection Principle: The **Extended Projection Principle** (EPP):

35) *Extended Projection Principle* (EPP)
    All clauses must have subjects. (i.e. the specifier of TP must be filled by a DP or CP)

The EPP works like the theta criterion, it is a constraint on the output of the X-bar rules. It requires that every sentence have a subject. Next, we must account for the fact that expletives violate the theta criterion.

One way of doing this is by claiming that expletives are not generated by the X-bar rules. Instead they are inserted by a special *expletive insertion* rule:

36) *Expletive insertion rule*
    Insert an expletive pronoun into the specifier of TP.

This rule applies when there is no other subject. If there is no theta marked subject and no expletive subject, then the EPP will filter the sentence out. The way in which we get around the theta criteria is by *ordering* the expletive insertion rule after the theta criterion has applied.

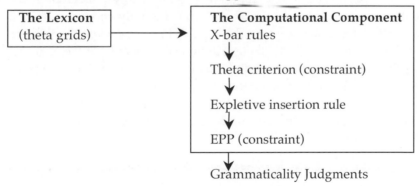

Since expletives are inserted *after* the theta criterion has applied, they can't be filtered out by it.

The model we've drawn here is very preliminary. In the next chapter, we will introduce a new kind of rule (the transformation – of which expletive insertion is a very special case) that will cause us to significantly revise this diagram.

You now have enough information to try Challenge Problem Sets 2, 3, 4, & 5

Two Kinds of *It*

There are two *it* pronouns in English. One is the expletive found with weather verbs. The other is the neuter pronoun *it* found in sentences like:

i) It bit me on the leg.

If you contrast the *it* in (i) with the ones in the weather verbs, you'll see that the *it* in (i) does take a theta role (agent) and does refer to something (probably an insect or some other animal). Not every sentence with an *it* involves an expletive.

5. SUMMARY

We started this chapter off with the observation that while X-bar rules capture important facts about constituency and cross-categorial generalizations, they overgenerate (that is they generate ungrammatical sentences). One way of constraining X-bar theory is by invoking lexical restrictions on sentences, such that particular predicates have specific argument structures, in the form of theta grids. The theta criterion rules out any sentence where the number and type of arguments don't match up one to one with the number and type of theta roles in the theta grid.

We also looked at one apparent exception to the theta criterion: theta role-less expletive pronouns. These pronouns only show up when there is no other subject, and are forced by the EPP. They escape the theta criterion by being inserted after the theta criterion has filtered out the X-bar rules.

By using lexical information (like theta roles) we're able to stop the X-bar rules from generating sentences that are ungrammatical. Unfortunately, as we'll see in the next chapter, there are also many sentences that the X-bar rules *cannot* generate. In order to account for these, we'll introduce a further theoretical tool: the movement rule.

IDEAS, RULES, AND CONSTRAINTS INTRODUCED IN THIS CHAPTER

i)   ***Selectional Restrictions***: Semantic restrictions on arguments.

ii)   ***Thematic Relations***: Semantic relations between a predicate and an argument – used as a means of encoding selectional restrictions.

iii)   *Agent*: The doer of an action (under some definitions must be capable of volition).

iv)   *Experiencer*: The argument that perceives or experiences an event or state.

v)   *Theme*: The element that is perceived, experienced or undergoing the action or change of state

vi)   *Goal*: The end point of a movement.

vii)   *Recipient*: A special kind of goal, found with verbs of possession (e.g., *give*).

viii)   *Source*: The starting point of a movement.

ix)   *Location*: The place an action or state occurs.

x)   *Instrument*: A tool with which an action is performed.

xi)   *Beneficiary*: The entity for whose benefit the action is performed.

xii)   *Proposition*: The thematic relation assigned to clauses.

xiii)   *Theta Role*: A bundle of thematic relations associated with a particular argument (DPs or CPs).

xiv)   *Theta Grid*: The schematic representation of the argument structure of a predicate, where the theta roles are listed.

xv)   *External Theta Role*: The theta role associated with subject DPs or CPs.

xvi)   *Internal Theta Role*: The theta role associated with objects or indirect objects.

xvii)   *The Theta Criterion*:
      a)   Each argument is assigned one and only one theta role.
      b)   Each theta role is assigned to one and only one argument.

xviii)   *Lexical Item*: Another way of saying "word." A lexical item is an entry in the mental dictionary.

xix)   *The Projection Principle*: Lexical information (like theta roles) is syntactically represented at all levels.

xx)   *Expletive (or Pleonastic) Pronouns*: A pronoun (usually *it* or *there*) without a theta role. Usually found in subject position.

xxi)   *Extended Projection Principle (EPP)*: All clauses must have subjects. Lexical information is syntactically represented.

xxii)   *Expletive Insertion*: Insert an expletive pronoun into the specifier of TP.

xxiii)   *The Lexicon*: The mental dictionary or list of words. Contains all irregular and memorized information about language, including the argument structure (theta grid) of predicates.

xxiv)   *The Computational Component*: The combinatorial, rule-based, part of the mind. Where the rules and filters are found.

xxv)   *The Model*:

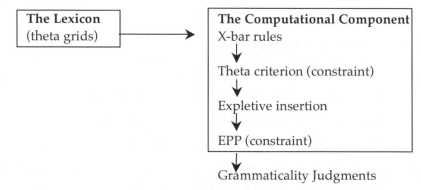

FURTHER READING

Gruber, Jeffrey (1965) Studies in Lexical Relations. Ph.D. dissertation, MIT.

Haegeman, Liliane (1994) *Introduction to Government and Binding Theory*. Oxford: Blackwell.

Marantz, Alec (1984) *On the Nature of Grammatical Relations*. Cambridge: MIT Press.

Williams, Edwin (1980) Predication. *Linguistic Inquiry* 11, 203–38.

Williams, Edwin (1994) *Thematic Structure in Syntax*. Cambridge: MIT Press.

GENERAL PROBLEM SETS

1. IDENTIFYING THEMATIC RELATIONS
[Data Analysis and Application of Skills; Basic]
Part 1: Identify the thematic relations associated with each DP or embedded CP in the following sentences. Each DP or CP may have more than one thematic relation associated with it.

a)   Shannon sent Dan an email.
b)   Jerid thinks that Sumayya cooked some beef waffles for him.
c)   Stacy hit a baseball to Yosuke.
d)   Jaime danced a jig.
e)   Yuko rubbed the pizza with a garlic clove.
f)   It's foggy in San Francisco.

Part 2: Draw the trees for (b–f), use CPs, DPs and TPs.

2. WARLPIRI[3]
[Data Analysis; Basic]
Consider the following data from Warlpiri:

a)   Lungkarda ka   ngulya-ngka   nguna-mi.
     bluetongue AUX   burrow-A   lie-NON.PAST
     "The bluetongue skink is lying in the burrow."

b)   Nantuwu   ka   karru-kurra   parnka-mi.
     horse   AUX   creek-B   run-NON.PAST
     "The horse is running to the creek."

c)   Karli   ka   pirli-ngirli   wanti-mi.
     boomerang AUX   stone-C   fall-NON.PAST
     "The boomerang is falling from the stone."

d)   Kurdu-ngku ka-jana pirli   yurutu-wana   yirra-rni.
     child-D   AUX   stone   road-E   put.NON.PAST
     "The child is putting stones along the road."

What is the meaning of *each* of the affixes (suffixes) glossed with -A, -B, -C, -D, and -E. Can you relate these suffixes to thematic relations? Which ones?

3. THETA GRIDS
[Data Analysis; Basic]
For each of the sentences below identify each of the predicates (including non-verbal predicates like *is likely*). Provide the theta grid for each. Don't forget: include only arguments in the theta grid; DPs and PPs that are adjuncts are not included. Index each DP, PP, CP argument with the theta role it takes. Assume that there are two different verbs *give* (each with their own theta grids) to account for (c) and (d); two different verbs *eat* (each with their own theta grids for (e) and (f); and two different verbs *ask* for (i) and (j).

---

[3] The data for this problem set comes from Ken Hale via Barb Brunson.

a) The stodgy professor left with his teaching assistant.
b) I played a tune on my iPod.
c) Molly gave Calvin a kiss.
d) Mercedes gave a test to the students in the lecture hall.
e) Pangur ate a cat treat.
f) Susan ate yesterday at the restaurant.
g) Gwen saw a fire truck.
h) Gwen looked at a fire truck.
i) Michael asked a question.
j) Adam asked if Hyacinth likes pineapples.
k) It is sunny in the dining room.
l) I feel it is unfortunate that television is so vulgar these days.
m) That Angus hates sushi is mysterious.

4. SINHALA[4]

[Data Analysis; Basic/Intermediate]

Two forms of the Sinhala verb appear in the data below and are identified in the glosses as A or B. (Data from Gair 1970.)

1) Provide a complete theta grid for each of the verbs in the following data. Be sure to primarily look at the second line of each piece of data, not the English translation.
2) Using indexes identify what theta role is assigned to each DP.
3) Discuss briefly (no more than 2 sentences) what kind of DP the suffix -*ṭə* attaches to.
4) What is the difference between *mamə* and *maṭə*? (Hint: the answer to this question is related to the answer to question (3).)
5) In terms of theta roles, what is the difference between the A and the B verb forms?

a) Mamə   kawi   kiənəwa.

    I   poetry   tell-A

    "I recite poetry."

b) Maṭə   kawi   kiəwenəwa.

    I   poetry   tell-B

    "I started reciting poetry (despite myself)."

---

[4] This problem is loosely based on one given to me by Barb Brunson. However, the data and questions have been altered. The data in this version of the problem set is taken directly from Gair, with some minor modifications to the glosses.

c) Lamea kataawǝ ahanǝwa.
     child   story   hear-A
     "The child listens to the story."

d) Lameaʈǝ kataawǝ æhenǝwa.
     child   story   hear-B
     "The child hears the story."

e) Mamǝ   naʈǝnǝwa.
     I   dance-A
     "I dance."

f) Maʈǝ   næʈǝenǝwa.
     I   dance-B
     "I dance (I can't help but do so)."

g) Hæmǝ irida   mǝ   mamǝ   kolǝmbǝ yanǝwa.
     every Sunday   EMPH   I   Columbo go-A
     "Every Sunday I deliberately go to Colombo."

h) Hæmǝ irida   mǝ   maʈǝ   kolǝmbǝ yæwenǝwa.
     every Sunday   EMPH   I   Columbo go-B
     "Every Sunday I experience going to Colombo."

i) Malli   nitǝrǝmǝ   aňḍǝnǝwa.
     brother   always   cries-A
     "Brother always cries."

j) Malliʈǝ   nitǝrǝmǝ   æňḍǝnǝwạ.
     brother   always   cries-B
     "Brother always bursts out crying without control."

k) Mamǝ   untǝ   baninǝwa.
     I   them   scold-A
     "I deliberately scold them."

l) Maʈǝ   untǝ   bænenǝwa.
     I   them   scold-B
     "I experienced scolding them."

m) Apiţə   pansələ peenəwa.

    we   temple   see-B

    "We saw the temple."

5. THETA CRITERION

[Data Analysis; Intermediate]

Show how each of the following sentences are violations of the theta criterion. Use theta grids to explain your answers.

a) *Rosemary hates.
b) *Jennie smiled the breadbox.
c) *Traci gave the whale.
d) *Traci gave a jawbreaker.
e) *placed the flute on the table.
f) *John placed on the table.
g) *John placed the flute.
h) *John placed the flute the violin on the table.
i) *The rock placed the sky with the fork.
j) *John placed the flute the table.

CHALLENGE PROBLEM SETS

CHALLENGE PROBLEM SET 1: IRISH AND THE THETA-CRITERION

[Data Analysis and Application of Skills; Challenge]

What problems do each of the following examples give for the theta criterion? (As a starting point, it may help to draw the theta grid for each verb and show what DP gets what role.) Please, not more than 3–4 sentences of discussion per example.

a) an fear a bhfaca mé é
    the man who saw I him
    "the man who I saw"

b) Rinceamar.
    Dance.1PL
    "We danced."

c) Ba-mhaith liom an teach a thógail.
    COND-good with-me the house its building
    "I would like to build the house."

CHALLENGE PROBLEM SET 2: OBJECT EXPLETIVES

[Critical Thinking; Challenge]

In the text above, it was observed that theta-role-less expletives primarily appear in subject position. Consider the following sentence. Is *it* here an expletive?

I hate it that you're always late.

How could you tell?

CHALLENGE PROBLEM SET 3: PASSIVES

[Data Analysis; Challenge]

Part 1: Write up the theta grids for the verbs in the following sentences. Assume there are two verbs *give* (give$_1$ is seen in (d), give$_2$ in (e)).

a)   John bit the apple.
b)   Susan forgave Louis.
c)   The jockey rides the horse.
d)   Phillip gave the medal to the soldier.
e)   Phillip gave the soldier the medal.

Part 2: English has a suffix *-en*, which when attached to verbs changes the structure of the sentence associated with them. This is called the **passive** morpheme. The following sentences are the passive equivalents of the sentences in part 1. The bracketed PPs starting with *by* are optional.

f)   The apple was bitten (by John).
g)   Louis was forgiven (by Susan).
h)   The horse was ridden (by the jockey).
i)   The medal was given to the soldier (by Phillip).
j)   The soldier was given the medal (by Phillip).

Describe in your own words what the *-en* passive suffix does to the theta grids of verbs. Pay careful attention to the last two examples, and to the optionality of the *by*-phrases.

CHALLENGE PROBLEM SET 4: HIAKI -WA[5]

[Data Analysis and Critical Thinking; Challenge]

Part 1: Consider the function of the suffix *-wa* in Hiaki (also known as Yaqui), a language spoken in Southern Arizona and Mexico. Look carefully at the data below, and figure out what effect this suffix has on the theta grids of

---

[5] Thanks to Heidi Harley for contributing this problem set.

Hiaki verbs. What English phenomenon is this similar to? (Data from Escalante 1990 and Jelinek and Escalante 2003.)

(Notes: Sometimes when -*wa* attaches to a verb, the form of the root changes (usually /e/ becomes /i/). This is a morphophonological phenomenon that you don't need to worry about. ACC refers to accusative case, INST means instrument, and PERF means perfective aspect (aspect plays no role in the answer to this problem). There is no nominative suffix in Hiaki.)

a)   Peo Huan-ta chochon-ak.
     Pete John-ACC punch-PERF
     "Pete punched John."

a') Huan chochon-wa-k.
     John punch-WA- PERF
     "John was punched."

b)   'Ume uusi-m uka kuchu-ta kuchi'i-m-mea bwa'a-ka.
     the children-PL the-ACC fish-ACC knife-PL-INST eat- PERF
     "The children ate the fish with knives."

b') 'U kuchu kuchi'i-m-mea bwa'a-wa-k.
     the fish knife-PL-INST eat-WA-PERF
     "The fish was eaten with knives."

c)   Peo bwiika.
     Pete sing
     "Pete is singing."

c') Bwiik-wa.
     sing-WA
     "Singing is happening." or "There is singing going on." or "Someone is singing."

Part 2: Not all verbs allow -*wa*. Consider the following pairs of sentences that show verbs that don't allow -*wa*. In terms of theta grids, what do these sentences have in common with each other that differentiates them from the ones that allow -*wa* (above in part 1).

a)   'U wikia chukte.
     the rope come.loose
     "The rope is coming loose."

a') *Chukti-wa.
     come.loose-WA
     "Coming loose is happening." or "There is coming loose going on." or "Something is coming loose."

b) 'U kaaro nasonte.
    the car damage
    "The car is damaged."

b') *Nasonti-wa.
    damage-WA
    "Damage is happening." or "There is damage going on." or "Something is getting damaged."

c) 'U kari veete-k.
    The house burn-PERF
    "The house burned."

c') *Veeti-wa-k.
    Burn-WA-PERF
    "Burning happened." or "There was burning going on." or "Something is getting burned."

d) 'U vachi bwase'e.
    The corn cook
    "The corn is cooking."

d') *Bwase'i-wa.
    cook-WA
    "Cooking happened." or "There was cooking going on." or "Something is being cooked."

CHALLENGE PROBLEM SET 5: ANTIPASSIVES

[Data Analysis and Critical Thinking; Challenge]

In many languages there is an operation that changes the theta grid of certain verbs, this operation is called the ***antipassive***.

Part 1: Here is some data from Inupiaq, an Inuit language of Canada and Alaska. Explain what adding the antipassive morpheme does to the theta grid of the verb. Verbs in Inupiaq agree with both their subjects and their objects. 3SUBJ-3OBJ means that the verb agrees with both a 3rd person subject and a 3rd person object. 3 means that the verb only agrees with a 3rd person subject. (Data from Seiler 1978.)

a) Aŋuti-m   umiaq   qiñig-aa   tirrag-mi.   *Active*
    man-ERG   boat-ABS   see-3SUBJ.3OBJ beach-at
    "The man sees the boat at the beach."

b)   Aŋun   (umiag-mik)   qiñiq-tuq   tirrag-mi.   *Antipassive*
     man-ABS   boat-INST   see-3   beach-at
     "The man sees (with a boat) at the beach."

Part 2: The following is some data from English. This might also be called an antipassive construction. How is it similar or different from the Inupiaq antipassive?

c)   I ate a basket of apples.
d)   I ate.

Part 3

Movement

chapter 9

Head-to-Head Movement

0. INTRODUCTION

Consider the relation between a verb and its object: According to X-bar theory, an object is the complement to V (sister to V, daughter of V'). This means that *no* specifier or adjunct can intervene between the complement and the head (if they did, the object would no longer be a complement).

The following sentence is from Modern Irish Gaelic, this is a Verb-Subject-Object (VSO) word order language:

1) Phóg Máire an lucharachán.
   Kissed Mary the leprechaun
   "Mary kissed the leprechaun."

In this sentence, the subject (a specifier) intervenes between the verb and the object; this sentence cannot be generated by X-bar theory. (Try to draw a tree where the specifier intervenes between the head and the complement – it's impossible.)

Now consider the following sentence from French:

2) Je mange souvent des   pommes.
   I eat   often   of.the apples
   "I often eat apples."

Souvent "often" intervenes between the verb and the object. If *souvent* is an adjunct it is appearing between a head and its complement. X-bar theory can't draw the tree for this one either.

In sum, X-bar theory *undergenerates*, it does not produce all the possible grammatical sentences in a language.

Although based on very different problems than the ones in (1) and (2), Chomsky (1957) observed that a phrase structure grammar (such as X-bar theory) cannot generate all the sentences of a language. He proposed that what was needed was a set of rules that change the structure (in very limited ways) generated by phrase structure rules. These rules are called *transformational rules*. Transformations take the output of X-bar rules (and other transformations) and change them into different trees.

The model of grammar that we are suggesting here takes the following form. You should read this like a flow chart. The derivation of a sentence starts at the top, and what comes out at the bottom is what you say.

3)   **The Computational Component**

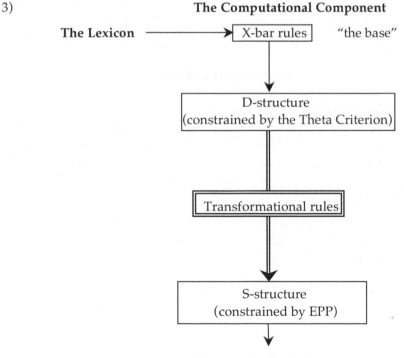

X-bar theory and the lexicon conspire together to generate trees. This conspiracy is called *the base*. The result of this tree generation is a level we call *D-structure* (this used to be called Deep Structure, but for reasons that need not concern us here, the name has changed to D-structure). You will never pronounce a D-structure. D-structure is also sometimes called the *underlying form* or *underlying representation* (and is similar in many ways to the underlying form found in phonology). The theta criterion filters out ungrammatical sentences at D-structure.

D-structure is then subject to the ***transformational rules***. These transformational rules can move words around in the sentence. We've actually already seen two of these transformational rules. In Chapter 7, we looked briefly at T to C movement in subject-aux inversion constructions, and affix lowering, which gets inflectional suffixes to lower to their verb. (In this chapter, we're going to look in more detail at these two rules.) The output of a transformational rule is called the ***S-structure*** of a sentence. The S-structure is filtered by the EPP, which ensures that the sentence has a subject. What are left are grammatical sentences.

In the version of Chomskyan grammar we are considering, we will look at two different kinds of transformations: movement rules and insertion rules. Movement rules move things around in the sentence. Insertion rules put something new into the sentence. This chapter is about one kind of movement rule: the rules that move one head into another, called ***head-to-head movement***. These transformational rules will allow us to generate sentences like (1) and (2) above. X-bar theory by itself cannot produce these structures.

Generative Power

Before we go any further and look at an example of a transformation, consider the power of this type of rule. A transformation is a rule that can change the trees built by X-bar theory. If you think about it, you'll see that such a device is extremely powerful; in principle it could do *anything*. For example you could write a changing rule that turns all sentences that have the word "red" in them to sentences with SOV order.

i) $[_{TP} \dots \text{red} \dots] \Rightarrow [_{TP} \text{S} [\text{O V}]]$

This rule would take a sentence like (ii) and change it into a sentence like (iii):

ii) The red book bores me.
iii) The red book me bores.

Similarly we could allow X-bar theory to generate sentences where the work "snookums" appears after every word, then have a transformation that deletes all instances of "snookums" (iv). (v) shows the D-structure of such a sentence. (vi) would be the S-structure (output) of the rule.

iv) "snookums" $\Rightarrow \varnothing$
v)   I snookums built snookums the snookums house snookums.

vi)   I built the house.

These are crazy rules. No language has a rule of these types. However, in principle, there is no reason that rules of this kind couldn't exist. We thus need to restrict the power of transformational rules. We do this two ways:

vii)   *Rules must have a motivation.* Frequently these motivations are output constraints. like the EPP that we saw in the last chapter, or morphophonological, like the ones we will propose in this chapter.

viii)   Not only are rules motivated by output constraints, they are restricted by them. *You cannot write a rule that will create a violation of an output constraint.*

As we go along we will consider specific ways to constrain transformational rules so that they don't overgenerate.

1. VERB MOVEMENT (V → T)

1.1 *French*

Let's return now to the problems we raised in the introduction to this chapter. Let's start with the sentence from French:

4)   Je mange souvent des   pommes.
     I   eat   often   of.the apples
     "I often eat apples."

In this sentence, an adjunct surprisingly appears between the head of VP and its complement. Compare this sentence to the English sentence in (5):

5)   I often eat apples.

In the English sentence, the adjunct does not intervene between the verb and the complement. The tree for (5) would look like (6).

6)

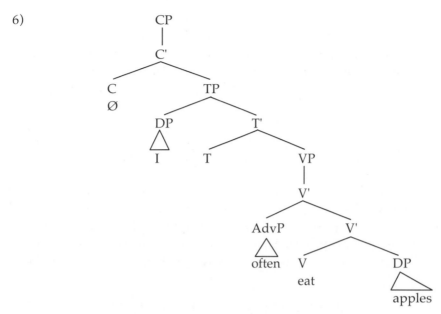

Notice the following thing about this structure. There is a head position that intervenes between the subject DP and the adverb *often*: this is the T position. T, you will recall, gives its inflection to the verb or surfaces as an auxiliary. Notice that in French (4), the thing that appears between the subject and the adverb is not T, but the tensed main verb.

Keeping this idea in the back of your mind now consider the following chart, which shows the relative placement of the major constituents of a French sentence with a tensed main verb (b), and English sentence with a tensed verb (a), and both languages with auxiliary constructions (c and d):

7)

a)	I	T	often	eat	apples
b)	Je	mange	souvent		des pommes
c)	I	Have	often	eaten	apples
d)	J'	Ai	souvent	mangé	des pommes

There are several things to observe about this chart. Recall from chapter 2, that auxiliaries are instances of the category T; as such, V' adjuncts are predicted to invariably follow them. This seems to be the case (c and d). What is striking about the above chart is that tensed main verbs in French also seem to occupy this slot, whereas in English, they follow the adverb. How can we account for this alternation? Let's assume that the form which meets X-bar theory (and happens to be identical to the English tree in (6)) is what is generated in *both* French and English. The difference between the two is that French has a special *extra* rule which moves its verbs out of the VP. More precisely, it moves them into the slot associated with T. This is the transformational rule we will call **V → T**; it is also known as **verb movement** or **verb raising.** This rule is informally stated in (8):

8)   *V → T movement:* Move the head V to the head T.

Before looking at an example, consider for a moment why this rule might apply. Much like the rule of affix lowering we introduced for English in chapter 7, this rule exists to get an inflectional affix on the verb. In fact, let's go one step further, let's claim that affix lowering and verb raising are really the same operation. Notice that they are in complementary distribution – a language either has one or the other. The difference between a verb raising language (French) and an affix lowering language (like English) might simply be one of a parameter. All languages have some version of this rule, some set the parameter to raise the verb to T, others set it to lower the T to the V.

9)   *Verb movement parameter:* Verbs raise to T *or* T lowers to V.

This provides a simple account of the difference between English and French adverbial placement.

Now, let's do a derivation for the French sentence *Je mange souvent des pommes.* The first step in the derivation is to build an X-bar structure, and insert all the words. This gives us the D-structure of the sentence:

10)

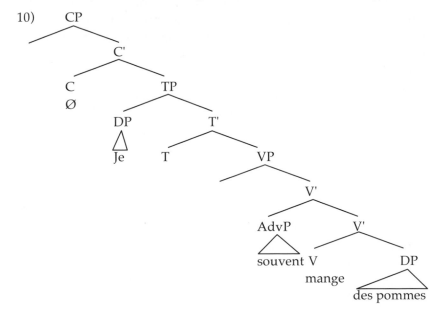

Notice that this D-structure is not a grammatical sentence of French (yet). In fact it has exactly the same word order as the English sentence in (5).

The next step in the derivation is to apply the transformation of Verb Movement. One typical way of representing a movement transformation is to draw a tree with an arrow.

11)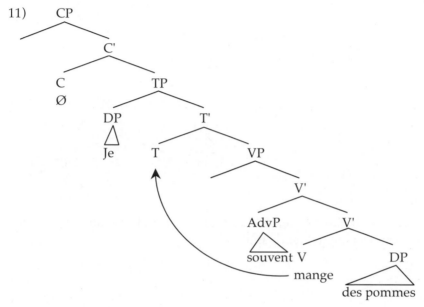

This results in the correct S-structure string:

12) Je mange$_i$ souvent t_i des pommes.

Yet at the same time, we can maintain X-bar theory. The t_i here stands for "trace" and sits at the D-structure position of the verb.

Consider now the related derivation for the English sentence *He often eats apples*. The D-structure is the same, except with English words:

13)

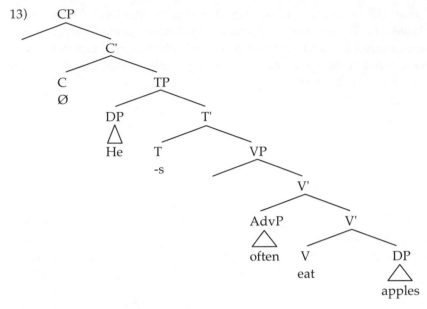

Since English is parameterized for affix lowering rather than verb raising, the inverse movement to French applies:

14)

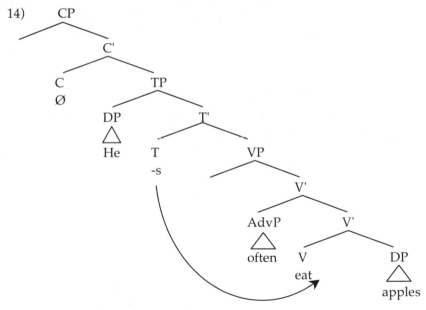

This results in the grammatical S-Structure:

15) He often eats apples.

What we have seen so far is a rather technical solution to a relatively small problem. Now, I'm going to show you that this solution can be extended. Recall our chart with adverb above in (7). Consider now the identical chart with negatives:

16)

a)	I	do	not	eat	Apples
b)	Je	ne-mange	pas		des pommes
c)	I	have	not	eaten	Apples
d)	Je	n'ai	pas	mangé	des pommes

Ignore for the moment the French morpheme *ne-*, which is optional in spoken French in any case. Concentrate instead on the relative positioning of the negatives *pas* and *not* and the verbs. The situation is the same as with the adverb *often*. All auxiliaries in both languages precede negation, as does the main verb in French. But in English, the main verb follows the negation.[1]

We can apply the same solution to this word order alternation that we did for adverbs: we will move the verb around the negation. The tree here will be slightly different, however. Let us assume that *not* heads a projection called NegP, and this projection is the complement of TP, and dominates VP.

17)

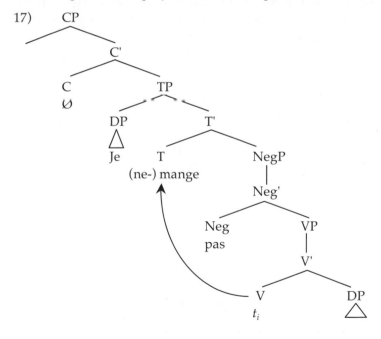

---

[1] For the moment, ignore the *do* verb. We will return to this below.

The transformation of verb movement then raises the verb around *pas* as represented by the arrow in (17).[2] Again this derives the correct word order.[3]

You now have enough information to try General Problem Sets 1 & 2

Observe that the alternation in position between an auxiliary and a tensed verb is not limited to French. Many (if not most) languages show this same alternation. Take for example the language Vata, a Kru language of West Africa. The underlying word order of Vata is SOV (data from Koopman 1984).

18) a)   A   la   saka li.
         we   have   rice eaten
         "We have eaten rice."

   b)   A   li   saka.
        we   eat   rice
        "We eat rice."

In the sentence with the overt auxiliary, the verb appears to the far right. When there is no auxiliary, the verb appears in the structural slot otherwise occupied by the auxiliary. This alternation can be attributed to verb raising. When there is an auxiliary (*la*), T does not require "support" from the verb, so the verb remains in its base generated position (19).

---

[2] An alternative to this is often found in the literature. In this alternative *ne-* heads the NegP and *pas* is in the specifier of NegP. The verb raises and stops off at the Neg head, (picking up *ne-* on the way) and then moves up to T. This alternative was presented in Pollock (1989).

[3] You might note that in English the comparable operation (affix lowering) does not apply around negation. We explore this issue in more detail below.

19)

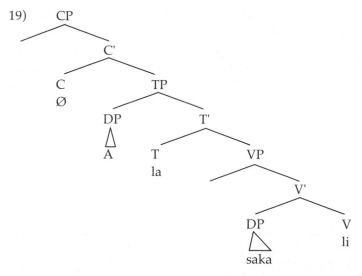

When there is no auxiliary, T requires support, and the verb raises around the object to T:

20)

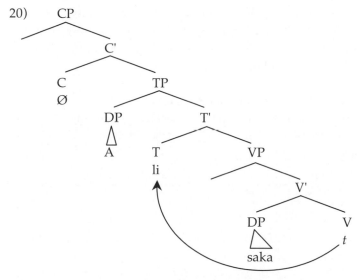

This, of course, is the correct word order (*A li saka*).

The transformational rule of V → T movement thus provides a simple, elegant and motivated account of cases where the verb shows up in the "wrong" position. The motivation for the verb to move (or the affix to lower) is intuitive: the need for the verb to get its inflection. This seems to correlate with the fact that in many languages there are positional alternations where auxiliaries (T) and tensed verbs alternate and are in complementary distribution. This also gives a straightforward account of certain cross-linguistic differences. We can account for the fact that English and French consistently differ in the relative placement of adverbs and negation with respect to tensed verbs. We derived this difference by appealing to a parameter which either has the verb raise to T, or T-affixes lower to the verb.

1.2 Irish

Now we'll turn to the other (more difficult) problem raised in the introduction to this chapter. This is the Verb-Subject-Object (VSO) order of Irish.

21) Phóg   Máire an lucharachán.
    Kissed Mary the leprechaun
    "Mary kissed the leprechaun."

As we observed above, there is no way that X-bar theory can generate a sentence of this type. This is true of every basic sentence in Irish. VSO order is found in every tensed sentence in Irish. It is also the basic order of about 9 percent of the world's languages, including languages from many different language families such as Tagalog, Welsh, Arabic, Mixtec, Mayan, Salish, Turkana, Maasai (to name only a few).

Digression on Flat Structure

Up until the early 1980s, most linguists considered VSO languages to simply be exceptions to X-bar theory. They proposed that these languages had a **flat structure**:

i)

This structure is called "flat" because there are no hierarchical differences between the subject, the object, and the verb. In other words, there are no structural distinctions between complements, adjuncts and specifiers. These sentences don't have a VP constituent. In (i) there is no single node dominating both the V and the second DP, but excluding the subject DP.

There is a delicate balance between a theory that is empirically adequate (one that accounts for all the data), like a theory that has *both* flat structure languages and X-bar languages, and one, which is explanatorily adequate and elegant (like pure X-bar theory). By claiming that these languages were exceptions, linguists were left with a considerably less elegant theory. Thus the race was on to see if there was some way to incorporate these languages into X-bar theory. Notice, however, that pure elegance alone is not sufficient cause to abandon an empirically adequate but inelegant theory like flat structure – we must also have empirical evidence (data) in favor of the elegant theory.

Flat structure makes the following predications:

a)   There is no VP constituent.
b)   There is no evidence for a hierarchical distinction between subjects and objects – they both have the same mother and mutually c-command one another.

It turns out that both these predications are wrong. First, if VSO languages have no VP in simple tensed clauses they should have no VPs in other clause types either. McCloskey (1983) observed for Irish, and Sproat (1985) for Welsh, that this is false.

ii)   Tá Máire [ag-pógail an lucharachán].
      Is Mary   ing-kiss the leprechaun
      "Mary is kissing the leprechaun."

In auxiliary sentences in Irish, there is a plausible candidate for a VP: the words bracketed in (ii). If this V + O sequence is a constituent, it should obey constituency tests. Two typical constituency tests from chapter 3, coordination and movement (clefting), show this:

iii)   Tá Máire [ag-pógail an lucharachán] agus [ag-goidú a ór].
       Is Mary [ing-kiss the leprechaun] and   [ing-steal his gold]
       "Mary is kissing the leprechaun and stealing his gold."

iv)   Is [ag-pógáil an lucharachán] atá Máire.
      It-is [ing-kiss the leprechaun] that.be Mary
      "It's kissing the leprechaun that Mary is."

These sentences show that the bracketed [V + O] sequence in (ii) is indeed a constituent, and a plausible VP.

Now, turn to the second prediction made by flat structure, where all the DPs are on a par hierarchically. This too we can show is false. Recall from chapter 5, that there is at least one phenomenon sensitive to hierarchical position: the distribution of anaphors. Recall that the antecedent of an anaphor must c-command it. If flat structure is correct, then you should be able to have either DP be the antecedent and either DP be the anaphor, since they mutually c-command one another (they are sisters):

v)

```
              TP
            /  |  \
          V   DP  DP
```

The data in (vi) and (vii) show that this is false. Only the object DP can be an anaphor. This means that the object must be c-commanded by the subject. Further it shows that the subject cannot be c-commanded by the object. Flat structure simply can't account for this.

vi) Chonaic Síle$_i$ í-fein$_i$.
    Saw   Sheila her-self
    "Sheila saw herself."

vii) *Chonaic í-fein$_i$ Síle$_i$.
    Saw   her-self Sheila
    "Sheila saw herself."

The flat structure approach, if you'll pardon the pun, comes up flat. It makes the wrong predictions. The verb raising approach proposed in the main text doesn't suffer from these problems. It maintains X-bar theory so both has a VP and a hierarchical distinction between subjects and objects.

You now have enough information to try General Problem Set 3

The failure of X-bar theory to account for 9 percent of the world's languages is a significant one! However, the theory of transformations gives us an easy out to this problem. If we assume that VSO languages are underlyingly SVO (at D-structure), then a transformational rule applies which derives the initial order.

22) SVO ⇒ VSO

How might we actually structurally implement this rule? Given the discussion in section 1.1 above, the answer should be obvious: we can use verb movement.

There is some straightforward evidence in favor of a verb movement approach to Irish word order: First, we see the same type of positional auxiliary/tensed verb word order alternations.

23) Tá Máire ag-pógáil an lucharachán.
    Is Mary ing-kiss the leprechaun
    "Mary is kissing the leprechaun."

24) Phóg Máire an lucharachán.
    kissed Mary the leprechaun
    "Mary kissed the leprechaun."

As in the French and Vata cases, with respect to a certain position (in Irish the initial position), auxiliaries and main verbs are in complementary distribution – evidence for V → T movement.

Unfortunately the situation here is not as straightforward as the French and Vata cases. If we try to draw the tree for (24) we immediately run into a problem.

25)

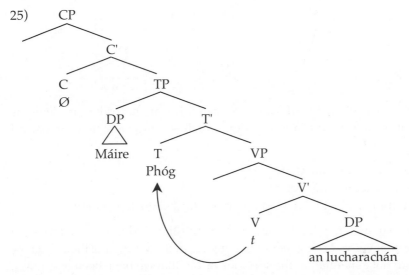

While moving the verb to T certainly accounts for the alternation between verbs and auxiliaries, it does not derive the correct VSO word order. Instead we get incorrect SVO order.

In all the sentences of Irish we've looked at, T (in the form either of an auxiliary or a raised tensed verb) seems to precede its specifier (the subject). One possibility to resolve this might be in exercising the parameters we looked at in chapter 6. So we might try putting the specifier of TP to the right in Irish:

26)

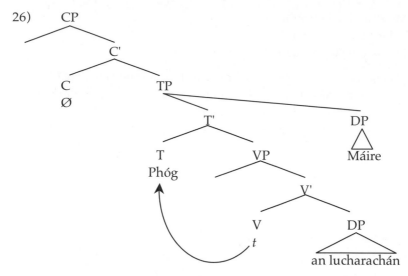

But this doesn't work, if you look carefully at the order of elements in 26 you'll see this results in VOS order, which is completely ungrammatical in Irish:

27) *Phóg an lucharachán Máire.
     kissed the leprechaun Mary
     (ungrammatical with the reading "Mary kissed the leprechaun.")

So X-bar parameters clearly aren't the solution. The only alternative is to claim that we've been generating subjects in the wrong position. That is, subjects are not generated in the specifier of TP, like we have been assuming. Instead, they are *underlyingly* generated in the specifier of VP.

The idea that subjects are generated in the specifier of VP is called the **VP-internal subject hypothesis**, and was first proposed by Hilda Koopman and Dominique Sportiche (1991). The idea has some thematic motivation. By assuming that subjects are generated inside the VP we can make the strong claim that theta roles are assigned entirely within the VP. We can encode this in the following constraint:

28) *The Locality Constraint on Theta Role Assignment*
     Theta roles are assigned within the projection of the head that assigns them (i.e., the VP or other predicate).

If we assume the VP-internal subject hypothesis, the derivation of VSO order is trivial: It involves a straightforward instance of V → T movement:

29)

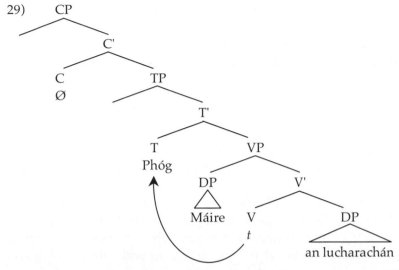

This derives the correct VSO order of Irish.

Now at this point your head is probably spinning and you are saying to yourself "Hold on, what about English, French, and Vata! In all those languages the subject precedes T." Alas, this is true. The solution to the conundrum lies easily within our grasp, however. Perhaps it is the case that in English, French, and Vata (but not the VSO languages) subject DPs *move* from the specifier of VP to the specifier of TP. A simple French sentence then would have two movements: one for the verb, one for the subject.

30)

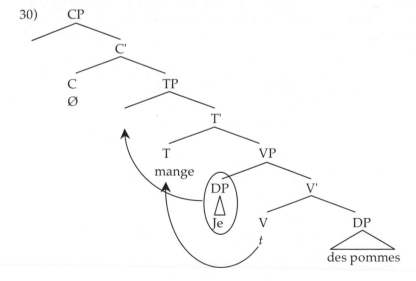

This second kind of movement is called ***DP movement*** and is the topic of the next chapter, where we'll discuss further evidence for VP-internal subjects. The correct formulation and motivations for DP movement are set out there. For now, we'll just observe that we have not argued ourselves into a corner; there is a way out.

You now have enough information to try General Problem Sets 4 & 5 and Challenge Problem Set 1

Let us summarize the (quite complicated) discussion up to now. In section 0, we saw that there are instances where X-bar rules fail to generate the correct orders of sentences. To solve this problem, we looked at a new rule type: the transformation. Transformations take a structure generated by X-bar theory and change it in restricted ways. We've looked at one such transformation: V → T. This rule has the function of movement a verb to the T head. It does so in order that the verb can support inflection. We also looked at the mirror image of verb movement: affix lowering, which lowers an inflectional suffix to the verb. These are in complementary distribution, so serve as tokens of the same rule. A language is parameterized as to whether it takes the raising or the lowering variant. The difference in word order between French and English negatives and sentences with adverbials can be boiled down to this parameter. The rule of verb movement itself can explain the fact that an adjunct (the adverb) appears between a head and its complement. Taken together with the VP-internal subject hypothesis, verb movement can also explain the very problematic basic VSO word order. This simple straightforward tool thus allows us to account for a very wide range of complicated facts.

2. T Movement (T → C)

Before leaving the topic of the movement of heads, we briefly return to a phenomenon somewhat obliquely discussed in chapter 7. This is the phenomenon known as *T → C* movement or subject-aux inversion. In yes/no questions in English (questions that can be answered with either a *yes* or *no*), auxiliary verbs invert with their subject:

31) a)   You *have* squeezed the toilet paper.
    b)   *Have* you squeezed the toilet paper?

In chapter 7, we claimed that this alternation is due to the presence of a special null question complementizer $\emptyset_{[+Q]}$. We observed that in many languages (such as Polish and Irish) yes/no questions aren't indicated with subject-aux inversion, but with a special form of the initial complementizer (recall Irish is VSO to start with, so subject-aux inversion would do nothing):

32) An bhfaca tú   an madra?
    Q   See   you the dog
    "Did you see the dog?"

We claimed that subject-aux inversion is a special case of these question complementizers. English doesn't have an overt (pronounced) question complementizer like the Irish *an*. Instead, English has a null $\emptyset_{[+Q]}$ complementizer. Being phonologically null, however, is a bit of a problem, since the difference in meaning between a statement and a question is encoded in something you can't hear. English employs a mechanism (which we now know is a transformation), that gives phonological content to that $\emptyset_{[+Q]}$ by moving T to it, *around the subject*:

33)

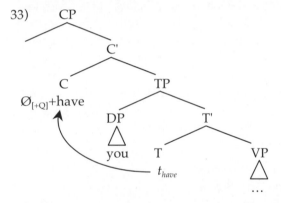

This kind of analysis is supported by the fact subject-aux inversion (T → C) is in strict complementary distribution with overt question complementizers as seen in the following embedded clauses:

34) a)   I asked *have* you squeezed the toilet paper.[4]
    b)   I asked whether you *have* squeezed the toilet paper.
    c)   *I asked whether *have* you squeezed the toilet paper.

---

[4] For many people this sentence is not grammatical unless the embedded clause is a direct quote. (That is, it would properly be written with " " around it.) This fact muddies the waters somewhat in this argument, as it may not be the case that T → C movement is allowed at all in embedded clauses in English. However, the same facts do hold true in other languages where subject-aux inversion in embedded clauses is more clearly instantiated.

So the process of subject-aux inversion must be a property triggered by complementizers. This rule is very similar to the rule of V → T movement. It is triggered by morphophonological requirements (such as the fact that something contentful must be pronounced, or that an affix needs a host). Both movements are instances of moving one head into another, so are considered instances of the same basic operation: *head-to-head movement*. This is a cover term for both V → T and T → C.

VSO as Raising to C?

In the previous section we claimed that Irish VSO order involves raising the verb to T. We were also forced to claim that subjects were generated VP internally. Notice that in English, we also have a VS order, found in yes/no questions. These VS orders we analyze as T → C movement, with the subject remaining in its more typical place in the specifier of TP. Why don't we analyze Irish VSO order the same way? Instead of having VP-internal subjects, why don't we simply have verbs raise to T, then do T → C in *all* Irish clauses. This too would derive VSO order. There is a very good reason for this. Recall that in English T → C movement is blocked when there is an overt complementizer. (You don't move T into the C, because it already has phonological content.) If Irish VSO really involves raising to C, then it should be the case that you do *not* get VSO order when there is an overt complementizer. This is false. You get VSO order even when there is a complementizer.

i) Duirt mé <u>gur</u> *phóg* **Máire** an lucharachán.
    Said I that kissed Mary the leprechaun
    "I said that Mary kissed the leprechaun."

This means that VSO must result from movement of the verb to some position lower than the complementizer. This is the analysis we argued for above, where V raises to T, and the subject is in the specifier of VP.

It appears as if V → T and T → C interact. In English, only auxiliaries ever occupy the T head as free-standing entities. Main verbs do not raise to T in English. So only auxiliaries undergo T → C movement. Main verbs never do:

35) a)   Have you squeezed the toilet paper?
    b)   *Squeezed you the toilet paper?

Contrast this to French. In French, main verbs undergo V → T movement. This means that when French does T → C movement, main verbs are predicted to also invert (because they are in T). This can be seen in the following tree:

36)

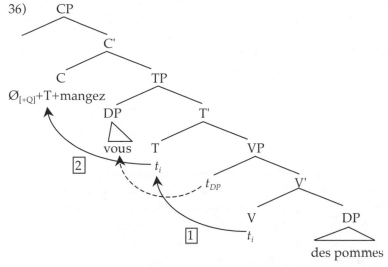

Movement $\boxed{1}$ is V → T movement. Movement $\boxed{2}$ is subsequent movement of the verb (in T) to C as part of T → C movement.

This prediction is borne out. Main verbs in French do invert in questions, but English main verbs do not.

37) a)   Mangez-vous des pommes?
    b)   *Eat you the apples?

To summarize, we have looked (again) at the transformation of T → C movement in more detail. We saw that it has a phonological motivation, and is similar in some ways to V → T movement. We also noticed that in a language (such as French) where V → T movement applies main verbs as well as auxiliary verbs undergo T → C.

You now have enough information to try General Problem Sets 6, 7 & 8 and
Challenge Problem Sets 2, 3, 4 & 5

3. *Do*-SUPPORT

In English, an interesting effect emerges when we try to question a sentence with no auxiliary:

38) a)   You eat apples.
    b)   Do you eat apples?

In sentences with no auxiliary, we insert a dummy (=meaningless) auxiliary in yes/no questions. There must be a reason for this. We have argued that in English, T lowers to attach to V, at the same time in questions, the transformation of T → C movement forces the same T to raise. This is a contradiction: we want T to raise and lower at the same time. The phenomenon of *do*-support appears to be an escape hatch for T. If we insert a dummy (contentless) auxiliary to support the inflectional affixes, then this dummy can undergo T → C movement. This is an insertion transformation. This transformation is called **do-*insertion*** or **do-*support***:

39) Do-*insertion:* When there is no other option for supporting inflectional affixes, insert the dummy verb *do* into T.

What triggers this transformation is different than what triggers the movement transformations. The movement transformations are motivated (triggered) by morphophonological concerns. Insertion transformations apply only in the case that there is nothing else you can do. They are, in essence, operations of ***last resort***, you only apply them when you absolutely have to and when no movement transformation can apply.

There are Two Verbs *Do* in English

Quite confusingly, English has two verbs *to do*. One is a main verb, meaning roughly "accomplish something," "perform an action." The other is a dummy (meaningless) auxiliary, which is inserted under "*do*-support." These are quite distinct entities. As can be seen by the fact that you can have both of them in one sentence:

i)   Did you do your homework?

Main verb *do* is not an auxiliary and is not in T, this can be seen by the fact that it cannot undergo T → C movement, and it follows *often* and *not*.

ii)   *Do you your homework?
iii)   You often do your homework.
iv)   You have not done your homework.

When invoking the *do*-insertion transformation, be careful that you only do it when dummy *do* is involved – not main verb *do*.

Do-support doesn't apply only in questions; it also shows up in negative sentences.

40) a)   I ate the apple.
    b)   I didn't eat the apple.

The negative morpheme *not* blocks the operation of affix lowering. The reasons for this are obscure. We will simply state it here as a stipulation.

4. MULTIPLE AUXILIARIES AND AFFIX-HOPPING IN ENGLISH

4.1 Multiple Auxiliaries

One issue still remaining in our discussion comes from the behavior of sentences in English with more than one auxiliary. Take the following sentence as an example:

41) Shannon should have been being fed at the table.

The placement of *should* is easy, it's in T, but where should the other auxiliaries in this sentence go? In chapter 7, challenge problem set 3, we suggested that one solution to this problem might be to treat auxiliaries as Vs that take other VPs as complements.

42)

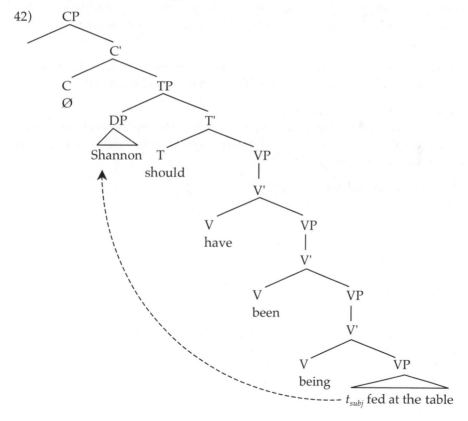

One piece of evidence for this approach is that these auxiliaries can follow negation and adverbs:

43) a)   Shannon should not have been being fed at the table.
    b)   Shannon should [_Adv_ never] have been being fed at the table.

Notice that negation cannot precede modals (which we will continue to treat as belonging to category T):

44) a)   *Shannon not should have been being fed at the table.
    b)   *Shannon did not should have been being fed at the table.

This shows that these auxiliaries are not in T.

   With this then, we have argued ourselves into a corner, since there are many instances where the auxiliary verbs *be* and *have* do appear to be in T because they precede negation:

45) a)   Shannon *has* not eaten.
    b)   Shannon *is* not eating.

There is a simple solution to this, auxiliary verbs (but not main verbs) raise in English. This means that the verb movement parameter needs to be modified:

46) *Verb Movement Parameter*: Option 1: All tensed verbs raise to T; Option 2: tensed Auxiliaries raise to T and T lowers to tensed main verbs.

English chooses the second option.

   Let's tree a number of sentences and see how this might work. Let's start with a simple sentence with a modal verb. We're continuing to treat modals as instances of the category T:

47) Shannon should eat.

48)

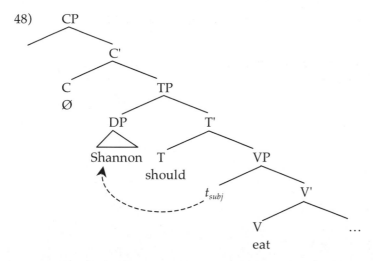

There is no verb movement in this sentence, the only movement is the shift of the subject DP from the specifier of the VP into the specifier of TP. Next let's contrast this with a sentence with a tense suffix and no auxiliary at all:

49) Shannon ate.

50)

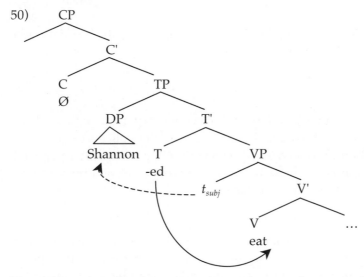

Here the -*ed* suffix lowers and attaches to the verb (this is followed by a morphological rule that turns *eat-ed* into *ate*). Finally here's the tree for a sentence with an auxiliary:

51) Shannon has eaten.

52)

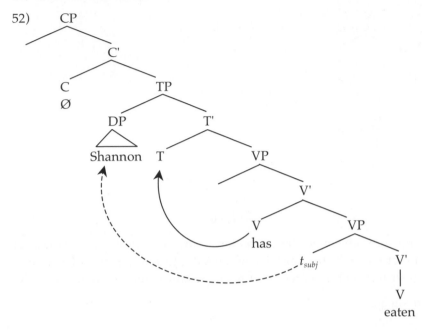

Here, because there is no modal in T and no suffix in T, the auxiliary *have* raises to T.

4.2 Affix-hopping

This analysis of multiple auxiliary constructions brings to light another property of English. Consider the shape of the verb that follows each of most common usages of the auxiliaries. When a verb follows a modal (category T with no lowering), it takes the same form as it would in a non-finite context (i.e., after *to*). We call this form the **base** form.

53) Shannon should *eat*. (cf. I want to *eat*.)   *modal*

When the verb follows the auxiliary *have* in its perfective usage (that is, when it marks that an event has a clear end-point), then the verb must appear in it's **past participle** form. This is usually marked with the *-en* or *-ed* suffix, although there are many verbs that have irregular participial forms. Be careful not to mix up the *-ed* suffix here with the past tense suffix; they are homophonous but they mean different things. To avoid this confusion we will indicate the past participle with *-en*.

54) Shannon has eaten.   *perfective*

When the verb is indication that the action has a portion that is on-going, we use the ***progressive*** form (this is sometimes also called a gerund, and the aspect is sometimes called imperfect).

55) Shannon is eating.   *progressive*

Finally, we have the form of the verb that is used for the passive voice. We'll look at the passive in more detail in later in chapter 10. Like the perfective, the passive uses the past participle, but follows the verb *be*:

56) The bread was eaten.   *passive*

For each English type of inflection, we have a distinct set of verbal forms. The suffix on the verb and the auxiliary together determine the meaning of the expression. When we have a tensed main verb (that is, a simple past or simple present), then the verb bears the appropriate tense morphology (*-s*, *-d*, or *-Ø*). When a modal (category T) such as *can* or *will* appears, then there is no morphology on the verb. When you have a perfective structure, we pair the auxiliary *have* with an *-en* participle. The progressive is a pairing of the verb *be* with an *-ing* progressive form. Finally the passive is a pairing of the verb *be* with an *-en* participle. This is summarized in the following chart.

57) a)   Simple Past and Present   V+*ed* / V+*s* / V+Ø
    b)   Modal   modal V
    c)   Perfective   *have* V+*en*
    d)   Progressive   *be* V+*ing*
    e)   Passive   *be* V+*en*

Notice what happens when we combine these patterns, the information about aspect and voice gets distributed in a systematic way:

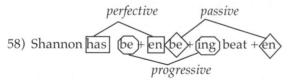

58) Shannon has be + en be + ing beat +en

We have a pattern of interleaving here, where the suffix associated with each verbal inflection is actually one verb or auxiliary down from the auxiliary that is associated with it. Chomsky, in what is perhaps his most famous book, (*Syntactic Structures* 1957) provided an account of this phenomenon known as Affix-hopping. The analysis we provide here, in terms of the affix lowering transformation we already have, is a modified version of Chomsky's.

Observe that the meaning "passive" cannot be described by the verb *be* alone, since *be* is found in both passives and progressives, and it cannot be described by just the suffix *-en*, since that is associated with both passives and perfectives. The notion of "passive" is only encoded when both the *be* and the *-en* suffix are present. Conversely, the meaning of *be* in isolation isn't clear as it can be found with multiple inflection types. One way of accounting for this is by having special lexical items that are syntactically decomposable (that is, they can be split into two different syntactic units). We can encode these as follows:

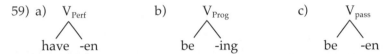

59) a) V_{Perf} b) V_{Prog} c) V_{pass}

     have -en   be   -ing   be   -en

Of course using these lexical items would result in the wrong word order. Chomsky's insight was that this contradiction could be resolved using a transformation: affix lowering (in combination with V→T movement). Let's start with a simple perfective sentence.

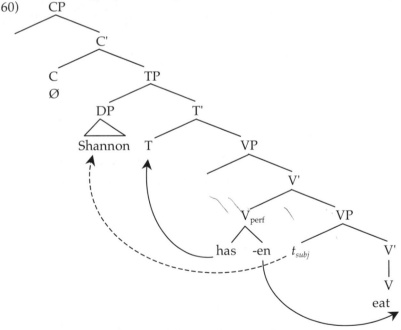

60)

In this tree, we have both verb (auxiliary) raising and affix lowering. The derivation of simple progressives and passive verb morphology is the same substituting *be+ing* and *be+en* in for the higher V. A more complicated example in (61):

61)

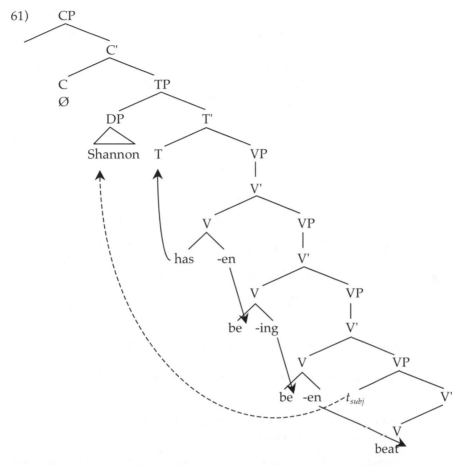

There are some things about these derivations which are still mysterious of course, For example, why lexical items that can be split this way exist and the precise motivation for the lowering the affixes (when they could, in principle, attach to the auxiliary they come with). Nevertheless this seems like a a good first approximation at capturing the complex behavior of English auxiliaries.

You now have enough information to try General Problem Set 9

5. SUMMARY

In this chapter we've looked at a range of phenomena (subject-aux inversion, word order differences among languages, and *do*-support) that support the basic notion that we need more than X-bar rules. We have introduced the transformational movement rules of V → T and T → C and the insertion rule of *do*-support to account for these phenomena.

APPENDIX: TESTS FOR DETERMINING IF A LANGUAGE HAS V → T OR AFFIX LOWERING

The following are tests that you can use to determine if a particular language shows verb raising or not. These tests work well on SVO languages, but don't work with SOV languages (such as Japanese).

A)   If the language shows Subj V *often* O order then it has V → T.

If the language shows Subj *often* V O order then it has affix lowering.

B)   If the language shows Subj V *not* O order then it has V → T.

If the language shows Subj *not* V O order then it has affix lowering.

C)   If main verbs undergo T → C movement, then the language has V → T.

IDEAS, RULES, AND CONSTRAINTS INTRODUCED IN THIS CHAPTER

i)   *Transformation*: A rule that takes an X-bar generated structure and changes it in restricted ways.

ii)   *D-structure*: The level of the derivation created by the base, and has had no transformations applied to it.

iii)   *S-structure*: The output of transformations. What you say.

iv)   *V → T movement*: Move the head V to the head T (motivated by morphology).

v)   *Verb Movement Parameter*: Option 1: all tensed verbs raise to T; Option 2: tensed auxiliaries raise to T and T lowers to tensed main verbs.

vi)   *The VP-internal Subject Hypothesis*: Subjects are generated in the specifier of VP.

vii)   *The Locality Constraint on Theta Role Assignment*: Theta roles are assigned within the projection of the head that assigns them (i.e., the VP or other predicate).

viii) $T \rightarrow C$ *Movement*: Move T to C, when there is a phonologically empty $\emptyset_{[+Q]}$ complementizer.

ix)   **Do-*insertion* (Do-*support*)**: When there is no other option for supporting inflectional affixes, insert the dummy verb *do* into T.

x)   *Stipulation*: Affix lowering is *blocked* by the presence of *not* in English.

xi)   *The Model*:

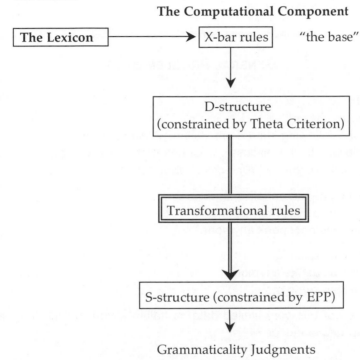

The Computational Component

The Lexicon   ⟶   X-bar rules   "the base"

D-structure (constrained by Theta Criterion)

Transformational rules

S-structure (constrained by EPP)

Grammaticality Judgments

FURTHER READING

Carnie, Andrew and Eithne Guilfoyle (2000) *The Syntax of Verb Initial Languages*. Oxford: Oxford University Press.

Emonds, Joseph (1980) Word order in Generative Grammar. *Journal of Linguistic Research* 1, 33–54.

Koopman, Hilda (1984) *The Syntax of Verbs: From Verb Movement Rules in the Kru Languages to Universal Grammar*. Dordrecht: Foris.

Koopman, Hilda and Dominique Sportiche (1991) The position of subjects. *Lingua* 85, 211–58.

Lightfoot, David and Norbert Hornstein (eds.) (1994) *Verb Movement.*
    Cambridge: Cambridge University Press.
McCloskey, James (1983) A VP in a VSO language. In Gerald Gazdar,
    Geoffrey Pullum, and Ivan Sag (eds.), *Order Concord and Constituency.*
    Foris, Dordrecht. pp. 9–55.
McCloskey, James (1991) Clause structure, ellipsis and proper government in
    Irish. *Lingua* 85, 259–302.
Ritter, Elizabeth (1988) A head movement approach to construct state noun
    phrases. *Linguistics* 26, 909–29.

GENERAL PROBLEM SETS

1. ITALIAN
[Data Analysis; Basic]
Consider the following data from Italian. Assume *non* is like French *ne*-
and is irrelevant to the discussion. Concentrate instead on the positioning
of the word *più*, 'anymore.' (Data from Belletti 1994.)

a) Gianni non ha più parlato.
    Gianni *non* has anymore spoken
    "Gianni does not speak anymore."

b) Gianni non parla più.
    Gianni *non* speaks anymore
    "Gianni speaks no more."

On the basis of this very limited data, is Italian a verb raising language or
an affix lowering language?

2. HAITIAN CREOLE VERB PLACEMENT
[Data Analysis; Basic]
Consider the following sentences from Haitian Creole. Is Creole a verb
raising language or an affix lowering language? Explain your answer.
(Data from DeGraff 2005.)

a) Bouki deja   konnen Boukinèt
    Bouki already knows   Boukinèt
    "Bouki already knows Boukinet."

b) Bouki pa konnen Boukinèt
    Bouki neg knows   Boukinèt
    "Bouki doesn't know Boukinèt."

3. FLAT VS. HIERARCHICAL STRUCTURE: BERBER

[Data Analysis; Advanced]

Consider the following data from Berber. Using your knowledge of binding theory, construct an argument that there is a VP in Berber, even though it is a VSO language. (Hint: When there is a VP, the subject c-commands the object, but when there is no VP, the two NPs asymmetrically c-command each other.) (Data From Choe 1987.)

a) Yutut   wrba$_k$ *ixfnns$_k$*
    hit   boy-NOM$_k$ himself$_k$
    "The boy$_k$ hit him$_k$"

b) *yutut   ixfnns$_k$ arba$_k$
    hit   himself$_k$ boy$_k$
    "himself$_k$ hit the boy$_k$"

4. WELSH

[Data Analysis; Basic]

Using the very limited data from Welsh below, construct an argument that Welsh has V to T movement. Do not worry about the alternation in the form of the word for "dragon," it is irrelevant to the answer to the question. (Data from Kroeger 1993.)

a) Gwelodd   Siôn   ddraig.
    saw.PAST   John   dragon
    "John saw a dragon."

b) Gwnaeth   Siôn   weld   draig.
    do.PAST   John   seen   dragon.GEN
    "John saw a dragon."

5. VP INTERNAL SUBJECTS: PRACTICE

[Application of Skills; Basic]

Using VP internal subjects, with movement to the specifier of TP where appropriate, and verb movement or affix lowering where appropriate, draw the trees for the following sentences:

a) Tiffany is not taking her syntax class until next year.
b) Christine likes wood furniture with a dark finish.
c) Les enfants   n'ont pas travaillé.   (French)
    the children have not worked
    "The children haven't worked."

d) Les enfants (ne)-travaillent pas.   (French)
    the children work   not
    "The children don't work."

6. AMERICAN VS. BRITISH ENGLISH VERB *HAVE*
[Critical Thinking; Basic/Intermediate]
English has two verbs *to have*. One is an auxiliary seen in sentences like (a):

a) I *have* never seen this movie.

The other indicates possession:

b) I never *have* a pen when I need it.

You will note from the position of the adverb *never* that the possessive verb *have* is a main verb, whereas the auxiliary *have* is raises to T.

Part 1: Consider the following data from American English. How does it support the idea that auxiliary *have* ends up in T, but possessive *have* is a main verb, and stays downstairs (i.e., has affix lowering applied)?

c) I have had a horrible day.
d) I have never had a pencil case like that!
e) Have you seen my backpack?
f) *Have you a pencil?

Part 2: Consider now the following sentence, which is grammatical in some varieties of British English:

g) Have you a pencil?

Does the possessive verb *have* in these dialects undergo V → T movement? How can you tell?

7. HEBREW CONSTRUCT STATE (N → D)
[Data Analysis; Intermediate]
Background: In the text above we considered two variations on head movement: V → T, and T → C. In an influential article in 1988, Ritter proposed that head movement might also apply inside DPs. More particularly she proposed that in many Semitic languages there is a rule of N → D movement. This applies in a possessive construction called the construct state. (Based on the analysis of Ritter 1988, data from Borer 1999.)

a) beit   ha-more
    house the-teacher
    "the teacher's house"

In the construct state, the noun takes on a special form (the construct):

b)   *Free form*   bayit   "house"
     Construct   beit   "house"

Ritter proposes that the construct arises when the noun moves into the determiner. The construct morphology indicates that this noun is attached to the determiner. A tree for sentence (a) is given below. The possessor noun sits in the specifier of the NP, the possessed N head undergoes head movement to D, where it takes on the construct morphology:

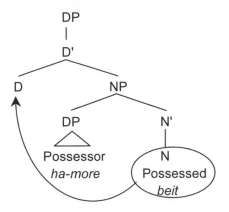

This results in the surface DP *[beit ha-more]*.

Part 1: Consider now the following evidence, how does this support Ritter's N → D analysis?

c)   *ha-beit ha-more
     the house the teacher
     "the house of the teacher"

Part 2: Now look at the positioning of adjectives. How does this support Ritter's analysis? Note in particular what noun the adjective modifies. (If you are having trouble with this question, trying drawing the tree of what the whole DP would look like before N → D movement applied.) M stands for "masculine", and F stands for feminine:

d)   more   kita   xadaS
     teacher-M   class-F new-M
     "a class's new teacher" or "the new teacher of a class"
          but: "*a new class's teacher" or "*the teacher of a new class"

8. ENGLISH[5]

[Data Analysis; Intermediate]
Consider the italicized noun phrases in the following sentences:

a) I ate *something spicy.*
b) *Someone tall* was looking for you.
c) I don't like *anyone smart.*
d) I will read *anything interesting.*

One analysis that has been proposed for noun phrases like the ones above involves generating elements like *some* and *any* as determiners, and generating elements *one* and *thing* as nouns (under N), and then doing head-to-head movement of the Ns up to D. The tree below illustrates this analysis:

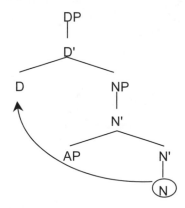

Give an argument in favor of this analysis, based on the order of elements within the noun phrase in general, and the order of elements in the noun phrases above.

9. ENGLISH TREES

[Application of Skills; Basic to Advanced]
Draw trees for the following English sentences; be sure to indicate all transformations with arrows.

a) I have always loved peanut butter.
b) I do not love peanut butter.
c) Martha often thinks Kim hates phonology.
d) Do you like peanut butter?
e) Have you always hated peanut butter?

---

[5] Thanks to Jila Ghomeshi for contributing this problem set.

f)   Are you always so obtuse?   *(Assume that AdjP can be a complement to T if it is a predicate, as in this case)*
g)   Will you bring your spouse?
h)   Has the food been eaten?
i)   Mike is always eating peanuts.

CHALLENGE PROBLEM SETS

CHALLENGE PROBLEM SET 1: FLOATING QUANTIFIERS
[Critical Thinking; Challenge]

In English, quantifiers normally appear before a DP. Up to this point in the book, we've been treating them as determiners. However, certain quantifiers can appear before determiners. One example is the quantifier *all*: *all the men*. In section 4 above, we argued that we can have stacked VPs. Let's extend that analysis and claim that we can have stacked DPs in certain circumstances (limited by the particular determiners involved). The structure of *all the men* is given below:

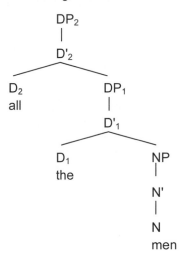

There are two DPs here (DP$_1$ and DP$_2$), in principle either of them could be moved to the specifier of TP. With this in mind provide an argument using the following data to argue that subjects in English start in the specifier of VP:

a)   All the men have gone.
b)   The men have all gone.

CHALLENGE PROBLEM SET 2: VERB MOVEMENT[6]

[Data Analysis; Challenge]

Based on the following data, do German and Persian exhibit V → T movement? Explain how you came to your answer.

German

a) Sprechen Sie Deutsch?
    speak   you German
    "Do you speak German?"

b) Ist er nach Hause gegangen?
    is he to   home gone
    "Has he gone home?"

c) Er sitzt nicht auf diesem Tisch.
    he sits not on   this   table
    "He does not sit on this table."

d) Sie soll nicht auf diesem Tisch sitzen.
    she must not on this   table sit
    "She must not sit on this table."

Persian

a) Rafti to   madrese?
    went you school
    "Did you go to school?"

b) Bâyad un biyâd?
    must   he come
    "Must he come?"

c) Man keyk na-poxtam.
    I   cake not-cooked
    "I did not bake cakes."

d) Un na-xâhad âmad.
    he not-will   come
    "He will not come."

---

[6] Thanks to Simin Karimi for contributing this data.

CHALLENGE PROBLEM SET 3: GERMANIC VERB SECOND
[Data Analysis and Critical Thinking; Challenge]
Background: Many of the languages of the Germanic language family exhibit what is known as **verb second** order (also known as V2). With V2, the main restriction on word order is that, in main clauses, the constituents may appear in essentially any order, as long as the verb is in the second position in the sentence. This is seen in the following data from German:

German (Vikner 1995)
a)   Die Kinder haben diesen Film gesehen.
      the children have this   film   seen
      "The children have seen this film."

b)   Diesen Film haben die Kinder gesehen.

One analysis of this phenomenon uses the specifier of CP as a "topic" position. The most topical constituent (the bit under discussion) is put in the specifier of CP (i.e., is moved there – we'll discuss this kind of movement in chapter 12). Whatever is in T then moves to the C head by T → C movement:

c)

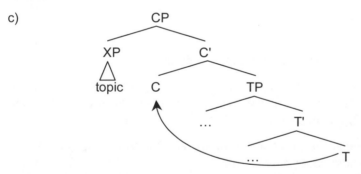

This puts T in second position. For the tree above and this problem set, assume that the VP and the TP have their heads on the right, but CP is left headed.

Part 1: Now consider the following data from embedded clauses in German.

d)   Er sagt [daß die Kinder diesen Film gesehen haben].
      He said that the children this   film   saw   have
      "He said that the children saw this film."

e)   *Er sagt [daß die Kinder haben diesen Film gesehen].

How does this data support the T → C analysis of V2? (Having trouble? Think about embedded *yes/no* questions in English.)

Part 2: Consider now the following sentence of German and compare it to the embedded clauses in part 1 above.

f)   Gestern sahen die Kinder den Film.
     Yesterday saw the children the film
     "The children saw the film yesterday."

Given what you now know about V2 and T → C movement in these languages, is German a V → T raising language or an affix lowering language?

Bonus: Is the data in part 1 above consistent with your answer? If not how might you make it consistent?

CHALLENGE PROBLEM SET 4: PROPER NAMES AND PRONOUNS
[Data Analysis; Challenge]
Consider the following data from English:

a)   Lucy
b)   *The Lucy
c)   *Smiths
d)   The Smiths
e)   Him
f)   *The him
g)   We linguists love a good debate over grammar.

Part 1: One possible analysis of proper names in English is that they involve head movement from an N position into a D position. How does the data in (a–d) above support this idea?

Part 2: Consider now the pronouns in (e–g). What category are they? N or D? Is there any evidence for movement?

CHALLENGE PROBLEM SET 5: ITALIAN N → D[7]
[Data Analysis and Critical Thinking; Challenge]
(You may want to do Challenge Question 4 before attempting this problem.)
In English, proper names cannot co-occur with determiners (e.g. *the John). However, in Italian proper names of human beings *can* occur with determiners as the following example shows. (The presence or absence of the determiner seems to be free or perhaps stylistically governed.)

---

[7] Jila Ghomeshi contributed this problem set based on data from Longobardi (1994).

a) i) Gianni mi   ha   telefonato.
        Gianni me   has   telephoned
        "Gianni called me up."

    ii) Il   Gianni   mi   ha   telefonato.
        the Gianni   me   has   telephoned
        "Gianni called me up."

Now, it has been argued that in the cases where the determiner does _not_ occur, the proper name has moved from N to D. Provide an argument to support this view, based on the following examples. (Note: for the purposes of this question treat possessive pronouns such as *my* as adjectives.)

b) i) Il   mio   Gianni ha   finalmente   telefonato.
        the   my   Gianni has   finally   telephoned

    ii) *Mio   Gianni   ha   finalmente   telefonato.
        my   Gianni   has   finally   telephoned

    iii) Gianni mio   ha   finalmente   telefonato.
         Gianni my   has   finally   telephoned

c) i) E'venuto   il   vecchio   Cameresi.
        came   the   older   Cameresi

    ii) *E'venuto   vecchio   Cameresi.
        came   older   Cameresi

    iii) E'venuto   Cameresi   vecchio.
         came   Cameresi   older

d) i) L' antica   Roma
        the ancient   Rome
        "Ancient Rome"

    ii) *Antica   Roma
        ancient   Rome

    iii) Roma   antica
         Rome   ancien

chapter 10

DP Movement

0. INTRODUCTION

In the last chapter, we looked at how certain basic word order facts could not be generated by X-bar theory alone. Instead, we saw that we need another rule type: the transformation. Transformations take X-bar trees and move elements around in them. The kind of transformation we looked at there moved heads into other heads. In this chapter, we are going to look at transformations that move NPs and DPs. (For the sake of convenience, I'm going to use NP to mean either NP or DP. Nothing turns on this usage. We could equally call the phenomenon DP-movement.)

Unlike head-to-head movement, where movement is motivated by word orders that cannot be generated using X-bar theory, the movement described here frequently takes X-bar generated trees and turns them into other acceptable X-bar generated trees. What motivates the movement is not a failure of X-bar theory, but instead the fact that certain DPs can appear in positions we don't expect from a thematic (theta role) perspective.

1. A PUZZLE FOR THE THEORY OF THETA ROLES

Try to sketch out the theta grid for the verb *to leave*. *Leave* requires one obligatory argument: an agent:

1) *leave*

Agent
DP
i

This can be seen from the following paradigm.

2) a) Bradley$_i$ left.
    b) Stacy$_i$ left Tucson.
    c) Slavko$_i$ left his wife.
    d) *It left. (where *it* is a dummy pronoun, not a thing)

The only obligatory argument for the verb *leave* is the agent, which is an external (subject) argument. Other arguments are possible (as in 2b and c) but not required. Now, note the following thing about the obligatory agent theta role. The agent role must be assigned to an argument *within the clause* that contains *leave*:

3) a) *[I want Bradley$_i$ [that left]].
    b) *John$_i$ thinks [that left].

When you try to assign the theta role to a DP that is outside the clause (such as the object *Bradley* or *John* in (3)) you get a stunningly ungrammatical sentence. We already have an explanation for this fact: in the last chapter we posited the following constraint:

4) *The Locality Constraint on Theta Role Assignment*
    Theta roles are assigned within the projection of the head that assigns them (i.e., the VP or other predicate).

This constraint requires that the DP getting the theta role be local to the predicate that assigns it. In the sentences in (3) the DP is actually in a different clause than the predicate that assigns it, so (4) predicts them to be ungrammatical.
     Now, look at the following sentence:

5) [John$_i$ is likely [to leave]].

John here is the agent of *leaving*, but the DP *John* appears in the main clause, far away from its predicate. Even more surprising is the fact that there seems to be no subject of the embedded clause. This is in direct violation of (4). The solution to this problem is simple: there is a transformation that takes the DP *John* and moves it from the lower clause to the higher clause.
     Let's spell this out in more detail. The theta grid for *is likely* includes only one argument: the embedded clause. This is seen in the fact that it can appear as the sole theta marked argument:

6) a)   [[That John will leave]ⱼ is likely].
    b)   It is likely [that John will leave]ⱼ.
    c)   *is likely*

Proposition
CP
j

Predicates Like *Is Likely*

In this chapter we're going to look at a number of predicates that consist of the auxiliary *be* and an adjective such as *likely* or *obvious*, as in *It is likely that Daphne like crème fraiche*. A few words are in order on how to tree this structure. In the last chapter, we argued that auxiliaries like *is* are generated in a V and then raise to the T node. The adjective *likely* (this is an adjective even though it ends in *-ly*, as only other adjectives, like *obvious, eager, easy*. etc., can appear in this position) is the complement of this verb. These adjectival predicates typically take a CP as a complement. We can tree these forms as below. We'll revise this slightly in chapter 14.

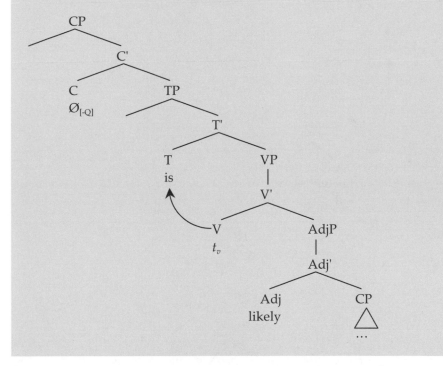

If this is the case, then in sentence (5), *John* is not receiving its theta role from *is likely*. This should be obvious from the meaning of the sentence as well.

There is nothing about *John* that *is likely*, instead it is what *John* is doing (his leaving) that *is likely*. The sentence is a clear violation of the locality condition on theta role assignment in its surface form. In chapter 8, we argued that the theta criterion applies before the transformation of expletive insertion occurs. Translated into our new terminology, this means that the theta criterion holds of D-structure. This means that <u>theta role assignment must also happen before all transformations.</u> We can arrange for *John*'s theta role to be assigned clause internally, at D-structure. The D-structure of the sentence would then look like (7) (Theta marking is indicated with a dotted large arrow):

7)

The subject DP is generated in the specifier of the embedded VP where it is assigned the agent theta role. How then do we derive the surface order? We need a transformation that moves this DP to the specifier of the main clause TP. This transformation is called **DP movement**:

8) *DP movement*
    Move a DP to a specifier position.

Notice that in the D-structure tree in (7) the specifier of the higher clause's TP is unoccupied. We can thus move the DP *John* into that position resulting in the tree in (9). (Note: the movement stops off in the specifier of the embedded TP and then moves on to the higher TP; we'll discuss why this happens in two hops shortly.)

9)

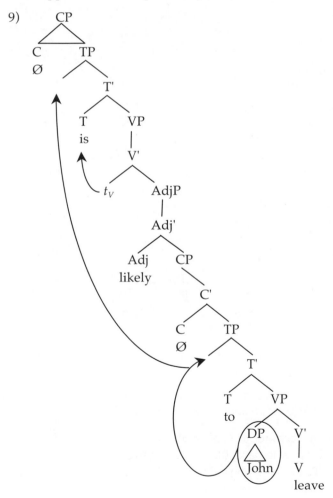

This particular instance of DP movement is frequently called *raising*, because you are raising the DP from the lower clause to the higher. The surface structure of this tree looks like (10) where there is a trace (marked *t*) left in each position that the DP has occupied.

10)

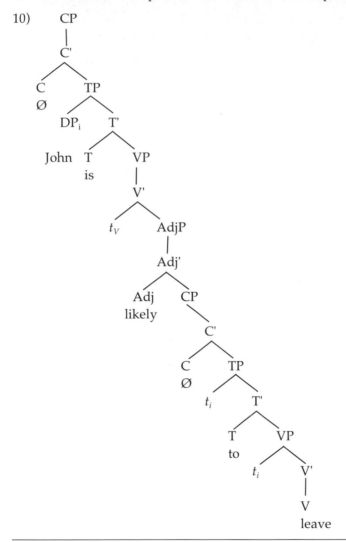

You now have enough information to try General Problem Set 1

As we stated in the last chapter, transformations are very powerful tools, and we want to limit their use. In particular we want to ensure that they only apply when required. Transformations thus need motivations or triggers. Look at the sentences in (11).

11) a) [That John will leave] is likely.
    b) It is likely that John will leave.

Recall back to the chapter on the lexicon, the presence of the theta-role-less *it* in (b) is forced by the Extended Projection Principle (EPP) – the requirement that the specifier of TP be filled by something (i.e., the requirement that there is a subject in every sentence). We might speculate then that the absence of a subject is the trigger for DP movement. The DP moves to the TP to satisfy the EPP. Since we have two TPs this applies twice. Ⓐ The DP moves from its theta position in the specifier of the embedded VP to the lower TP to satisfy this TP's EPP requirement. Then it moves on to the higher TP to satisfy its requirements Ⓑ.

12)

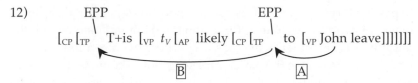

This explanation seems to work at least partially well. And we'll adopt it for theory-internal reasons to motivate the movement to the embedded specifier at the least. In section 3, we revisit this question and see that the EPP is only a partly satisfactory motivation for DP movement, and will posit an approach using "Case." First, however, let's look at the other main situation that involves DP movement: Passives.

2. PASSIVES

The sentence given in (13) is what is called an ***active*** sentence in traditional grammar:

13) The policeman kissed the puppy.   *Active*

The sentence given in (14) by contrast is what is called a ***passive***:

14) The puppy was kissed by the policeman.   *Passive*

These two sentences don't mean exactly the same thing. The first one is a sentence about a policeman (*the policeman* is the topic of the sentence); by contrast (14) is a sentence about a puppy (*the puppy* is the topic). However, they do describe the same basic event in the world with the same basic participants: there is some kissing going on, and the kisser (agent) is *the policeman* and the kissee (theme) is *the puppy*. At least on the surface then, these two sentences seem to involve the same thematic information.

On closer examination however, things change. Notice that in the passive sentence, the agent is represented by an optional prepositional phrase headed by *by*. This is an adjunct; as discussed in the chapter on the lexicon, adjuncts are not included in the basic theta grid and are not subject to the theta criterion. If the agent here is an adjunct and not subject to the theta criterion it should be optional. This is indeed the case:

15) The puppy was kissed.

It thus seems that passives and actives have different thematic properties. Actives have an agent and a theme, whereas passives lack the agentive theta role in their theta grids.

The explanation for this is not syntactic, instead it is a morphological issue. The passive form of a verb takes special morphology. In English, there are two main passive suffixes. One is (unfortunately) homophonous with the past tense suffix *-ed*. The other is the *-en* suffix. These two are allomorphs of each other. We will use *-en* as the basic form, so as not to confuse the passive morpheme with the past tense. There is a simple morphological operation that derives a passive verb from an active one:

16) kiss+en → kissed, beat+en → beaten, etc.

This morphological operation doesn't only affect the outward pronunciation of the word, it also affects the meaning. More particularly it affects the theta grid of the verb. Whenever the *-en* suffix is present, there is no DP. One way of thinking of this is that the *-en* absorbs (or is itself assigned) the agent role.[1]

17) a)   *kiss*

Agent	Theme
DP	DP

b)   *kiss+en (→ kissed)*

Agent	Theme
DP	DP
-en	

Now, let's look at the word order in the passive and active. In the active, the theme argument appears in object position; in the passive it appears in the subject position. One possible analysis of this is to claim that the theme is

---

[1] This technically is a violation of our locality constraint as the *-en* is introduced by a different V than its theta assigner. For the moment we'll simply assume that any VP inside a clause counts as the domain for theta role assignment for that main verb in that clause.

generated in object position in both actives and passives, but then is moved to subject position in passives.

Here is a sample derivation. The D-structure of the passive sentence looks like (18). The dotted arrows in this tree represent theta (θ) assignment, not movement. Because *-en* absorbs the agent role, there is only one DP in this sentence (*the puppy*), the one that gets the theme role. Even if there is a *by* phrase (e.g., *by the policeman*) it does not get its theta role from the verb, it is an adjunct, and adjuncts are never included in theta grids. The theme is the internal argument (i.e., it is not underlined in the theta grid), so it does not appear in the specifier of the VP, it must appear as the complement, like other internal theta roles .

18)

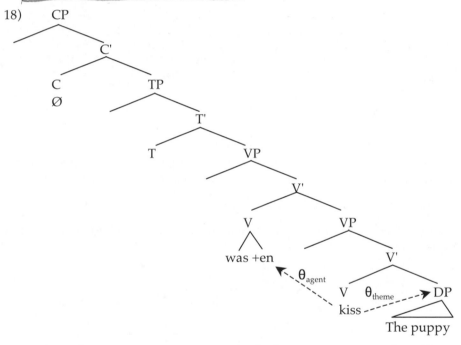

Now, like the raising sentences we looked at in section 1, the EPP is not satisfied here. There is nothing in the specifier of TP. The surface order of the passive can then be derived by DP movement (and head movement of the auxiliary and lowering of the affix).

19)

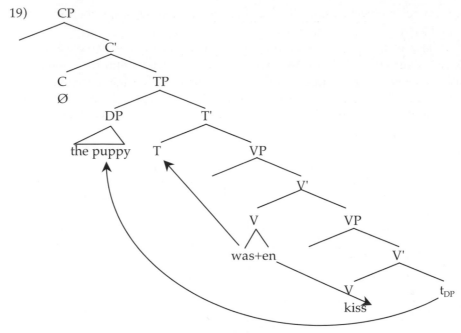

The DP *the puppy* moves to satisfy the EPP.

As mentioned above, passives often also occur with what appears to be the original external argument in a prepositional phrase marked with *by*.

20) The puppy was kissed by the policeman

We treat these *by*-phrases as optional adjuncts. We draw these *by*-phrases in by adjoining them to V':

21)

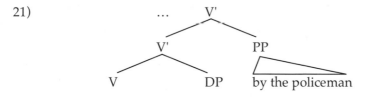

You now have enough information to try General Problem Set 2. You can also try Challenge Problem Sets 1 & 2

Movement or Underlying External Theme?

One might ask why it isn't simpler to say that the passive morpheme just deletes the agent and makes the theme an external argument in the theta grid.

i)

Agent	Theme	→	Theme
DP	DP		DP

Then the D-structure of the sentence will put the theme into the subject position right from the start with no movement. This is impossible, however, if you look at passives of sentences that take clausal complements. Take the active sentence in (ii):

ii)   Wilma considers [Fredrick to be foolish].

In this sentence, *Wilma* is the experiencer of *consider*, and *Fredrick* is the external theta role of the predicate *is foolish*. When *consider* is made into a passive, the subject of the lower clause raises to become the subject of the main clause:

iii) Fredrick$_i$ is considered t_i to be foolish.

Notice that *Fredrick* is never theta-marked by the verb *consider*. As such there is no way to make it the external argument like in (i). Because of cases like (iii), the movement account is preferred.

3. CASE

Up until now, we've motivated the movement of DPs using the EPP. In this section, we look at some data that shows that we might need an additional mechanism to account for movement.

Let's start with raising: as we saw in the last chapter, one way to satisfy the EPP is by inserting an expletive. For some reason this option isn't available in raising environments:

22) *It is likely John to leave.   (cf. *It is likely that John left*)

Nor does it explain why *only* the subject DP of an embedded clause can satisfy the EPP; object DP may not move to satisfy this requirement:

23) *Bill$_i$ is likely John to hit t_i.

The same kind of mystery appears in passives. It isn't clear why it isn't simply permissible to satisfy the EPP by inserting an expletive:

24) *It was kissed the puppy.[2]

Our theory predicts that such sentences should be acceptable. In order to explain why they are not, we are going to have to add a new theoretical tool: *Case*.

   In many languages, nouns bearing various grammatical relations take special forms. For example, in Japanese, subjects are marked with the suffix *-ga*, objects are marked with *-o* and indirect objects and certain adjuncts with *-ni*:

25) Asako-ga   ronbun-o   kai-ta.
    Asako-NOM   article-ACC   wrote-PAST
    "Asako wrote the article."

26) Etsuko-ga   heya-ni   haitte-kita.
    Etsuko-NOM   room-DAT   in-came
    "Etsuko came into the room."

These suffixes represent *grammatical relations* (see chapter 4). The three most important grammatical relations are *subject, object*, and *indirect object*. Notice that these are *not* the same as thematic relations. Thematic relations represent meaning. Grammatical relations represent how a DP is functioning in the sentence syntactically. The morphology associated with grammatical relations is called *case*. The two cases we will be primarily concerned with here are the *nominative case*, which is found with subjects, and the *accusative case*, found with objects.

   English is a morphologically poor language. In sentences with full DPs, there is no obvious case marking. Grammatical relations are represented by the position of the noun in the sentence:

27) a)   Jennifer swatted Steve.
    b)   Steve swatted Jennifer.

There is no difference in form between *Jennifer* in (27a), where the DP is functioning as a subject, and (27b), where it is functioning as an object. With pronouns, by contrast, there is a clear morphological difference, as we observed in chapter 1.

---

[2] This sentence becomes grammatical if you put a big pause after *kissed*, but notice that in this circumstance, the *it* is not a dummy, but refers to the *puppy*.

28) a)   She swatted him.
    b)   He swatted her.

Most pronouns in English have different forms depending upon what case they are in:

29) *Nominative*   I   you   he   she   it   we   you   they
Objective *Accusative*   me   you   him   her   it   us   you   them

Can this be extended to full DPs? Well, consider the general poverty of English morphology. The first and second persons in the present tense form of verbs don't take any overt suffix:

30) a)   I walk.
    b)   You walk.   (cf. He/She/It walks. You walked.)

But one wouldn't want to claim that (30a and b) aren't inflected for tense. Semantically they are. These forms can only refer to the present, they can't refer to the past or the future. We are thus forced to claim that there is an unpronounced or null present tense morpheme in English. It seems reasonable to claim that if there are null tense suffixes, there are also null case suffixes in English. Indeed, in the system we are proposing here all nouns get case – we just don't see it overtly in the pronounced morphology. This is called **abstract Case**. (Abstract Case normally has a capital C to distinguish it from morphological case.)

   Case, then, is a general property of Language. Furthermore it seems to be associated with a syntactic phenomenon – the grammatical function (relations) of DPs. If it is indeed a syntactic property, then it should have a structural trigger. In the case theory of Chomsky (1981), DPs are given Case if and only if they appear in specific positions in the sentence. In particular, nominative case is assigned in the specifier of finite T, and accusative case is assigned as a sister to the verb (prepositions also assign what is often called "Prepositional case" to their complement DP): [3]

31)   NOMinative case   Specifier of finite T
        ACCusative case   Sister to transitive V
        PREPositional case   Assigned by a preposition

   Case serves as our motivation for DP movement. You can think of Case as being like a driver's license. You can't drive without a license, and you can only get a license at the Department of Motor Vehicles. So you have to

---

[3] This is an almost ridiculous oversimplification. There are many prepositional cases (datives, locatives, ablatives, jussives, etc.). We abstract away from this here. We are also ignoring the genitive case normally associated with possessive constructions.

go there to get the license. A DP needs a license to surface in the sentence, and it can only get a license (Case) in specific positions. If it isn't in one of those positions, it must move to get Case. A DP without Case can't drive. This is called the *Case filter*:

32) *The Case filter*
     All DPs must be marked with a Case.
     If a DP doesn't get Case the derivation will crash.

One standard way of implementing the Case filter is by using a mechanism known as feature checking. This is based on a notion taken from phonology. The idea is that words are composed of atomic features. A word like *he* is composed of features representing its person, its number, its gender etc. We can represent these features in a matrix:

33) *he*
$$\begin{bmatrix} \text{masculine} \\ \text{3rd person} \\ \text{singular} \\ \text{nominative} \end{bmatrix}$$

Similarly, we will claim that Case assigners like T have a feature matrix:

34) T (*is*)
$$\begin{bmatrix} \text{present} \\ \text{3rd person} \\ \text{singular} \\ \text{nominative} \end{bmatrix}$$

You'll notice that both of these feature matrices have a feature [nominative]. The Case filter becomes a requirement that a noun like *he* be close enough to a Case assigner like *is*, to check that the noun has the right features. The noun must be close to its Case assigner:

35)   ...   *Nominative Case*

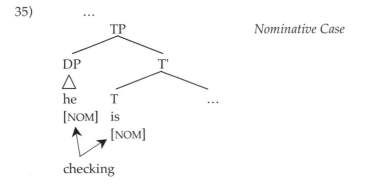

36)   *Accusative Case*

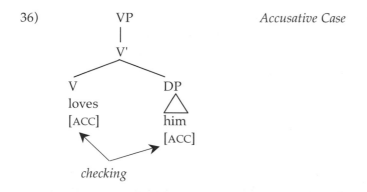

checking

Ergative/Absolutive Languages

In this book, we are looking exclusively at languages that take nominative and accusative cases. These are a fairly common kind of language in the western hemisphere. In nominative/accusative languages, the same case is assigned to the subjects of transitives and the subjects of intransitives (nominative case); a different case (accusative) is assigned to the objects of intransitives.

i)   *Nom/Acc languages*

	Nom	Acc
Trans	Subject	Object
Intrans	Subject	

However, there is a huge class of languages that does not use this case pattern, including many Polynesian, Australian, and Central American languages. These languages, called "Ergative/Absolutive" languages, mark the object of transitives and the subject of intransitives using the same case (absolutive); subjects of transitives are marked with a different case: ergative.

ii)   *Erg/Abs languages*

	Erg	Abs
Trans	Subject	Object
Intrans		Subject

From the perspective of structural case theory, these languages are a mystery and the subject of great debate. They don't fit the theory presented here. Even more mysterious are those languages that use *both* Nom/Acc and Erg/Abs case systems (under different circumstances). This is a topic of a lot of current research in syntax now.

37)   PP   *Prepositional Case*

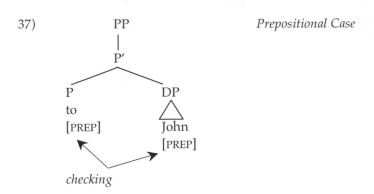

checking

If the noun and the Case assigner are not local (that is, the noun is not in the specifier or complement of the Case assigner), then the feature won't be checked and the Case filter violated. We'll use this notion of locality in feature checking again in chapter 11, when we look at *wh*-movement.

You now have enough information to try General Problem Set 3

---

4. RAISING: REPRISE

Let's now return to the raising sentences we were looking at in section 1, and we'll expand the paradigm to include the following:

38) a) It is likely that Patrick left.
   b) That Patrick left is likely.
   c) *Patrick is likely that t_i left.
   d) *It is likely Patrick to leave.
   e) *Patrick to leave is likely.
   f) Patrick is likely t_i to leave.

Sentences (38a–c) involve a tensed (finite) embedded clause. Sentence (38a) shows that one can satisfy the EPP with an expletive, provided the embedded clause is finite. Sentence (38d) shows that an expletive won't suffice with a non-finite embedded clause. Sentence (38b) shows that a tensed clause can satisfy the EPP, but a non-finite one cannot (38e). Finally, we see that raising is possible with a non-finite clause (38f) but not a finite one (38c). This is quite a complicated set of facts, but it turns out that the distribution turns on a single issue. Above we saw that DPs are assigned nominative Case only in the specifier of finite T. (In other words, non-finite T does not have a [NOM] feature, whereas finite T does.) Sentences (38d–f) are *non-finite*. This means that the DP *Patrick* cannot get nominative Case in the specifier of the embedded clause. The ungrammaticality of (38d and e) are now explained: *Patrick* is not getting Case, so the sentence violates the Case filter. In sentence (38f) by contrast, the DP has moved to the specifier of the *finite* main clause T; it can receive Case here, so the sentence is grammatical:

39)

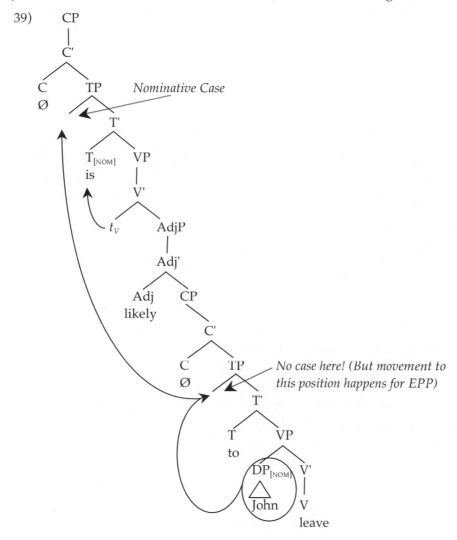

John starts out where it gets its theta role (the specifier of VP), then it moves to the specifier of the embedded TP, where it satisfies the EPP for that TP. But this is not a case position, the T *to* shows that the clause is non-finite. So the DP moves from this position to the specifier of the higher TP, where it can check its nominative Case. This is a pattern that is repeated over and over again. DPs always move from positions where they can't check Case (but where they get a theta role) to positions where they get Case.

The distribution of raising in sentences (39a–c) is also now explained. These clauses have an embedded finite T. As such the DP *Patrick* can get nominative Case in the specifier of embedded T. It does not have to move. If it did move, it would move without reason, as it already has Case.

You now have enough information to try General Problem Set 4 and Challenge Problem Set 3

---

5. PASSIVES: REPRISE

Case theory also allows an explanation of passive constructions. However, this requires an additional piece of machinery to be added to the passive morphology. Only active transitive verbs can assign accusative Case:

40) He kissed her.

Passive verbs cannot:

41) a)   She was kissed.
    b)   *She was kissed him.[4]
    c)   *It was kissed her.   (where *it* is an expletive)

It thus appears that not only does the passive suffix absorb the verb's external theta role, it also absorbs the verb's ability to assign accusative Case. This is a rough version of what is called **Burzio's Generalization** (after Burzio 1986): *A predicate that assigns no external theta role cannot assign accusative Case.* The passive morpheme thus has the following two functions:

42) The passive morpheme *-en*
    a)   absorbs a verb's external theta role.
    b)   checks a verb's [ACC] Case feature.

Recall that the *-en* suffix lowers and attaches to the V. This movement also creates a local configuration. The verb and the *-en* suffix are adjacent. In fact, the *-en* is closer to the verb than the DP.

---

[4] This sentence is also a violation of the theta criterion.

43)   ...

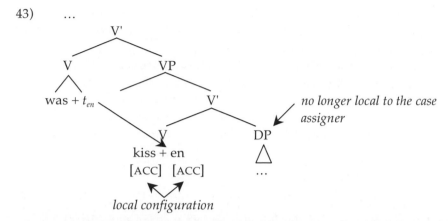

Since the *-en* absorbs the accusative case, there is now no case for the DP, so it must move to get Case. With this in mind, reconsider the passive sentence we looked at in section 2:

44)

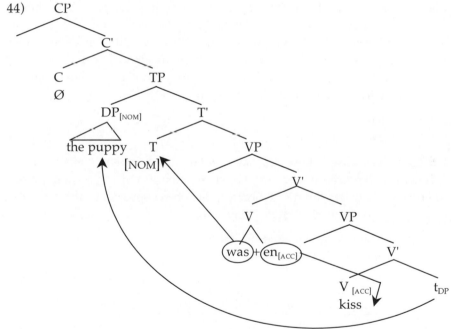

The passive morphology has conspired to absorb both the accusative case and the external theta role. This means that there is no DP in the specifier of the finite T. There is a Case position open so the theme DP can move to the specifier of TP. Now we have the trigger for DP movement in passives: A DP moves to get Case from its Caseless theta position to the nominative

Case assigning specifier of TP. Notice that this DP now moves for two reasons. First it moves to satisfy the EPP, but it also must move to get Case.

Inherently Passive Verbs: Unaccusatives

One of the interesting discoveries of the 1980s was the fact that there is a set of verbs in many languages that are inherently passive. That is they have only an internal argument, and they don't assign accusative case. These are called *unaccusative verbs* (or less commonly *ergative verbs*). Compare the two sentences in (i) and (ii)

i)   Stacy danced at the palace.
ii) Stacy arrived at the palace.

The first sentence is a regular intransitive (often called *unergative*) where *Stacy* bears an external agent theta role. The sentence in (ii) by contrast has no external theta role. *Stacy* is a theme that originates in the object position of the sentence. *Stacy* is then raised to subject position to satisfy the Case filter, just like a passive. These predicates are passive without having any passive morphology. The arguments for this are well beyond the scope of this textbook. But note the following two differences between the predicates in (i) and (ii). The unergative predicate in (i) can optionally take a direct object. Unaccusative predicates cannot (something that is predicted, if their subject is underlyingly an object):

iii) Stacy danced a jig.
iv) *Stacy arrived a letter.

Unaccusatives also allow an alternative word order (called **there** *inversion*) where the underlying object remains in object position. Since unergative subjects aren't generated in object position, they aren't allowed to appear there with *there* inversion.

v)   *There danced three men at the palace.
vi) ?There arrived three men at the palace.

You now have enough information to try General Problem Set 5

---

6. CLOSING UP A LOOSE END

In the last chapter, we were forced to argue (on the basis of evidence from the VSO language Irish) that subject DPs were generated in the specifier of VP not TP.

45)   TP   *Irish*

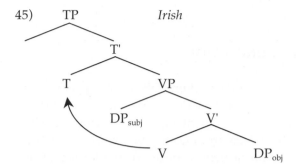

The problem, then, was why subject DPs appear before T in languages like English. The solution should now be clear: All subject DPs move to the specifier of finite T to get Case. In actives and intransitives, this is from the specifier of VP. In passives, the movement is from the underlying object position.

46)   TP   *English*

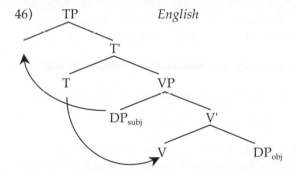

The difference between SVO languages like English and VSO languages is in where nominative Case is assigned. In SVO languages, nominative Case is assigned in the specifier of finite T. In VSO languages, nominative Case is assigned when the DP is immediately c-commanded by finite T (which allows it to remain inside VP).

46)   TP   ─ Nominative Case position for English

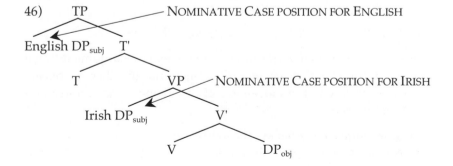

You now have enough information to try General Problem Sets 6–9

7. CONCLUSION

In this chapter, we've looked at situations where DPs don't appear in the positions we expect them to (given our knowledge of theta theory). We have argued that these sentences involve movement of DPs to various specifier positions. The motivation for this comes from Case. The Case filter requires all DPs to check a Case in a specific structural position. We looked at two situations where DPs don't get Case in their D-structure position. In raising structures, a DP is in the specifier of an embedded clause with non-finite T. In this position, it can't receive Case so it raises to the specifier of the finite T in the higher clause. We also looked at passive structures. The passive morpheme does two things: it takes the role of external argument and absorbs the verb's ability to assign accusative Case. This results in a structure where there is no subject DP, and the object cannot receive Case in its base position. The DP must move to the specifier of T to get Case.

IDEAS, RULES, AND CONSTRAINTS INTRODUCED IN THIS CHAPTER

i)   *DP Movement*: Move a DP to a specifier position.

ii)   *Raising*: A specific instance of DP movement. The DP moves from the specifier of an embedded non-finite T to the specifier of a finite T in the main clause where it can get Case.

iii)   *case (lower case c)*: The special form DPs get depending upon their place in the sentence.

iv)   *Case (capital C)*: The licensing that a DP requires: Nominative is found on subjects (specifier of finite T). Accusative is found on objects (complement to V).

v)   *The Case Filter*: All DPs must be marked with Case.

vi)   *Passives*: A particular verb form where the external argument (often the agent or experiencer) is suppressed and the theme appears in subject position. The movement of the theme is also an instance of DP movement.

vii)   *The Morphology of Passives*: The suffix *-en*:
a) absorbs a verb's external theta role
b) absorbs a verb's ability to assign accusative Case to its sister.

viii)   ***Burzio's Generalization***: The idea that if a verb does not assign an external argument (i.e., is passive or unaccusative), then it can't assign accusative case.

ix)   ***Unaccusatives***: Inherently passive verbs like *arrive*.

FURTHER READING

Baker, Mark, Kyle Johnson, and Ian Roberts (1989) Passive arguments raised. *Linguistic Inquiry* 20, 219–51.

Burzio, Luigi (1986) *Italian Syntax.* Dordrecht: Reidel.

Chomsky, Noam (1995) *The Minimalist Program.* Cambridge: MIT Press.

Jaeggli, Osvaldo (1986) Passive. *Linguistic Inquiry* 17, 587–622.

Perlmutter, David and Paul Postal (1984) The 1-Advancement Exclusiveness Law. In David Perlmutter and Carol Rosen (eds.), *Studies in Relational Grammar.* Chicago: University of Chicago Press. pp. 81–125.

Sportiche, Dominique (1988) A theory of floating quantifiers and its corollaries for constituent structure. *Linguistic Inquiry* 19, 425–49.

GENERAL PROBLEM SETS

1. HAITIAN CREOLE

[Data Analysis and Critical Thinking; Intermediate]

In the text, we suggested that DP movement leaves what is called a trace (*t*) at the D-structure position of the DP. In English, you can't hear this trace. Now consider the following data from Haitian Creole. (Data from Déprez 1992.)

a)   Sanble   Jan   pati.
     seems   John left
     "It seems that John left."

b)   Jan sanble li pati.
     John seems he leave
     "John seems he to have left."

c)   *Jan sanble pati.

Questions:

1)   How does this data support the idea that raising constructions involve movement from the lower clause to the higher clause, and the movement leaves a trace?

2) Is sentence (b) a violation of the theta criterion? How might we make
    sure that it isn't?

2. ARIZONA TEWA
[Data Analysis; Basic]
The following data is from Arizona Tewa (Data from Kroskrity 1985):

a) hẹ'i sen né'i 'enú mánk^{hw}ẹ́di.
    that man this boy 3.3.hit
    "That man hit this boy."

b) né'i 'enú hẹ'i sen-di   'ók^{hw}ẹ́di.
    This boy that man-DAT 3.PASS.hit
    "This boy was hit by that man."

c) na:bí k^{w}iyó   hẹ'i p'o   mánsunt'ó.
    my   woman that water 3.3.drink
    "My wife will drink that water."

d) hẹ'i p'o   nasunti.
    that water 3.PASS.drunk
    "That water was drunk."

1) Determine the X-bar parameter settings for Tewa.
2) Draw trees for (a) and (c). Assume Tewa is an affix lowering language.
3) Describe in your own words the differences between (a) and (b) and
    between (c) and (d)
4) Draw the trees of (b) and (d) showing all the movements.

3. PERSIAN ACCUSATIVE CASE[5]
[Data Analysis and Critical Thinking; Intermediate]
In the text above, we claimed that some verbs have an accusative feature
[ACC] that must get checked by a complement DP. In English, we only
see the realization of this feature on pronouns. This question focuses
on the [ACC] feature in Persian.

Background: Persian is an SOV language. There is no Case distinction
among Persian pronouns. For example, the pronoun *man* "I, me" doesn't
change whether it is a subject, object of a preposition or possessor
(see (a) below). (iii) shows that possessors are linked to head nouns
with a vowel glossed as EZ (for *Ezâfe*).

---

[5] Thanks to Jila Ghomeshi for contributing this problem set.

a) i) *Man*   ruznâme   xarid-am.
        I   newspaper bought-1SG
        "I bought a newspaper."

    ii) Simâ   az   *man*   ruznâme   xâst.
        Sima   from   me   newspaper wanted.3SG
        "Sima wanted a newspaper from me."

    iii) Ruznâme-ye   *man*   injâ-st.
         newspaper-EZ me   here-is
         "My newspaper is here."

Hypothesis: It looks like the clitic *-râ* (which is pronounced as *-o* or *-ro*, depending on whether the preceding word ends in a vowel or not) is the realization of the [ACC] feature based on examples like the following:

b) i) Man   jiân-o   didam.
        I   Jian-RÂ   saw.1SG
        "I saw Jian."

    ii) *Man   jiân   did-am.
        I   Jian   saw-1SG

c) i) Jiân   man-o   did.
        Jian   I-RÂ   saw.3SG
        "Jian saw me."

    ii) *Jiân   man   did.
        Jian   I   saw.3SG

d) i) Jiân in   ketâb-o   xarid.
        Jian this book-RÂ   bought.3SG
        "Jian bought this book."

    ii) *Jiân in   ketâb   xarid.
        Jian this book   bought.3SG

One possible analysis is that Persian verbs have an [ACC] feature that gets checked by *-râ*. That is, *-râ* contributes the [ACC] feature to the DP that can be used to check the feature of the verb.

The problem: Not all direct objects show up with *-râ*. Yet we don't want to say that the ones without *-râ* don't check the [ACC] feature of the verb.

e) i) Jiân   ye ketâb xund.
        Jian   a book   read.3SG
        "Jian read a book."

ii) Jiân   ketâb-o   xund.
    Jian   book-RÂ   read.3SG
    "Jian read the book."

f) i) Man   se-tâ   qalam   xarid-am.
        I   three   pen   bought-1SG
        "I bought three pens."

    ii) Man   se-tâ   qalam-o   xarid-am.
        I   three   pen-RÂ   bought-1SG
        "I bought the three pens."

g) i) Jiân   pirhan   xarid.
        Jian   shirt   bought.3SG
        "Jian bought a shirt."

    ii) Jiân   pirhan-o   xarid.
        Jian   shirt-RÂ   bought.3SG
        "Jian bought the shirt."

Suggest a solution to this problem.

4. TURKISH

[Data Analysis, Critical Thinking; Advanced]
In this chapter, we argued that the reason DPs raise from embedded clauses to main clauses is that they cannot get Case in the embedded clause. Consider the following data from Turkish. What problems does this cause for our theory? Is there a simple way to explain why Turkish nouns raise? (Data from Moore 1998.)

a) Biz süt   içiyoruz.
    we milk   drink
    "We are drinking milk."

b) Biz$_i$ sana [$_{CP}$ t$_i$ süt içtik] gibi göründük.
    We you-DAT   milk drank like appear
    "We appear to you [$_{CP}$ drunk milk]."

5. IMPERSONALS IN UKRAINIAN, KANNADA, AND IRISH

[Data Analysis; Intermediate]
(The Ukrainian and Kannada data are taken from Goodall 1993. The Ukrainian data originally comes from Sobin 1985. The Kannada data is originally from Cole and Sridhar 1976. The Irish data is slightly modified from Stenson 1989.)

Many languages contain a construction similar to the passive called *the impersonal passive*. Consider the following data from Ukrainian, Kannada, and Irish. Pay careful attention to the Case marking on the various nouns.

a) Cerkvu   bulo zbudovano v 1640 roc'i.   *Ukrainian*
    Church-ACC   was built   in 1640 year
    "The Church was built in the year 1640."

b) Rama-nannu   kollalayitu.   *Kannada*
    Ramma-ACC   kill.PASS
    "Rama was killed."

c) Buaileadh   iad   sa gcluife   deireanach. *Irish*
    beat.PAST.PASS   them.ACC   in the game last
    "They were beaten in the last game."

What is the difference between these impersonal passive constructions and more traditional passives of English? Suggest a parameter that will account for the difference between languages like Ukrainian, Kannada, and Irish and languages like English. (Hint: the parameter will have to do with the way the passive morphology works.)

6. ENGLISH
[Application of Skills; Basic to Advanced]
Draw the D-structure trees for the following sentences. Be explicit about what transformations derived the S-structure tree (if any). Recall that we have the following transformations: Expletive insertion, DP movement (both raising and passive), affix lowering, verb movement, T → C movement, and *do*-support/insertion. Annotate the D-structure tree with arrows to show the derivation of the S-structure.

a) Marie is likely to leave the store.
b) The money was hidden in the drawer.
c) Donny is likely to have been kissed by the puppy.
d) It seems that Sonny loves Cher.
e) Has the rice been eaten?

7. ENGLISH UNGRAMMATICAL SENTENCES
[Application of Skills; Basic to Intermediate]
Explain why the following sentences are ungrammatical. Some sentences may have more than one problem with them.

a)   *It seems Sonny to love Cher.
b)   *Bill was bitten the dog.
c)   *Donny is likely that left.

8. UNACCUSATIVES AND PASSIVES
[Critical Thinking; Advanced]
In a textbox above, we mentioned the existence of a class of verbs that are essentially inherently passive. These are called unaccusatives. A surprising property of unaccusative verbs is that they don't allow passivization.[6] (Data from Perlmutter and Postal 1984.)

a)   The Shah slept in a bed.
b)   The bed was slept in by the Shah.
c)   Dust fell on the bed.   *unaccusative*
d)   *The bed was fallen on by the dust. *unaccusative*

Similar effects are seen in the following Dutch sentences. Sentence (e) is not unaccusative (we call these "unergatives"), while sentence (f) is. Both these sentences are impersonal passives. English doesn't have this construction, so they are difficult to translate into English.

e)   In de zomer wordt er hier vaak gezwommen.
     "In the summer, there is swimming here."

f)   *In de zomer wordt er hier vaak verdronken.
     "In the summer, there is drowning here."

Your task is to figure out why passives of unaccusatives (like c, d, and f) are not allowed. The following data might help you:

g)   Bill was hit by the baseball.
h)   *Was been hit by Bill by the baseball. (passive of a passive)
i)   Bill gave Sue the book.
j)   Sue was given the book by Bill.
k)   *The book was been given by Bill by Sue. (passive of a passive)

---

[6] Strictly speaking, the data in (a–d) do not involve passivization, since the NP that is moved comes from inside a PP. The technical term for these constructions is pseudo-passivization. The differences between pseudo-passivization and passivization are not relevant to this problem set.

9. ICELANDIC QUIRKY CASE
[Data Analysis and Critical Thinking; Advanced]
In Icelandic, some verbs assign irregular case marking to particular arguments. For example, the verb *hjálpað* "help" assigns dative case to its theme argument. (Data from Zaenen, Maling, and Thráinsson 1985.)

a) Ég hjálpaði honum.
    I helped him-DAT
    "I helped him."

This kind of irregular case marking is called **quirky Case** and it seems to be linked to the theta grid of the particular predicate. The dative case is obligatorily linked with whatever noun takes the theme role:

hjálpað "help"

Agent	Theme
DP	DP
i	K

Dative Case

Now consider the following data from Icelandic DP movement constructions.

b) Honum$_k$ var hjálpað t_K.
    him-DAT was helped
    "He was helped."

c) Ég tel honum$_k$ [t_k hafa verið hjálpað t_k i prófinu].
    I believe him-DAT have been helped   in the-exam
    "I believe him [to have been helped in the exam]."

What problem does this cause for the theory of DP movement we have proposed above? Can you think of a solution? (A number of possibilities exist, be creative.)

CHALLENGE PROBLEM SETS

CHALLENGE PROBLEM SET 1: MIDDLES AND PASSIVES
[Critical Thinking; Challenge]
Middles are English constructions that are little bit like passives. An example of an active/middle pair is seen below:

a) I cut the soft bread.
b) The soft bread cuts easily.

In (b), the theme appears in the subject position. One analysis of this order has the theme undergoing DP movement to subject position.

Consider now the following triplet of sentences. The first sentence is called a middle, the second an active, and the third a causative.

c) The boat sank.   *middle*
d) The torpedo sank the boat.   *active*
e) The captain sank the boat (with a torpedo).   *causative*

Part 1: Describe the relationship between the active, middle, and causative in terms of their theta grids.

Part 2: Now consider the passives of sentences (c–e). Why should sentence (f) be ungrammatical, but (g) and (h) grammatical?

f) *Was sunk (by the boat).
    (also * It was sunk by the boat, where *it* is an expletive)
g) The boat was sunk by the torpedo.
h) The boat was sunk by the captain (with a torpedo).

CHALLENGE PROBLEM SET 2: PASSIVES AND DOUBLE OBJECTS
[Critical Thinking; Challenge]
(For more information on the phenomenon discussed in this problem set, see Larson 1988.) English has two constructions that surface with ditranstive verbs. One is called the prepositional construction, the other the double object construction:[7]

a) I sent a book to Louis.   *prepositional*
b) I sent Louis a book.   *double object*

It is possible to make passives out of these constructions. But some additional restrictions on how passives work are needed. Consider the following data and posit a restriction on DP movement in passives to account for the ill-formedness of the ungrammatical sentences. Pay careful attention to sentence (g).

---

[7] There is a great deal of literature that tries to derive the double object construction from the prepositional construction using NP movement (see for example Larson 1988). The relationship between the two constructions is not relevant to the question in this problem set, but is an interesting puzzle in and of itself.

c)   A book was sent to Louis.
d)   *Louis was sent a book to.
e)   *To Louis was sent a book.[8]
f)   Louis was sent a book.
g)   *A book was sent Louis.

CHALLENGE PROBLEM SET 3: TWO KINDS OF RAISING
[Critical Thinking; Challenge]
In the text, we proposed that subjects of non-finite clauses can raise to the subject position of finite clauses in sentences like (a):

a)   John$_i$ seems [t_i to have left].

This kind of raising is sometimes called **subject-to-subject raising**. Now consider the following sentence:

b)   Bill wants John to leave.

This sentence should be ungrammatical, because *to* is a non-finite T, so can't assign Case to *John*. One hypothesis that has been proposed to account for this says there is also a process of **subject-to-object raising**:

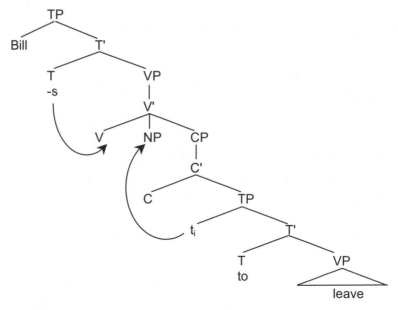

How does the following data support this analysis?

---

[8] This may be marginally acceptable in poetic or flowery speech. Assume for the purposes of this problem set that this is ungrammatical.

c) John wants Bill to leave.
d) John wants him to leave.
e) John believes him to have been at the game.
f) ?John$_i$ believes himself$_i$ to have been at the game.
g) *John$_i$ believes him$_i$ to have been at the game.
h) He is believed (by John) to have been at the game.

chapter 11

Wh-movement

0. INTRODUCTION

In chapter 10, we looked at DPs that were appearing in positions where they didn't get theta roles. Instead, the DP surfaced in a derived position. That is, they were moved from the position where they got a theta role to a position where they could get Case. The trigger for this movement was the requirement that DPs check their Case feature, as Case can only be assigned in specific structural positions. In this chapter, we turn to another kind of phrasal movement, one where DPs already have Case. DPs (and other phrases) can move for a different reason to form what are called **wh-*questions.***

There are several different kinds of questions, only two of which we are concerned with in this book. The first kind is the familiar *yes/no question* that we looked at in the chapter on head movement:

1)   a)   Are you going to eat that bagel?
     b)   Do you drink whisky?
     c)   Have you seen the spectrograph for that phoneme?

The answers to these questions cannot be other than *yes, no, maybe* or *I don't know.* Any other response sounds strange:

1') a') #Pizza/ ✓yes
    b') #Scotch/ ✓no
    c') #Syntactic tree/ ✓no

The other kind of question is called a *wh*-question. These questions take their name from the fact that the words that introduce them (mostly) begin with the letters <*wh*> in English: *who/whom*, *what*, *when*, *where*, *why*, *which*, and *how*. The responses to these kind of questions cannot be *yes* or *no*. Instead they must be informative phrases.

2) a) When did you do your syntax homework?   #yes / ✓yesterday
    b) What are you eating?   #no/ ✓a bagel
    c) How is Louise feeling?   #yes/ ✓much better

How these questions are formed is the focus of this chapter.

Who and *Whom*

In traditional prescriptive grammar, there are two *wh*-phrases that refer to people: *who* and *whom*. *Who* is used when the *wh*-phrase originates in subject position and gets nominative Case. *Whom* is the accusative version. In most spoken dialects of Canadian and American English this distinction no longer exists, and *who* is used in all environments. For the sake of clarity, I use *who(m)* to indicate that the *wh*-phrase originated in object position, but you should note that from a descriptive point of view *who* is perfectly acceptable in object position for most speakers today.

---

1. MOVEMENT IN *WH*-QUESTIONS

If you look closely at a statement and a related *wh*-question, you'll see that the *wh*-phrase appears in a position far away from the position where its theta role is assigned. Take for example:

3) a) Becky bought the syntax book.
    b) What did Becky buy?

The verb *buy* in English takes two theta roles, an external agent and an internal theme. In sentence (3a), *Becky* is the agent, and *the syntax book* is the theme. In sentence (3b) *Becky* is the agent and *what* is the theme. In the first sentence, the theme is the object of the verb, in the second the theme is at the beginning of the clause. The situation becomes even more mysterious when we look at sentences like (4):

4) What did Stacy say Becky bought?

In this sentence *what* is still the theme of *bought*, yet it appears way up at the beginning of the main clause. This would appear to be a violation of the locality constraint on theta role assignment introduced in chapter 9.

The situation becomes murkier still when we look at Case. Recall that accusative Case is assigned when a DP is the sister to a V:

5)   Matt [$_{VP}$ kissed her$_{ACC}$].

But in *wh*-questions the accusative form (like *whom*) is not a sister to V:

6)   Whom$_{ACC}$ did Matt kiss?

So it appears as if not only are these *wh*-phrases not in their theta positions, but they aren't in their Case positions either.

Given what we've seen in the previous two chapters, this looks like another case of movement – this one with different triggers again. Let's start with the issue of where *wh*-phrases move to. One position that we've had for a while, but have not yet used, is the specifier of CP. This is the place *wh*-phrases move to:

7)

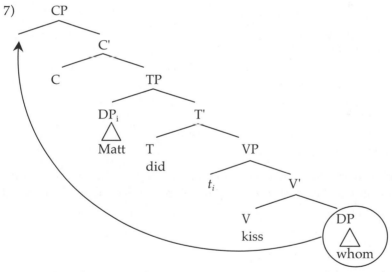

Notice that what moves here is an entire phrase. You can see this if you look at slightly more complex *wh*-questions:

8)   a)   [To whom] did Michael give the book?
     b)   [Which book] did Michael give to Millie?

When you move an entire phrase, it cannot be an instance of head-to-head movement (by definition), so this must be movement to a position other

than a head, in this case we have the empty specifier of CP. The element
that is moved can be a DP, a PP, or an AdvP.

The movement to the specifier of CP accounts for another fact about
the word order of *wh*-questions: they also involve T → C movement
(in main clauses):

9) a) Who(m) are you meeting?
    b) *Who(m) you are meeting?

The *wh*-phrase appears to the left of the auxiliary in C. This means that the
wh-phrase must raise to a position higher than C. The only position available
to us is the specifier of CP:

10)

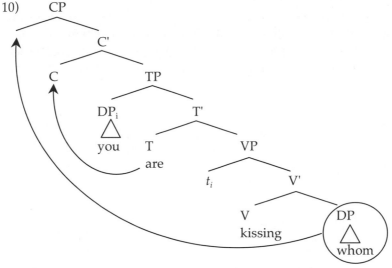

The fact that *wh*-movement is to the CP specifier position can also be
seen in languages that allow both a *wh*-phrase and an overt complementizer,
such as Irish:

11) Cad a^L tá sa   seomra?
    What C-*wh* is in-the room
    "What is in the room?"

In Irish, the *wh*-phrase *cad* "what" appears to the left of the complementizer
a^L, supporting the idea that the *wh*-phrase is in the specifier of CP, the only
position available to it. A similar fact is seen in Bavarian German
(Bayer 1984):

12) I woass ned wann dass da Xavea kummt.
    I know not when that the Xavea comes
    "I don't know when Xavea is coming."

In English the only thing allowed to appear in C is an inverted auxiliary, other complementizers are not:

13) a) *I asked what that she kissed?
    b) *I asked what whether she kissed?

This follows simply from the assumption that the only complementizer that is compatible with *wh*-movement in English is null. In other languages this complementizer has phonological content (e.g., Irish a^L or Bavarian German *dass*).

Let's now consider the possible motivations for *wh*-movement. In chapter 9, we triggered T $\rightarrow$ C movement with a [+Q] feature that was part of the complementizer. DP movement, in chapter 10, was triggered by a Case feature. We can do the same thing, here, for *wh*-questions, by proposing a feature that triggers *wh*-movement. Let's call this feature [+WH]. It resides in the C of a *wh*-sentence. In some languages (such as Irish), there are special forms of complementizers that represent these features:

14) [–Q, –WH] *go*
    [+Q, –WH] *an*
    [+Q, +WH] a^L

You get the *go* complementizer when the sentence is not a *yes/no* or *wh*-question. You get the *an* complementizer in *yes/no* questions and a^L in *wh*-questions. The form of the complementizer is dependent upon the features it contains (McCloskey 1979).

A *wh*-phrase moves to the specifier of CP to be near the [+WH] feature. Another way to phrase this is to say that *wh*-phrases move into the specifier of CP to check the *wh*-feature, just like we moved DPs to the specifier of TP to check a [NOM] Case feature in chapter 10. We can formalize *wh*-movement the following way:

15) *Wh-movement*
    Move a *wh*-phrase to the specifier of CP to check a [+WH] feature in C.

Let's do a derivation for the following sentence:

16) Who(m) did Matt kiss?

The D-structure of this sentence will look like (17):

17)

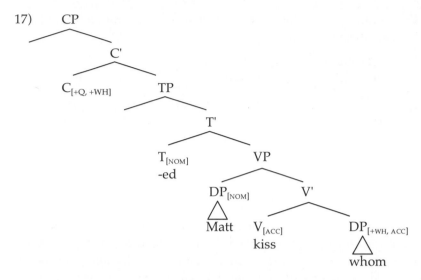

Matt and *whom* both get their theta roles in these D-structure positions. *Whom* also gets its Case in this base position. Three other operations apply: There is DP movement of *you* to the specifier of TP to check the [NOM] feature. There is insertion of *do* to support the *-ed* and we get T → C movement to fill the null [+Q] complementizer:

18)

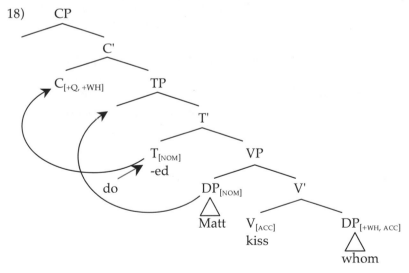

Wh-movement applies to check the [+WH] feature:

19)

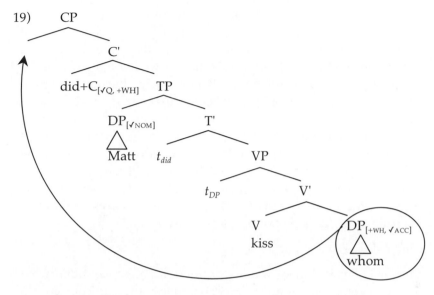

This results in the surface string in (20a) and the tree in (20b).

20) a) Who(m) did Matt kiss?

    b) CP

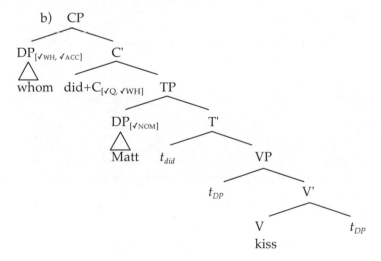

Traces and *Wanna*-contraction

You may have noticed that I have been marking the position that movement occurs from with a *t* (coindexed with the word it replaces). The *t* here stand for "trace." Later in this chapter we'll see that traces are required to block certain kinds of illicit movement. But an important question is whether there is any reality behind the notion "trace." This is especially important in a theory like Generative Grammar which claims psychological underpinnings. Finding evidence for something that is not pronounced is remarkably difficult. However, there is some straightforward evidence for traces. First a little background: In spoken varieties of English (both standard and non-standard), function words often contract with nearby words. One such contraction takes non-finite T (*to*) and contracts it with a preceding verb like want:

i)   I want to leave → I wanna leave.

This phenomenon is called **wanna-*contraction***. Now consider what happens when you have *wh*-movement and *wanna*-contraction going on at the same time. *Wanna*-contraction is permitted when the *wh*-movement applies to an object:

ii)   Who(m)ᵢ do you wanna kiss *t*ᵢ.

But look what happens when you try to do *wanna*-contraction, when *wh*-movement targets the subject:

iii) Whoᵢ do you want *t*ᵢ to kiss the puppy?
iv) *Who do you wanna kiss the puppy?

English speakers have very strong judgments that *wanna*-contraction is impossible when the subject is *wh*-questioned. Why should this be the case? If we have traces, the explanation is simple: the trace intervenes between the *to* and the verb. It blocks the strict adjacency between the verb and the *to*, thus blocking contraction:

v)   Whoᵢ do you want tᵢ to kiss the puppy?

The theory of traces, provides a nice explanation for this fact. For an alternate view see Pullum (1997).

Now let's do a more complicated example. This one involves DP movement, *wh*-movement and T → C movement:

21) Who was kissed?

The D-structure of this sentence is given in (22). This sentence is a passive.

22)

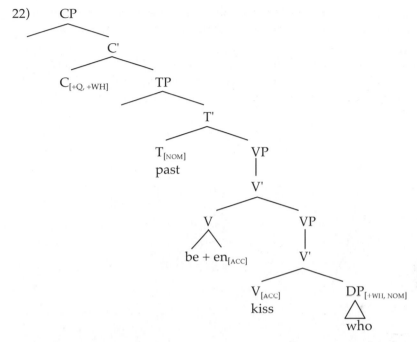

Who is the only argument in the sentence (a theme) and it starts out as a complement to the verb. The suffix *-en* lowers to the verb and absorbs both the agent theta role and the verb's accusative case. Also the auxiliary raises to T to support the tense:

23)

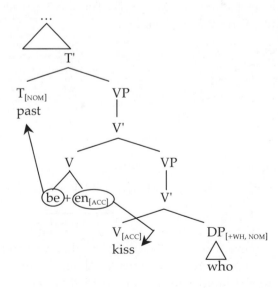

Since *-en* has taken the verb's [ACC] feature, *who* cannot get Case in its base position. It must move to the specifier of TP to check nominative Case:

24)

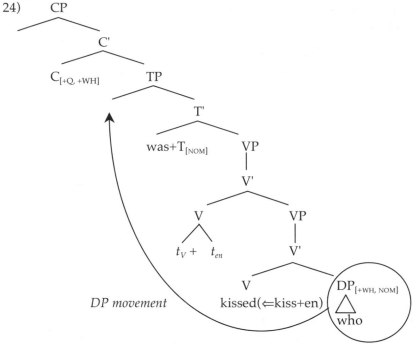

Once this DP has checked its Case features, it can move on to the specifier of CP for *wh*-feature checking (A). The auxiliary also undergoes T → C movement (B) for the [+Q] feature:

25)

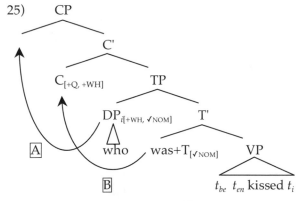

These two movements are "vacuous" in that *who* and *was* are in the order *who was* … both before movements A and B and after them. However, the feature checking requirements force us to claim that both movements occur anyway.

You now have enough information to try Challenge Problem Set 1

Wh-movement can also apply across clauses. Next, we'll do a derivation of a sentence where the *wh*-phrase moves from an embedded clause to the specifier of a main clause CP.

26) Who(m) do you think Jim kissed?

The D-structure of this sentence will look like (27). In this tree, *who(m)* is theta marked by the verb *kiss*, and gets its internal theme theta role in the object position of that verb:

27)

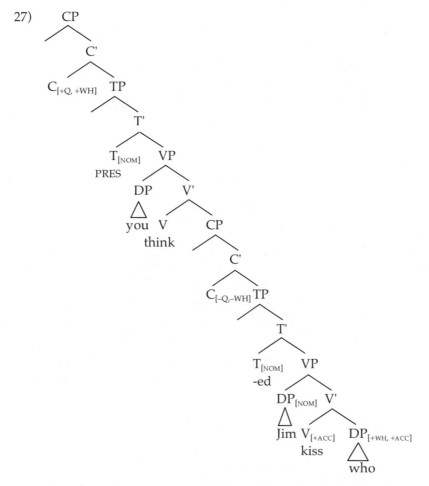

The T suffix *-ed* needs support, so it undergoes affix lowering and the present tense feature on the higher T that requires *do*-insertion. The [+Q] feature on the C also triggers T → C movement. The DP *Jim* moves from the specifier of the embedded VP to the specifier of the embedded TP for EPP and Case reasons. The DP *you* does the same in the higher clause.

28)

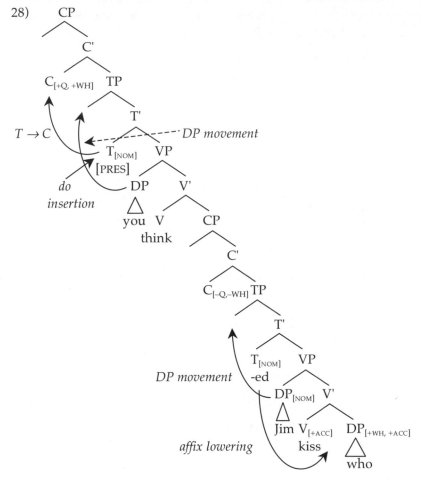

Finally we have *wh*-movement. For reasons that will become clear towards the end of this chapter, we do this movement in two hops, moving first to the specifier of the embedded CP, then on to the higher CP to check that C's [+WH] feature.

29)

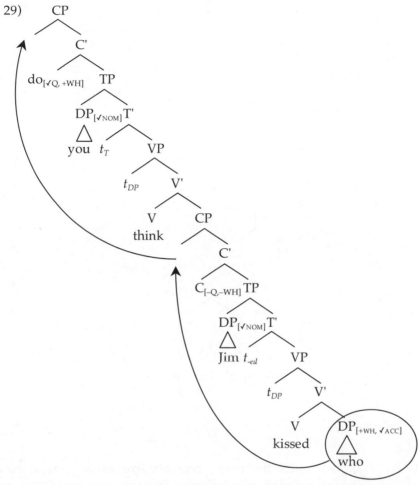

This derives the correct S-structure, where the *wh*-phrase is in initial position:

30)

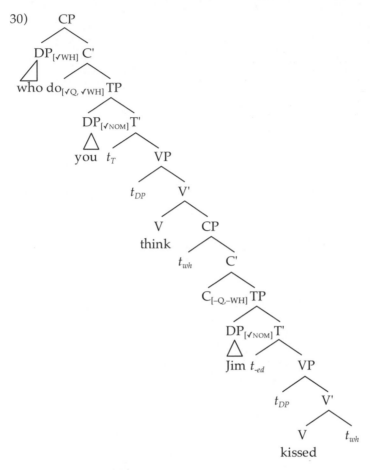

Let's do one more derivation, this time a sentence like the one above, but where the *wh*-phrase stops in the specifier position of the embedded CP:

31) I wonder who Jim kissed.

The main difference between this sentence and (26) lies in the nature of the main verb. In (26) the verb was *think*, that subcategorizes for a CP headed by C$_{[-Q, -WH]}$ (32a). The verb *wonder*[1] differs in that it subcategorizes for a CP headed by C$_{[-Q, +WH]}$, that is the embedded clause has *wh*-movement in it (32b):

---

[1] We have to assume that there is another verb *wonder*, found in sentences such as *I wonder if Bill left* that selects for a CP headed by C$_{[+Q,-WH]}$.

32) a)   *think*

Agent	Proposition
DP	CP_[–Q, –WH]

b)   *wonder*

Agent	Proposition
DP	CP_[–Q, +WH]

The D-structure for (31) is given in (33); it differs minimally from (27) only in the main verb and the feature structures of the two complementizers. The DPs all get their theta roles in these D-structure positions.

33)

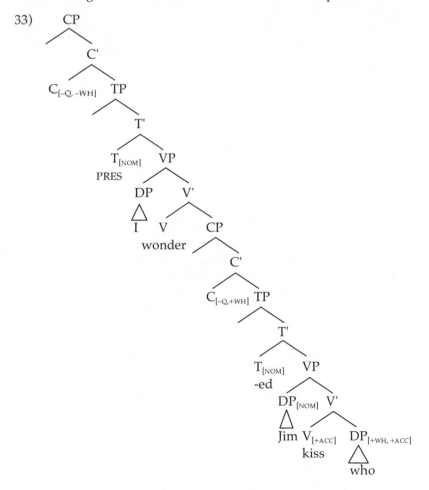

Just as in the previous example, *who* gets its case in its base position; the *-ed* and null PRES affixes lower to the Vs and the two agent DPs (*you* and *Jim*) move to their respective specifiers of TP to get case.

34)

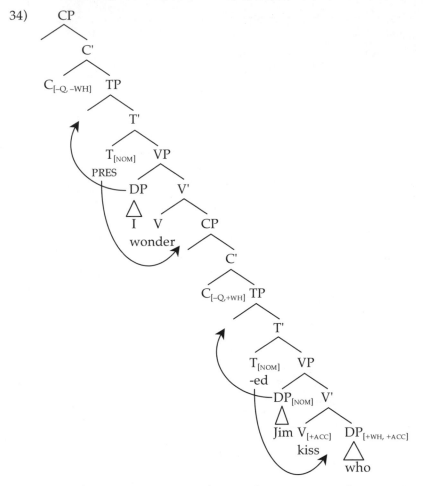

Finally we have movement of the *wh*-phrase. Notice that it only goes to the specifier of the embedded CP. This is because of the featural content of the Cs. The embedded CP is [+WH], the main clause CP is [–WH].

No T → C Movement in Embedded Clauses

In the main text, we've noticed that *wh*-movement and T → C movement often go hand in hand. One surprising fact about English is that this is not true of embedded *wh*-questions. When a *wh*-question is embedded the subject does not invert with the auxiliary (i.e., no T → C movement):

i) I wonder what he has done?
ii) *I wonder what has he done?

In other words, in embedded clauses there is no $C_{[+Q, +WH]}$. One simple explanation for this is that theta grids simply can't contain $C_{[+Q]}$.

35)

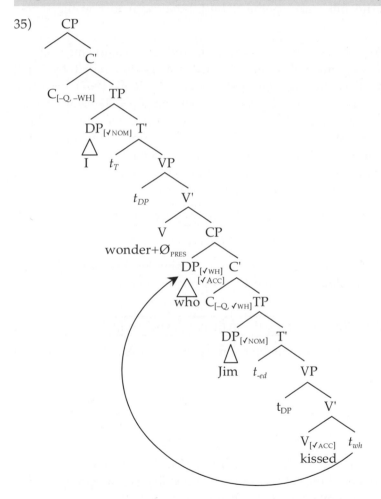

You now have enough information to try General Problem Sets 1–3

2. ISLANDS

Wh-movement isn't entirely free. There are constraints on what categories you can move *out* of (the categories that contain the *wh*-phrase). Compare the following two sentences, one of which has *wh*-movement out of a simple complement CP (36a). The other (36b) moves a *wh*-phrase out of a clause that is contained *inside a DP*:

36) a)   What$_i$ did Bill claim [$_{CP}$ that he read t_i in the syntax book]?
    b)   *What$_i$ did Bill make [$_{DP}$ the claim [$_{CP}$ that he read t_i in the syntax book]]?

In sentence (36a), we see that *wh*-movement **out** of a complement clause is grammatical, but movement out of a CP that is dominated by a DP is horrible (36b). This phenomenon, first observed by Ross (1967), has come to be known as the **Complex DP Island** phenomenon. The word **island** here is meant to be iconic. Islands are places you can't get off of (without special means like a plane), they are surrounded by water, so you are limited in where you can move: You can only move about within the confines of the island. Islands in syntax are the same. You cannot move *out* of an island, but you can move around within it. DPs are islands.

37) *What$_i$ did Bill make [$_{DP}$ the claim [$_{CP}$ that he read t_i in the syntax book]]?

Complex DP Island

The example in (37) involves a CP that is a complement to the N head. The same effect is found when the CP is a relative clause (i.e., an adjunct to the N):

38) *[Which cake]$_i$ did you see [$_{DP}$ the man [$_{CP}$ who baked t_i]]?

We can characterize this phenomenon with the following descriptive statement:

39) *The Complex DP constraint*
    * wh$_i$ [... [$_{DP}$ ... t_i ...] ...]

You now have enough information to try General Problem Set 4

There are many other kinds of islands. One of the most important is called a **wh-*island***. First, observe that it is possible to move a *wh*-phrase to the specifier of an embedded CP, when the C is [+WH]:

40) I wonder [$_{CP}$ what$_i$ C$_{[-Q, +WH]}$ [$_{TP}$ John bought t_i with the $20 bill]].

It is also possible to move (another) *wh*-phrase to the specifier of the main CP:

41) [$_{CP}$ How$_k$ do [$_{TP}$ you think [John bought the sweater t_k]]]?

However, look at what happens when you try to do both (move one *wh*-phrase to the embedded specifier, and the other to the main CP specifier):

42) *[$_{CP}$ How$_k$ do [$_{TP}$ you wonder [$_{CP}$ what$_i$ [$_{TP}$ John bought t_i t_k]]]]?

This sentence is wildly ungrammatical – even though we have only done two otherwise legitimate transformations. Now this isn't a constraint on having two *wh*-phrases in a sentence. Two *wh*-phrases are perfectly acceptable in other contexts:[2]

43) a)   How do you think John bought what?
     b)   I wonder what John bought how.

It seems then to be a <u>constraint on *moving*</u> both of them. The same kind of example is seen in (44a) and (44b):

44) a)   I wonder [$_{CP}$ what$_i$ [$_{TP}$ John kissed t_i]].
     b)   [$_{CP}$ Who$_k$ did [$_{TP}$ you think [$_{TP}$ t_k kissed the gorilla]]]]?

Movement of either the subject (44b) or the object (44a) to the specifiers of the CPs is acceptable. However, movement of both results in terrible ungrammaticality:

45) *[$_{CP1}$ Who$_k$ did [$_{TP}$ you wonder [$_{CP2}$ what$_i$ [$_{TP}$ t_k kissed t_i]]]]?

The central intuition underlying an account of these facts is that <u>once you move a *wh*-phrase into the specifier of a CP</u>, then that CP becomes <u>an island for further extraction</u>:

46) I asked [$_{CP}$ what$_i$ John kissed t_i]   *wh*-island

Movement out of this *wh*-island results in ungrammaticality. We can express this with the following descriptive statement:

47) *Wh-island Constraint*
     * wh$_i$ [… [$_{CP}$ wh$_k$ [… t_i …] …] …]

This constraint simply says that you cannot do *wh*-movement (in the schematic in (47) this is represented by the wh$_i$ and the coindexed t_i) and skip around a CP that has another *wh*-phrase (wh$_k$) in its specifier.

---

[2] If you have trouble with this judgment, try stressing the word *what* in (41) and *how* in (42).

We're going to discuss this particular island in much greater detail in the next section.

Subjects are another kind of island. Consider the following sentence; it has a CP in its subject position (48a). When you try to *wh*-move the *wh*-equivalent to *several rioters* (*who* in 48b), the sentence becomes ungrammatical.

48) a)   [$_{TP}$ [$_{CP}$ That the police would arrest <u>several rioters</u>] was a certainty].
    b)   *Who$_i$ was [$_{TP}$ [$_{CP}$ that the police would arrest t_i] t_{was} a certainty]?

This is called the *subject condition*:

49) *The Subject Condition*.
    *wh$_i$ ... [$_{TP}$ [$_{CP}$ ... t_i ...] T ...]

We have one final island to consider. Consider a conjunction like that in (50a). Here we have two DPs conjoined with each other. *Wh*-moving either of these DPs results in ungrammaticality (50b and c).

50) a)   I liked Mary and John.
    b)   *Who$_i$ did you like Mary and t_i?
    c)   *Who$_i$ did you like t_i and John?

The same is true if you try to do *wh*-movement from within another structure that is conjoined, such as a conjoined VP in (51):

51) a)   I [$_{VP}$ ate some popcorn] and [$_{VP}$ drank some soda].
    b)   *What$_i$ did you eat t_i and drink some soda?
    c)   *What$_i$ did you eat some popcorn and drink t_i?

The island condition that governs these situations is called the *Coordinate Structure Constraint*:

52) *Coordinate Structure Constraint*:
    *wh$_i$ ... [$_{XP}$ [$_{XP}$ ... t_i ...] conj [$_{XP}$ ...]] ...
    or *wh$_i$ ... [$_{XP}$ [$_{XP}$ ...] conj [$_{XP}$ ... t_i ...]] ...
    or *wh$_i$ ... [$_{XP}$ [$_{XP}$ ...] conj t_i] ...
    or *wh$_i$ ... [$_{XP}$ t_i conj [$_{XP}$ ...]] ...

We thus have four environments out of which *wh*-movement cannot occur: Complex DPs, Subjects, CPs with a *wh*-word in their specifier and out of a conjunct in a coordination. These environments are the subject of much research in syntactic theory right now. In the next section, we will look at one possible explanation for some of these island effects (although the account does not account for all of them by any means). This account refers to a constraint known as the Minimal Link Condition.

3. THE MINIMAL LINK CONDITION

3.1 Wh-islands and the Minimal Link Condition

Island phenomena beg for explanation. Let's consider *wh*-islands in some detail. As we noticed above, in questions with multiple *wh*-phrases, the movement of each *wh*-phrase is allowed independently of each other:

53) a) I wonder [$_{CP}$ what$_i$ [$_{TP}$ John kissed t_i]].
    b) [$_{CP}$ Who$_k$ did [$_{TP}$ you think [$_{TP}$ t_k kissed the gorilla]]]]?

However, when you combine the movements the sentence becomes nearly incomprehensible:

54) *[$_{CP1}$ Who$_k$ did [$_{TP}$ you wonder [$_{CP2}$ what$_i$ [$_{TP}$ t_k kissed t_i]]]]?

Recall from earlier discussion that syntactic operations like to either be local (for example, anaphors must be bound within their clause – a local relation; similarly theta roles are assigned within their VP – another local relation) or create localities (for example, DPs move to get close or local to their case assigner; affixes move to get close or adjacent to their host; and *wh*-phrases move to get near a [+WH]). In the next chapter, we will consider a unified approach to movement that tries to capture at least the last set of cases. What is important here is that our grammars seem to like relations that are close. With this intuition in mind, think about *wh*-islands. *Wh*-phrases move to get in the specifier of a C$_{[+WH]}$ so let's hypothesize that there is a further restriction, movement must always target the nearest *potential* position. This is another locality condition: the Minimal Link Condition (MLC):

55) *Minimal Link Condition (MLC) (intuitive version)*
    Move to the closest potential landing site.

In (54) there are two CPs, but both the *wh*-phrases start in the embedded clause. This means that for both *wh*-phrases the embedded CP (CP2) is the closest potential landing site. Here's an abbreviated D-structure of (54), the potential landing sites for the wh-phrase are underlined:

56) [$_{CP1}$ __ C$_{[+WH]}$ [$_{TP}$ you Ø$_{[PRES]}$ wonder [$_{CP2}$ __ C$_{[+wh]}$ [$_{TP}$ who -ed kiss what]]]]?

If we start by moving *what* to this position, we can check off *what*'s *wh*-feature, and this move meets the minimal link condition because the movement has targeted the closest potential landing site:

57) [$_{CP1}$ __ C$_{[+WH]}$ [$_{TP}$ you Ø$_{[PRES]}$ wonder [$_{CP2}$ what$_k$ C$_{[\checkmark wh]}$ [$_{TP}$ who -ed kiss t_k]]]]?

Now the other *wh*-phrase in this sentence has to check[3] its *wh*-features, but the closest potential position is filled by *what*. While movement to the specifier of CP1 would allow it to check its [+WH] feature, this would be a violation of the MLC, as the movement skips the first potential position:

58) [CP1 __ C[+WH] [TP you Ø[PRES] wonder [CP2 what$_k$ C[✓wh] [TP who -ed kiss t_k]]]]?

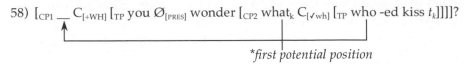

                                        first potential position

Even though the specifier of CP2 is filled with *what*, it still counts as the closest position. But since it is occupied, *who* can't move there, so there is no way for the [+WH] feature to be checked. Notice that it doesn't matter what order we apply the operations in. If we move *who* first, stopping off in the specifier of CP2 (thus meeting the MLC), then that specifier is occupied by the trace, so there is no place for the what to move to:

59) [CP1 who$_i$ C[+WH] [TP you Ø[PRES] wonder [CP2 t_i C[✓wh] [TP t_i -ed kiss what]]]]?

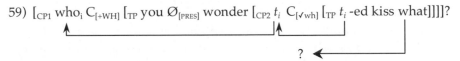

The MLC thus explains the ungrammaticality of *wh*-islands: When you have multiple *wh*-phrases that require movement, movement of at least one of them will be blocked by the MLC because the closest potential landing site will be occupied by the other.

Before moving on to look at the utility of the MLC in other domains, it's worth noting how the grammaticality of a sentence like (60) is derived when we have a constraint like the MLC. This sentence looks like we have non-local movement. The word *who* gets its theta role in the embedded clause yet ends up in the specifier of the higher CP:

60) [CP Who$_i$ do you think [CP2 [TP t_i kissed the gorilla]]]?

This should be a violation of the MLC, since the *wh*-phrase ends up in the specifier of a CP that is higher up in the tree. You will recall from the tree in (29) that we said that *wh*-movement that crosses clause boundaries does so in two hops: First to the specifier of the lower CP, then on to the higher CP.

61) [CP Who$_i$ do you think [CP2 t_i [TP t_i kissed the gorilla]]]?

---

[3] We return to sentences like *I wonder who loves what* where there appears to be no movement in section 4.

We now have an explanation for why this is the case: The MLC requires that all movement be local. In order to maintain this locality the movement happens in two hops. This phenomenon is called *successive cyclic movement*. In the problem sets section of this chapter there is a question on Irish (General Problem Set 6) that shows a morphological correspondence to successive cyclic movement.

You now have enough information to try General Problem Sets 5 & 6 and Challenge Problem Sets 2 & 3

It should be noted before we go on that the MLC does not explain all island effects, only the *wh*-islands. Accounting for other island types is a hot topic of research in syntax today.

3.2 The MLC in DP Movement and Head Movement

The MLC has usage above and beyond that of *wh*-islands. We can use it to account for a variety of other locality effects with DP and head movement too.

The verbs *is likely* and *seem* both have empty subject positions and allow the subject-to-subject raising variant of DP movement.

62) a)   Mark$_i$ is likely [t$_i$ to have left].
    b)   Mark$_i$ seems [t$_i$ to have left].

Consider now what happens when you embed one of these in the other. It is only possible for DP movement to occur to the *lower* of the two case positions. (63a) shows the D-structure. (63b) shows the grammatical S-structure where the DP shifts to the lower position, and expletive insertion applies at the higher position. (63c) and (63d) show ungrammatical forms, where the DP has shifted to the higher of the two positions. This kind of movement is ungrammatical, whether or not (63d vs. 63c) expletive insertion applies in the lower specifier of TP.

63) a)   __ seems [that ___ is likely [Mark to have left]].
    b)   It seems [that Mark$_i$ is likely [t$_i$ to have left]].
    c)   *Mark$_i$ seems that is likely [t$_i$ to have left].
    d)   *Mark$_i$ seems that it is likely [t$_i$ to have left].

When two Case positions are available movement has to target the closer (lower) one. The MLC condition explains these facts as well.

64) *[$_{TP}$ Mark$_i$ seems that   [$_{TP}$ it is likely [t$_i$ to have left]]].

first potential nominative position

Sentences (63c and d) are ungrammatical because the movement goes beyond the closest potential position, which is occupied by an expletive into a higher position. It is as if the expletive creates a "case-island" for the purposes of DP movement.

A similar effect is seen in head-movement. Recall from chapter 9 that in French we have both T → C movement and V → T movement. These two operations had to happen in tandem if we have a yes/no question with a main verb and no auxiliary:

65) a)   [$_{CP}$ C$_{[+Q]}$ [$_{TP}$ vous T$_{[pres]}$ [$_{VP}$ t$_{vous}$ mangez des pommes]]]
             you   eat   of.the apples

   b)   [$_{CP}$ C$_{[+Q]}$ [$_{TP}$ vous T$_{[pres]}$ [$_{VP}$ t$_{vous}$ mangez des pommes]]]

             T → C   V → T

   c)   Mangez vous des pommes?
        "Do you eat apples?"

(65a) is roughly the D-structure of the sentence (with the subject DP moved from the specifier of TP for case). We have two instances of head movement (65b). First V → T applies, then T → C to give the C content, this results in the surface string in (65c). Consider what would happen if the intermediate T position were occupied by an auxiliary (66a) and we tried to do head-movement of the verb around it (66b), this would give us the ungrammatical string in (66c):[4]

66) a)   [$_{CP}$ C$_{[+Q]}$ [$_{TP}$ vous avez [$_{VP}$ t$_{vous}$ mangé des pommes]]]
             you   have   eaten   of.the apples

   b)   [$_{CP}$ C$_{[+Q]}$ [$_{TP}$ vous avez [$_{VP}$ t$_{vous}$ mangé des pommes]]]

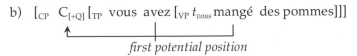

             first potential position

---

[4] For ease of reading these diagrams I'm leaving out the stacked verb analysis of auxiliary constructions and just generating auxiliaries in T; this does not change the MLC effect.

c) *Mangé vous avez des pommes
    eaten   you have

The ungrammaticality of (66c) follows easily, the V → C movement has skipped the intermediate T (occupied by *avez*). This T position is the first potential landing site for the verb. This is thus a violation of the Minimal Link Condition.[5]

      You now have enough information to try Challenge Problem Set 4

    The MLC then doesn't only explain *wh*-islands, it also extends to other locality restrictions on movement, such as the requirement that DP movement always target the closest case position and the requirement that head movement not skip intervening heads. Notice that in each of these cases what counts as a "potential landing site" is different. The same basic constraint holds, but the conditions for each type of movement are different. This discovery was made by Luigi Rizzi in his famous book *Relativized Minimality* (1990). There are two things that are vague about our preliminary definition of the MLC above: the precise definition of "closest" and the precise definition of "potential landing site." Nevertheless for most people our preliminary definition should be intuitive and sufficient. For people who prefer more precision here is a definition that is more formal and defines closest in terms of c-command and relativizes the landing site to the type of movement:

67) *The Minimal Link Condition (formal)*
    Movement of some item β can target some position α of type δ if and only if
    i)   α c-commands β
    ii)   there is no γ, also of type δ, such that α c-commands γ, and γ c-commands β.
    iii) δ is defined as:
        (a) A head if β = a head.
        (b) The specifier of TP if β = a DP with an unchecked [NOM].
        (c) The complement of the V if β = a DP with an unchecked [ACC].
        (d) The specifier of CP if β = *wh*-phrase with an unchecked [+WH] feature.

Conditions (i) and (ii) of this version of the MLC firm up what is meant by "closest." Here closeness is defined in terms of c-command, where there

---

[5] This instance of the MLC is sometimes known by an older name: The Head Movement Constraint (HMC), which was invented by Travis (1984); the HMC was the inspiration behind the MLC.

can be no intermediate c-commanding landing site of the relevant type intervening between the item that's moving and its landing site. The way that this is defined is actually nearly identical to the definition of *government* given way back in chapter 4. In fact, the MLC is often assumed to be the successor to the government relation.[6] Condition (iii) defines the kind or type of landing site relative to each type of movement.

4. ECHO QUESTIONS (*WH*-IN-SITU) IN ENGLISH

You may have noticed in the previous section that the MLC, when applied to *wh*-movement, in essence prevents any clause from having two moved *wh*-phrases. Does this mean that a clause can't have two *wh*-phrases at all? Obviously not:

68) Who loves who(m)?

This sentence is grammatical, even though the second *wh*-phrase does not move. This is a phenomenon called *wh*-in-situ (from the Latin *in situ* "in place"). We also see *wh*-in-situ in sentences with only one *wh*-phrase:

69) Shelly loves who?   (If this is not grammatical for you, stress *who*.)

We might ask why the *wh*-phrase in (69) and the second *who* in (68) don't move to check their [+WH] features. The answer is simple, these are not *wh*-questions and these apparent *wh*-phrases are [–WH]. These are *echo-questions*. Echo questions are not requests for new information; instead they are requests for confirmation of something someone has heard. Consider sentence (68) in a conversational context:

70) *Daniel*:   Hey, I just heard that Shelly loves Ferdinand.
    Andrew: Shelly loves who?
    Daniel: You heard me, Shelly loves Ferdinand.

It's clear from this snippet of discussion that Andrew is incredulous about Shelly loving Ferdinand and was asking for confirmation of what he heard. This is very different from a request for information. There are two relevant properties of echo-questions (i) they don't involve movement, but (ii) they do involve a special intonation, where the in-situ *wh*-phrase is stressed. Since echo questions don't involve movement, they aren't going to be subject

---

[6] The term "govern" had two usages in the 1980s and early 1990s: one as a structural relation (as defined in chapter 4); the other was as a constraint on the grammar. It is this latter usage that the MLC replaces.

to the MLC (explaining the grammaticality of (68) and other examples like it). While yes/no questions and *wh*-questions have some kind of syntactic licensing echo questions seem to be licensed by intonation and stress. In this regard they are similar to intonational questions that don't have subject/aux inversion such as (71) (where the rising curve is meant to indicate raised intonation and the italics represent stress on the words):

71)

Fred saw a spaceship in *the linguistics lounge*?

Note that this question again has a subtly different meaning from the one with subject/aux inversion and *do*-support (*Did Fred see a space ship in the linguistics lounge?*). The sentence with subject/aux inversion is a request for information. (71) is an expression of doubt and a request for confirmation.[7] How such phonological licensing is encoded into the syntactic tree is very controversial. One solution is that, like *wh*-questions and yes/no questions, echo questions and intonational questions involve a special complementizer. We can indicate this as $C_{[+INT]}$. The [+INT] feature doesn't trigger any movements, but it instructs the phonology to put a rising intonation curve on the clause that follows the C. The stress has to do with contrastive focus. In English contrastively focused material is stressed.

Wh-in-situ in English (and in closely related languages) seems to be largely limited to echo-question contexts.[8] However, *wh*-in-situ is the norm for real *wh*-questions in languages such as Chinese and Japanese. These languages appear to have no *wh*-movement at all. This will be a major topic of the next chapter.

5. CONCLUSION

In this chapter, we looked at a third kind of movement transformation: *Wh*-movement. This process targets *wh*-phrases and moves them to the specifier

---

[7] In fact, many people distinguish these using special punctuation in emails and informal writing. A yes/no question is indicated with a simple question mark (?), but an echo or intonational question is usually indicated with a combination of two (or more) question marks with an exclamation mark in between (?!?).

[8] There are contexts however, which involve a multiple *wh*-question interpretation. For example, a police officer might ask a suspect *"When did you convince your accomplice to hide the money where?"* or a parent might ask a teenager *"Who were you with where?"*. These kinds of in-situ questions will receive the same treatment as in-situ *wh*-questions in languages such as Japanese and Chinese to be discussed in the next chapter.

of CPs. This movement is triggered by the presence of a [+WH] feature in C. Movement is always from a Case position to the specifier of CP. *Wh*-movement is not totally unrestricted; there is a locality constraint on the movement: the MLC. Movement must be local, where local is defined in terms of closest potential landing site. We saw further that the MLC might be extended to other types of movement.

In the next chapter, we're going to continue this trend and look at movement processes in general and the similarities between them, as well as briefly delve into the interaction between the syntax and the formal interpretation (semantics) of the sentence.

IDEAS, RULES, AND CONSTRAINTS INTRODUCED IN THIS CHAPTER

i)   **Wh-*movement***: Move a *wh*-phrase to the specifier of CP to check a *wh*-feature in C.

ii)   *Island*: A phrase that contains (dominates) the *wh*-phrase, and that you may not move out of.

iii)   *The Complex DP Constraint*: *wh_i [… [$_{DP}$ … t_i …] …]

iv)   *Wh-island Constraint*: * wh_i [… [$_{CP}$ wh_k [… t_i …] …] …]

v)   *The Subject Condition*: *wh_i … [$_{TP}$ [$_{CP}$ … t_i …] T …]

vi)   *Coordinate Structure Constraint*:
        *wh_i … [$_{XP}$ [$_{XP}$ … t_i …] conj [$_{XP}$ …]] …
        or *wh_i … [$_{XP}$ [$_{XP}$ …] conj [$_{XP}$ … t_i …]] …
        or *wh_i … [$_{XP}$ [$_{XP}$ …] conj t_i] …
        or *wh_i … [$_{XP}$ t_i conj [$_{XP}$ …]] …

vii)   *Minimal Link Condition (MLC)**(intuitive version)*: Move to the closest potential landing site.

viii)   *The Minimal Link Condition (formal)*:
        Movement of some item β can target some position α of type δ if and only if
        i)   α c-commands β
        ii) there is no γ, also of type δ, such that α c-commands γ, and γ c-commands β.
        iii) δ is defined as
             (a) A head if β = a head

        (b) The specifier of TP if β = a DP with an unchecked [NOM].

        (c) The complement of the V if β = a DP with an unchecked [ACC].

        (d) The specifier of CP if β = *wh*-phrase with an unchecked [+WH] feature.

ix)   **Wh-*in-situ***: when a *wh*-phrase does not move.

x)   ***Echo-Questions and Intonational Questions***: Question forms that are licensed by the phonology (intonation and stress) and not by the syntax, although they may involve a special C.

FURTHER READING

Baltin, Mark (1981) Strict bounding. In C. L. Baker and John McCarthy (eds.) *The Logical Problem of Language Acquisition*. Cambridge: MIT Press. pp. 257–95.

Cheng, Lisa (1997) *On the Typology of Wh-Questions*. New York: Garland Press.

Chomsky, Noam (1977) On *wh*-movement. In Peter Culicover, Thomas Wasow, and Adrian Akmajian (eds.), *Formal Syntax*. New York: Academic Press. pp. 71–132.

Chomsky, Noam (1986a) *Barriers*. Cambridge: MIT Press.

Chomsky, Noam and Howard Lasnik (1978) A remark on contraction. *Linguistic Inquiry* 9, 268–74.

Cinque, Guglielmo (1981) *Types of A' Dependencies*. Cambridge: MIT Press.

Koopman, Hilda (1984) *The Syntax of Verbs*. Dordrecht: Foris.

Lasnik, Howard and Mamoru Saito (1984) On the nature of proper government. *Linguistic Inquiry* 15, 235–89.

Lightfoot, David (1976) Trace theory and twice moved NPs. *Linguistic Inquiry* 7, 559–82.

Manzini, Maria Rita (1992) *Locality: A Theory and Some of its Empirical Consequences*. Cambridge: MIT Press.

Richards, Norvin (1997) What Moves Where When in Which Language? Ph.D. dissertation, MIT.

Rizzi, Luigi (1990) *Relativized Minimality*. Cambridge: MIT Press.

Ross, J. R. (Haj) (1967) Constraints on Variables in Syntax. Ph.D. dissertation, MIT.

Travis, Lisa deMena (1984) Parameters and Effects of Word Order Variation. Ph.D. dissertation, MIT.

GENERAL PROBLEM SETS

1. ENGLISH MOVEMENT SENTENCES
[Application of Skills; Basic to Advanced]

For each of the following sentences, give the D-structure tree and annotate it with arrows indicating what transformations have applied. The sentences may have head-to-head movement, *do*-insertion, expletive insertion, DP movement and *wh*-movement.

a)   What is bothering you?
b)   Who has seen my snorkel?
c)   How was the plot discovered by the authorities?
d)   Which animals appear to have lost their collars?
e)   What did Jean think was likely to have been stolen?
f)   Car sales have surprised the stockbrokers.
g)   Have you seen my model airplane collection?
h)   Can you find the lightbulb store?
i)   John was bitten by an advertising executive.
j)   It is likely that Tami will leave New York.
k)   Tami is likely to leave New York.
l)   It seems that Susy was mugged.
m) Susy seems to have been mugged.
n)   What did you buy at the supermarket?
o)   I asked what Beth bought at the supermarket.
p)   What is it likely for Beth to have bought at the supermarket?
     (Treat the PP *for Beth* as appearing the specifier of the embedded TP.)
q)   What is likely to have been bought at the supermarket?

2. BINDING THEORY
[Critical Thinking; Basic]

In chapter 5, you were asked why the sentence below causes a problem for the binding theory. Remind yourself of your answer, and then explain how the model of grammar we have proposed in this chapter accounts for this fact.

   Which pictures of himself does John despise?

3. BINDING AND SCRAMBLING[9]

[Critical Thinking; Intermediate/Advanced]

You should complete Problem Set 2 before attempting this problem set.

Modern Persian has a kind of movement often called **scrambling**. Your task in this problem set is to figure out whether scrambling is DP movement, head-to-head movement or *wh*-movement. The Persian word *hamdiga* means "each other" and is an anaphor. Assume that anaphors are subject to the binding theory of chapter 4, and that they must be in argument positions to be bound. Sentence (a) shows the basic order. Sentences (b) and (c) show the surface word order after scrambling has applied. The scrambled sentences mean almost exactly the same thing as (a). HAB stands for "habitual." Recall that $_{i/*k}$ means that the sentence is okay with the DP having the index $_i$ but not with the index $_k$.

a)   Mo'allem-â$_k$ fekr   mi-kon-an   [$_{CP}$ ke [$_{T'}$ [$_{vP}$ bachche-hâ$_i$
      teacher-PL thought HAB-do-3PL   that   child-PL

[$_{vP}$ aks - â -ye hamdiga$_{i/*k}$ - ro be modir   neshun dâd-an]]]].
   picture-PL-EZ each other - RÂ to principal sign   gave-3PL
"The teachers$_k$ think that the children$_i$ showed [each other's]$_{i/*k}$ pictures to the principal."

b)   Mo'allem-â$_k$ [aks-â-ye hamdiga$_{i/*k}$-ro]$_m$ fekr mi-kon-an [$_{CP}$ ke [$_{T'}$ [$_{vP}$ [bachche-hâ$_i$] [$_{vP}$ t$_m$ be modir neshun dâd-an]]]].

c)   [Aks-â-ye hamdiga$_{i/*k}$-ro]$_m$ mo'allem-â$_j$ fekr mi-kon-an [$_{CP}$ ke   [$_{T'}$ [$_{vP}$ bachche-hâ$_i$ [$_{vP}$ t$_m$ be modir neshun dâd-an]]]].

4. PICTURE DPs

[Critical Thinking; Intermediate/Advanced]

Why is the grammaticality of the following sentence surprising? Does the theory we have presented in this chapter predict this to be acceptable? What constraint should this sentence violate.

Who(m) did you see a picture of?

5. LOCALITY

[Data Analysis; Basic]

Why is the following sentence ungrammatical?

*Who$_j$ did [$_{TP}$ George try to find out [$_{CP}$ what$_i$ [$_{TP}$ t$_j$ wanted t$_i$]]]?

---

[9] This problem set was contributed by Simin Karimi.

Draw a tree showing the exact problem with this sentence. Be precise about what constraint rules it out.

6. IRISH[10]
[Data Analysis; Advanced]
Irish has a number of different complementizer forms. In declarative clauses (statements), it uses the complementizer *go/gur*. As discussed in the text above, when there is a question, this complementizer switches to the *wh*-form a^L. (The idea behind this problem set is taken from McCloskey 1979.)

a) Ceapann tú   go   bhuailfidh an píobaire an t-amhrán
    think   you that play.FUT   the piper   the song
    "You think that the piper will play the song."

b) Caidé a^L cheapann tú a^L bhuailfidh an píobaire?
    What WH think   you WH play.FUT   the piper
    "What do you think the piper will play?"

Note carefully the number of a^L complementizers in sentence (b). (b) provides evidence that *wh*-phrases stop off in intermediate specifiers of CP (for MLC reasons). Explain why. You need to make the assumption that the complementizer a^L only shows up when a *wh*-phrase has at one point shown up in its specifier.

CHALLENGE PROBLEM SETS

CHALLENGE PROBLEM SET 1: WHO ATE THE PIZZA?
[Critical Thinking; Challenge]
In the text we suggested that subject questions involving an auxiliary have vacuous movement of both the *wh*-phrase (to the specifier of CP) and the auxiliary (to $C_{[+Q, +WH]}$), even though that leaves the subject *wh*-phrase and auxiliary in the same order they'd be in if they'd stayed in the TP:

---

[10] This problem set was suggested by an anonymous Blackwell reviewer.

a)

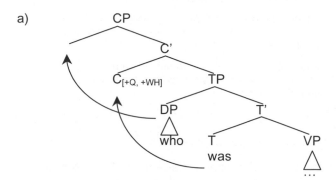

We suggested this was the case so that we could maintain the feature checking requirements hold here too.

Consider however the following sentence. Notice that the tense morphology is not realized as *did*, but on the main verb *ate*.

b)   Who ate the pizza?

Question 1: Explain why this is an argument against the vacuous movement shown in (a).

Question 2: If there is no vacuous movement, what then are we to make of the complementizer in subject questions? Is it [+Q, +WH]? Is there some way to explain why the complementizers with subject *wh*-questions are different than complementizers with object and adjunct wh-questions (which do show both *wh*-movement and T → C movement)?

CHALLENGE PROBLEM SET 2: IRISH
[Data Analysis; Challenge]
Some dialects of English allow a kind of *wh*-construction, where the base position of the *wh*-phrase is filled by a ***resumptive pronoun*** (the idea behind this problem set is taken from McCloskey 1991):

This is the book$_i$ that the police are arresting everyone who reads it$_i$.

In Modern Irish, this kind of construction is very common. Modern Irish has two different *wh*-complementizers (notice that these are *not* wh-phrases, which go in the specifier of CP, these are complementizers): a^L, a^N. The complementizer a^L is found in sentences like (a). Sentence (i) shows a simple sentence without *wh*-movement using the non-*wh*-complementizer *go*. Sentences (ii) and (iii) show two possible forms of the question. (ii) has the question moved only to an intermediate CP specifier. (iii) has the *wh*-phrase moved to the topmost specifier.

a) i)   Bíonn fios   agat i gconaí [$_{CP}$ **go** bhuailfidh an píobaire an t-amhrán].
         be.HAB know at.2.S always   that play.FUT the piper   the song
         "You always know that the bagpiper will play the song."

    ii) Bíonn fios   agat i gconaí [$_{CP}$ caidé$_i$ **a^L**   bhuailfidh an píobaire t_i].
         be.HAB know at.2.S always   what$_i$ COMP play.FUT the piper t_i
         "You always know what the bagpiper will play."

    iii) [$_{CP}$ Cáidé$_i$ **a^L** [$_{TP}$ bhíonn fios   agat i gconaí [$_{CP}$ t_i **a^L** bhuailfidh an píobaire t_i]]]?
         What COMP be.HAB know at.2.S always t_j COMP play.FUT the piper t_i
         "What do you always know the piper will play?"

Now the distribution of the complementizer a^N seems to be linked to the presence of a resumptive pronoun. Consider the (ii) sentences in (b) and (c). Both show resumptive pronouns and the complementizer a^N:

b) i)   Bíonn fios   agat i gconaí [$_{CP}$ caidé$_i$ **a^L**   bhuailfidh an píobaire t_i].
         be.HAB know at.2.S always   what$_i$ COMP play.FUT the piper t_i
         "You always know what the bagpiper will play."

    ii) [$_{CP}$Cén Píobaire$_j$ **a^N** [$_{TP}$ mbíonn fios agat i gconaí [$_{CP}$caidé$_i$ **a^L** bhuailfidh **sé$_j$** t_i]]]?
         Which piper COMP be.HAB know at.2.S always what$_i$ COMP play.FUT he
         "Which bagpiper do you always know what he will play?"

c) i)   Tá   máthair an fhir   san   otharlann.
         Be.PRES mother the man.GEN in.the hospital
         "The man's mother is in the hospital."

    ii) Cé$_i$ **a^N** bhfuil   **a$_i$** mháthair san   otharlann?
         who COMP be.PRES his mother   in.the hospital
         "Who is (his) mother in the hospital?"

The a^N complementizer and the resumptive pronouns are boldfaced in the above examples. Where precisely does the a^N-resumptive strategy appear? In what syntactic environment do you get this construction?

CHALLENGE PROBLEM SET 3: SERBIAN/CROATIAN/BOSNIAN[11]
[Critical Thinking; Challenge]
In this chapter, we have proposed that a *wh*-phrase appears in the specifier of CP, to check a [WH] feature. Our analysis of locality conditions requires that only one *wh*-phrase can appear in the specifier of CP. Consider the following data from Serbian/Croatian/Bosnian. Assume that this language is SVO at D-structure. (Data from Bošković 1997 as cited in Lasnik 1999a.)

---

[11] This problem set was contributed by Simin Karimi.

a)   Ko šta gdje kupuje?
     who what where buys
     "Who buys what where?"
b)   *Ko kupuje šta gdje?
c)   *Ko šta kupuje gdje?
d)   *Ko gdje kupuje šta?

What problems does this data raise for our analysis? Can you see a way around these problems?

CHALLENGE PROBLEM SET 4: FRENCH NEGATION
[Critical Thinking; Challenge]
We've argued that in French the verb raises to T, and that T raises to C in yes/no questions. Further in this chapter, we've argued that head movement is subject to the Minimal Link Condition. In previous chapters we've treated the French word *pas* as the head of NegP as in (a). Consider an alternative where *pas* isn't the specifier of NegP but is an adjunct to the VP as in (b):

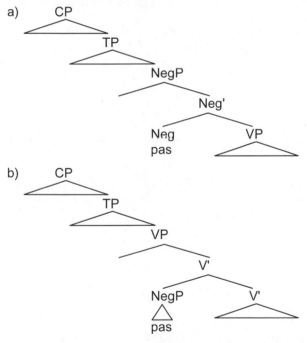

Keep in mind the restriction in the MLC that the moving element can't skip potential landing sites that c-command it. Recall that V → T movement jumps over the word *pas*:

c) Je n'aime pas t_V des   pommes.
    I   like   not   of.the apples.
    "I don't like apples"

Does this argue for the analysis in (a) or the analysis in (b)? Explain your answer.

chapter 12

A Unified Theory of Movement

0. INTRODUCTION

At the beginning of this book, we looked at rules that generate the basic phrase structure of human syntax. These rules generated trees that represent hierarchical structure and constituency. These trees have particular mathematical properties that we investigated in chapters 4 and 5. In chapter 6, we saw that stipulated phrase structure rules missed some very basic generalizations, and refined them into X-bar phrase structure rules. The X-bar rules, being very general, allow us (informed by parameter settings) to generate a wide variety of trees, and capture structural differences between heads, complements, adjuncts, and specifiers. In chapter 7, we extended the rules to various clause types, complementizers, and DPs. In chapter 8, we saw that, in fact, the X-bar rules actually generated too many structures, and that we had to constrain their power. The device we use to limit them is a semantic one: the thematic properties of predicates (stored in the lexicon) and the theta criterion. What results from the output of the X-bar schema and the lexicon is called D-structure. The theta criterion holds of D-structures, as do the binding conditions. In chapters 9, 10, and 11, we saw a variety of cases where lexical items either could not be generated where they surfaced by X-bar theory (e.g., head-adjunct-complement ordering in French) or appeared in positions other than the ones predicted by theta theory. We developed a new kind of rule: the movement rule or transformation, which moves items around from their base position in the D-structure to the actual position they appear in on the surface. There are three movement transformations: Head-to-head movement (T → C and V → T), DP movement, and *wh*-movement. In each of these cases movement occurs because it *has* to. Each movement has a trigger or motivation. Heads move to fill empty [Q] features or to take an inflectional suffix. DPs move to check case features. *Wh*-phrases move to be near the [WH] feature. We also posited two insertion transformations: *Do*-support and expletive insertion. The output of the transformations is called S-structure, which is itself subject to several constraints: the Case filter, the EPP and the Subjacency Constraint. The model (flowchart) of the grammar looks like (1).

1)

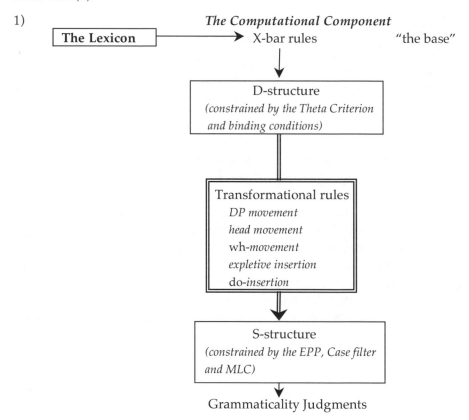

The Computational Component

The Lexicon ⟶ X-bar rules   "the base"

D-structure
(constrained by the Theta Criterion and binding conditions)

Transformational rules
  DP *movement*
  head *movement*
  wh-*movement*
  expletive insertion
  do-*insertion*

S-structure
(constrained by the EPP, Case filter and MLC)

Grammaticality Judgments

This straightforward model can generate a large number of sentence types. It is also a system with explanatory adequacy, which makes specific predictions about how a child goes about acquiring a language (via parameters).

This is a fairly complete and simple system, but we might ask if the system can be made even simpler. Are we missing any generalizations here?

Recent work in syntactic theory that answers this question suggests we might unify the different types of movement into a single rule type with a slight reorganization of the architecture of the grammar.

> **The Minimalist Program**
> The system of grammar described in this chapter is a very cursory look at some of the principles underlying the most recent version of generative grammar: The Minimalist Program (Chomsky 1993, 1995). The Minimalist Program is motivated not only by the search for explanatory adequacy but also for a certain level of formal simplicity and elegance. What is outlined here is by no means a complete picture, but is meant to give you a taste of what current work is striving towards.

1. MOVE

In this book we've proposed the following motivations for transformations:

2) a) Head movement   *to get a suffix or fill null* [+Q]
    b) DP movement   *to check case features* [NOM] *or* [ACC]
    c) *Wh*-movement   *to check a* [+WH] *feature*

Notice that while there are significant differences between the motivations for the various types of movement, there is one overwhelming similarity. The movements all occur so that one item can appear near another. In the case of head movement the V or T head needs to appear as part of the same word as the place it moves to. With *wh*-movement, the *wh*-phrase needs to be near the [WH] feature, just as DP movement occurs so the DP can check its Case feature with T or V. All the motivations for movement then seem to be *locality constraints*. That is, two items must be near or *local* to one another. This is a trend that we've seen before in previous chapters.

  If all the movement types are motivated by locality, then there isn't really a significant difference between the rule types. Perhaps we can unify them into a single rule: *Move.* Move says simply "move something" (but only if you have to):

3) *Move (very informal version)*
    Move something somewhere.

Now of course, this is a bit vague and we'll have to sharpen it up in some way. In particular, we will want to constrain the rule so there isn't just random movement all over the sentence. So the next step is to formulate a constraint that motivates and forces this transformation to apply (in all the different circumstances).

Let's take *wh*-movement as our paradigm case. In *wh*-movement the *wh*-phrase moves to the specifier of CP so as to be local with a [WH] feature. Another way to think of this, as we suggested in chapter 11, is to say that both the *wh*-phrase and the complementizer have a [+WH] feature, and they need to compare them, or *check* them. Checking of features can only occur in a local configuration. In this case we have what is called a *specifier–head configuration* for reasons that should be obvious from the following partial tree.

4)

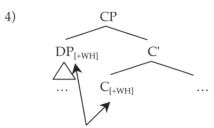

Specifier–head checking configuration

The constraint that forces this movement to occur is called the **Principle of Full Interpretation** (Chomsky 1993, 1995).

5) *Full Interpretation (FI)*
    Features must be checked in a local configuration.

6) *Local Configuration (preliminary)*
    [WH] features: Specifier–head configuration.

We can extend this to the other cases of movement too. As we suggested in chapter 10, imagine that Case is not simply an ending, but is also a feature. A subject DP bears a [NOM] Case feature. Imagine also that the heads of the phrases that assign case (T and V) also bear this feature (although they don't show it morphologically). We can thus reduce the Case filter to full interpretation: Nominative Case is feature checking like that in (7) and accusative Case is like that in (8):

7)

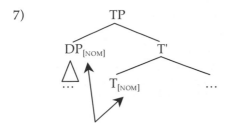

Specifier–head checking configuration

8)

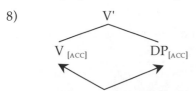

Head–complement checking configuration

Case and Agreement

The notion that T bears some kind of Case feature often troubles people, since Case is an inherently nominal kind of inflection and T seems to be associated with verbal material. One clever solution to this problem is to claim that verbal items like T do in fact bear Case; we just call case on verbs "agreement." In fact, cross-linguistically, there does seem to be some kind of correlation between the kinds of agreement markers that are found on verbs and the case marking on the subjects. Languages with ergative/absolutive case marking systems often also have ergative/absolutive agreement. So we could claim that [NOM] when on a noun is case, but when on T or a V is agreement, thus at least partly motivating the structure in (7) and (8).

Finally, we can extend this to the head movement cases. Instead of claiming that verbs move to pick up inflectional suffixes in V → T movement, let's claim that both the V and the T head bear some kind of abstract inflectional features (e.g., [±past]). This allows us to capture the behavior of verbs with null T morphology as well as that of ones with affixes. When the verb and T check these features against one another then the suffix representing that tense feature (or agreement feature) is allowed to surface on the verb. The local configuration in this setting is within the head itself (a relationship which is called a head–head configuration):

9)

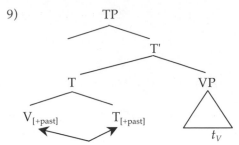

Head/Head checking configuration

Similarly, both T and C bear a [+Q] feature, and they must be in a head–head checking relationship:

10)

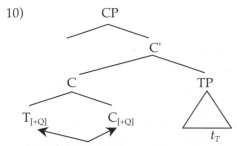

Head/Head checking configuration

Local Configuration is thus defined in terms of features. The particular configuration required is determined by which feature is being used. This is very similar to the way in which we formally defined the conditions on the Minimal Link Condition in the previous chapter, where the intervening categories were relativized to the kind of feature being checked by the element that is moving. (11) is a summary of these local configurations.

11) *Local Configuration*:
    [WH], [NOM] features: Specifier–head configuration.
    [ACC] features: Head–complement configuration.[1]
    [PAST], etc., [Q] features: Head–head configuration.

With this in place we actually have a very elegant transformational system. We have combined our three movement rules into one: Move and two constraints: full interpretation and the Minimal Link Condition. In previous chapters, we've already argued that constituent structure is created by a few very limited phrase structure rules, which are constrained by the theta criterion

---

[1] In the next chapter we will claim that [ACC] is actually checked in a specifier–head configuration like [NOM], this will allow us to create a phrase structure system that accounts for double object verbs and dative constructions.

and the lexical entries of categories. Computationally speaking, this is a surprisingly simple system of grammar.

2. EXPLAINING CROSS-LINGUISTIC DIFFERENCES

The system outlined above in section 1, is simple and elegant. It does however, make the unfortunate prediction that all languages will have exactly the same set of transformational rules (although they can still differ in phrase structure, due to the parameters). This is clearly not the case. English does not have V → T movement. Many other languages lack passive and raising. Still others appear to lack *wh*-movement. Take the case of Mandarin Chinese (data from Huang 1982; tone is omitted).

12) a) Ni xiang chi sheme?
        you want eat what
        "What do you want to eat?"

    b) *Sheme ni xiang chi?
        what you want eat
        "What do you want to eat?"

    c) Ni kanjian-le shei?
        you see-ASP who
        "Who did you see?"

    d) *Shei ni kanjian-le?
        who you see-ASP
        "Who did you see?"

Chinese appears to have no *wh*-movement. As we discussed in the last chapter this is called **wh-*in-situ***. The Chinese case differs from English, however, in that these are not echo-questions. These are real *wh*-questions. As such they should have [+WH] features on their Cs and on the *wh*-phrases. Why, then, is it the case that the unchecked [+WH] features on the *wh*-phrases don't violate Full Interpretation? They have not moved so they are not in a local configuration with their C. Full Interpretation predicts that (12a) should be ungrammatical and (12b) should be grammatical – the exact opposite of the facts.

Our solution to this problem is going to surprise you. We're going to claim that in Chinese the *wh*-phrase does move, you just don't hear it! This requires a refinement of our grammar model.

Ferdinand de Saussure (a linguist from the late nineteenth century) observed that every linguistic expression consists of two parts: the signifier and the signified. For our purposes, this roughly corresponds to the phonological or *phonetic form* of the sentence (abbreviated as PF) and its semantic or *logical form* (LF). We call these "forms" the *interface levels*, because they represent the interface with the phonological system and with the interpretive system respectively. This means that when we're computing the grammaticality of a sentence we're really computing two distinct things: its sound (for the purposes of a syntactician this means the sequence of the words) and its meaning. To a certain degree these interface levels are computed together, but they also diverge from one another. When we look at the question cross-linguistically, we see that any particular PF order of elements does not directly correspond to some specific meaning. For example, the English sentence *I saw the man* and the Irish sentence *Chonaic mé an fear* (literally *Saw I the man*) <u>mean</u> the same thing, but they have different word orders. One way to represent this conundrum is by having two separate levels in our model of grammar that correspond to these interface levels. These levels represent the final products of our computation, so they should appear at the end of the derivation. This gives us a more refined model of the grammar than the one we saw in (1):

13)   **The Lexicon** ⟶ X-bar rules   The Base

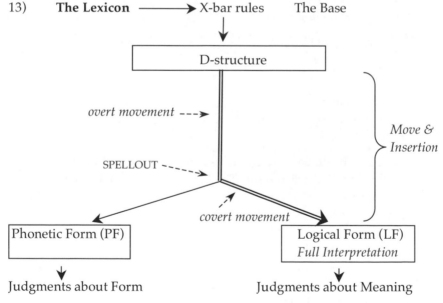

Let me draw your attention to some of the important differences between this model[2] and the model we had in (1). First of all you'll note that there is

---

[2] This model isn't entirely an accurate representation of Chomsky's minimalist model. I have retained the notion of D-structure here. In Chomsky's version,

no S-structure. In the old model, S-structure was the level from which we drew grammaticality judgments. In this new model it is the interface levels PF and LF that give us well-formedness judgments (judgments about form) and semantic judgments respectively. Some of the derivation applies in tandem generating both the PF and the LF; these operations apply on the "stem" of the upside down Y. Then there is a point at which the derivation branches into operations that are purely about form and sound and operations that are purely about meaning. This branching point is called *SPELLOUT* (usually in all capital letters). After SPELLOUT, the derivation proceeds along two distinct paths, one generating the PF, the other the LF. Chomsky (1993) makes two important claims. First he claims that Full Interpretation is a constraint that holds of sentences at LF. Second, he claims that exactly the same operations that happen between D-structure and SPELLOUT can also happen between SPELLOUT and LF (in (13) this is indicated by means of the double line that extends from D-structure to SPELLOUT and from SPELLOUT to LF). Move can apply anywhere along this double line.

At first this may seem counterintuitive, but the kinds of movement can happen *after* SPELLOUT; that is, after the pronounced order has been created, and the "form" portion of the sentence is sent off to PF. This is a mind-bending notion, but actually allows us to make the following remarkable claim about cross-linguistic variation: *Every instance of feature-checking motivated movement happens in every single language.* Why would we want to do such a thing? Let us assume, not uncontroversially, that the kinds of meaning determined by the syntax are universally held by all humans. This is *not* to say that all humans have identical world-views or identical perceptions of events etc.; we are not making such a strong claim here. This is not a claim about cultural or personal interpretations. This is simply a *limited* statement that all humans have a notion of what it means to express a declaration, a yes/no question, a *wh*-question, a passive, a sentence with raising, etc. These kinds of constructions, and relationships such as constituency and the binding conditions *do* seem to be universal in interpretation even if they do have different forms cross-linguistically.

---

the X-bar rules are replaced by an operation called Merge and there is no D-structure. In Chomsky's model the constraints we've claimed to be D-structure constraints (The Theta Criterion and the binding conditions) are handled differently. Getting rid of D-structure involves some tricky argumentation that lies beyond the scope of this textbook. Once you are finished reading this book have a look at some of the suggested readings at the end that will take you onto this more advanced material. This aside the diagram in (13) is a fair representation of how many linguists working within the minimalist program is structured.

Let us call such basic interpretations ***universal semantics***. If, as we have hypothesized throughout this book, this basic semantic content is determined by our X-bar phrase structure system (which creates constituents) and the movement operations (which check to make sure that there is a featural correspondence among the words in the constituent structure), then universal semantics should be generated the same way in every language. Yet it goes without saying, that every language has different (yet narrowly limited) ways of expressing that universal semantics. The Y model gives us a straightforward way of accounting for this. The differences between languages are in when that movement occurs: before SPELLOUT or after. Essentially there are two kinds of movement, movement that happens between D-structure and SPELLOUT (called *overt* movement) and movement that happens between SPELLOUT and LF (called *covert* movement). Since covert movement happens after the branching off to the PF (phonology) component, you simply can't hear it happen! The differences between languages then, are in when they time specific instances of the general operation Move. English times those instances involving [WH] features overtly before SPELLOUT, Chinese times those same movements covertly, after SPELLOUT. This can be simply encoded in a parameter:

14) Wh-*parameter*: Overt / Covert
    (English sets at "Overt," Chinese sets at "Covert")

This parameter determines whether movement applies before S-structure or after:

15)

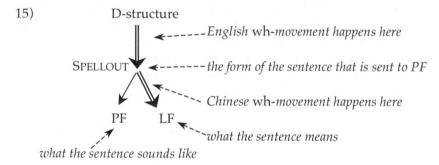

To make this clearer let us abstractly show each step of the derivation for Mandarin Chinese and English (I'm abstracting away from *do*-insertion, etc.):

16)

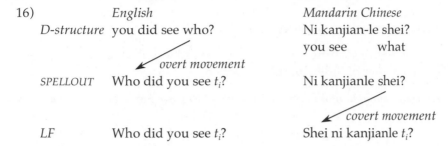

	English	*Mandarin Chinese*
D-structure	you did see who?	Ni kanjian-le shei?
		you see what
SPELLOUT	Who did you see t_i?	Ni kanjianle shei?
LF	Who did you see t_i?	Shei ni kanjianle t_i?

You'll notice that the order of elements in the LFs of this sentence is identical in both languages, but the SPELLOUT form is different. You never hear the LFs. You only hear the SPELLOUT forms. The LFs are identical because the two sentences (in the two languages) mean the same thing.

This kind of analysis has a nice side effect. It also allows us to get rid of the odd-man-out of transformations: Affix (T) lowering. This was the only movement that we looked at that ever went downwards. It also appeared to be in complementary distribution with V-movement. If a language has one, then it doesn't have the other. This is suspicious; when we find items in complementary distribution, it suggests they are really instances of the same thing. With the system described above we can get rid of the affix lowering account of English. English doesn't have affix lowering. Instead, it has V → T movement like any other language, only in English it is timed covertly, so you never hear it.

17)

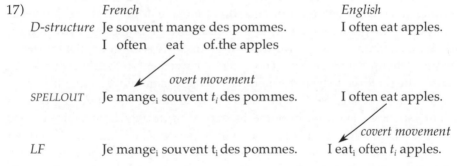

	French	*English*
D-structure	Je souvent mange des pommes.	I often eat apples.
	I often eat of.the apples	
SPELLOUT	Je mange$_i$ souvent t_i des pommes.	I often eat apples.
LF	Je mange$_i$ souvent t_i des pommes.	I eat$_i$ often t_i apples.

Again, these sentences mean the same thing, so they have identical LFs. The word order in the two sentences is different, so the SPELLOUTs are different. Again this is encoded in a parameter:

18) *Verb movement parameter*: Overt / Covert
(French sets at Overt; English sets at Covert)[3]

In this view of things, differences in the word order of the world's languages reduce to a matter of timing in the derivation.

You now have enough information to try General Problem Sets 1 & 2 and Challenge Problem Sets 1 & 2

---

3. SCOPE, COVERT MOVEMENT, AND THE MLC

At first blush the whole notion of a movement you cannot hear seems pretty suspicious (just like empty words that you can't hear seems suspicious). There is some evidence it does exist, however. This evidence comes from the behavior of *wh*-questions in Japanese and from English sentences with quantifiers.

3.1 MLC Effects in Wh-in-situ *Languages*

Let's compare two hypotheses. One is the covert movement hypothesis proposed above in section 1. That is, in languages like Mandarin Chinese and Japanese, *wh*-phrases move just as in English, but they move covertly, so that you don't hear the movement. The other hypothesis (on the surface less suspicious) is simply that *wh*-phrases don't move in Mandarin and Japanese. Consider the predictions made by these two hypotheses with respect to island conditions and the MLC. Island effects are seen in English precisely because there is movement. Too long a movement (violating the MLC) causes the sentence to be ill-formed. When there is no movement, obviously, no violations of the MLC will occur. Now compare our two hypotheses about Japanese. The first hypothesis, according to which there is (covert) movement, predicts that Japanese will show MLC violations. The other hypothesis predicts that no violations will appear since there is no *wh*-movement. The following sentence is only ungrammatical with the meaning

---

[3] Of course if you assume this, you can't claim that tense suffixes are generated in T, otherwise there is no way to get them onto the verb overtly. Chomsky (1993) gets around this problem by hypothesizing that the features that trigger movement aren't actual morphological items, like *-ed*, but instead are merely abstract features [+past]. The morphology on the verb is simply base generated on the verb in the lexicon and the features associated with it are checked at LF.

indicated (it is grammatical with other meanings, such as an echo-question interpretation).

19) *[Nani-o   doko-de   katta   ka]   oboete-iru   no?
     what-ACC   where-at   bought Q   remember   Q
     "What do you remember where we bought?"

If this data can be explained by the MLC, then we know that movement occurs – even if we can't hear it – because this constraint is sensitive to movement.

You now have enough information to try General Problem Set 3 and Challenge Problem Set 3

3.2 English Quantifiers and Scope

If LF is truly a semantic construct, we expect to find some semantic correlations to covert movement. One typical assumption about semantics is that there are some similarities between it and the semantics expressed by formal logic. With this in mind consider the following discussion of English quantifier scope.

We call words like *every* and *all* **universal quantifiers.** In formal logic these are represented by the symbol ∀. Words like *some* are **existential quantifiers** and are represented by the symbol ∃. In logic, quantifiers are said to hold **scope** over constituents containing variables. Variables are items that stand for arguments in the meaning of the sentence. The logical representation of an expression like *Everyone dances* is:

20) $\forall x$ [x dances]

This means that for every (∀) person you choose (represented by x), then that person (x) dances. The quantifier ∀ has scope over the variable x. This is indicated by the brackets that surround *[x dances]*. One popular interpretation of the logical relation of scope is that it corresponds directly to the syntactic relation of c-command. So at LF the structure of (20) is (21):

21)

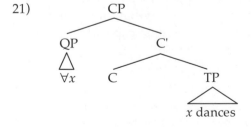

The quantifier phrase (QP) c-commands the TP, thus is holds scope over it. The quantifier is said to bind the variable it holds scope over. (In logic, this is represented as having the first x next to the $\forall$, and then the other x inside the brackets.) In the notation we have used up to now in this book, we could translate this using indexes:

22) $\forall x_i [x_i \text{ dances}]$

However, since the logical notation is more common for drawing LFs we will use it here.)

An interesting phenomenon arises when we look at sentences with more than one quantifier. The following sentence is ambiguous in English:

23) Everyone loves someone.

This can have two meanings. The first meaning is that for every person in the world there is some other person who they love: Mary loves John, Bill loves Susy, Rose loves Kim, ..., etc. The other meaning is that there is one person in the world that everyone else in the world loves: Mary loves John, Bill loves John, Rose loves John, ..., etc. Using a pseudo-logical paraphrase we can represent these two meanings as (24). The actual logical representations are given in (25):

24) a)   For every person x, there is some person y, where x loves y.
    b)   For some person y, every person x loves y.

25) a) $\forall x (\exists y [x \text{ loves } y])$
    b) $\exists y (\forall x [x \text{ loves } y])$

In logical notation, you'll notice that the difference between the two meanings lies in the order of the quantifiers, which reflects the embedding of the structure. The universal quantifier in (25a) is said to have **wide scope**, whereas in (25b) it has **narrow scope**.

In chapter 3, we claimed that if a sentence is ambiguous, then there are two tree structures for the sentence. It would be nice if we could draw two different trees that represent the two meanings of these sentences. As mentioned above, one hypothesis about scope phenomena is that they reflect c-command. That is, a quantifier has scope over everything it c-commands.[4] Consider the meaning in (24a). We can easily see this scope when we draw the simplified tree (QP stands for Quantifier Phrase):

[4] A full discussion of the semantics and structure of scope lies well beyond the purview of this book. See Heim and Kratzer (1998) for more on this complicated topic.

26)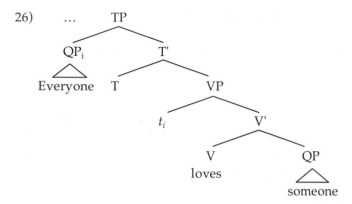

Everyone here c-commands *someone*, so the wide scope reading for the universal quantifier is derived. The narrow scope reading is more difficult, if this hypothesis is correct, then in the tree for (24b) *someone* must c-command *everyone*. The only way to get this fact is to move the quantifier. This kind of movement is called **quantifier raising** or **QR**.

27)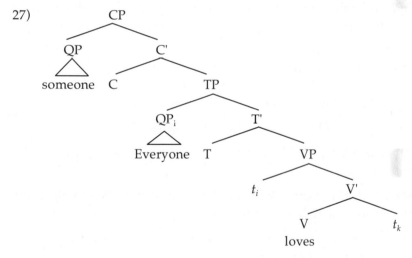

In this QR sentence, *someone* c-commands *everyone*, and so has scope over it. This derives the narrow scope reading for the universal quantifier. Obviously, this quantifier raising analysis cannot be overt. The surface string for this ambiguous sentence is *everyone loves someone* (not **someone everyone loves*). In order to get the second meaning for this sentence we need to propose movement you can't hear, in other words, covert movement. Covert movement thus has independent justification.

You now have enough information to try Challenge Problem Set 4

4. CONCLUSION

In this chapter we made the big jump from three movement rules with different but similar motivations to a single rule with a single motivation (Full Interpretation). We also claimed that cross-linguistic variation in movement, when we assume a universal semantics, requires that movement can both be overt (before SPELLOUT) and covert (after SPELLOUT). The Y model with Saussurian interface levels (LF and PF) allows this to occur. We also looked very briefly at an example from quantifier scope that provides independent support for the notion of covert movement.

IDEAS, RULES, AND CONSTRAINTS INTRODUCED IN THIS CHAPTER

i)   *Move (very informal version)*: Move something somewhere.

ii)   *Full Interpretation*: Features must be checked in a local configuration.

iii)   *Local Configuration*:
        [WH], [NOM] features: Specifier–head configuration.
        [ACC] features: Head–complement configuration.
        [PaST] etc, [Q] features: Head–head configuration.

iv)   *Logical Form (LF)*: The semantic/interpretive system.

v)   *Phonetic Form (PF)*: The component of grammar where word order is expressed.

vi)   *SPELLOUT*: The point at which the derivation divides into form (PF) and meaning deriving structures (LF).

vii)   *Overt Movement*: Movement between D-structure and SPELLOUT (heard/pronounced movement).

viii)   *Covert Movement*: Movement between SPELLOUT and LF (silent movement).

ix)   **Wh-***Parameter*: Overt/Covert.

x)   *Verb Movement Parameter*: Overt/Covert.

xi)   *Universal Quantifier ($\forall$)*: Words such as *every, each, all, any*. *Identifies all the members of a set.*

xii)   ***Existential Quantifier (∃)***: Words like *some*, or *a*. *Identifies at least one member of a set.*

xiii)   ***Scope***: A quantifier's scope is the range of material it c-commands.

xiv)   ***Wide vs. Narrow Scope***:Wide scope is when one particular quantifier c-commands another quantifier. Narrow scope is the opposite.

xv)   ***Quantifier Raising (QR)***: A covert instance of Move that moves quantifiers.

FURTHER READING

Cheng, Lisa (1997) *On the Typology of Wh-questions*. New York: Garland Press.

Chomsky, Noam (1991) Some notes on economy of derivation and representation. In Robert Friedin (ed.), *Principles and Parameters in Comparative Grammar*. Cambridge: MIT Press. pp. 417–54.

Chomsky, Noam (1993) A Minimalist program for linguistic theory. In Kenneth L. Hale and Samuel J. Keyser (eds.), *The View from Building 20*. Cambridge: MIT Press. pp. 1–52.

Chomsky, Noam (1995) *The Minimalist Program*. Cambridge: MIT Press.

Heim, Irene and Kratzer, Angelika (1998) *Semantics in Generative Grammar*. Oxford: Blackwell.

Huang, C.-T. James (1982) Logical Relations in Chinese and the Theory of Grammar. Ph.D. dissertation, MIT.

May, Robert (1985) *Logical Form*. Cambridge: MIT Press.

Saito, Mamoru and Howard Lasnik (1994) *Move Alpha: Conditions on Its Application and Output*. Cambridge: MIT Press.

GENERAL PROBLEM SETS

1. FRENCH
[Data Analysis; Basic]
Go back and look at all the French data in chapter 9 and determine if French has overt or covert DP movement. Explain your answer.

2. IRISH
[Data Analysis; Basic]
Go back and look at all the Irish data in chapters 9, 11 and determine whether Irish has overt or covert *wh*-movement, overt or covert DP movement and overt or covert head movement.

3. PF MOVEMENT
[Creative and Critical Thinking; Advanced]
In the text above, we proposed that some movement was covert. That is, it happened between SPELLOUT and LF. This movement affects meaning, but it doesn't affect how the sentence is pronounced. Can you think of any kind of movement that might occur just on the PF branch of the model? That is, are there any phenomena that affect only how the sentence is pronounced, but not its meaning?

CHALLENGE PROBLEM SETS

CHALLENGE PROBLEM SET 1: SERBIAN/CROATIAN/BOSNIAN
[Data Analysis; Challenge]
Compare the data in challenge problem set 3 of chapter 11 with their English Equivalents:

a)   *Who what where buys?
b)   Who buys what where?
c)   *Who what buys where?
d)   *Who where buys what?

Using the terms "covert movement" and "overt movement," explain the difference in parameter setting between Serbo-Croatian and English.

CHALLENGE PROBLEM SET 2: NEPALI AND MONGOLIAN
[Data Analysis; Challenge]
Consider the following data from Nepali and Mongolian (data from Erin Good and Amy LaCross respectively). Do these languages have overt or covert *wh*-movement? How can you tell?

Nepali:

a)   Timilai uu   kahile aunche   jasto-lagcha?

    you   she when coming   think

    "When do you think she is coming?"

b)   Timi kahile aaunchau?

    you   when   coming

    "When are you going to come?"

c)   Ramle Sitale kun   manche ayecha bhaneko sochecha?

      Ram   Sita which man   came said   think?

      "Which man did Ram think that Sita said came?"

Mongolian:

d)   Ekč   jamar   hɔl hix   ve?

     older-sister   which-one food make C$_{[+Q]}$

     "Which food will the older sister make? "

CHALLENGE PROBLEM SET 3: ECHO QUESTIONS IN ENGLISH
[Critical Thinking; Challenge]
Give an argument that echo questions in English involve no movement
at all (neither overt nor covert), and thus are very different from the covert
movement found in languages like Chinese and Japanese. Hint: The
evidence will come from the MLC: The following sentence might help you:

a)   Who does John think loves *what*?

CHALLENGE PROBLEM SET 4: SCOPE OF NEGATION
[Data Analysis, Creative and Critical Thinking; Challenge]
The following sentence is ambiguous:

a)   The editor did not find many mistakes in the paper.

This can either mean

i)   The editor isn't very good, and although there were many mistakes he
      didn't find them.
ii)   The editor searched thoroughly for mistakes, but the paper didn't have
      many mistakes in it.

We can express these variations in meaning using scope. With meaning (i),
we have a situation where *many* has scope over negation (i.e. *many*
c-commands *not* (¬) or in logic: MANYx [¬ find (editor, x)]). (That is, *many*
has wide scope). By contrast the narrow scope reading (ii), *not* c-commands
many (¬ find (editor, MANYx).

Part 1: Draw the LF tree for each of the meanings. Keep in mind
that the word order for (i) will not be the same as the SPELLOUT order,
you are drawing the tree for the LF which includes movement that is covert.
Also assume that only quantifiers move; negation does not move.

Part 2: Consider now the passive form of this sentence:

b)   Many mistakes were not found in the paper by the editor.

This sentence is not ambiguous. It only has one meaning: wide scope
for many (that is, the meaning in (i) above). This sentence can never have
the meaning in (ii) above. Why should this be the case? (Hint: ask yourself

if it is possible to create an LF with negation c-commanding *many* for (b). Remember negation does not move.)

Part 3: English passives involve overt DP movement from the complement of V to the specifier of TP. Explain why it is crucial that this movement be overt, in explaining why *many* cannot have narrow scope (reading ii) at LF.

Optional really advanced question: Are the traces of DP movement variables? How can you tell?

Part 4

Advanced Topics

chapter 13

Expanded VPs

0. INTRODUCTION

In chapters 1–12, we sketched out the major theoretical tools assumed by the majority of syntacticians operating in the principles and parameters framework. The next few chapters take us away from these agreed-upon areas, and focus on important material that is both more controversial and more advanced. The discussion in these chapters is going to be more open-ended. Do not expect a perfect answer or even an answer that can be considered "right." Instead our discussion will consider some major lines of thought about these more difficult topics.

1. THE PROBLEM OF DITRANSITIVE VERBS[1]

In chapters 2 and 8, we discussed a number of ditransitive verbs, such as *put* of subcategory $V_{[DP \_ DP \, PP]}$, *give* of subcategory $V_{[DP \_ DP \, \{DP/PP\}]}$, and *tell* of subcategory $V_{[DP \_ DP \, \{CP/DP\}]}$. In many cases the third argument of these verbs seems to function like a complement, aside from the fact that it is not immediately adjacent to the verb. For example, no adjunct may intervene between the two post-verbal DP arguments of the verb *give*:

---

[1] Many thanks to Heidi Harley for allowing me access to her teaching materials for the preparation of this chapter.

1) a) *Josh gave Clay carefully a book.
    b) Josh gave Clay a book carefully.

However, we know from our study of X-bar theory in chapters 6 and 7, that
(i) we are only ever allowed one complement and (ii) complements of verbs
must be adjacent to that verb. This follows from the fact that X-bar theory
requires trees to be strictly binary branching. So the place to attach
these "second" complements is a mystery (2):

2)

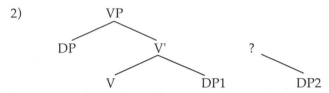

Even if we were to allow ternary branching as in (3), a different problem
emerges. In (3) the two DPs c-command one another, thus we might expect
a symmetry between them in terms of binding relationships.

3)

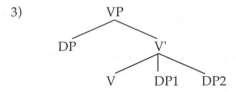

Barss and Lasnik (1986) showed that there is actually a clear asymmetry
between these two DPs, as if the first one c-commanded the second, but not
vice versa. This can be seen in examples (4a and b) where we have a typical
anaphor–antecedent relationship (principle A). As you can see the indirect
object *Justin* can bind a direct object anaphor; but the reverse is not possible.
If the structure of the sentence were (3), then the anaphor should be able
to appear in either position because the two DPs symmetrically c-command
one another.

4) a) Briana showed Justin$_i$ himself$_i$ in the mirror.
    b) *Briana showed himself$_i$ Justin$_i$ in the mirror.

These facts show that in terms of c-command relationships the two DPs
must be in a configuration like that in (5):

5)

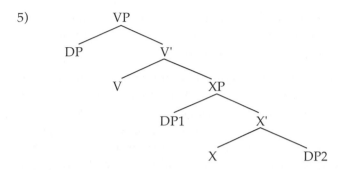

It's only in a configuration like (5) where DP1 c-commands DP2, but DP2 does not c-command DP1. Of course the obvious question that arises then lies in the nature of the category labeled X in (5). We address this question in the next section.

You now have enough information to try General Problem Set 1

2. LIGHT VERBS

There is reason to think that what appear to be morphologically simple verbs in English may in fact be morphologically complex. In particular, we're going to claim that verbs that assign an agentive theta role consist of two parts; a verbal root and what we call a *light verb*. Light verbs are essentially auxiliaries (in that they head their own VP) and they are part of the complex that surfaces as a simple verb in English. To see this at work, we need to turn to other languages where the morphological complexity of verbs is more obvious on the surface.

In Japanese (6a), Hiaki (6b), Malagasy (6c), we see that certain simple verbs in English correspond to morphologically complex structures in these languages. These each consist of (at least) a verb root and some other morpheme that speakers report as either marking agentivity, or making the root into a full verb. I have abbreviated this light verb element, following Chomsky (1995) as "v". This is usually called *little v* to contrast it to lexical verb roots which are of category *big V*.

6) a) Keiko-wa   pizza-o   ag-**e**-ta.
        Keiko-TOP   pizza-ACC   rise-**v**-PAST
        "Keiko raised the pizza."

    b) Huan   u'usit-ta   ee-**tua**-k.
        Juan   child-ACC   feel-**v**-PAST
        "Juan teased the child."

c) M-**an**-sasa   ny lamba   amin ny savony   Rasoa.
    PAST-**v**-wash   the clothes   with the soap   Rasoa
    "Rasoa washes the clothes with the soap."

A number of scholars have suggested that even in English, agentive verbs are bimorphemic. There is a verb root that indicates the lexical meaning of the word and a light verb that roughly means "cause." So a verb like *clean* really means something like "to cause to be clean." Kratzer (1996) suggests that agentive theta roles are not assigned by the verb, but by the light verb[2] contained within it. So if we take a verb like *clean*, this is really composed of the little verb v meaning "cause" (CAUSE) which assigns the agent role, and takes a VP as a complement (we will refer to the theta role assigned to this VP as "predicate") and the lexical root √CLEAN, which takes the theme as a complement:

7) CAUSE   √CLEAN

Agent	Predicate
DP	VP
i	j

Theme
DP
K

So the tree for the sentence *Ryan cleaned the window* contains a vP dominating a VP. The subject DP moves for the usual case and EPP reasons. In order to create the verb *clean* out of CAUSE and √CLEAN there is head movement of the V into the v category. The affix *-ed* either lowers on to the v+V head (as we did in chapter 9) or is attached to the V to start with, and there is covert movement of the v+V to T (as we did in chapter 12) – we'll indicate these options with a dotted curved line.

You now have enough information to try General Problem Set 2

[2] Kratzer actually calls the category *voice*, and suggests that it is of the same category as the auxiliary verb that introduces the passive discussed in chapter 10.

8)

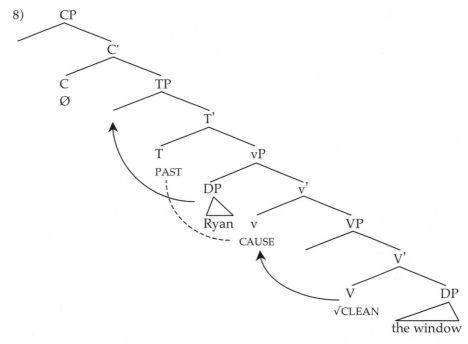

The evidence for this separation of agents from their roots comes from the behavior of phrasal idioms. Marantz noticed that while there are sentential idioms (the verb plus all the arguments as in *The pot called the kettle black*[3]) and verb+object idioms (such as *kick the bucket*[4]), there are no subject+verb idioms. Similarly, we find that while the meaning of the object can change the interpretation of the verb, as in (9), the subject never does so (10).

9) a) kill a bug   = end the life of the bug
    b) kill a conversation   = cause the conversation to end
    c) kill an evening   = while away the time span of the evening
    d) kill a bottle   = empty the bottle
    e) kill an audience   = entertain the audience

10) a) John laughed
    b) The audience laughed
    c) The manager laughed
    d) The bug laughed

---

[3] For the information of non-native English speakers: this means "to speak hypocritically."
[4] For the information of non-native English speakers: this means "to die."

This suggests that there is a tight link between the verb and its object that it doesn't share with its subject. If we adopt the little v approach, these facts follow directly: the verb root has the object in its theta grid but the agent is never in the theta grid of the verb root, so an idiomatic meaning cannot form around it.

You now have enough information to try Challenge Problem Sets 1 & 2

With this light verb approach for simple transitives, let's consider how this might extend to datives. It is a relatively simple matter to substitute little v and big V in for the verb and X in the tree in (5) giving (11):

11)

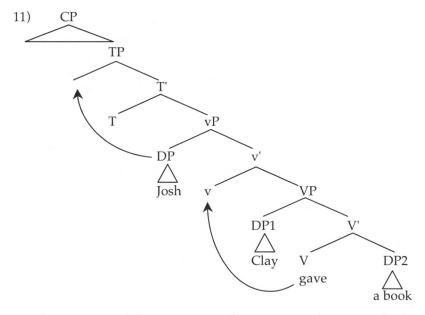

Head movement of the V to v gives the correct spellout order (*Josh gave Clay a book*). It also accounts for the asymmetric c-command effects between the two post-verbal DPs. There are however, a number of problems with this analysis still. One thing that is a bit of a mystery is how case gets assigned to the two NPs, especially the one that is labeled DP1 in (11). To find an explanation for this, we turn now to a different, yet equally puzzling phenomenon involving object positioning.

3. OBJECT SHIFT

The following pair of sentences with embedded infinitive clauses from two dialects of Irish show an interesting alternation in the position of the object and in the case marking of the object. Sentence (12a) represents the order of elements in the northern dialects of Irish (mainly Ulster). You will note that the object appears before the verb (and the particle a^L) and bears accusative case – the case we normally associate with being the complement to the verb. In sentence (12b), which is found in literary Irish and in southern (Munster) Irish, by contrast, the object appears after the verb, but it takes a genitive case marking.[5]

12) a) Ba mhaith liom   [$_{CP}$ Seán   *an abairt* a^L scríobh].
         C good with.1.S   John   the sentence.ACC TRAN write
         "I want John to write the sentence."

    b) Ba mhaith liom [$_{CP}$ Seán a^L scríobh *na habairte*].
         C good with.1.S   John   TRAN   write   the sentence.GEN
         "I want John to write the sentence."

Both these sentences are surprising. As we've seen in earlier chapters, Irish seems to typically put its heads before its complements (determiners precede Ns, prepositions precede DPs, etc.). With this in mind, (12b) displays the expected word order; but we get the unexpected genitive case marking on the object. (12a) has the opposite problem, the order of the verb and its complement DP are reversed from what we'd expect in a head-initial language, but the object at least bears the correct case.[6]

    We find a similar variation in literary Irish when we look at main clauses in different aspects.[7] In the progressive aspect (13b), objects follow the main verb and take the genitive case. In the recent perfective (13a), objects precede the main verb (and the particle a^L), and take the accusative case:

13) a) Tá   Seán tar eis *an abairt* a^L scríobh.
         be.PRES John PERF   the sentence TRAN write
         "John has just written the sentence."

    b) Tá   Seán ag   scríobh *na habairte*.
         be.PRES John PROG write   the sentence
         "John is writing the sentence."

---

[5] In traditional grammars, this is typically taken to be a result of the fact that the infinitival verb in Irish is "nominal" in nature. This account doesn't explain the accusative case in the Northern dialects, so we will leave it aside here.

[6] This order and case marking are also available in the Southern dialects if there is no overt subject for the embedded clause. (See McCloskey 1980 for a survey of the phenomenon).

[7] Aspect refers to the duration of an event and whether it is completed or not.

This kind of alternation, known as **object shift**, is not an esoteric property of Irish; it is found in a wide variety of languages. Take the embedded clauses below taken from German (data from Diesing 1992); in particular focus on the order of negation and the DP referring to "the cat":

14) a)   … weil ich *nicht* [DP eine einzige Katze] gestreichelt habe
          since I   not   a   single cat   petted   have
      "… since I have not petted a single cat"

    b)   … weil ich [DP die Katze] *nicht* streichle
          since I   the cat   not   pet
      "… since I did not pet the cat"

The conditions for object shift here are different from the Irish example (the alternation is around negation instead of around the verb; and the alternation seems to be linked to definiteness/specificity rather than case), but this also appears to be a case of object alternation.

We can even find a related alternation in English. Consider complex verbs like *blow up* in English. With full NPs, the direct object can either precede or follow the particle up (15a and b), but with pronouns the particle must appear in the middle of the complex verb (15c and d):

15) a)   I blew up the building.
    b)   I blew the building up.
    c)   *I blew up it.
    d)   I blew it up.

These alternations in object position all differ in their specifics, but clearly we have some kind of movement operation that affects the position of objects.

The Irish case is particularly illustrative, as it shows an alternation in case marking. Accusative case is only available in the shifted position. Building upon a proposal of Pollock (1989) and Chomsky (1991) we can propose that there is a special functional category whose sole purpose is accusative case assignment. The name of this category is **AgrO** (standing for Object Agreement); (the basic idea behind this name being that the case assigner is usually the constituent that agrees with the object). The head of AgrO in Irish is the particle a^L,[8] which follows the shifted object. For Irish object shift then, we have a structure where the object moves from the position where it gets its theta role to this shifted position where it gets accusative case:

---

[8] This is a different a^L from the one seen in the exercises in chapter 11. It is simply homophonous in the same way that the English infinitive marker *to* is homophonous to the preposition *to*.

16)

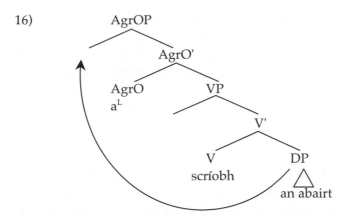

AgrOP seems to be located between VP and vP.[9] This can be seen in the following sentence from Scots Gaelic (a language closely related to Irish), where the shifted object appears before the a^L AgrO morpheme but after the light verb *bhith*:

17) Bu toigh leam   [$_{CP}$ sibh a^L bhith air   ***an dorus*** a^L dhùnadh].
    be like with me   you AGR v   PERF the door AGR close
    "I'd like you to have shut the door."[10]

You now have enough information to try General Problem Sets 3 & 4 and Challenge Problem Set 3

Leaving aside the upper portion of the tree, the structure of the expanded VP then is at least as follows

18)

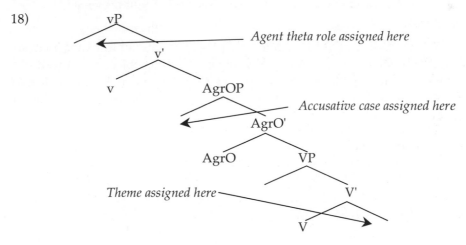

---

[9] As first observed by Koizumi (1993).
[10] Data from Adger (1996).

This is quite a radical shift in structure from the simple VP we've had up to now. So it is worth considering if this proposal makes any predictions. One elegant argument for this expanded structure comes from the work of Lasnik (1999a). In many languages there are phenomena where a string that has already been uttered is omitted in subsequent structures where it would otherwise have to be repeated word for word. For example, we get sentences like (19):

19) Darin will eat a squid sandwich but Raiza won't.

The second CP here *[Raiza won't]* is obviously missing the VP *[eat a squid sandwich]* as that is what Raiza won't do. One typical explanation for this phenomenon is that there is a special rule of **ellipsis** that allows the deletion of VPs under identity with an antecedent VP:

20) Darin will [eat a squid sandwich]ᵢ but Raiza won't [eat a squid sandwich]ᵢ.

There is one variant of the ellipsis phenomenon that puzzlingly doesn't delete the entire VP. This is called, for reasons that need not worry us here, **pseudogapping**. In pseudogapping constructions the accusative DP is left behind:

21) Darin will eat a squid sandwich, and Raiza will *a peanut butter one*.

This isn't simply deleting a verb: everything but the accusative-marked DP is deleted from the second VP (example from Lasnik 1999a).

22) The DA proved Jones guilty and the assistant DA will ~~prove~~ *Smith* ~~guilty~~.

The split vP-AgrOP-VP architecture provides a straightforward analysis of this. Pseudogapping is indeed VP ellipsis – but the object has moved out of the VP into AgrOP, but the verb and all other material remains inside the VP, and gets deleted. The object survives ellipsis because it has shifted outside of the VP.

23)

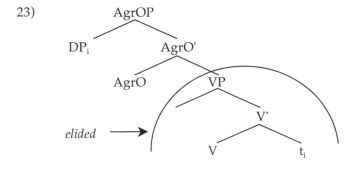

Regular VP ellipsis is really vP ellipsis, which is why the object disappears in those contexts.

Object shift to a VP-external AgrOP also explains a puzzling fact in a phenomenon called ***Antecedent Contained Deletion*** (ACD). ACD is a special case of ellipsis, where an elided VP is contained within a DP that is itself contained within the VP that serves as the antecedent for the ellipsis, as schematized in (24). An example of ACD is given in (25):

24) $[_{VP}$ ... $[_{DP}$ ... $[_{CP}$ ... $[_{VP}$ ---$]_i$ ...$]$ $]$ $]_i$

25) Brandon $[_{VP}$ read every book that Megan did $[_{VP}$ ...$]]$.

ACD has the property of infinite regress. The antecedent of the ellipsis contains the ellipsis, so how can the content of the elided VP ever be recovered? The antecedent of the gap also contains that gap. Object shift provides an elegant solution to this problem.[11] The DP containing the gap is always an object, so it shifts out of the antecedent VP into the specifier of AgrOP. After this happens the elided VP is no longer contained within its own antecedent so the problem of infinite regress vanishes, as the actual gap is no longer contained within the VP antecedent.

26)

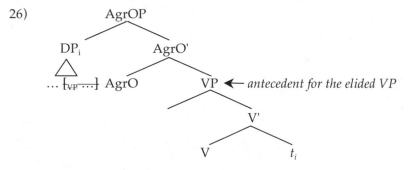

4. DITRANSITIVES: REPRISE

Let's now return to ditransitive verbs. For verbs where the final argument is a PP and CP we have a straightforward account of where all the arguments get theta roles and case. First let's look at a verb like *tell* which can take both a DP and a CP complement. First we have the theta grids for the little v and the root √TELL.

---

[11] See Hornstein (1994).

27) CAUSE

Agent	Predicate
DP	AgrOP
i	J

√TELL

Theme	Proposition
DP	CP
k	l

Given a sentence like *Nate told Brandon that Kimberly drove an SUV*, we have a D-structure tree as in (28) (leaving aside the details of tense inflection).

28) CP

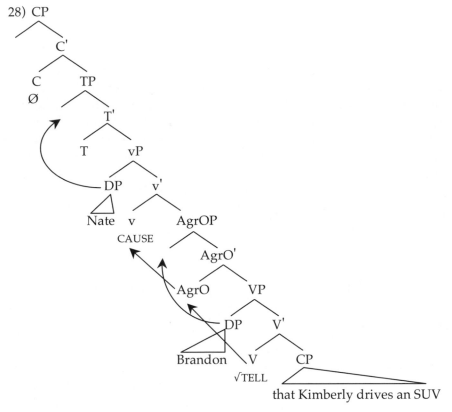

that Kimberly drives an SUV

The root moves through AgrO and into CAUSE; it must stop in AgrO on its way up to the little v in order to meet the MLC. The DP *Brandon* shifts to the specifier of AgrOP to get case.

A similar analysis can be applied to verbs like *put* that take a PP second complement, as in the sentence *Briana put the mug on the counter*:

29) CP

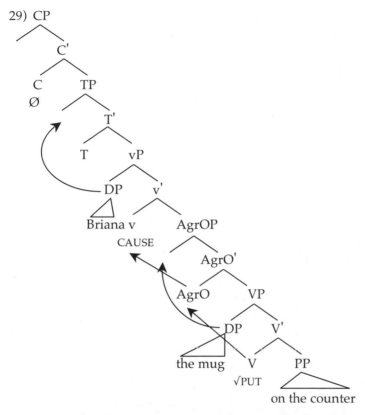

The last kind of ditransitive is more difficult. This is the case of *give*. *Give* allows two possible argument structures one with a DP theme and PP goal (as in *Jason gave the tape recorder to Maria*). This version of *give* presumably has a structure like that in (28). The other version of *give* takes two DP complements (*Jason gave Maria the tape recorder*). There are two puzzles with this kind of construction. First we have the obvious question of the source of accusative case for the goal DP. Second, more curious, is the fact that the indirect object goal precedes the direct object theme. If the theme moves to the specifier of AgrOP for case, then the goal must be moving to a higher position than that. One possibility that has been proposed is that goals can be introduced by two distinct mechanisms. One is via a preposition like *to*. The other is using another light verb, this one meaning LOCATE or POSSESS instead of CAUSE. This second mechanism could be paired with another case assigning functional category, this time for indirect objects (AgrIOP).[12]

---

[12] Collins and Thráinsson (1996).

Under such a story the architecture of the complex VP for a verb like *give* looks like (30).

30) CP

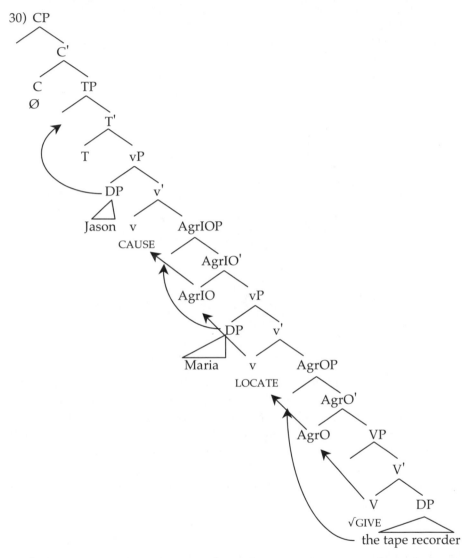

Each DP moves to its case position, and the root √GIVE moves through AgrO, Locate, AgrIO, into CAUSE. This gives the correct surface order.

There are, of course, a number of open issues here, not the least of which is the relationship between the two structures for the verb *give*. However, these complex split VP structures seem to provide a mechanism for explaining the hierarchical properties of ditransitive verbs, the case marking of their arguments and provide an explanation for such diverse facts as pseudogapping, Antecedent Contained Deletion, and object shift. In the next chapter, we see that the AgrO category also helps us in providing a landing site for a new kind of DP movement (subject to object raising).

You now have enough information to try General Problem Sets 5 & 6

IDEAS, RULES, AND CONSTRAINTS INTRODUCED IN THIS CHAPTER

i)   ***Light verbs (little v)***: the higher part of a complex verb, usually meaning CAUSE (or LOCATE in the case of ditransitive double object verbs).

ii)   ***Object Shift***: the phenomenon where accusatively marked objects shift leftwards.

iii)   ***AgrO***: the head that checks accusative case in the split VP system.

iv)   ***(VP) Ellipsis***: A process that deletes a VP (or vP) under identity with a previously uttered identical VP.

v)   ***Pseudogapping***: A variety of ellipsis where the accusative object is not deleted.

vi)   ***Antecedent Contained Deletion (ACD)***: A kind of ellipsis where the antecedent of the ellipsis contains the ellipsis site.

FURTHER READING

Adger, David (1996) Aspect, agreement and Measure Phrases in Scottish Gaelic. In Robert Borsley and Ian Roberts (eds.), *The Syntax of the Celtic Languages*. Cambridge: Cambridge University Press. pp. 200–2.

Barss, Andy and Howard Lasnik (1986) A note on anaphora and double objects. *Linguistic Inquiry* 17, 347–54.

Beck, Sigrid and Kyle Johnson (2004) Double objects again. *Linguistic Inquiry* 35, 97–124.

Chomsky, Noam (1991) Some notes on economy of derivation and representation. In Robert Freidin (ed.), *Principles and Parameters in Comparative Grammar*. Cambridge: MIT Press. pp. 417–54.

Chung, Sandra (1976) An object creating rule in Bahasa Indonesia. *Linguistic Inquiry* 7, 1–37.

Collins, Chris and Hoskuldur Thráinsson (1996). VP internal structure and object shift in Icelandic. *Linguistic Inquiry, 27*, 391–444.

Den Dikken, Marcel (1995) *Particles: On the Syntax of Verb-Particle, Triadic, and Causative Constructions*. Oxford: Oxford University Press

Diesing, Molly (1992) *Indefinites*. Cambridge: MIT Press.

Harley, Heidi (2002) Possession and the double object construction. *Yearbook of Linguistic Variation* 2, 29–68.

Hornstein, Norbert (1994) An argument for Minimalism: the case of antecedent contained deletion. *Linguistic Inquiry* 25, 455–80.

Iatridou, Sabine (1990) About Agr(P). *Linguistic Inquiry* 21, 551–7.

Johnson, Kyle (1991) Object positions. *Natural Language and Linguistic Theory* 9, 577–636.

Koizumi, Masatoshi (1993) Object Agreement Phrases and the split VP hypothesis. *MIT Working Papers in Linguistics* 18, 99–148.

Kratzer, Angelika (1996) Severing the external argument from its verb. In Johan Rooryck and Laurie Zaring (eds.), *Phrase Structure and the Lexicon*. Dordrecht: Kluwer. pp. 109–37.

Larson, Richard (1988) On the double object construction. *Linguistic Inquiry* 19, 335–91.

Lasnik, Howard (1999a) *Minimalist Analyses*. Oxford: Blackwell.

Marantz, Alec (1984). *On the Nature of Grammatical Relations*. Cambridge: MIT Press.

McCloskey, James (1980) Is there raising in Modern Irish? *Eriú* 31, 59–99.

Pesetsky, David (1994) *Zero Syntax: Experiencers and Cascades*. Cambridge: MIT Press.

Pollock, Jean-Yves (1989) Verb movement, Universal Grammar and the structure of IP. *Linguistic Inquiry* 20, 365–424.

Stechow, Arnim von (1996) The different readings of *wieder* 'again': A structural account. *Journal of Semantics* 13, 87–138.

GENERAL PROBLEM SETS

1. NPIs and Double Object Verbs

[Data Analysis and Critical Thinking; Intermediate]

The words *anything* and *anyone* are negative polarity items, and must be licensed by a negative word like *no one* or *nothing*. Explain how the following data supports the structure given above in the main text in (5). (Hint: think structural relations). (Data from Barss and Lasnik 1986.)

a) Amanda gave no one anything.
b) *Amanda gave anyone nothing.

2. COMPLEX VERBS
[Data Analysis and Critical Thinking; Intermediate]
Sentence (a) is from Persian and sentence (b) is from Chicheŵa. Explain how these data support the idea that verbs are really composed of a v and a V.

a) Kimea az ra'ise edâre   da'vat **kard**
    Kimea of boss   office   invitation **v**
    "Kimea invited the office boss."

b) Mtsikana   anagw-**ets**-a   kuti mtsuko
    Girl   fall-**v**   that waterpot
    "The girl knocked over that waterpot."

3. PARTICLES
[Data Analysis and Critical Thinking; Advanced]
Using the split vP-AgrOP-VP system, explain the verb-particle facts of English given in example (15). Assume that a verb like *blow up* is structured as in (i) and that the *blow* portion of this complex verb can move independently of the preposition/particle *up*. You do <u>not</u> have to explain why the shifted order is obligatory with pronouns and not with DPs.

i)

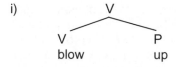

4. THETA GRIDS
[Application of Skills; Intermediate]
The theory involving AgrOP requires that we modify the lexical entries given in the text above in (7). Provide new theta grids for little v meaning CAUSE and the root √CLEAN that take into account AgrOP.

5. TREES
[Application of Skills; Intermediate to Advanced]
Using split VP structures and AgrOP draw the trees for the following sentences:

a) Susan sent the package to Heidi.
b) Carolyn sent Heidi a package.
c) Peter placed the letter in the envelope.
d) I asked Mike if he had seen the Yeti.
e) I bought some flowers for Manuel.
f) I bought Manuel some flowers.

6. Applicatives in Bahasa Indonesia
[Data Analysis; Advanced]
Consider the following data from Bahasa Indonesia (Chung 1976). This language has two orders that are similar to the prepositional order and the double object orders of English *give* type verbs. What is interesting is the presence in the construction with two DPs of a morpheme in the verb that is typically called the applicative (APPL), explain how this data is evidence for the split VP approach proposed in (30).

a) Saja mem-bawa surat itu kepada Ali.
   I   CAUSE-bring letter the to   Ali
   "I brought the letter to Ali."

b) Saja mem bawa-kan   Ali surat itu.
   I   CAUSE-bring-APPL   Ali letter the
   "I brought Ali the letter."

CHALLENGE PROBLEM SETS

CHALLENGE PROBLEM SET 1: THAT DOG DOESN'T HUNT
[Critical Thinking; Challenge]
Consider the idiom: *That dog doesn't hunt* (meaning "that solution doesn't work"). Is this a counter-example to the claim that there are no subject-verb idioms in English? (As a matter of contrast: notice that in verb + object idioms the subject can be any possible DP: John kicked the bucket, The man kicked the bucket.

CHALLENGE PROBLEM SET 2: AGAIN
[Critical Thinking; Challenge]
As discussed in von Stechow (1996) and Beck and Johnson (2004) the following sentence is ambiguous:

   John opened the door again.

It can have either of the following meanings:

i)   The door was open before (perhaps opened by Susan) and now it's open again due to John's action.
ii) John opened the door before, and he did it again.

Keeping in mind the principle of modification, explain how this data is evidence for a little v meaning CAUSE and the split VP hypothesis.

CHALLENGE PROBLEM SET 3: AGRS
[Creative Thinking; Challenge]
In the chapter above we proposed AgrO and AgrIO, there may well be evidence that case is not assigned by TP, but by an AgrSP. In particular

it has been proposed that the EPP is a property of TP, but case is assigned lower in the structure, in an AgrSP:

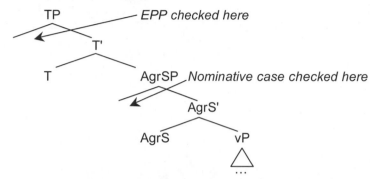

Part 1: Using the following data from English argue for an AgrS in the position suggested above. Assume *there* is an expletive (without a theta role.)

a) There was a man arriving at the station when I pulled up.
b) There were four men arriving at the station when I pulled up.

Part 2: The following data from Scots Gaelic was given above as evidence for the position of AgrO between v and V. This data also contains evidence for AgrS. Explain what it is. (Scots Gaelic data from Adger 1996.)

c) Bu toigh leam   [cₚ sibh aᴸ   bhith air   an doras aᴸ   dhúnadh.]
    be like with me   you AGR v   PERF the door AGR close
     "I'd like you to have shut the door."

chapter 14

Raising, Control,
and Empty Categories

0. INTRODUCTION

The following two sentences look remarkably alike:

1) a) Jean is likely to leave.
    b) Jean is reluctant to leave.

But these sentences are structurally very different. Sentence (1a) is a raising sentence like those we saw in chapter 10. Sentence (1b), however, is a different matter. This is what we call a *control sentence*; it does not involve any DP movement. We will claim there is a special kind of null DP in the subject position of the embedded clause. Syntacticians call this special DP *PRO*, which stands for "null pronoun." The differences between these two constructions are schematized below.

2) Jean$_i$ is likely [t_i to leave].   *subject-to-subject raising*

3) Jean is reluctant [PRO to leave].   *(subject) control*

The bracketed diagram in (3) shows the DP raising construction we looked at in chapter 10. The structure in (4), which has no movement, is the control construction. The evidence for this kind of proposal will come from the thematic properties of the various predicates involved. In addition to contrasting the sentences in (1a and b), we'll also look at the differences between sentences like (4a and b):

4) a) Jean wants Brian to leave.
    b) Jean persuaded Brian to leave.

Again, on the surface these two sentences look very similar. But, again, once we look at these in more detail we'll see that they have quite different structures. We will claim that *Brian* in (4a) raises to the object position of the verb *wants*. This is called **subject-to-object raising**, and was discussed in an exercise in the last chapter. The structure of the sentence in (4b) parallels the structure of the control sentence in (1b). Both *Jean* and *Brian* are arguments of the verb *persuade*, there is no raising, but there is a PRO in the subject position of the embedded clause.

5) Jean wants Brian$_i$ [t_i to leave].   *subject-to-object raising*

6) Jean persuaded Brian [PRO to leave].   *object control*

The construction in (6) is called **object control** (because the object "controls" what the PRO refers to).

This chapter ends with a short discussion of the various kinds of empty elements we've looked at so far (null heads, PRO, traces, etc.), and introduces a new one which is found in languages like Spanish and Italian.

1. RAISING VS. CONTROL

1.1 Two Kinds of Theta Grids for Main Predicates

If you look at the following two sentences, you will see that the predicate *is likely* only takes one argument: a proposition.

7) a) [That Jean left] is likely.   *clausal subject*
    b) It is likely [that Jean left].   *extraposition*

Sentence (7a) shows the proposition *that Jean left* functioning as the predicate's subject. Sentence (7b) has this embedded clause as a complement, and has an expletive in subject position. For reasons having to do with the history of generative grammar, but that need not concern us here, the first construction (7a) is often called a **clausal subject** construction, and the second (7b) an **extraposition** construction. The theta grid for the predicate is given in (8). As is standard (see chapter 8), expletives are not marked in the theta grid, as they don't get a theta role.

8) *is likely*

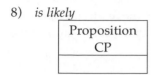

Proposition CP

We assume that the D-structures of the sentences given in (7) are identical. These sentences have the embedded clause as a complement to the predicate, and nothing in the subject position:

9)

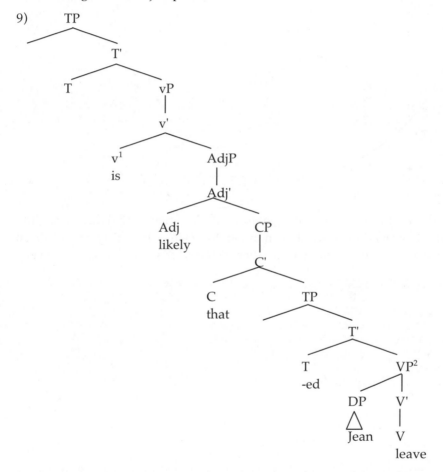

---

[1] This little v isn't CAUSE because it doesn't introduce an agent. It probably means something like "be in the state of …"

[2] To keep this tree down to a reasonable size, I'm abbreviating the vP-VP tree here simply as VP.

In the clausal subject construction, the embedded CP moves to the specifier of TP, presumably to satisfy the EPP requirement that every clause have a subject: [3]

10)   TP

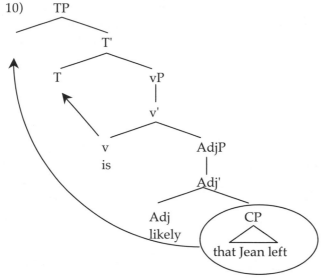

(10) shows the SPELLOUT for sentence (7a). Sentence (7b) has a slightly different derivation, instead of moving the clause to satisfy the EPP, an expletive *it* is inserted into the specifier of TP as seen in the SPELLOUT in (11):

---

[3] We haven't discussed the possibility of moving CPs before. Since this is movement for the EPP, it may well be a variant of DP movement. This analysis of clausal subjects (involving movement) is not uncontroversial. Some researchers generate these CPs directly in the specifier of TP at D-structure. We move it from the complement position to ensure parsimony with the analysis of expletive and raising constructions discussed below. We should also note that not all raising verbs allow the clausal subject construction. For example, *seem* and *appear* do not *[[that Jean left] seems]*. I leave it as an exercise for you to figure out why this might be the case.

11)

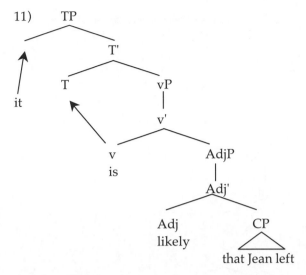

Observe that the embedded clause is finite in both these sentences. This means that its subject gets nominative Case. As we saw in the chapter 10, if the embedded clause is non-finite (as in 12), then the subject must move to get Case. Fortunately, *is likely* does not have an external (subject) theta role, but does have a nominative Case feature to check. This means that the specifier of the higher TP is available for Case feature checking. This is a typical raising construction.

12) ____ is likely [Jean to leave].

13)

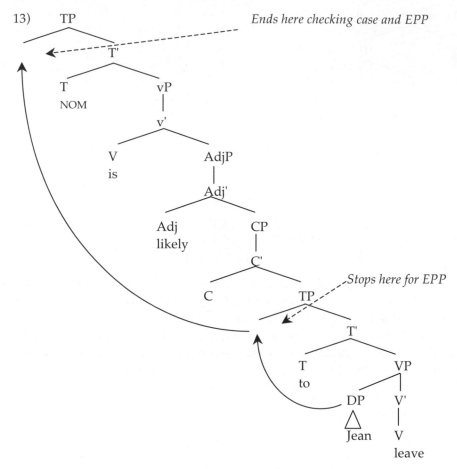

As we noted in chapter 10, the *Jean* in this sentence gets its theta role from *leave*. *Jean* is going *to leave*, she isn't *likely*. What *is likely* is the whole proposition of Jean leaving. With *is likely* then, there is only one theta role assigned (to the embedded clause). Three possible sentences emerge with this structure: clausal subject, extraposition and raising.

Let's contrast this with the predicate *is reluctant*. If you think carefully about it, you'll notice that this predicate takes two arguments. The person who is reluctant (the experiencer) and what they are reluctant about (the proposition):

14) *is reluctant*

Experiencer DP	Proposition CP

This means that, unlike *is likely*, *is reluctant* assigns a theta role to its subject. Because of this both clausal subject and extraposition (expletive) constructions are impossible. The specifier of TP of the main clause is already occupied by the experiencer (it moves there to get Case), so there is no need to insert an expletive or move the CP for EPP reasons. This explains why the following two sentences (an extraposition and a clausal subject example) are ill-formed with the predicate *is reluctant*:

15) a)   *It is reluctant [that Jean left].   (where *it* is an expletive)
    b)   *[that Jean left] is reluctant.

Both of these sentences seem to be "missing" something. More precisely they are both missing the external experiencer role: the person who is reluctant. Consider now the control sentence we mentioned above in the introduction:

16) Jean is reluctant to leave.

Jean here is the experiencer, and the embedded clause is the proposition:

17) a)   *is reluctant*

Experiencer	Proposition
DP	CP
i	k

    b)   Jean$_i$ is reluctant [to leave]$_k$.

So *Jean* is theta marked by *is reluctant*. Note, however, that this isn't the only predicate in this sentence. We also have the predicate *leave*, with the following theta grid:

18) *leave*

Agent
DP
M

Who is this theta role assigned to? It also appears to be assigned to the DP *Jean*:

19) Jean$_{i/m}$ is reluctant [to leave]$_k$.

As we saw in chapter 8, the theta criterion only allows one theta role per DP. This sentence seems to be a violation of the theta criterion, as its subject DP gets two theta roles. How do we resolve this problem? The theta criterion says that there must be a one-to-one mapping between the number of theta roles and the number of arguments in a sentence. This sentence has three theta roles (agent, experiencer, and proposition), but only two arguments. The logical conclusion, if the theta criterion is right – and we have every reason to believe it is, since it makes good predictions otherwise – is that there is actually a third DP here (getting the surplus agent theta role); you just can't hear it. This DP argument is called PRO (written in capital letters). PRO only appears in the subject positions of non-finite clauses. The structure of a control construction like (19) is given below. Indices mark the theta roles from the theta grids in (17) and (18):

20)

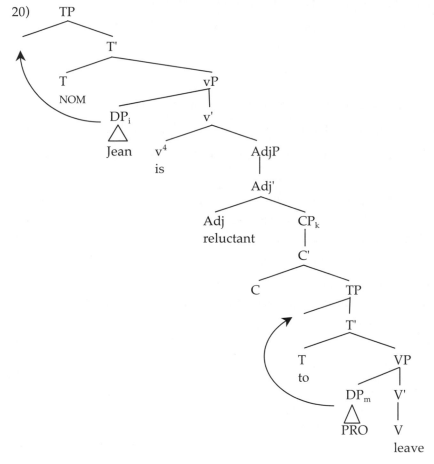

You'll notice that PRO is appearing in a position where no Case can be assigned. We return to this below, as well as to the question of why PRO must obligatorily refer to *Jean*.

Before looking at any more data it might be helpful to summarize the differences between control constructions and raising constructions. The main predicate in a raising construction does not assign an external

---

[4] Again this is not CAUSE, this little v probably means something like "perceive."

theta role (it has an empty specifier of TP at D-structure). The subject of the embedded clause is Caseless, and raises to this empty position for Case checking (and to satisfy the EPP). In control constructions, the main clause predicate *does* assign an external argument. There is no raising; the external theta role of the embedded predicate is assigned to a null Caseless PRO. This is summarized in the following bracketed diagrams:

21) a)   *no theta role*   *Agent*

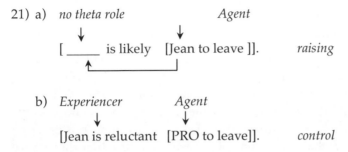

b)   *Experiencer*   *Agent*

[Jean is reluctant   [PRO to leave]].   *control*

1.2 Distinguishing Raising from Control

One of the trials of being a syntactician is learning to distinguish among constructions that are superficially similar, but actually quite different once we dig a little deeper. Control and raising constructions are a perfect example. There are, however, some clear tests we can use to distinguish them. First, note that whether you have a raising or control construction is entirely dependent upon the main clause predicate. Some main clause predicates require raising, others require control (and a few rare ones can require both). The tests for raising and control then, mostly have to do with the thematic properties of the main clause's predicate.

To see this we'll contrast our two predicates *is likely*, which is a raising predicate, and *is reluctant,* which takes a control construction.

The most reliable way to distinguish raising constructions from control constructions is to work out the theta grids associated with the matrix predicates. If the matrix predicate assigns an external theta role (the one that is underlined, the one that appears in subject position), then it is not a raising construction. Take for example:

22) a)   Jean is likely to dance.
    b)   Jean is reluctant to dance.

Contrast the role of *Jean* in these two sentences (as we did above in section 1.1). In the second sentence *is reluctant* is a property we are attributing to *Jean*. In (22a), however, there is nothing about *Jean* that *is likely*. Instead, what *is likely* is Jean's dancing.

One nice test that works well to show this is the behavior of idioms. Let's take the idiom *the cat is out of the bag*. This construction only gets its idiomatic meaning ("the secret is widely known") when the expression is a whole. When it's broken up, it can only get a literal interpretation ("the feline is out of the sack"). You can see this by contrasting the meanings of the sentences in (23):

23) a)   The cat is out of the bag.
    b)   The cat thinks that he is out of the bag.

Sentence (23b) does not have the meaning "the secret is widely known." Instead our first reading of this sentence produces a meaning where there is actual cat-releasing going on. The subject of an idiom must at some point be local to the rest of the idiom for the sentence to retain its idiosyncratic meaning. We can use this as a diagnostic for distinguishing raising from control. Recall that in the D-structure of a raising construction the surface subject of the main clause starts out in the specifier of the embedded TP. Therefore in raising constructions, at D-structure, the subject of an embedded sentence is local to its predicate:

24) [_____ is likely [Jean to dance]].

If D-structure is the level at which we interpret idiomatic meaning, then we should get idiomatic meanings with raising constructions.[5] With control constructions, on the other hand, the subject of the main clause is never in the embedded clause, so we don't expect to get idiomatic readings. This is borne out by the data.

25) a)   The cat is likely to be out of the bag. *(idiomatic meaning)*
    b)   The cat is eager to be out of the bag. *(non-idiomatic meaning)*

We can thus use idiom chunks like *the cat* in (25) to test for raising versus control. If you get an idiomatic reading with a predicate, then you know raising is involved.

Another test you can use to distinguish between raising and control constructions is to see if they allow the extraposition construction. Extraposition involves an expletive *it*. Expletives are only allowed in non-thematic positions, which are the hallmark of raising:

26) a)   It is likely that Jean will dance.

---

[5] This is not an implausible hypothesis. Idioms have the feel of lexical items (that is, their meaning must be idiosyncratically memorized, just like the meanings of words). Remember that the lexicon is the source of the material at D-structure, so it makes sense that D-structure is when idiomatic meanings are inserted.

b)   *It is reluctant that Jean will dance.

At the end of this chapter, there is a problem set (general problem set 4) where you are asked to determine for a list of predicates whether or not they involve raising or control. You'll need to apply the tests discussed in this section to do that exercise.

1.3 What is PRO?

You may have noticed a fairly major contradiction in the story we've been presenting. In chapter 10, we claimed that DPs always need Case. However, in this section we've proposed that PRO can appear in the specifier of non-finite TP. This is not a Case position, so why are we allowed to have PRO here? Shouldn't PRO get Case too? It is, after all, a DP. Chomsky (1981) claims that the reason PRO is null and silent is precisely *because* it appears in a Caseless position. In other words PRO is a very special kind of DP, it is a Caseless DP, which explains why it can show up in Caseless positions, like the specifier of non-finite TP.

Why do we need PRO? If we didn't have PRO, then we would have violations of the theta criterion. Notice that what we are doing here is proposing a null element to account for an apparent hole in our theory (a violation of either the theta criterion or the Case filter). There is good reason to be suspicious of this: It seems like a technical solution to a technical problem that is raised only by our particular formulation of the constraints. Nonetheless, it does have a good deal of descriptive power. It can account for most of the data having to do with embedded infinitival clauses. Until a better theory comes along, the PRO hypothesis wins because it can explain so much data.

You now have enough information to try General Problem Set 1

---

2. TWO KINDS OF RAISING, TWO KINDS OF CONTROL

2.1 Two Kinds of Raising

Up to this point we have been primarily looking at raising from the subject of an infinitive complement clause to the specifier of a main clause TP. This raising happens so the DP can get Case. However, raising doesn't have to target the specifier of TP; there are other instances of DP raising where the DP ends up in other positions. Consider the verb *want*. *Want* can take an accusatively marked DP:

27) a) I want cookies.
    b) Jean wants Robert.
    c) Jean wants him.

Want can also take an infinitive CP complement (sentence (28) is an instance of a control construction.)

28) I$_i$ want [PRO$_i$ to leave].

This flexible verb can also show up with both an accusatively marked DP and an infinitive complement:

29) I$_i$ want [Jean$_j$ to dance]$_k$.

Think carefully about the theta grids of the verbs here. *Jean* is the agent of *dance*, *I* is the experiencer of *want*, and the proposition *Jean to dance* takes up the second theta role of *want*.

30) a) *dance*

Agent
DP
J

    b) *want*

Experiencer	Proposition
DP	CP
i	k

Notice that *Jean* does not get a theta role from *want*; it only gets one from *dance*. This means that this is not a control construction. You can see this if we apply our idiom test to the sentence: [6]

31) I want the cat to be let out of the bag.

Although the judgment isn't as clear here, it is possible to get the idiomatic reading of *the cat to be let out of the bag*.

Since this isn't a control construction, then how does the DP *Jean* get Case? The embedded TP is non-finite, so its specifier is not a Case position. The answer to this puzzle is the DP raises to the object position of *want*, where it can get accusative Case.

---

[6] The extraposition test will not work here. Remember expletives are usually only found in subject position (because of the EPP). *Jean* here is found in object position, so extraposition can't apply.

32) TP

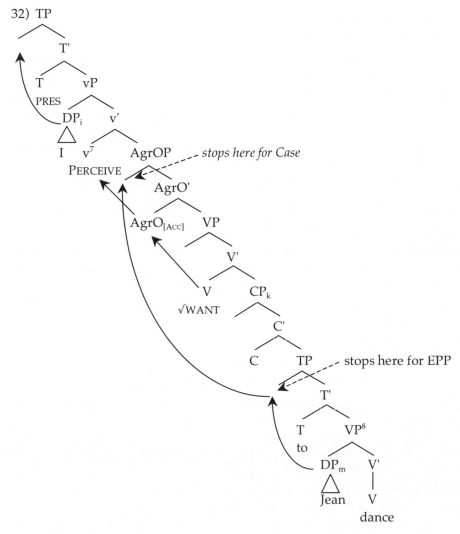

The verb root raises through AgrO into v. The DP *Jean* moves first to the specifier of the embedded TP for EPP reasons, then moves on to the specifier of AgrOP where it gets accusative case.

We can see that this is the right analysis of these facts by looking at the Case-marking a pronoun would get in these constructions. Since the DP shows up as the specifier of AgrOP with an [ACC] Case feature, we predict it will take accusative Case. This is correct:

---

[7] This v is not CAUSE, as there is no agent role here. This v probably means something like perceive.

[8] Again this VP is an abbreviation for vP and VP.

33) a)   I want *her* to dance.
    b)   *I want *she* to dance.

Binding theory also provides us with a test for seeing where the DP is. Recall the fundamental difference between a pronoun and an anaphor. In the binding theory we developed in chapter 5, an anaphor must be bound within its clause, whereas a pronoun must be free. What clause a DP is in determines whether it is an anaphor or a pronoun. We can use this as a test for seeing where a DP appears in the tree structure. We are considering two hypotheses: (34a) has the DP in the object position of *want* (just as in (32)), whereas (34b) has the DP in the subject position of the non-finite TP.

34) a)   I want Jean$_i$ [t$_i$ to dance].
    b)   I want [Jean to dance].

If we can have a bound anaphor, instead of *Jean*, then we know that the pronoun must be in a different clause from its antecedent, since pronouns cannot be bound within their own clause. Similarly we predict that if an anaphor is OK, then the DP is within the same clause as its antecedent. The data supports (34a).

35) a)   *Jean$_i$ wants her$_i$ to be appointed president.
    b)   Jean$_i$ wants her$_j$ to be appointed president.
    b)   ?Jean$_i$ wants herself$_i$ to be appointed president.

These forms exhibit a second kind of raising, which we might call subject-to-object raising.

Subject-to-object Raising = Exceptional Case Marking (ECM)

In the early work on generative grammar, in the 1960s and 1970s, the construction we have been looking at here was treated in a very similar manner to the analysis presented here. It was also called subject-to-object raising. In the 1980s and early 1990s (in what was called GB theory), there was a period of time when these constructions got a different analysis. Instead of raising the infinitival subject to object position, the subject was left inside the embedded clause (in the specifier of TP), and the verb was allowed to "exceptionally" Case mark into the embedded clause. Thus for that period of time, these constructions were called *Exceptional Case Marking* (or *ECM*) constructions. Today, we have gone back to the original subject-to-object raising analysis. Can you think of some way that we can distinguish the ECM from subject-to-object raising analyses?

You now have enough information to try General Problem Sets 2 & 3

2.2 Two Kinds of Control

In section 1, we contrasted sentences like (36a) and (36b). These sentences differed in terms of their argument structure and in what movement if any applies. (36a) is a raising construction, where *Jean* gets its theta role only from *to leave*, and raises for Case reasons to the specifier of the main clause TP. In (36b), *Jean* gets a theta role from *is reluctant*, and there is no movement. Instead there is a null Caseless PRO in the specifier of the tenseless clause.

36) a)   Jean$_i$ is likely [t_i to leave].
    b)   Jean$_i$ is reluctant [PRO$_i$ to leave].

In this subsection, we'll make a similar claim about the structures in (37).

37) a)   Jean wants Robert$_i$ [t_i to leave].
    b)   Jean persuaded Robert$_i$ [PRO$_i$ to leave].

Sentence (37a) is an instance of subject-to-object raising. Sentence (37b), while on the surface very similar to (37a), is actually also a control construction. There are two major kinds of control constructions. To see this I'll put the two (b) sentences side by side in (38). (38a) is what we call **subject control**, because the subject DP of the main clause is co-referential with PRO. (38b) is **object control**, where the main clause object is co-referential with PRO.

38) a) (=36b) Jean$_i$ is reluctant [PRO$_i$ to leave].   *subject control*
    b) (=37b) Jean persuaded Robert$_i$ [PRO$_i$ to leave].   *object control*

Consider first the thematic properties of the raising construction:

39) Jean$_i$ wants Robert$_j$ [t_j to leave]$_k$.

We are now well familiar with the theta grid for *to leave*, which takes a single agent argument. The theta grid for the subject-to-object raising verb *want* is repeated below:

40) a)   *leave*

Agent
DP
i

  b)   *want*

Experiencer	Proposition
DP	CP
i	k

Robert is the agent of *leave*, but is not an argument of *want*. In section 2.1 above, we used the idiom test to show that this is the case. Now, contrast this situation with the object control verb *persuade*:

41) Jean$_i$ persuaded Robert$_m$ [PRO$_j$ to leave]$_k$.[9]

The DP *Robert* in this sentence *is* theta marked by *persuade*. So in order not to violate the theta criterion we have to propose a null PRO to take the agent theta role of *leave*.

42) a) *leave*

Agent
DP
j

  b) *persuade*

Agent	Theme	Proposition
DP	DP	CP
i	m	k

We can see this again by comparing the idiomatic readings of subject-to-object raising vs. object control.

43) a) Jean wants the cat to get his/Bill's tongue.

  b) #Jean persuaded the cat to get his/Bill's tongue.

Sentence (43a) is slightly odd, but it does allow the idiomatic reading, but (43b) only takes the literal (non-idiomatic) meaning.

Control = Equi

In early versions of generative grammar – in particular, the ones before the invention of theta roles – the phenomenon we are calling control was called *Equi-NP Deletion* or *Equi* for short. This is just another name for the same phenomenon.

2.3 Summary of Predicate Types

In this section we've argued for four distinct types of embedded nonfinite constructions: subject-to-subject raising, subject-to-object raising, subject control and object control. Which construction you get seems to be dependent upon what the main clause predicate is. For example, *is likely*

---

[9] The indices on this sentence mark theta roles (as marked in the grid in (42)). They do not mark coindexing. In this sentence, the index $_m = _j$ (m and j are the same index).

requires a subject-to-subject raising construction whereas *is reluctant* requires a subject control construction. It should be noted that some verbs allow more than one type of construction. For example, the verb *want* allows either subject control, or subject-to-object raising:

44) a) Jean$_i$ wants [PRO$_i$ to leave].   *subject control*
    b) Jean wants Bill$_i$ [t$_i$ to leave].   *subject-to-object raising*

An example of these types is given in (45) and a summary of their properties in (46):

45) a) Jean is likely to leave.   *subject-to-subject raising*
    b) Jean wants Robert to leave.   *subject-to-object raising*
    c) Jean is reluctant to leave.   *subject control*
    d) Jean persuaded Robert to leave.   *object control*

46) a) *subject-to-subject raising*
    - Main clause predicate has one theta role (to the proposition), and no external (subject) theta role
    - DP movement of embedded subject to the specifier of TP for EPP and Case
    - Allows idiomatic readings
    - Allows extraposition

    b) *subject-to-object raising*
    - Main clause predicate assigns two theta roles (an external agent or experiencer and a proposition)
    - Main clause predicate has an [ACC] Case feature
    - DP movement of the embedded clause subject to the specifier of AgrOP for Case reasons
    - Allows idiomatic readings

    c) *subject control*
    - Main clause predicate assigns two theta roles (external agent or experiencer and proposition)
    - Caseless PRO in embedded clause
    - No DP movement for Case
    - Does not allow idiomatic readings or extraposition

    d) *object control*
    - Main clause predicate assigns three theta roles (external agent or experiencer, an internal theme and a proposition)
    - Caseless PRO in embedded clause
    - No DP movement for Case
    - Does not allow idiomatic readings or extraposition

You now have enough information to try General Problem Sets 4 & 5, and Challenge Problem Set 1

3. CONTROL THEORY

In chapter 5, we developed a set of noun types (anaphors, pronouns, R-expressions) that have different properties with respect to how they get their meanings. R-expressions get their meaning from the discourse or context and can never be bound; anaphors are bound by antecedents within their clauses; and pronouns can either be bound by antecedents outside their clause or be free. In this section, we consider the troubling question of what kind of DP PRO is. Unfortunately, we are going to get a bit of a mixed answer.

Let us start by defining some terminology. This terminology is subtly similar to that of the binding theory, but it is different. If PRO gets its meaning from another DP, then PRO is said to be **controlled**. This is identical to the notion **coreferent** and very similar to the notion **bound** (we will make this distinction clearer below). The DP that serves as PRO's antecedent is called its **controller**.

We are going to contrast two different kinds of PRO. The first kind is called **arbitrary PRO** (or PRO_{arb}). The meaning of this pronoun is essentially "someone":

47) [PRO_{arb} to find a new mate], go to a dating service.

Arbitrary PRO is not controlled by anything. Arbitrary PRO is a bit like an R-expression or a pronoun, in that it can get its meaning from outside the sentence.

Non-arbitrary PRO (henceforth simply PRO) also comes in two different varieties. On one hand we have what is called **obligatory control**. Consider the sentence in (48). Here, PRO must refer to *Jean*. It can't refer to anyone else:

48) Jean$_i$ tried $PRO_{i/*j}$ to behave.

There are other circumstances where PRO does not have to be (but can be) controlled. This is called **optional control**, and is seen in (49):

49) Robert$_i$ knows that it is essential [$PRO_{i/j}$ to be well-behaved].

PRO here can mean two different things. It can either refer to Robert or it can have an arbitrary PRO_{arb} reading (indicated in (49) with the subscript $_j$). You can see this by looking at the binding of the following two extensions of this sentence:

50) a) Robert$_i$ knows that it is essential [PRO$_i$ to be well-behaved on his$_i$ birthday].

b) Robert$_i$ knows that it is essential [PRO$_j$ to be well-behaved on one's$_j$ birthday].

(50a) has the controlled meaning (as seen by the binding of *his*), (50b) has the arbitrary reading (as seen by the presence of *one's*).

With this in mind let's return to the central question of this section. Is PRO an anaphor, a pronoun, or an R-expression? We can dismiss the R-expression option right out of hand. R-expressions must always be free. PRO is only sometimes free (= not controlled). This makes it seem more like a pronoun; pronouns can be both free or bound. The data in (49) seems to support this, PRO is behaving very much like a pronoun. Compare (49) to the pronoun in (51).

51) Robert$_i$ knows it is essential [that he$_{i/j}$ is well-behaved].

You'll notice that the indexing on (51) which has a pronoun, is identical to the indexing on PRO in (49). We might hypothesize then that PRO is a pronoun. This can't be right, however. Recall that we also have situations where PRO must be bound (= controlled) as in the obligatory control sentence *Jean$_i$ tried PRO$_{i/*j}$ to behave.* This makes PRO look like an anaphor, since anaphors are obligatorily bound. Williams (1980) suggests that in obligatory control constructions PRO must be c-commanded by its controller, just as an anaphor must be c-commanded by its antecedent. However, as should be obvious, this can't be right either. First, as noted above, we have situations where PRO is free (as in 47); anaphors can never be free. Second, if we take the binding theory we developed in chapter 5 literally, PRO and its controller *Jean*, are in different binding domains, violating Principle A.[10] We thus have a conundrum: PRO doesn't seem to be an R-expression, a pronoun, or an anaphor. It seems to be a beast of an altogether different color.

Since the distribution of PRO does not lend itself to the binding theory, an entirely different module of the grammar has been proposed to account for PRO. This is called **control theory**. Control theory is the bane of professional theoreticians and students alike. It is, quite simply, the least

---

[10] Recall from chapter 5 that our definition of binding domain as a clause is probably wrong. One might even hypothesize on the basis of data like *Jean is likely to behave herself* that the definition of binding domain requires some kind of tensed clause, rather than just any kind of clause. I leave as an exercise the implications of such a move.

elegant part of syntactic theory. We'll have a brief look at it here, but will come to no satisfying conclusions.

First let's observe that some parts of control are sensitive to syntactic structure. Consider what can control PRO in (52):

52) [Jean$_i$'s father]$_j$ is reluctant PRO$_{j/*i}$ to leave.

If you draw the tree for (52), you'll see that while the whole DP *Jean's father* c-commands PRO, *Jean* by itself does not. The fact that *Jean* cannot control PRO strongly suggests that there is a c-command requirement on obligatory control, as argued by Williams (1980). This said, the structure of the sentence doesn't seem to be the only thing that comes into play with control. Compare now a subject control sentence to an object control one:

53) a)   Robert$_i$ is reluctant [PRO$_i$ to behave].   *subject control*
    b)   Susan$_j$ ordered Robert$_i$ [PRO$_{i/*j}$ to behave].   *object control*

In both these sentences PRO must be controlled by *Robert*. PRO in (53b) cannot refer to *Susan*. This would seem to suggest that the closest DP that c-commands PRO must control it. In (53a), *Robert* is the only possible controller, so it controls PRO. In (53b), there are two possible controllers: *Susan* and *Robert*. But only *Robert*, which is structurally closer to PRO, can control it. This hypothesis works well in most cases, but the following example shows it must be wrong:

54) Jean$_i$ promised Susan$_j$ [PRO$_{i/*j}$ to behave].   *subject control*

In this sentence it is *Jean* doing the behaving, not *Susan*. PRO must be controlled by *Jean*, even though *Susan* is structurally closer. So structure doesn't seem to be the only thing determining which DP does the controlling.

One hypothesis is that the particular main clause predicate determines which DP does the controlling. That is, the theta grid specifies what kind of control is involved. There are various ways we could encode this. One is to mark a particular theta role as the controller:

55) a)   *is reluctant*

<u>Experiencer</u>	Proposition
DP	CP
controller	

b) *persuade*

Agent	Theme	Proposition
DP	DP	CP
	controller	

c) *promise*

Agent	Theme	Proposition
DP	DP	CP
controller		

In this view of things, control is a thematic property. But a very careful look at the data shows that this can't be the whole story either. The sentences in (56) all use the verb *beg*, which is traditionally viewed as an object control verb, as seen by the pair of sentences in (56a and b), where the (b) sentence shows an embedded tense clause paraphrase:

56) a) Louis begged Kate$_i$ [PRO$_i$ to leave her job].
   b) Louis begged Kate that she leave her job.
   c) Louis$_i$ begged Kate [PRO$_i$ to be allowed [PRO$_i$ to shave himself]].
   d) Louis$_i$ begged Kate that he be allowed to shave himself.

Sentences (56c and d), however, show subject control. The PROs in (c) must be controlled by the subject *Louis*. The difference between the (a) and the (b) sentence seems to be in the nature of the *embedded* clause. This is mysterious at best. Examples like these might be used to argue that control is not entirely syntactic or thematic, but may also rely on our knowledge of the way the world works. This kind of knowledge, often referred to as *pragmatic* knowledge,[11] lies outside the syntactic system we're developing. The study of the interaction between pragmatics, semantics and syntax is one that is being vigorously pursued right now, but lies beyond the scope of this book. See the further reading section below for some places you can go to examine questions like this in more detail.

You now have enough information to try Challenge Problem Set 2

---

[11] See for example Landau's (1999) dissertation.

4. ANOTHER KIND OF NULL SUBJECT: "LITTLE" *pro*

In chapter 8, we made the claim that all sentences require subjects, and encoded this into the EPP. However, many languages appear to violate this constraint. Take, for example, these perfectly acceptable sentences of Italian:

57) a)   Parlo.
      speak.1SG
      "I speak."

   b)   Parli.
      speak.2SG
      "You speak."

The subject DP in these sentences seems to be missing. But there is no ambiguity here. We know exactly who is doing the talking. This is because the verbs are inflected with endings that tell us who the subject is. This phenomenon is called either ***pro-drop*** or ***null subjects***. Ideally, we would like to claim that a strong constraint like the EPP is universal, but Italian (and many other languages) seem to be exceptions. One technical solution to this issue is to posit that sentences in (57) actually do have DPs which satisfy the EPP. Notice again that this is merely a technical solution to a formal problem.

You might think that the obvious candidate for this empty DP would be PRO. But in fact, PRO could not appear in this position. Remember PRO only appears in Caseless positions. We know that Italian subject position is a Case position, because you can have an overt DP like *io* in (58).

58) Io parlo.
   I speak.1SG
   "I speak."

So linguists have proposed the category *pro* (written in lower-case letters). *pro* (called ***little pro*** or ***baby pro***) appears in Case positions; PRO (called ***big PRO***) is Caseless.

English doesn't have *pro*. This presumably is due to the fact that English doesn't have a rich agreement system in its verbal morphology:

59) a)   I speak.
   b)   You speak.
   c)   He/she/it speak<u>s</u>.
   d)   We speak.
   e)   They speak.

In English, only third person forms of verbs take any special endings. One of the conditions on *pro* seems to be that it often appears in languages with rich agreement morphology.[12] The means we use to encode variation among languages should now be familiar: parameters. We use this device here again in the ***null subject parameter***, which governs whether or not a language allows *pro*. Italian has this switch turned on. English has it set in the off position.

You now have enough information to try General Problem Set 6

5. SUMMARY

We started this chapter with the observation that certain sentences, even though they look alike on the surface, can actually have very different syntactic trees. We compared subject-to-subject raising constructions to subject control constructions, and subject-to-object raising constructions to object control constructions. You can test for these various construction types by working out their argument structure, and using the idiom test. Next under consideration was the issue of what kind of DP PRO is. We claimed that it only showed up in Caseless positions. We also saw that it didn't meet any of the binding conditions, and suggested it is subject, instead, to control theory. Control theory is a bit of a mystery, but may involve syntactic, thematic, and pragmatic features. We closed the chapter by comparing two different kinds of null subject categories: PRO and *pro*. PRO is Caseless and is subject to the theory of control. On the other hand, *pro* takes Case and is often "licensed" by rich agreement morphology on the verb.

IDEAS, RULES, AND CONSTRAINTS INTRODUCED IN THIS CHAPTER

i)   ***PRO (big PRO)***: A null (silent) DP found in Caseless positions (the specifier of non-finite TP).

ii)   **pro** (***Little* pro** *or **Baby* pro**): A null (silent) DP often found in languages with "rich" agreement. *pro* does get Case.

iii)   ***Clausal Subject Construction***: A sentence where a clause appears in the specifier of TP. E.g., *[That Jean danced the rumba] is likely*.

[12] This not a universally true statement. Many Asian languages allow *pro*-drop even though they don't have rich agreement systems. For discussion, see Huang (1989).

iv) **Extraposition**: A sentence (often an alternate of a clausal subject construction) where there is an expletive in the subject position and a clausal complement. E.g., *It is likely that Jean danced the rumba.*

v) **Subject-to-subject Raising**: A kind of DP movement where the subject of an embedded non-finite clause moves to the specifier of TP of the main clause to get nominative Case. E.g., *Jean$_i$ is likely t$_i$ to dance.*

vi) **Subject-to-object Raising** (*also called* **Exceptional Case Marking** *or* **ECM**): A kind of DP movement where the subject of an embedded non-finite clause moves to the complement of the verb in the main clause to get accusative Case. E.g., *Jean wants Bill$_i$[t$_i$ to dance].*

vii) **Control Theory**: The theory that governs how PRO gets its meaning. There appear to be syntactic factors (the controller must c-command PRO), thematic factors (what DP does the controlling is dependent upon what main clause predicate is present), and pragmatic factors involved.

viii) **Pragmatics**: The science that looks at how language and knowledge of the world interact.

ix) **Subject Control** (*also called* **Equi**): A sentence where there is a PRO in the embedded non-finite clause that is controlled by the subject argument of the main clause. E.g., *John$_i$ is reluctant PRO$_i$ to leave.*

x) **Object Control**: A sentence where there is a PRO in the embedded non-finite clause that is controlled by the object argument of the main clause. E.g., *John persuaded Bill$_i$ PRO$_i$ to leave.*

xi) **Obligatory vs. Optional Control**: Obligatory control is when the PRO must be controlled: *Jean$_i$ is reluctant PRO$_i$ to leave.* Optional control is when the DP can be controlled or not: *Robert$_i$ knows that it is essential [PRO$_{i/j}$ to be well behaved].*

xii) **PRO$_{arb}$**: Uncontrolled PRO takes an "arbitrary" reference. That is, it means something like *someone.*

xiii) **Null Subject Parameter**: The parameter switch that distinguishes languages like English, which require an overt subject, from languages like Italian that don't, and allow *pro.*

FURTHER READING

Brame, Michael (1976) *Conjectures and Refutations in Syntax and Semantics.* Amsterdam: Elsevier.

Bresnan, Joan (1972) Theory of Complementation in English. Ph.D. dissertation, MIT.

Chomsky, Noam (1965) *Aspects of the Theory of Syntax.* Cambridge: MIT Press.

Chomsky, Noam (1981) *Lectures on Government and Binding.* Dordrecht: Foris.

Hornstein, Norbert (1999) Movement and control. *Linguistic Inquiry* 30, 69–96.

Hyams, Nina (1986) *Language Acquisition and the Theory of Parameters.* Dordrecht: D. Reidel.

Jaeggli, Osvaldo and Kenneth Safir (eds.) (1989) *The Null Subject Parameter.* Dordrecht: Kluwer Academic Publishers.

Landau, Idan (1999) Elements of Control. Ph.D. dissertation, MIT.

Manzini, Maria Rita (1983) On control and control theory. *Linguistic Inquiry* 14, 421–46.

Petter, Marga (1998) *Getting PRO under Control.* The Hague: Holland Academic Graphics.

Postal, Paul (1974) *On Raising.* Cambridge: MIT Press.

Rizzi, Luigi (1982) *Issues in Italian Syntax.* Dordrecht: Foris.

Rosenbaum, Peter S. (1967) *The Grammar of English Predicate Complement Constructions.* Cambridge: MIT Press.

Williams, Edwin (1980) Predication. *Linguistic Inquiry* 11, 203–38.

GENERAL PROBLEM SETS

1. THE EXISTENCE OF PRO
[Critical Thinking; Intermediate]
How does the following sentence provide support for the existence of PRO in the subject position of the non-finite clause?

a)   [To behave oneself in public] is expected.

Consider now the following sentence. Does it provide support for the existence of PRO? How?

b)   Robert$_i$ knew [$_{CP}$ that it was necessary [$_{CP}$ PRO$_i$ to behave himself$_i$]].

2. RAISING TO OBJECT

[Critical Thinking; Intermediate]
We claimed that subject-to-object raising targets the specifier of AgrOP as the landing site of the movement for Case. Consider the following sentences, keeping in mind that *out* and *incorrectly* modify the main verb. How do these sentences support the idea that subject to object raising lands in AgrOP? Draw the tree for sentence (b).

a)   She made Jerry out to be famous.
b)   Mike expected Greg incorrectly to take out the trash.

3. ICELANDIC PRO AND QUIRKY CASE

[Data Analysis and Critical Thinking; Intermediate/Advanced]
Background. In order to do this question it will be helpful to have reviewed the discussion of floating quantifiers in chapter 10, and to have done the question on Icelandic quirky Case in chapter 10.

As discussed in chapter 10, in English, it is possible to "float" quantifiers (words like *all*) that modify subject arguments:

a)   The boys don't all want to leave.

Icelandic also allows floating quantifiers, but with a twist. The quantifier takes endings indicating that it has the same Case as the DP it modifies. Recall from the last chapter that certain verbs in Icelandic assign irregular or "quirky" Cases to their subjects. The verb *leiddist* "bored" is one of these. In sentence (b), the subject is marked with its quirky dative Case. The floating quantifier *öllum* "all" is also marked with dative. (Data from Sigurðsson 1991.)

b)   Strákunum leiddist öllum   í skóla.
     boys.DAT   bored all.DAT   in school
     "The boys were all bored in school."

We might hypothesize then, that floated quantifiers must agree with the noun they modify in terms of Case.

The question. Now consider the following control sentence. What problems does the following sentence hold for our claim that PRO does not get Case? Can you relate your solution to the problem of Icelandic passives discussed in the problem sets of chapter 10? Note that the noun in the main clause here is marked with nominative rather than dative Case.

c)   Strákarnir vonast til að PRO leiðast ekki öllum í skóla.
     boys.NOM hope for to   bore not all.DAT in school
     "The boys hope not to be bored in school."

4. ENGLISH PREDICATES

[Application of Skills; Intermediate]

Using your knowledge of theta theory and the tests of extraposition and idioms determine if the predicates listed below are subject-to-subject raising (SSR), subject-to-object raising, (SOR), subject control (SC), or object control (OC). **Some predicates fit into more than one category**. (The idea for this problem set comes from a similar question in Soames and Perlmutter 1979.)

is eager	is believed	seems	is ready
persuaded	urged	requested	hoped
expect	force	tell	advise
ask	assure	imagine	promise
want	is likely	consent	imagine
encouraged	intended		

5. TREES AND DERIVATIONS

[Application of Skills; Intermediate to Advanced]

Draw trees for the following sentences, annotate your trees with arrows so that they show all the movements, and write in all PROs with appropriate coindexing indicating control. You may wish to do this problem set *after* you have completed problem set 4.

a) Jean wants Bill to do the Macarena.
b) Robert is eager to do his homework.
c) Jean seems to be in a good mood.
d) Rosemary tried to get a new car.
e) Susan begged Bill to let her sing in the concert.
f) Susan begged to be allowed to sing in the concert.
g) Christina is ready to leave.
h) Fred was believed to have wanted to try to dance.
i) Susan consented to try to seem to have been kissed.
j) Alan told me who wanted to seem to be invincible.
k) What did John want to eat?

6. IRISH *pro*

[Data Analysis; Advanced]

Irish is a null subject language.

a) Rinceamar.
    Dance.3PL.PAST
    "We danced."

Consider the following Irish sentences and discuss how Irish *pro*-drop differs from that found in Italian:

b) Tá mé.
    Am I
    "I am."

c) Táim.
    Am.1SG
    "I am."

d) *Táim   mé.
    Am.1SG I
    "I am."

CHALLENGE PROBLEM SETS

CHALLENGE PROBLEM SET 1: IS EASY
[Critical Thinking; Challenge]
Consider the following sentences:

a) This book is easy to read.
b) John is easy to please.

Is *is easy* a raising or a control predicate or both? If it is a raising predicate, which argument is raised? If it is a control predicate, where is the PRO? What kind of PRO is it?

CHALLENGE PROBLEM SET 2: CONTROLLERS
[Critical Thinking; Challenge]
Williams (1980) claimed that obligatorily controlled PRO requires a c-commanding controller. What problem do the following sentences hold for that hypothesis?

a) To improve myself is a goal for next year.
b) To improve yourself would be a good idea.
c) To improve himself, Bruce should consider therapy.
d) To improve herself, Jane went to a health spa.

chapter 15

Advanced Topics
in Binding Theory

0. A QUICK REVIEW OF CHAPTER 5 BINDING THEORY

In chapter 5, we sketched out a brief version of the binding theory that allowed us to see the utility of structural relations and to give us a tool to probe the c-command structures in a tree. That chapter contained a number of simplifications. It isn't very hard to find counter examples to the theory proposed there. In this chapter, we give binding relations a slightly more nuanced look.

First let us review some of the basics from chapter 5. Binding theory concerns the distribution of types of DPs with respect to each other. It is partly a semantic study (looking at coreference) and partly a syntactic study (looking at the structural considerations that govern the coreferential possibilities). Recall that coreference is defined in terms of binding which is both coindexing and c-command. When a DP is both c-commanded by and coindexed with another DP, we say the first DP is bound by the second. We have three major types of DPs. R-expressions are full DPs that get their reference from external sources and may not be bound (Principle C); Anaphors are DPs that must get their meaning from another local DP in the sentence (i.e., must be bound) and are governed by Principle A. Pronouns lie between the two. Pronouns may be coreferent with another DP in the sentence, but need not be. To the extent that they may be coreferent they must find their antecedent outside the clause they are contained in (Principle B). In chapter 5, we defined locality in finding an antecedent by making reference to the clause as the binding domain. In this chapter, this is perhaps the most major part of the theory that we'll have cause to revise. Just as we defined the MLC relativistically by the type of element we were moving, we will define binding domain relativistically according to the type of DP that is involved. We will also consider the question of what level of representation the binding principles hold at in the model of the grammar we've been exploring.

The version of the binding theory I give you here is loosely based on the one found in Chomsky's (1986b) *Knowledge of Language*, but with an eye towards more recent developments in the theory.

1. LEVELS OF REPRESENTATION

In chapter 5, we claimed that the binding domain was a clause (CP). This nicely accounts for the ungrammaticality of sentences like (1) below:

1) *Chris$_i$ said [$_{CP}$ that himself$_i$ was appealing].

However, on the face of it, this runs into trouble with sentences such as:

2) Chris$_i$ wants himself$_i$ to be appealing.

Assuming that *himself* is the subject of the predicate *to be appealing*, here the binding relation seems to cross clause boundaries. However, the analysis we developed of subject to object raising in the previous chapter solves this problem. If the DP *himself* moves to the specifier of the AgROP for case reasons it moves out of the CP where it gets its theta role. Once it is part of the higher clause structure its new binding domain contains the antecedent *Chris*. In (3) the old binding domain is shown with the rightmost arc. The raising of the DP extends this to the higher CP

3) 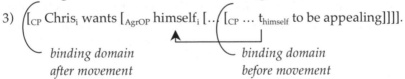[$_{CP}$ Chris$_i$ wants [$_{AgROP}$ himself$_i$ [.. [$_{CP}$ ... t$_{himself}$ to be appealing]]]].

        binding domain   *binding domain*
        after movement   *before movement*

This fact then suggests that the binding principles hold after movement has applied. Given the model that we sketched in chapter 12, this would be the level of LF. This makes a fair amount of sense, since binding is at least partly a semantic relation and LF is the level that interacts with the conceptual/semantic component of the grammar.

Were things so simple however! If you did general problem set 2 in chapter 11, you will have learned that there is at least some evidence that binding principles hold before movement. Take the sentence in (4):

4)   [Which pictures of himself$_i$] did Chris$_i$ like?

The *wh*-moved DP here contains an anaphor (*himself*). This anaphor is only c-commanded by its antecedent **before** the movement:

5)   C$_{[+Q,+WH]}$ Chris$_i$ did like [which pictures of himself$_i$]   (D-structure)

In chapter 11, this was taken to be evidence that the binding principles held at D-structure, before movement.

So we have an apparent contradiction here. Raising sentences such as (2) provide an argument for the claim that the binding principles happen after movement, but *wh*-questions such as (4) suggest that binding principles happen before movement. The theory of movement we have, however, provides a straightforward solution, if we make a minor adjustment to our assumptions. We have up to now been marking the source of movement with a *t* for trace. Let us consider the possibility that these traces have more to them than this. Chomsky (1993) suggested that movement was really an operation of copying, where you don't pronounce the original copy. So for example, when we do *wh*-movement in a sentence like (4), the LF of the sentence is really as in (6) where the DP in outline font is the trace and isn't pronounced.

6)   [Which pictures of himself$_i$] did Chris$_i$ like [Which pictures of himself$_i$]?

In this view, movement consists of two parts, a copying operation which duplicates part of the tree and then puts the copy somewhere in the tree and then an operation that (usually) silences the original. The technical name for the two DPs in (6) is the **chain**. Chains are the combination of the moved copy and any silent originals (traces) they leave behind.

With this technology in hand we have a simple account of the timing dilemma we sketched above. Binding principles all hold at LF. We can claim that at LF at least one link in the chain (one copy or original) is subject to the binding principles. In a sentence like (6), the version of the anaphor in the trace is c-commanded by *Chris*, this version is present at LF, it just isn't pronounced. Binding principle A is met because one copy of the anaphor is c-commanded by a local antecedent.

In the case of sentences like (2), a different copy of the anaphor is locally c-commanded by its antecedent. This time it is the moved copy that meets the binding principle A:

7)   Chris$_i$ wants himself$_i$ [... [$_{CP}$ ... himself$_i$ to be appealing]]].

Defining the binding principles over the chains of DPs rather than over DPs themselves solves this timing problem. We can claim that the binding principles hold of LF representations and that, in the case of anaphors, at least one copy must appear in the right binding configuration:

8) Binding Principle A (revised): One copy of an anaphor in a chain must be bound within its binding domain.

An exercise at the end of the chapter asks you to consider if the same property is true of pronouns and Principle B.

You now have enough information to try Challenge Problem Set 1

---

2. THE DEFINITION OF BINDING DOMAIN

2.1 A Miscellany of Domain Violations

There is significant reason for thinking that our definition of binding domain in terms of clauses is far too simplistic. Consider the following sentences. In most major dialects of English, sentence (9b) is ungrammatical with co-indexation between *Heidi* and *herself*, despite the fact that sentence (9a), which is very similar in structure to (9b) is entirely grammatical. (There is a dialect of English, spoken mainly in the western US, where (9b) is acceptable. If you are a speaker of that dialect, bear with me and assume that the judgments given here are correct. There is a problem set about this alternate dialect at the end of this chapter.)

9) a) Heidi$_i$ believes any description of herself$_i$.
   b) *Heidi$_i$ believes Martha$_k$'s description of herself$_i$.

In both (9a) and (9b), the anaphor is c-commanded by a coindexed antecedent contained in the same clause as the anaphor. By all of the definitions and constraints we have looked at so far (9b) should be acceptable, but it isn't.

The next set of sentences we need to consider has the reverse problem. Recall from chapter 5 that pronouns must be free within their binding domain. (10) is ungrammatical with the coindexation given because the pronoun and its c-commanding antecedent are in the same clause:

10) *Heidi$_i$ likes her$_i$.

But a pronoun inside an embedded CP is okay with coindexation or without it:

11) Heidi$_i$ thinks that she$_{i/k}$ has won.

We explained this phenomenon in terms of the clause serving as the binding domain. Pronouns must be free within their immediate clause. Consider now the following problem sentence:

12) Heidi likes her violin.

(12) is ambiguous in precisely the same way that (11) is. *Her* can be bound by *Heidi* or not:

13) a)   Heidi$_i$ likes her$_i$ violin.
    b)   Heidi$_i$ likes her$_k$ violin.

The interpretation in (13a) is particularly surprising, since *her* and *Heidi* are both dominated by the same CP, so are both in the same binding domain. The indexation in (13a) should be a violation of principle B, yet the sentence is entirely acceptable.

To round off our survey of binding puzzles, consider the sentence in (14). This sentence is acceptable, contrary to all principles of the binding theory:

14) Heidi$_i$ thinks that pictures of herself$_i$ should be hung in the Louvre.

The anaphor is not in the same clause as its antecedent at all. This should be a clear principle A violation, yet the sentence is reasonably acceptable.

2.2 Anaphors

The problem in every case that we have looked at has to do with the definition of binding domain. Let us start to probe this question by looking more closely at the difference between (9a and b). The main difference between the two sentences seems to be the presence of the extra DP *Martha* that intervenes between the anaphor and its antecedent in the unacceptable form. However, not just any intervening DP will do:

15) Heidi$_i$ gave a present to herself$_i$.

In (15) *a present* intervenes between the antecedent and the anaphor (and furthermore it c-commands the antecedent, but it doesn't intervene in the binding possibilities the way the middle DP does in (9b). The DP that causes the problems seems to be the DP in the specifier of another DP (i.e., the possessor DP). Possessor DPs in the specifier position of another DP are a little like the "subject" of those DPs.

16) a)   The army's destruction of the palace
    b)   The army destroyed the palace.

There seems to be a real parallel between (16a) and (16b). The DP that interferes with binding seems to be the "subject" of the DP. A similar pattern with the subject of a TP is seen in control vs. subject-to-object raising constructions in (17):

17) a)   Heidi wants to kiss herself.[1]
    b)   *Heidi$_i$ wants Fred to kiss herself$_i$.

The ungrammaticality of (17b) seems to be due to the presence of *Fred*. One hypothesis that might work is to claim that the binding domain is either a CP (to account for cases like (9a, 10 or 11) or a DP (as in 9b and 17). But then we are left with the question of determining which one is appropriate in which context. The answer to this seems to make reference to this intermediate "subject." Chomsky (1986b) proposes a revision to the binding theory where the binding domain of an anaphor can change depending upon whether there is a *potential antecedent* (= "subject"). What we find when we look at sentences like those in (9) is that the binding domain seems to be a DP, when that DP has a potential antecedent (as in 9b):

9′) b)   *Heidi$_i$ believes ([$_{DP}$ Martha$_k$'s description of herself$_i$].
                                    ↑
                     potential antecedent

This sentence is ungrammatical because the DP here is the binding domain –it contains the potential antecedent *Martha* (note, not the actual antecedent, just a potential[2] one). This means that the anaphor is not bound in its binding domain, and is a violation of principle A.

But now consider (9a) again. Here the anaphor can be bound by *Heidi*. The main difference between this sentence and (9b) is that the object DP contains no potential antecedent for the anaphor. The first potential antecedent is the actual antecedent. So the binding domain for this sentence is the whole clause.

9′) a)   ([$_{CP}$ Heidi$_i$ believes [$_{DP}$ any description of herself$_i$].
              ↑
     potential antecedent

---

[1] (17) of course has a PRO in it that does the binding, but it is worth noting the parallel in any case.
[2] The notion of "potential" antecedent is very loose. The potential antecedent need not agree with the anaphor, nor must it even be a semantically plausible antecedent.

a)   *Heidi$_i$ believes Art's description of herself$_j$.
b)   *Heidi$_i$ dislikes the TV's depiction of herself$_j$.

The only principle seems to be that it is in the specifier of the DP or TP.

The surprising result that binding domains for anaphors seem to be able to shift around depending upon whether there is an antecedent or not is captured in our revised principle A below:

18) *Binding Principle A* (final): One copy of an anaphor in a chain must be bound within the smallest CP or DP containing it and a potential antecedent.

This version of principle A makes an interesting prediction about the distribution of anaphors that appear in the subject position of an embedded clause. Let us make the reasonable assumption that an anaphor can't serve as its own antecedent, or that a DP dominating the anaphor can't serve as that anaphor's antecedent.[3] If we have an embedded clause where the anaphor is in the subject, the smallest CP containing a subject is the main clause. This means that a DP can bind an anaphor in an embedded clause if that anaphor is inside the subject position. Quite surprisingly, this is true: such sentences are grammatical (19 below and 14 above):

19) $[_{CP}$ Heidi$_i$ said $[_{CP}$ that $[_{DP}$ pictures of herself$_i$] were embarrassing]].

This DP does not count as a potential antecedent because it dominates the anaphor.

This CP does not count as the binding domain for the anaphor because it does not contain a potential antecedent.

This is the first potential antecedent for the anaphor (it is also the actual antecedent).

This is the binding domain for the anaphor as it is the smallest CP or DP containing a potential antecedent.

When we add a possessor within the embedded subject, the binding domain shifts:

20) *$[_{CP}$ Heidi$_i$ said $[_{CP}$ that $[_{DP}$ Martha$_k$'s pictures of herself$_i$] were embarrassing]].

potential antecedent

smallest DP or CP containing the anaphor and a potential antecedent

This is a truly surprising result, but one that follows directly from the binding principle in (18).

---

[3] This is known as the *i-within-i* condition, the details of which need not concern us here.

Before leaving this topic, it's worth noting that this binding principle does leave one sentence unexplained, and this is a fairly important sentence at that. The ungrammaticality of sentence (1) (repeated here as 21) is now a mystery:

21) *Chris$_i$ said [$_{CP}$ that himself$_i$ was appealing].

According to the principle in (18) this should be acceptable. If *himself* can't count as its own potential antecedent, then the smallest CP or DP containing a potential antecedent for the anaphor is the main clause (with the actual antecedent *Chris* serving as the potential antecedent). This means that *himself* would be bound within its binding domain so the sentence should be grammatical contrary to fact. In order to account for (21) we are going to have to appeal to something other than the binding principle in (18). Fortunately, there is a relatively simple solution to this problem. The anaphor in (21) is in the specifier of TP, this is the position where nominative case is assigned. Notice that English does not have any nominative anaphors (*heself, *sheself, *Iself* etc.) Perhaps the ungrammaticality of (21) is not due to any binding principle violations but is a simple case conflict instead. *Himself* is accusative in case, but it is in a position that is associated with nominative case.

You can now try General Problem Set 1 and Challenge Sets 2 & 3

2.3 Pronouns

Our definition of binding domain as the smallest CP or DP containing a potential antecedent seems to work well for anaphors, but unfortunately it doesn't fare so well for our examples with pronouns. Take the examples in (13) (repeated here as 22):

22) a)   Heidi$_i$ likes her$_i$ violin.
    b)   Heidi$_i$ likes her$_k$ violin.

Here again we have a case where a DP is acting like a binding domain. Recall that pronouns must be free within their binding domain. In order to explain the grammaticality of (22a), the pronoun must be in a different binding domain than its antecedent. The obvious candidate for this is the DP [*her violin*]. But in the previous section we argued the binding domain was the smallest DP or CP containing a potential antecedent. Assuming that pronouns can't be their own antecedents, the DP [*her violin*] contains no such potential antecedent, so it can't be a binding domain. By the potential antecedent definition the binding domain is the whole CP, which would mean that in (22a) the pronoun would be bound by *Heidi* within its domain in violation of principle B. Yet the sentence is grammatical. Chomsky (1986b) came up with an ingenious solution to this problem. He suggested that that binding domains for pronouns and anaphors are defined differently. The difference lies in the inherent nature of the DP types. Anaphors are DPs that want to bound so they are going to look for the closest potential antecedent. Pronouns by contrast want to be free! So they are going to look for structures **without** an antecedent if they can find them. So the DP [*her violin*] is the smallest DP or CP that does not contain a potential antecedent:[4]

23) [$_{CP}$ Heidi$_i$ likes ([$_{DP}$ her$_i$ violin]].

           ↑
    smallest DP or CP <u>not</u> containing a potential antecedent

This constraint is encoded in (24):

24) ***Binding Principle B*** (nearly final): A pronoun must be free within the smallest CP or DP containing it but <u>not</u> containing a potential antecedent.

The fact that binding domain is defined differently for pronouns and anaphors not only reflects that they are different animals with different requirements, but more importantly explains the contrasts outlined in section 2.1.

But the definition in (24) still has a problem. Under this definition there is no way to explain the ungrammaticality of (25):

25) *Heidi$_i$ likes her$_i$.

This is because under (24) there is no way to define a binding domain for *her*. In (25) there is no DP or CP that contains *her*, is not *her* itself, and does not contain a potential antecedent. The binding domain for (25) is undefined under (24). In order to correct for this we need to add a rider clause to (24), such that if no CP or DP without a potential antecedent can be found, then the root (main clause) CP counts:

26) ***Binding Principle B*** (final): A pronoun must be free within the smallest CP or DP containing it but <u>not</u> containing a potential antecedent. If no such category is found, the pronoun must be free within the root CP.

With this definition, the ungrammaticality of (25) is explained. The main clause CP acts as the binding domain, and the pronoun is bound within this domain in violation of principle B.

---

[4] Violin isn't a potential antecedent as it doesn't asymmetrically c-command *her*, and neither *her* nor the DP containing *her* can be the potential antecedent.

This approach makes a very interesting prediction. Recall sentence (19) from above, repeated here as (27):

27) [$_{CP}$ Heidi$_i$ said [$_{CP}$ that [$_{DP}$ pictures of herself$_i$] were embarrassing]].

One surprising fact is that for most speakers, anaphors like those in (27) can freely alternate with pronouns:

28) [$_{CP}$ Heidi$_i$ said [$_{CP}$ that [$_{DP}$ pictures of her$_i$] were embarrassing]].

Under our old theory – where the binding domains for pronouns and anaphors were identical – the fact that both (27) and (28) are grammatical would be a real puzzle. Under the older approach, pronouns and anaphors were by definition in complementary distribution (pronouns had to be free in their clause, anaphors had to be bound in their clause). The fact that (27) and (28) can both exist shows that the domains for the binding principles are more nuanced. The definitions have to allow for a situation, where the anaphor in (27) is bound by *Heidi* in its binding domain, but where the pronoun is free in its binding domain in the structurally identical (28). But if binding domains are defined relativistically (relative to the type of the DP involved), then (27) and (28) do not form a contradiction. In (27) the smallest DP or CP containing a potential antecedent is the main clause CP. In (28) the smallest DP or CP not containing an antecedent is the DP [*pictures of her*]. So the anaphor in (27) can be bound in its domain, while the pronoun in the exact same position in (28) can be free in its domain.

You now have enough information to try General Problem Set 2

IDEAS, RULES, AND CONSTRAINTS INTRODUCED IN THIS CHAPTER

i)   *The Copy Theory of Movement*: Movement is a two-part operation. First the moved element is copied and put into the surface position; second the original is made silent (but is still structurally present).

ii)   *Chain*: The moved copy and all its traces.

iii)   *Potential Antecedent*: A DP in the specifier of TP or another DP. The potential antecedent cannot be the anaphor or pronoun itself, nor can it be a DP that contains the anaphor or pronoun.

iv)   *Binding Principle A* (final): One copy of an anaphor in a chain must be bound within the smallest CP or DP containing it and a potential antecedent

v)   ***Binding Principle B*** (final): A pronoun must be free within the smallest CP or DP containing it but <u>not</u> containing a potential antecedent. If no such CP or DP can be found, the pronoun must be free within the root CP.

FURTHER READING

Büring, Daniel (2005) *Binding Theory*. Cambridge: Cambridge University Press.

Chomsky, Noam (1986b) *Knowledge of Language: Its Nature, Origins and Use*. New York: Praeger.

GENERAL PROBLEM SETS

1. BINDING DOMAIN FOR ANAPHORS
[Application of Skills; Intermediate]
Draw the trees for each of the following sentences, then identify the binding domain of the anaphors. For the ungrammatical forms, explain why the sentence is ungrammatical. In all cases assume that *John* and *himself* are coindexed. Assume the judgments given:

a)   John loves himself.
b)   John loves pictures of himself.
c)   *John loves Mary's pictures of himself.
d)   *John thinks that Mary loves himself.
e)   *John thinks that Mary's depiction of himself is wrong.
f)   John thinks that most depictions of himself are wrong.
g)   Which pictures of himself does John like?
h)   John seems to like pictures of himself.
i)   John believes himself to be the best at baseball.
j)   John wants to congratulate himself.

2. BINDING DOMAIN FOR PRONOUNS
[Application of Skills; Intermediate]
Draw the trees for each of the following sentences, then identify the binding domain of the pronouns. For the ungrammatical forms, explain why the sentence is ungrammatical. In all cases assume that John and the pronoun are coindexed. Assume the judgments given:

a)   *John loves him
b)   John loves his puppy.

c)   John asked if the unflattering description of his work would be published in the paper.
d)   John asked if his essay would be published in the paper.
e)   *John wants to kiss him.
f)   *John believes him to be fantastic.

CHALLENGE PROBLEM SETS

CHALLENGE PROBLEM SET 1: PRONOUNS
[Critical Thinking; Challenge]
We argued above that at least one link of a movement chain containing an anaphor must meet principle A of the binding theory and be bound within its binding domain. Is this true for pronouns as well? Provide examples to support your answer.

CHALLENGE PROBLEM SET 2: POSSESSIVE PRONOUNS
[Critical Thinking; Challenge]
Up to now we've treated possessive pronouns as being of category D. One alternative is that pronouns like *his* are really bimorphemic and take the form below:

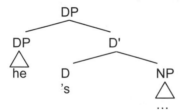

And then there are morphological rules that turn *he's* into *his* (and *she's* into *her*, etc.). Using our definition of "potential antecedent," how does the following sentence argue for the tree above instead of treating *his* as a D? Assume the judgment given.

  *Mary doesn't like his pictures of himself.

CHALLENGE PROBLEM SET 3: WESTERN AMERICAN DIALECTS OF ENGLISH
[Critical Thinking; Challenge]
For most speakers of English the sentence below is ungrammatical with the indexation given. However, there is a significant dialect area in the western United States (Andy Barss has found speakers from Arizona, California and New Mexico that all have this judgment) where this sentence is typically judged as fully acceptable. What minor adjustment must we make to principle A to explain the grammaticality of this sentence in this dialect?

  Heidi$_i$ doesn't like Nate's pictures of herself$_i$.

Part 5

Alternatives

chapter 16

Lexical-Functional Grammar

0. ALTERNATIVE THEORIES

The first fifteen chapters of this textbook are an introduction to syntactic theory from one particular perspective. That is the perspective of the Chomskyan Principles and Parameters (P&P) approach (and its descendant: Minimalism). While a large number of syntacticians (perhaps even a majority) operate using the assumptions and formalisms we've developed so far in this book, not everyone does. In this chapter and the next, we look at two other popular formalisms: *Lexical-Functional Grammar (LFG)* and *Head-Driven Phrase Structure Grammar (HPSG)*.

In many ways, these theories have the same basic goals and assumptions as P&P syntax. LFG and HPSG are considered to be generative grammars, just like P&P. Where all these theories differ is in the precise formulation of the rules and constraints. We will have something to say about choosing among formalisms at the end of chapter 17, but to a great degree it comes down to a matter of the range of phenomena one wants to account for and one's preferred means of formal expression. My inclusion of these approaches is not meant to imply that they are better than P&P, nor to imply that P&P is better than them. They should simply be viewed as alternatives.

As a beginning syntactician, you might wonder why you should bother looking at alternative approaches. After all, a significant part of the literature and research being done in syntax uses the assumptions and formalisms developed in the first fifteen chapters. Shouldn't we just pick one formalism and stick with it? To be honest, most researchers do just this; they do their work within only one formalism. For example, I do almost all of my research within the P&P approach. But this doesn't mean that I shouldn't be familiar with other formalisms too. An important body of work is conducted in these formalisms, and their results are often directly relevant to work being done in Chomskyan P&P syntax. Being able to interpret work done in these alternative approaches is a very useful skill (and unfortunately, one rarely taught to beginning syntacticians). The results found in other approaches to syntax have often affected the development of P&P theory. For example, the lexical approach to passives (whereby the passive morphology affects the thematic and case assigning properties of the underlying verbal morphology) replaced an earlier purely transformational approach to passives. This idea was borrowed from LFG. Similarly, the idea of feature checking is directly related to the notion of unification found in both LFG and HPSG. So I encourage you to keep an open mind and consider the advantages of being familiar with more than one formalism.

1. C-STRUCTURE

One major part of LFG is almost identical to the approach taken in the rest of the book. This is the idea that the words of a sentence are organized into constituents, which are represented by a tree, and generated by rules. In LFG, these trees are called the *c-structure*, and are roughly equivalent to the S-structure in P&P.[1] Many LFG theorists adopt X-bar theory, but it is not as strictly applied to all languages. For example, LFG posits a flat (VP-less) structure for many VSO languages (Kroeger 1993) and "free word order" or "non-configurational" languages like Warlpiri (Simpson 1991). This said, most LFG c-structures look just like the S-structure trees we have built elsewhere in this book. There is one major exception to this: since there is no movement, there are (for the most part) no traces (nor are there any other null elements).

---

[1] Because LFG doesn't use transformations, there is no D-structure. Phrase structure rules directly build the c-structure (= S-structure). Displaced items are dealt with in other ways. See below.

2. FUNCTIONS

As you might guess from its name, there are two driving forces in Lexical-Functional Grammar: the lexicon (which we explore in section 3 below) and functions. The notion of function is borrowed from math and computer science. A *function* is a rule that maps from one item to another.[2] There are really two kinds of functions in LFG, which can be a bit confusing. The first kind are called **grammatical functions** and are things like subject, object, etc. We called these grammatical relations in chapter 4. When a practitioner of LFG talks about functions, they are primarily talking about grammatical functions. The other kind of function refers to the principles that map between the different parts of the grammar, such as the mapping between the c-structure and the structure that represents the grammatical functions. This is called an *f-structure*. We are going to look at grammatical functions here, then turn to the mapping relations in section 4.

In P&P syntax, grammatical functions or relations are read off of the tree. That is, you know what the subject of a sentence is by looking for the NP that is in the specifier of TP. In LFG, grammatical functions are not defined by a tree; instead, they are primitive notions (meaning they can't be derived somehow). Every sentence has an f-structure that represents grammatical functions. In the f-structure, a particular NP will be identified as being the subject of the sentence, quite independent of the tree structure associated with the sentence. In the sentence *Diana loves phonology*, *Diana* is equated with the SUBJ grammatical function. This equation is usually represented in what is called an *Attribute Value Matrix (AVM)*; the item on the left is the attribute or function, the item on the right is the value attributed to that function:

1) [SUBJ   [PRED[3]   'Diana']]

Attributes can have various kinds of values, including other AVMs. For example, the value for the SUBJ function in sentence (2) is itself a matrix containing other functions:

2)   The professor loves phonology.

---

[2] If you are unfamiliar with this notion you might want to consult a good "mathematics for linguists" textbook, such as Allwood, Andersson and Dahl (1977).

[3] The term PRED here is a bit confusing, since 'Diana' is an argument of the clause. PRED here can be, very loosely, translated as the semantic head of the AVM.

3)

$$\begin{bmatrix} \dots & \\ \text{SUBJ} & \begin{bmatrix} \text{PRED} & \text{'professor'} \\ \text{DEF} & + \\ \text{NUM} & \text{sng} \end{bmatrix} \end{bmatrix}$$

In the embedded AVM, the function PRED tells you the lexical content of the subject NP, DEF tells you if it is definite or not, NUM tells you the number, etc. These are all properties of the subject. You'll notice that more than just grammatical functions are represented in these structures; various kinds of other features (like definiteness, etc.) are as well.

Once you combine all the AVMs for all the parts of a sentence you get the f-structure, containing all the sentence's featural and functional information. Where does all this featural information come from? Most of the information that is combined into the f-structure comes from the lexical entries of all the words in the sentence. The lexicon thus plays an important role in this theory.

3. THE LEXICON

The lexicon is where a lot of the work in LFG is done. All the information that ends up in an f-structure starts out in the lexical entries of the words that compose the sentence.

The rough equivalent to a theta grid in LFG is the **a-structure** or argument structure.[4] As in P&P syntax, the a-structure is part of the lexical entry for the predicate. Simplifying somewhat, the lexical entry for the inflected verb *loves* is seen in (4). For the moment, ignore the arrows; I'll explain these below in section 4.

4) *loves:*   V $(\uparrow\text{PRED}) = $ 'love $<(\uparrow\text{SUBJ}),(\uparrow\text{OBJ})>$'
$(\uparrow\text{TENSE}) = $ present
$(\uparrow\text{SUBJ NUM}) = $ sng
$(\uparrow\text{SUBJ PERS}) = $ 3rd

This lexical entry says that *love* is a verb that means 'love', and takes two arguments, an obligatory subject and an obligatory object (as contained within the < > brackets). The parentheses here do *not* mean "optional" – as both arguments are, indeed, obligatory. It also tells us that *loves* is

---

[4] This is a gross over-simplification, I'm ignoring a large number of mapping operations here. I'm also ignoring the complexities of inflectional morphology and how they interact with the featural structure. See Bresnan (2001) or Falk (2001) for extensive discussion.

the present tense form. (The lexical entry for *loved* would have a different value for TENSE.) Finally it tells us that the subject is third person singular ((↑SUBJ NUM) means "my subject's number is …").

All lexical items bring some information to the sentence. For example, we know that the determiner *the* is definite and such information is contained in its lexical entry.

5)   *the:* D   (↑DEF) = +

Functional and featural information comes with the lexical item when it is inserted into the c-structure (as we will see below).

4. F-STRUCTURE

F-structures, as noted above, are the set of all the attribute value pairs for a sentence. Perhaps the easiest way to see this is to look at an example. We use again the sentence *the professor loves phonology*. An f-structure for this sentence is given in (6):

6)
$$\begin{bmatrix} \text{PRED} & \text{'love <SUBJ, OBJ>'} \\ \text{TENSE} & \text{present} \\ \text{SUBJ} & \begin{bmatrix} \text{DEF} & + \\ \text{NUM} & \text{sng} \\ \text{PRED} & \text{'professor'} \end{bmatrix} \\ \text{OBJ} & \begin{bmatrix} \text{PRED} & \text{'phonology'} \end{bmatrix} \end{bmatrix}$$

The topmost PRED function tells you what the predicate of the sentence is. It also contains information about the a-structure of the sentence. The TENSE feature tells you about the tense of the sentence. The SUBJ and OBJ functions have submatrices (containing information on their internal structure) as values.

C-structures must be related to f-structures somehow. This is accomplished with the use of variables. Consider the simple c-structure in (7). Each lexical item is followed by the information it contributes by virtue of its lexical entry. Each node in the tree is marked with a *variable* ($f_1, f_2, f_3, \ldots$, etc.). These will be used in mapping to the f-structure. Again, ignore the arrows for the moment.

7)

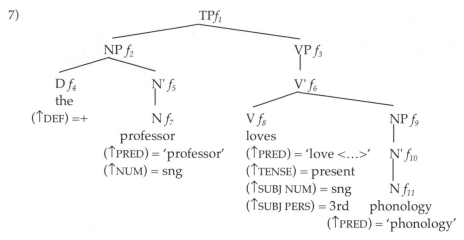

Each of these variables corresponds to a pair of matrix brackets in the f-structure. There is *no* one-to-one correspondence here. Multiple nodes in the tree can correspond to the same (sub)AVM:

8)

$$f_1, f_3, f_6, f_8, \begin{bmatrix} \text{PRED} & \text{'love <SUBJ, OBJ>'} \\[4pt] \text{TENSE} & \text{present} \\[4pt] \text{SUBJ} & f_2, f_4, f_5, f_7, \begin{bmatrix} \text{DEF} & + \\ \text{NUM} & \text{sng} \\ \text{PRED} & \text{'professor'} \end{bmatrix} \\[4pt] \text{OBJ} & f_9, f_{10}, f_{11}, \; [\text{PRED} \quad \text{'phonology'}] \end{bmatrix}$$

This means that the information contained in nodes f_2, f_4, f_5, f_7 contribute the SUBJ features to the sentence. f_9, f_{10}, f_{11}, provide the OBJ info, etc.

The mapping formally happens through what is called an *f-description*. The f-description is set out with *functional equations*. These equations tell us, for example, that the subject of the sentence f_1 corresponds to the constituent f_2. This is written as:

9) $(f_1 \text{SUBJ}) = f_2$

The fact that the subject NP (f_2) is definite is encoded in D node (f_4):

10) $f_2 = f_4$

When a node is a head, or simply passes information up the tree (e.g., V' or V), then a simple equivalence relation is stated:

11) $f_3 = f_6$

These functional equations control how information is mapped through the tree and between the tree and the f-structure. Each piece of information in the f-structure comes from (various places in) the tree as controlled by the functional equations in the f-description.

In order to make this clearer, as a notational device, c-structures are often annotated with their functional equations. There is a useful device that is used to clarify these annotations. These are **metavariables**. Metavariables are variables that stand for other variables. There are two metavariables:

12) a)   ↓ means "this node"
    b)   ↑ means "my mother" (immediately dominating node)

So the equation ↑=↓ means "all of the features I have also belong to my mother" – in other words, a head. The notation (↑SUBJ)=↓ means "I represent the subject function of my mother".

We also saw these arrows in lexical entries. They mean the same thing here. (↑PRED) = 'love' means "the terminal node that I fill has the predicate value of 'love'."

Here is the c-structure in (7) repeated below as (13) with the functional equations annotated using metavariables:

13)

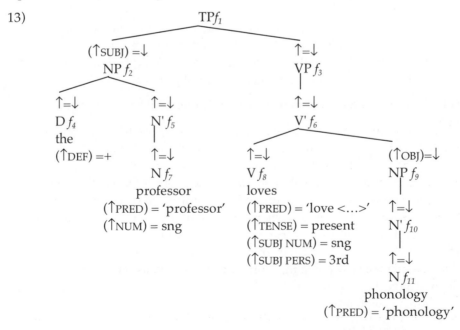

Unification is the idea that features and functions coming from disparate places in the tree must be compatible with one another. Take, for example, the fact that the verb specifies that its subject must be third person singular (as marked by the suffix -*s*). If the subject has number or person features, then those features must match the verb's subject features in the f-structure. This is forced by the fact that the f-structure (in mathematical terms) solves for, or is the solution to, the set of functional equations known as the functional description. If the features didn't match, then the f-structure wouldn't unify. Notice that this is a very similar notion to the idea of feature checking, discussed in chapter 12. Feature checking also ensures compatibility of features coming from different parts of the sentence. Minimalism simply uses movement, rather than functional equations, to guarantee this. Both systems have their advantages; LFG's system has a certain mathematical precision and elegance that P&P movement and feature checking do not. By contrast, P&P/Minimalism is able to derive word order differences between languages from feature checking and movement. Minimalism thus provides a slightly more explanatory theory of word order than LFG, which uses language-specific phrase structure rules. It is not at all clear which approach is preferable.

There are a number of constraints on f-structures. Three of these conspire together to result in the LFG equivalent of the theta criterion:

14) a) *Uniqueness*: In a given f-structure, a particular attribute may have at most one value.
    b) *Completeness*: An f-structure must contain all the governable grammatical functions that its predicate governs.
    c) *Coherence*: All the governable grammatical functions in an f-structure must be governed by a local predicate.

(14a) is also the constraint that forces unification. All f-structures must meet these constraints.

4.1 Why F-structures?

We now have a fairly detailed sketch of the basics of LFG. Before turning to some implementations of the model dealing with some of the empirical issues we've looked at elsewhere in this book, it is worth considering why the LFG model uses f-structures. The answer is fairly straightforward: Information about a particular grammatical function may come from more than one place in the tree and, more importantly, the sources of information do not have to be constituents. Falk (2001) gives the example of the pair of following sentences:

15) a) The deer are dancing.
    b) The deer is dancing.

The form of the subject noun is identical in both of these sentences. However, in terms of meaning, it is plural in (15a) and singular in (15b). Let's assume that the lexical entry for the form 'deer' lacks any specification for number:

16) *deer* N   (↑PRED) = 'deer'

The number associated with the subject function in the sentences in (15) comes from the auxiliary:

17) a)   *are* T   (↑TENSE) = present
                   (↑SUBJ NUM) = pl
    b)   *is* T   (↑TENSE) = present
                   (↑SUBJ NUM) = sg

While the number comes from the auxiliary, it is only really a property of the subject. The NUM feature still gets mapped to the SUBJ function, because of the functional annotation (↑SUBJ NUM) = pl. Similar facts are seen in "free word order" or "non-configurational" languages, like the aboriginal Warlpiri language spoken in Australia. Contra the principle of modification we discussed in chapter 3, in Warlpiri, words that modify one another do not have to appear as constituents on the surface. Since information can come from various parts of the tree, this points towards a system where functional information is not read directly off the tree; instead, an f-structure-like level is motivated.[5]

You can now try General Problem Set 1

---

5. Assorted Phenomena

Having now quickly laid out the fundamentals of LFG (c-structure, f-structure, the lexicon, etc.), we turn to how various phenomena discussed in other parts of this book are treated in LFG.

---

[5] It is worth briefly mentioning how P&P deals with these same facts. At D-structure, these units do form constituents. A transformation, known as **scrambling** (see the problem sets in chapter 11), then reorders the elements so they don't surface as constituents. Both approaches achieve essentially the same results with different underlying assumptions.

5.1 Head Mobility

In chapter 9, we analyzed alternations between the position of a tensed verb and the position of auxiliaries in languages like French, Vata, or Irish as involving head-to-head movement. In French, the main verb alternates in its position relative to adverbs, depending upon the presence or absence of an auxiliary. When an auxiliary is present, the verb stays in its base position. When there is no auxiliary, the verb moves to T. Although LFG has no movement, it has a related account of these phenomena. LFG simply posits that tensed verbs and untensed participial forms belong to different categories. This is called *head mobility*. Tensed verbs are of category T, whereas untensed forms are of category V:

18) a) *mange* T (↑PRED) = 'eat <(↑SUBJ), (↑OBJ)>'
                     (↑TENSE) = present
     b) *mangé* V (↑PRED) = 'eat <(↑SUBJ), (↑OBJ)>'
     c) *ai*   T (↑TENSE) = present[6]

19) a)   b)

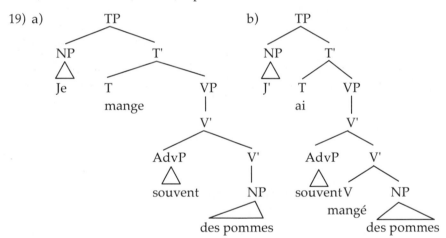

You'll notice that in (19a) the VP has no head V. This is allowed in LFG, but not in P&P theory (as it violates the endocentric properties of X-bar theory).

In English, both participles and tensed verbs are of the category V; only auxiliaries are of category T:

20) a) *eat*   V (↑PRED) = 'eat <(↑SUBJ), (↑OBJ)>'
                    (↑TENSE) = present
     b) *eaten* V (↑PRED) = 'eat <(↑SUBJ), (↑OBJ)>'
     c) *have*   T (↑TENSE) = present

---

[6] The sentence *J'ai souvent mangé des pommes* also bears what are called aspect features. We leave these aside here.

This means that both the participle and the tensed form will appear in the VP and no outward appearance of head movement will arise.

5.2 Passives

LFG's basic grammatical functions allow us to do passives in just one step, which all happens in the lexicon. In LFG there is no syntactic component to passives. Instead there is a simple lexical change associated with the passive morphology:

21) a) *kiss*   V $(\uparrow \text{PRED}) = \text{'kiss} <(\uparrow \text{SUBJ}), (\uparrow \text{OBJ})>'$

                       +en   ⇓   ⇓

    b) $kissed_{\text{pass}}$V $(\uparrow \text{PRED}) = \text{'kiss} < \quad \varnothing \quad (\uparrow \text{SUBJ}) >'$

When the lexical entry in (21b) is inserted into a c-structure, the original object is directly placed into the subject position. There is no movement.

5.3 Raising and Control

Before getting into LFG's analysis of raising and control constructions, we need to introduce the theory's treatment of non-finite complements. In most versions of LFG, these are not treated as CPs. Instead, they are most often treated as VP constituents. The special category VP' has been created to host *to*. Nearly identical c-structures are used for both raising and control:

22)

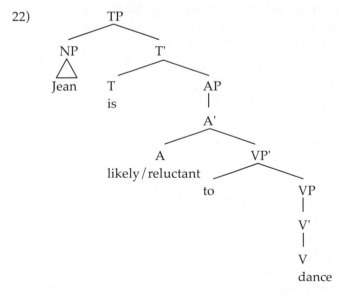

The differences between control and raising constructions are expressed in lexical entries and f-structures, not in the phrase structure (c-structure) as in P&P.

Let's start with control constructions.[7] LFG uses a special grammatical function to represent non-finite complements. Since embedded predicates in these constructions don't have their subject expressed overtly, they are considered **open functions** (that is, they are missing an argument). The grammatical function used to represent open functions is XCOMP (or XADJU in the case of adjuncts). Predicates like *is likely* and *is reluctant* select for XCOMPS in their lexical entries. The lexical entry for *reluctant* is given in (17):

23) *reluctant*   A $(\uparrow\text{PRED})$ = 'reluctant $<(\uparrow\text{SUBJ}), (\uparrow\text{XCOMP})>$'

Reluctant takes a thematic subject and an open function as its arguments. When we combine this with a predicate such as *dance*, we get an f-structure like the following for the sentence *Jean is reluctant to dance*:

24)   *
$$
\begin{bmatrix}
\text{SUBJ} & [\ \text{PRED} \quad \text{'Jean'}\ ] \\
& \\
\text{PRED} & \text{'reluctant} <(\uparrow\text{SUBJ}), (\uparrow\text{XCOMP})>' \\
\text{TENSE} & \text{present} \\
\text{XCOMP} & \begin{bmatrix} \text{SUBJ} & \text{??????} \\ \text{PRED} & \text{'dance} <(\uparrow\text{SUBJ})>' \end{bmatrix}
\end{bmatrix}
$$

This f-structure is ill-formed, because it violates the principle of completeness: The subject function of the XCOMP is not filled. This is resolved using the LFG equivalent of control: **functional control**. Functional control is indicated with a curved line linking the two functions.

25)
$$
\begin{bmatrix}
\text{SUBJ} & [\ \text{PRED} \quad \text{'Jean'}\ ] \\
& \\
\text{PRED} & \text{'reluctant} <(\uparrow\text{SUBJ}), (\uparrow\text{XCOMP})>' \\
\text{TENSE} & \text{present} \\
\text{XCOMP} & \begin{bmatrix} \text{SUBJ} & [\quad] \\ \text{PRED} & \text{'dance} <(\uparrow\text{SUBJ})>' \end{bmatrix}
\end{bmatrix}
$$

This indicates that the subject of the main clause is also the subject of the non-finite complement. Functional control is licensed by the lexical

---

[7] I am simplifying the situation here. The range of phenomena P&P theory groups as "control" constructions divides into two groups in the LFG analysis: functional control and anaphoric control, which have different properties. We won't distinguish these here. See Falk (2001) or Bresnan (2001) for explanations of the difference.

entry of the main clause verb. Here is a revised lexical entry for *reluctant* that contains a control equation (a statement that licenses the curved line in (25):

26) *reluctant*   A   (↑PRED) = 'reluctant <(↑SUBJ), (↑XCOMP)>'
                              (↑SUBJ) = (↑ XCOMP SUBJ)

In English, the second line of this entry stipulates that the subject of the main predicate is identical to the subject of the XCOMP. Notice that this is essentially the equivalent of the thematic analysis of control discussed in chapter 14, and suffers from the same empirical problems as a thematic analysis (see the discussion in chapter 14 to remind yourself of these facts).

In control constructions, the controller must *f-command* the controllee. One node f-commands another if it is less deeply embedded in the f-structure (inside fewer square brackets).

Interestingly, raising constructions have a similar analysis. They also involve functional control. The difference between them and more traditional control constructions is simply that the subject argument of the raising predicate is non-thematic (doesn't get a theta role – indicated by writing it outside the < > brackets), and it is linked to a particular argument in its complement's argument structure (as indicated by the second line of the lexical entry). To see this, consider the lexical entry for *likely*:

27) *likely*   A   (↑PRED) = 'likely <(↑XCOMP)> (↑SUBJ)'
                              (↑SUBJ) = (↑XCOMP SUBJ)

The first line of this lexical entry puts the subject argument outside the angle brackets (< >), indicating that it doesn't get a theta role. The second line specifies that the argument which fills this function is the thematic subject of the open function. Again, in the f-structure this is indicated with a curved line. The following is the f-structure for *Jean is likely to dance*:

28)
$$
\begin{bmatrix}
\text{SUBJ} & [\ \text{PRED} \quad \text{'Jean'}\ ] \\[2mm]
\text{PRED} & \text{'likely} <(↑\text{XCOMP})>, (↑\text{SUBJ})' \\
\text{TENSE} & \text{present} \\
\text{XCOMP} & \begin{bmatrix} \text{SUBJ} & [\quad] \\ \text{PRED} & \text{'dance} <(↑\text{SUBJ})>' \end{bmatrix}
\end{bmatrix}
$$

The difference between the raising and the control sentence simply reduces to a matter of argument structure.

5.4 Wh-*movement: Long Distance Dependencies*

The sharing of feature structures (as expressed by the curved line) is also used to define long distance dependencies such the relationship between a *wh*-phrase and the gap (or trace) it is associated with. There is a special grammatical function: FOCUS, which is found in *wh*-constructions. I'll abstract away from the details, but in English, this function is associated with the specifier of CP. The element taking the FOCUS function must share features with some argument (this is forced on the sentence by the constraint of coherence). The following is the f-structure for the sentence *Which novel do you think Anne read?* (COMP is the function assigned tensed embedded clauses.)

29)

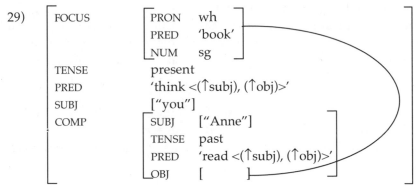

The FOCUS shares the features of the OBJ function of the complement clause, indicating that they are identical.

There is much more to *wh*-dependencies in LFG than this simple picture. For example, LFG has an account of island conditions based on f-structures. There is also an explicit theory of licensing *wh*-dependencies. For more on this see the readings in the further reading section at the end of the chapter.

You can now try Challenge Problem Sets 1–3

---

6. CONCLUSION

This concludes our whirlwind tour of Lexical-Functional Grammar. A single chapter does not give me nearly enough space to cover the range and depth of this theory, and as such doesn't give LFG the opportunity to really shine. I've glossed over many details and arguments here, but I hope this chapter gives you enough information to pursue further reading in this alternative framework. Remember that the results derived in frameworks like LFG can give us insights about the way human language works. If we're clever enough, we should be able to incorporate these insights into the P&P or Minimalist framework, too. Similarly, a student of LFG should be able to use the insights of Minimalism or P&P to inform their theorizing. Remember that syntactic theories are only hypotheses about the way syntax is organized. We really don't know which approach, if any of these, is right. So by looking at other theoretical approaches we question our basic assumptions, and consider new alternatives.

IDEAS, RULES, AND CONSTRAINTS INTRODUCED IN THIS CHAPTER

i)   *C-structure*: Constituent structure. The tree in LFG. Roughly equivalent to S-structure in P&P.

ii)   *Grammatical Function*: Same thing as a grammatical relation. Common grammatical functions: SUBJ = subject; OBJ = object; PRED = predicate; XCOMP = open complement (non-finite clause); COMP = closed complement (finite embedded clause); FOCUS = the function associated with *wh*-phrases

iii)   *F-structure*: The level of representation where grammatical functions are unified.

iv)   *Attribute Value Matrix (AVM)*: A matrix that has an attribute (or function) on the left and its value on the right. The set of all AVMs for a sentence form the sentence's f-structure.

v)   *A-structure*: Argument structure. The LFG equivalent of the theta grid.

vi)   *Variables*: LFG uses variables (f_1, f_2, f_3, ..., etc.) for each node on the c-structure which are used in the mapping between c-structure and f-structure.

vii)   *Functional Equation*: An equation that maps one variable to another (e.g., $(f_1 \text{SUBJ}) = f_2$ says that f_2 maps to f_1's SUBJ function).

viii)   *F-description*: The set of all functional equations. Defines the mapping between c-structure and f-structure.

ix)   *Annotated C-structure*: A c-structure annotated with the functional equations which map it to the f-structure.

x)   *Metavariable*: A variable over variables. $\uparrow$ = my mother's variable, $\downarrow$ = my variable.

xi) $\uparrow=\downarrow$: "All the functional information I contain, my mother also contains."

xii) $(\uparrow SUBJ)=\downarrow$, $(\uparrow OBJ)=\downarrow$: "I am the subject of the node that dominates me" or "I am the object of the node that dominates me."

xiii)   **Unification**: All the features and functions associated with the f-structure must be compatible. (Similar to feature checking in P&P.)

xiv)   **Uniqueness**: In a given f-structure, a particular attribute may have at most one value.

xv)   **Completeness**: An f-structure must contain all the governable grammatical functions that its predicate governs.

xvi)   **Coherence**: All the governable grammatical functions in an f-structure must be governed by a local predicate.

xvii)   **Head Mobility**: The idea that lexical items can take different categories depending upon their features. E.g., a tensed verb in French is of category T, whereas an untensed one is a V. This derives head-to-head movement effects.

xviii) **Lexical Rule of Passives**: Passives in LFG are entirely lexical. There is no syntactic movement:

xix)   **Open function** (XCOMP): A function with a missing argument (e.g.,
a   non-finite clause).

xx)   **Functional Control**: The LFG equivalent of control, indicated with a curved line linking two AVMs in an f-structure.

xxi)   **Raising vs. Control**: In LFG raising vs. control reduces to a lexical difference. The SUBJ function in raising constructions isn't thematic, but is in control constructions.

FURTHER READING

Bresnan, Joan (2001) *Lexical-Functional Syntax*. Oxford: Blackwell.

Dalrymple, Mary, Ronald Kaplan, John Maxwell and Annie Zaenen (eds.) (1995) *Formal Issues in Lexical-Functional Grammar*. Stanford: CSLI Publications.

Falk, Yehuda N. (2001) *Lexical-Functional Grammar: An Introduction to Parallel Constraint-Based Syntax*. Stanford: CSLI Publications.

Kaplan, Ronald (1995) The formal architecture of Lexical-Functional Grammar. In Mary Dalrymple et al. (eds.), *Formal Issues in Lexical-Functional Grammar*. Stanford: CSLI Publications. pp. 7–27.

Kaplan, Ronald and Joan Bresnan (1982) Lexical-Functional Grammar: A formal system for grammatical representation. In Joan Bresnan (ed.), *The Mental Representation of Grammatical Relations*. Cambridge: MIT Press. pp. 173–281.

A lot of material on LFG can be found on the web:

http://www-lfg.stanford.edu/lfg

http://www.essex.ac.uk/linguistics/LFG/

Further reading on other theories:

Edmondson, Jerold and Donald A. Burquest (1998) *A Survey of Linguistic Theories* (3rd ed.). Dallas: Summer Institute of Linguistics.

Sells, Peter (1985) *Lectures on Contemporary Syntactic Theories*. Stanford: CSLI Publications.

GENERAL PROBLEM SET

1. ENGLISH
[Application of Skills; Intermediate]
Draw the annotated c-structures and f-structures for the following sentences. (It may also be helpful to write out lexical entries for each of the words detailing the information each word contributes):

a)   Susie loves the rain.
b)   Joan thinks that Norvin is likely to write a paper.
c)   What have you read?

CHALLENGE PROBLEM SETS

CHALLENGE PROBLEM SET 1: ICELANDIC (AGAIN)
[Critical Thinking; Challenge]
Go back to the questions on quirky case in Icelandic in previous chapters and review the data. These data caused problems for us with our case driven theory of movement and our theory of PRO. Do these same problems arise in LFG? Why or why not?

454 Alternatives

CHALLENGE PROBLEM SET 2: TRANSFORMATIONS OR NOT?
[Critical Thinking; Challenge]
Construct the design for an experiment that would distinguish between a transformational approach, and a non-transformational approach like LFG.

CHALLENGE PROBLEM SET 3: WANNA-CONTRACTION
[Critical and Creative Thinking; Challenge]
How might LFG account for *wanna*-contraction (see chapter 11) if it doesn't have movement or traces?

chapter 17

Head-Driven Phrase Structure Grammar

0. INTRODUCTION

Another major formalism for syntactic theory is **Head-Driven Phrase Structure Grammar** or **HPSG**. HPSG is also a generative theory of grammar. It shares with P&P and LFG the goal of modeling how human Language is structured in the mind. HPSG and LFG in particular have many things in common. For example they both make use of a highly enriched lexicon, and the Attribute Value Matrix (AVM) notation we saw with LFG.[1]

As with our discussion of LFG, a short chapter like this cannot hope to properly cover the rich variety of work done in HPSG. In order to get a fuller picture you'll need to look at some of the primary sources of material listed in the further reading section at the end of this chapter; in particular, Sag, Wasow and Bender (2003) is a very accessible work. Another small caveat is in order before we launch into the details of the theory. For pedagogical reasons, I have couched the presentation here so that someone who has read the first 15 chapters of this book can relate the material here to what they already understand. Sometimes in order to do this, I've had to use metaphors and analogies that many practitioners of HPSG would disagree with. For example, I often state that some theoretical device in HPSG is the "equivalent" of something else in P&P or LFG. By this, I generally mean "does roughly the same kind of work;" I do not mean that they are necessarily notationally or empirically equivalent – as they are not.

---

[1] With some significant differences in notation and assumptions.

1. FEATURES

The basic tool of linguistic description in HPSG is **features**. There are a couple of notational systems for features; I adopt here the one used in Sag, Wasow and Bender (2003).[2] Much of the argumentation in this chapter is also taken from that book.

Features enable linguistics to talk about such information as the category of a word, what other words it must appear with (i.e., its theta grid), and what level in the tree the node is (in HPSG, bar levels are treated as features). As in LFG, features are paired with a value in an AVM, and again like LFG, features can take feature structures as values (1):

1) [AGR   [NUM   pl]]

The AVM in (1) says that the agreement feature for the word involves a number feature that is plural in value.

Feature structures come of a variety of types. First we have types that indicate the *word* vs. *phrase* status of every constituent in a tree (thus roughly equivalent to the notion of bar level). The features for a node are next divided into three major classes: the values of the feature SYN are structures relevant to the syntax, ARG-ST (argument structure) feature structures represent the theta grid, and the value of a SEM feature structure represents the semantic properties of the node.

Let us first talk about SYN feature structures. SYN feature structures tell us about the formal grammatical properties of the node. They tell us the syntactic category of the node, any inflectional properties of the node, what other elements the node must combine with, etc. The feature that determines the category of the node and its inflectional properties is called the HEAD feature. The feature that restricts what kind of nodes appear in the specifier position is called the SPR feature, and the feature that restricts what kind of nodes appear in the complement position is the COMPS feature. To see how this works, let us take a partial lexical entry for the word *letter*. This example is taken from Sag and Wasow (1999: 132):

---

[2] It should be noted that many of the ideas in Sag, Wasow and Bender (2003) diverge from the conception of HPSG presented in Pollard and Sag (1994); many HPSG researchers would disagree with the particulars presented here. In particular see Richter (2000) for discussion of the differences among various kinds of HPSG.

2)

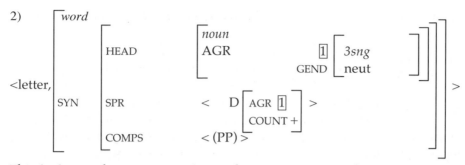

This looks much more intimidating than it actually is. The lexical entry is an ordered list of the form of the word and the large AVM. Ordered lists are represented with angled brackets (< >). At the top we have *word*, which tells us, obviously, that this is a word and not a phrase. Below this we have the SYN feature whose value is described by the AVM containing the HEAD, SPR, and COMPS features. The HEAD feature tells us what kind of lexical item this is. It is a *noun*, it triggers neuter and third person agreement. The SPR feature gives us an ordered list of the items that may or must appear in the specifier position of any projection of this noun. The ordered list in this lexical entry contains only one item: a count noun determiner. The boxed number found both in the HEAD feature and in this SPR feature (⒈) is called a *(coreference) tag*. Tags are used to indicate that certain substructures of an overall structure are identical. The tag ⒈ in the description of the HEAD feature refers to the object described by the AVM that follows it. The ⒈ in the SPR feature indicates that whatever the agreement features of the head are, they must be identical for the specifier. This means that since the noun is third person singular, the determiner must also be singular:

3) a)   this (sg) letter (sg)
    b)   *these (pl) letter (sg)

The idea of structural identity (as expressed by coreference tags) does much of the work that Functional Control does in LFG and feature checking does in P&P – and more. For instance, it allows HPSG to have a non-transformational analysis of raising and to eliminate PRO in control constructions.

Notice that the specifier is not optional in this lexical entry. In English, with singular count nouns, specifiers are not optional:

4) a)   I gave her the letter.
    b)   I gave her a letter.
    c)   *I gave her letter.

Finally, we have the COMPS feature, which says that we may have an optional PP complement:

5) a) a letter about computer software
    b) a letter from the president

The next major feature is the ARG-ST feature. Its value is an ordered list of all the arguments associated with the word and represents the theta grid of the word. You might observe that there is a redundancy between ARG-ST features, and the SPR/COMPS features. As we will see below in section 2, this is acceptable because they are treated differently by the rules which combine words into sentences. As we will see, we need the ARG-ST feature for binding reasons, independent of the SPR/COMPS features.[3] An example of the ARG-ST feature for the verb *love* is given in (6):

6) <*love*,   [ARG-ST < NP, NP>]>

We can impose various kinds of selectional restrictions on this representation, of course. For example, the verb *loves* requires that its subject be third person singular. We can encode this by inserting an AVM with this specification into the first NP slot in the ARG-STR list.

7) <*loves*,   [ARG-ST < [NP [AGR 3s]], NP>]>

Finally we have the SEM (semantic) features. These give us information about how the word and sentence are to be interpreted. For example, MODE tells us the semantic type of the node (proposition, interrogative, directive, referential item). The INDEX features are like the indices we used in chapter 5: They mark the various participants or situations described in the sentence. Last, we have the RESTR (restriction) feature, which tell us the properties that must hold true for the sentence to be true. Again, this looks a bit like our theta grids from chapter 8. Unfortunately we don't have the space to cover this interesting aspect of HPSG in any detail.

The complete lexical entry for the noun *letter* is given in (8), showing all these features. The largest AVM in this structure is known as the noun's *SYN-SEM structure*.

---

[3] Other arguments for distinguishing ARG-STR from COMPS and SPR can be found in Manning and Sag (1998).

8)

<letter,

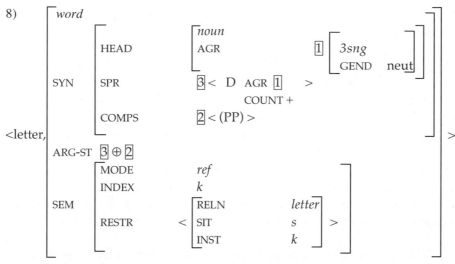

Each word in the lexicon has a rich lexical entry like this that specifies the features and feature structures it brings to the sentence. This lexical entry tells us that this item is a *word*; its SYN feature specifies that it is a *noun* with a 3sng, neuter HEAD feature. Since it is a count noun, the SPR feature requires that it take a count determiner, which must agree with the HEAD | AGR feature (indicated by the tag 1). It may also take an optional PP COMPS (complement). The specifier and complement features are related in the ARG-ST feature by the tags 3 and 2 (I'll discuss the ⊕ symbol below). The SEMantic features, which don't really concern us much here, indicate that the item is *ref*erential and is assigned the index *k*. The RESTR feature tells us what the word means and what context it can appear in. (Again see Sag, Wasow and Bender (2003) for a more complete description of all these features.)

2. THE LEXICON

Needless to say, there is a lot of information stored in lexical entries in HPSG grammars. In many cases this information is redundant or predictable. For example, for any count noun (such as *letter* or *ball* or *peanut*), there are two forms: a singular form and a plural form. Ideally we don't really want two complete lexical entries, as the information in one is predictable from the other. While memory is cheap, it would be nice to reduce the amount of redundancy or predictable information contained in each lexical entry. HPSG does this in a number of ways.[4]

First, like LFG, HPSG has lexical rules that can change the shape of lexical entries. Take for example the plural rule that derives the lexical entries for plurals out of uninflected nouns. (The F_{NPL} notation refers to a function that does the actual morphology. For example, F_{NPL} applied to *cat*, will result in *cats*, but F_{NPL} applied to *child* will give you *children*.)

9)   *Plural Rule*

$$< \boxed{1}, \begin{bmatrix} noun \\ \text{ARG-ST} < [\text{count }+] > \end{bmatrix} > \Rightarrow < F_{NPL}(\boxed{1}), \begin{bmatrix} word \\ \text{SYN [HEAD [AGR [NUM pl]]]} \end{bmatrix} >$$

This rule says that given any basic count noun root $\boxed{1}$, you can create a plural lexical item that has an identical feature structure, except with plural number.

Similar rules can be applied to do derivation (such as deriving the noun *dancer* from the verb *dance*), or to do grammatical function-changing operations like the passive. In the following rule (taken from Sag and Wasow 1999: 235) the symbol ⊕ means "an append of lists." For more on this notion, see the references below, but for our purposes it roughly corresponds to an ordering of the AVMs. You'll see that the rule does three things: (i) it puts the verb ($\boxed{1}$), into a passive form; (ii) it puts the first argument (NP$_i$) into an optional *by*-phrase (don't worry about the details of the feature structure for the *by*-phrase); (iii) it moves all the other arguments ($\boxed{a}$) up in the ARG-ST list, the ⊕ symbol showing that the arguments are strictly ordered with respect to one another. The big gray arrows in the following rule are not part of the rule itself; I've just written them in to point out the important parts of the rule.

10) *Passive Rule*

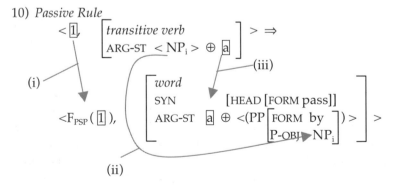

---

[4] One of which we don't have the space to discuss here: *inheritance hierarchies*. These are discussed at length in Sag and Wasow (1999) and other sources on HPSG.

There is one further area of redundancy in the lexicon, which we already noted in section 1 above. The information about the number of arguments a word takes appears twice in the SYN-SEM structure. It appears once in the ARG-ST feature and once in the SPR/COMPS features. This redundancy is solved by the *Argument Realization Principle* (11), which builds the SPR and COMPS features out of the ARG-ST feature:

11) *Argument Realization Principle (ARP):* A word structure satisfies the following feature structure description:

$$
\begin{bmatrix}
\text{SYN} & \begin{bmatrix} \text{SPR} & \boxed{1} \\ \text{COMPS} & \boxed{2} \end{bmatrix} \\
\text{ARG-ST} \ \boxed{1} \ \oplus \ \boxed{2}
\end{bmatrix}
$$

The equivalence of the SPR/COMPS features and the ARG-ST feature is indicated by the tags $\boxed{1}$ and $\boxed{2}$. The first argument is mapped to the SPR feature, the second to the COMPS feature. This principle says that you map the first argument of the argument structure into the SPR position, and the second one into the COMPS position.

HPSG, then, shares with LFG a rich lexicon with many lexical rules. This is where the similarities end, however. In LFG, we used functions and functional equations to map constituency (c-structure) onto the functional representation (f-structure). In HPSG, like P&P theory and as we'll see below, functional (= featural) information is read directly off the constituent tree instead of using mapping principles.

3. RULES, FEATURES, AND TREES

HPSG differs from LFG in at least one significant regard: it is *compositional*. By that we mean that the way in which the meaning of the sentence is determined is by looking at the constituent structure associated with the sentence. HPSG shares this assumption with P&P. The meaning of a sentence in HPSG and P&P can be calculated by taking each node, and using constituency to determine what modifies what. Relationships between words are directly encoded into constituency. In LFG, we instead used functional equations to calculate the relationships between words.

In all three theories (HPSG, LFG, and P&P), the end of the sentence should involve a *saturation, satisfaction,* or *unification* of the features introduced by the words.[5] In Minimalism, this was accomplished by feature checking via the construction of the phrase structure tree and via movement. In LFG, this is accomplished by functional equations that map to an f-structure. In HPSG, by contrast, all feature satisfaction occurs by combining words into constituents. Constituency is introduced by phrase structure rules.[6] These rules look a little different than the ones we used in chapters 3, 6, and 7, but they do similar work. There are three basic rules (which are roughly equivalent to the complement rule, the adjunct rule and the specifier rule of X-bar theory). The first of these is the **Head Complement Rule**. This takes a head (marked with H) word, and if it is in sequence with a number of arguments that match its COMPS requirements, licenses a phrase with an AVM like its own, except that those COMPS features have been checked off and deleted.[7]

12) *Head Complement Rule*

$$\begin{bmatrix} phrase \\ \text{COMPS} < > \end{bmatrix} \rightarrow \quad \text{H} \begin{bmatrix} word \\ \text{COMPS} < \boxed{1}, \dots, \boxed{n} > \end{bmatrix} \boxed{1} \quad \dots \quad \boxed{n}$$

Notice that the tags $\boxed{1}$, ..., $\boxed{n}$ on the head must be identical to the tags of the phrases that follow. This means that the element(s) on the right hand side of the head must be selected for in the COMPS portion of the head word. The resulting category (the *phrase*) has had its COMPS features erased. (Thus making the satisfaction of features like COMPS very much like feature checking.) The output of this rule – when applied to a transitive verb

---

[5] The exact characterization of how this works is a matter of some debate in HPSG, with various formal proposals in different versions of the theory. In early HPSG this was done with unification (see chapter 16), as is the version found in Sag and Wasow (1999). In Pollard and Sag (1994) well-formed feature structures are licensed by *conjunction* (or more accurately the conjunctive satisfaction of all the principles of the grammar). The distinctions between these approaches need not concern us here, which is why I've adopted the neutral term *satisfaction* (or saturation) to get at the underlying idea. See Richter (2000) for a discussion of the formal apparatus underlying these issues.

[6] Phrase structure rules are actually a shorthand notation for more complicated principles. See Pollard and Sag (1994) for more discussion.

[7] For expository ease, I'm occasionally lapsing into the metaphors and terminology of Minimalism, which are not accepted by practitioners of HPSG. I do this so that you can relate the ideas of HPSG to what you have previously seen in this book; this doesn't mean that the ideas are entirely equivalent. For example, the notions of checking and deletion suggest a derivational approach to syntax which is not necessarily a part of HPSG. For more on the philosophical and methodological assumptions underlying HPSG see Pollard and Sag (1994).

and an NP – is seen in (13). For ease of exposition, I've omitted most of the featural information here, leaving just the relevant features present.

13)

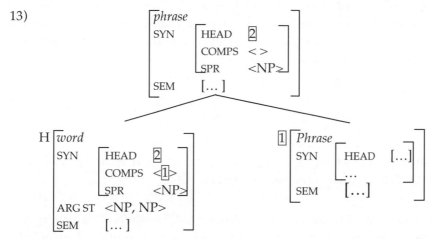

The resulting phrase is what we would label a V' in P&P syntax. The rule combines a head with an item that satisfies one of its COMPS requirements. It then licenses a phrase lacking that COMPS requirement.

One thing to notice about (13) is that the head features of the head word become the head features of the entire phrase, just like the syntactic category of a head is passed up the tree to the phrase level in the X-bar theory of chapter 6. In HPSG this due to the ***Head Feature Principle***:

14) *Head Feature Principle (HFP)*: The HEAD value of any headed phrase is identical to the HEAD value of the head daughter.

You'll also notice that the SPR feature of the head daughter is also transferred up to the mother node. This is triggered by the ***Valence Principle*** (Sag, Wasow and Bending 2003):

15) *Valence Principle*: Unless the rule says otherwise, the mother's SPR and COMPS values are identical to those of the head daughter.

Semantic Feature Flow

The distribution of syntactic feature values is governed by our three phrase structure rules. Semantic feature values also flow up the tree. This is governed by two principles. We won't go into these in detail, but here they are for your reference:

i) *Semantic Compositionality Principle*
    In any well-formed phrase structure, the mother's RESTR value is the sum of the RESTR values of the daughters.

ii) *Semantic Inheritance Principle*
    In any headed phrase, the mother's mode and index values are identical to those of the head daughter.

Adjuncts are introduced by the **Head Modifier Rule**. This rule makes reference to the special feature MOD. The MOD feature is contained in the SYN-SEM structure of the modifier and is linked to the thing it modifies with a tag, allowing modifiers to impose selectional restrictions on the phrases they modify. The rule takes a *phrase* (equivalent to our X' level) and licenses another *phrase* (X').

16) *Head Modifier Rule*

$$[phrase] \quad \rightarrow \quad H\,\boxed{1}\,[phrase] \quad \begin{bmatrix} phrase \\ \text{HEAD}\,[\text{MOD}\,\boxed{1}] \end{bmatrix}$$

Specifiers are introduced using the third rule, which also takes a *phrase* (X') and licenses a *phrase* (however, this time equivalent to our XP). The S node in HPSG is a projection of the verb (i.e., is licensed as a mother of the VP by this rule). Just as in X-bar theory, the HFP allows this rule to be non-category specific.

17) *Head Specifier Rule*

$$\begin{bmatrix} phrase \\ \text{SPR} <\,> \end{bmatrix} \quad \rightarrow \quad \boxed{1} \quad H\begin{bmatrix} phrase \\ \text{SPR} <\,\boxed{1}\,> \end{bmatrix}$$

This rule takes a phrase with a non-empty SPR value and combines it with an item that satisfies that value, and generates a phrase without an SPR value.

On an intuitive level, these rules take as inputs the lexical entries for words and output sentences where the information has been combined into a meaningful whole. In the next two sections, we turn to a variety of phenomena discussed in this book and look at how HPSG accounts for them.

4. BINDING

HPSG does not use the notion c-command to determine binding relations. Instead, binding makes reference to the ARG-ST list in the SYN-SEM structures. Because of the rules discussed above in section 3, arguments on the left side of an ARG-ST ordered list will always be higher in the tree than ones further to the right on the list. As such the binding conditions in HPSG are based on precedence in the ARG-ST list. This is accomplished with the notion *outrank*.

18) *Outrank*: A phrase A *outranks* a phrase B just in the case where A's SYN-SEM structure precedes B's SYN-SEM structure on some ARG-ST list.

Anaphors are marked with a special feature: ANA. [ANA +] nodes are subject to the HPSG equivalent of principle A:

19) *Principle A:* An [ANA +] SYN-SEM structure must be outranked by a co-indexed SYN-SEM structure.

Pronouns, which are [ANA −] are subject to principle B.

20) *Principle B*: An [ANA −] SYN-SEM structure must not be outranked by a co-indexed SYN-SEM structure.

Because of the direct mapping between the ARG-ST and the tree, this will give us essentially the same results as the c-command analysis given in chapter 4. For a discussion of the important differences between a c-command analysis and an ARG-ST analysis, see Pollard and Sag (1992).

5. LONG DISTANCE DEPENDENCIES

In this section, we look briefly at how HPSG deals with long distance dependencies between the surface position of *wh*-phrases and the position with which they are thematically associated. P&P uses movement to capture this relation. LFG uses functional control. HPSG uses a feature: GAP.[8] This is a feature like COMPS or SPR that indicates that an argument is required by the SYN-SEM structure and is missing. The presence of a non-empty GAP feature indicates that an argument is not filling the expected complement position. This is encoded in a revised version of the argument realization principle, where the sequence ② ⊖ ③ is a list where the elements on the list ③ have been removed from ②. This principle allows you to optionally map an argument to he GAP feature rather than the COMPS feature.

---

[8] Also called SLASH.

21) *Revised ARP*[9]

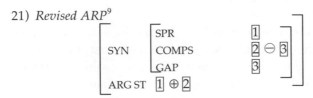

This guarantees that any argument that could appear on the COMPS list can appear on the GAP list instead. Just as we needed principles for passing head features, valence features and semantic features up the tree, we also need a principle to make sure GAP features make it up to the top of the tree: *The GAP Principle*. (Formulation again taken from Sag, Wasow and Bender (2003).)

22) *The GAP Principle*

This principle encodes the idea that a mother's GAP feature represents the union of all the GAP values of its daughters.

    Let's do an example. Because we don't have the space to introduce HPSG analyses of head movement or *do*-support, we'll use topicalization, rather than a *wh*-question as an example of a long distance dependency. Topicalization has the same basic properties as other *wh*-movement (subject to island constraints, etc.). The sentence we'll do is seen in (23). This sentence is grammatical if we put contrastive stress on the first NP.

23) <u>That boy</u>, we saw …

In a normal sentence, an NP (filled by *that boy*) occupies the COMPS position of the verb *saw*. In this sentence, by contrast, the COMPS position is empty. Instead there is an NP in the GAP feature. The NP *we* satisfies the verb's SPR feature. The GAP value is percolated up the tree by the GAP principle which results in a tree like (24): [10]

---

[9] This particular formulation only allows *wh*-extraction from object position. As something to think about, you might consider how HPSG would go about dealing with subject extraction (as seen in the Irish data in chapter 11).

[10] You might consider whether gap feature percolation is really different from movement or is simply a notational variant. What kind of evidence might you propose to distinguish the two approaches?

24)
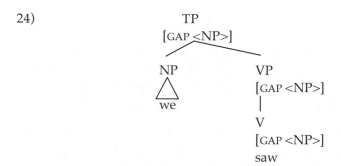

TP
[GAP <NP>]

NP
we

VP
[GAP <NP>]
|
V
[GAP <NP>]
saw

The GAP feature associated with the S node must be satisfied someway. This is accomplished with the *Head Filler Rule*.

25) *The Head Filler Rule*

$$\begin{bmatrix} phrase \\ GAP < > \end{bmatrix} \rightarrow \boxed{1}\begin{bmatrix} phrase \\ GAP < > \end{bmatrix} \quad H\begin{bmatrix} phrase \\ FORM \ fin \\ SPR < > \\ GAP < \boxed{1} > \end{bmatrix}$$

This rule satisfies the GAP feature, by adding the missing NP at the top of the tree:

26)

TP
[GAP < >]

NP
That boy

TP
[GAP <NP>]

NP
we

VP
[GAP <NP>]
|
V
[GAP <NP>]
saw

You can now try General Problem Set 1 and Challenge Problem Sets 1 & 2

IDEAS, RULES, AND CONSTRAINTS INTRODUCED IN THIS CHAPTER

Some of the definitions here are taken from Sag, Wasow and Bender (2003) or the first edition of that book (Sag and Wasow 1999).

i) **Features**: These do the work of determining what can combine with what.

    a) Bar-level-like features tell us what hierarchical level the node is at.

    b) The SYN feature structures gives us the syntactic info about the node.

        i) The HEAD feature gives the category and inflectional info.

        ii) The COMPS feature tells us what complements appear in the structure.

        iii) The SPR feature tells us what appears in the specifier.

        iv) The GAP feature tells us if there is a long distance dependency.

    c) The ARG-ST feature is the HPSG equivalent of the theta grid. Binding relations are defined against this.

    d) The SEM feature structures tell us the semantic information about the constituent, and come in a variety of types.

ii) **(Coreference) Tags**: Numbers written in boxes (e.g., ①) that show that two items are identical in a SYN-SEM structure or between SYN-SEM structures.

iii) **SYN-SEM Structure**: The set of AVMs for a node, containing all the SYN, SEM and ARG-ST features.

iv) **Plural Rule**:

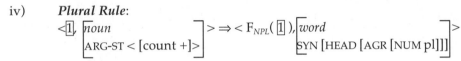

v) **Passive Rule**:

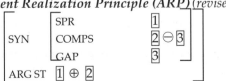

vi) **Argument Realization Principle (ARP) (revised)**:

$$\begin{bmatrix} \text{SYN} & \begin{bmatrix} \text{SPR} & ① \\ \text{COMPS} & ② \ominus ③ \\ \text{GAP} & ③ \end{bmatrix} \\ \text{ARG ST} & ① \oplus ② \end{bmatrix}$$

vii)   ***Compositional***: The idea that the semantics of the sentence can be read off of the constituency tree. This idea is shared by P&P and HPSG, but is rejected by LFG.

viii)   ***Feature Satisfaction*** (*sometimes loosely called* **Unification**): The idea that all the features in a SYN-SEM structure must match. The rough equivalent of feature checking in P&P/Minimalism.

ix)   ***Head Complement Rule***:

$$\begin{bmatrix} phrase \\ \text{COMPS} < > \end{bmatrix} \rightarrow \text{H} \begin{bmatrix} word \\ \text{COMPS} < \boxed{1}, \dots, \boxed{n} > \end{bmatrix} \boxed{1} \ \dots \ \boxed{n}$$

x)   ***Head Feature Principle***: The HEAD value of any headed phrase is identical to the HEAD value of the head daughter.

xi)   ***Valence Principle***: Unless the rule says otherwise, the mother's SPR and COMPS values are identical to those of the head daughter.

xii)   ***Semantic Compositionality Principle***: In any well-formed phrase structure, the mother's RESTR value is the sum of the RESTR values of the daughters.

xiii)   ***Semantic Inheritance Principle***: In any headed phrase, the mother's mode and index values are identical to those of the head daughter.

xiv)   ***Head Modifier Rule***:

$$[phrase] \rightarrow \text{H} \boxed{1} [phrase] \quad \begin{bmatrix} phrase \\ \text{HEAD} [\text{MOD} \ \boxed{1}] \end{bmatrix}$$

xv)   ***Head Specifier Rule***:

$$\begin{bmatrix} phrase \\ \text{SPR} < > \end{bmatrix} \rightarrow \boxed{1} \quad \text{H} \begin{bmatrix} phrase \\ \text{SPR} < \boxed{1} > \end{bmatrix}$$

xvi)   ***Outrank***: A phrase A outranks a phrase B just in the case where A's SYN-SEM structure precedes B's SYN-SEM structure on some ARG-ST list.

xvii)   ***Principle A***: An [ANA +] SYN-SEM structure must be outranked by a coindexed SYN-SEM structure.

xviii) ***Principle B***: An [ANA −] SYN-SEM structure must not be ranked by a coindexed SYN-SEM structure.

xix)   ***The GAP Principle***: $[\text{GAP} \ \boxed{1} \oplus \dots \oplus \boxed{n}]$

$$[\text{GAP} \ \boxed{1}] \quad \dots \quad [\text{GAP} \ \boxed{n}]$$

xx) **The Head Filler Rule**:

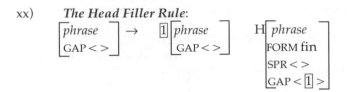

$$\begin{bmatrix} phrase \\ \text{GAP} < > \end{bmatrix} \rightarrow \boxed{1}\begin{bmatrix} phrase \\ \text{GAP} < > \end{bmatrix} \quad \text{H}\begin{bmatrix} phrase \\ \text{FORM fin} \\ \text{SPR} < > \\ \text{GAP} < \boxed{1} > \end{bmatrix}$$

FURTHER READING

Borsley, Robert (1996) *Modern Phrase Structure Grammar*. Oxford: Blackwell.

Gazdar, Gerald, Ewan Klein, Geoffrey Pullum and Ivan Sag (1985) *Generalized Phrase Structure Grammar*. Cambridge: Harvard University Press.

Manning, Christopher and Ivan Sag (1998) Argument structure, valence and binding. *The Nordic Journal of Linguistics* 21, 107-44.

Pollard, Carl and Ivan Sag (1992) Anaphors in English and the scope of Binding Theory. *Linguistic Inquiry* 23, 261-303.

Pollard, Carl and Ivan Sag (1994) *Head-Driven Phrase Structure Grammar*. Stanford: CSLI Publications and Chicago: The University of Chicago Press.

Richter, Frank (2000) A Mathematical Formalism for Linguistic Theories with an Application in Head-Driven Phrase Structure Grammar. Ph.D. dissertation, University of Tübingen.

Sag, Ivan and Thomas Wasow (1999) *Syntactic Theory: A Formal Introduction* (1st ed.). Stanford: CSLI Publications.

Sag, Ivan, Thomas Wasow and Emily Bender (2003) *Syntactic Theory: A Formal Introduction* (2nd ed.). Stanford: CSLI Publications.

GENERAL PROBLEM SET

1. ENGLISH
[Application of Skills; Intermediate]

Create an HPSG-style lexicon for the words in (a) and then draw a tree using the rules and lexical entries for the sentence (b).

a) the, kitten, tore, toilet, paper
b) The kitten tore the toilet paper.

You may abbreviate your SYN-SEM structures using tags.

CHALLENGE PROBLEM SETS

CHALLENGE PROBLEM SET 1: SUBJECT-AUX INVERSION
[Critical Thinking; Challenge]
How might HPSG go about doing subject-aux inversion? (Hint: consider a lexical rule.) Assume that auxiliary verbs select for other verbs in their ARG-ST features.

CHALLENGE PROBLEM SET 2: ISLAND CONSTRAINTS
[Critical Thinking; Challenge]
In this chapter, we didn't talk at all about how HPSG might account for island constraints. Propose a constraint on the GAP principle that might account for them.

Conclusions
and Directions
for Further Study

We started this textbook with the question of what a person needs to know about their language in order to understand a simple sentence. We hypothesized that some of language is innate and other parts are parameterized. In the first twelve chapters of this book, we sketched out some of the major research threads in one approach to syntax: the principles and parameters (P&P) view. In part 1, we looked at how rules generate hierarchical tree structures. These structures are geometric objects with mathematical properties. We looked at one set of phenomena (binding) that is sensitive to those properties. In part 2, we looked at a more sophisticated view of tree structures, developing X-bar theory, and the thematic (lexical) constraints on it such as theta theory. In part 3, we looked extensively at how problematic word orders, such as passives, raising, VSO languages, and *wh*-questions could all be accounted for using movement. In chapter 12, we brought these threads together and started looking at the unified approach to movement. Part 4 addressed three more advanced topics in syntax. We looked at split VP/vPs and the way they account for ditransitives and object shift; we looked at raising and control; and we revisited binding theory and came up with a more sophisticated version of the binding theory. Part 5 of this book changed direction slightly. We looked, ever so briefly, at two popular alternatives to P&P/Minimalism. This was so that you could read papers and books written in those alternatives, as well as giving you a taste for other, related, ways we can approach topics in syntax.

Congratulations for getting through all this material. I hope this book has whetted your appetite for the study of syntax and sentence structure and that you will pursue further studies in syntactic theory. To this end, I've appended a list of books that can take you to the next level.

Cook, V. J. and Mark Newson (1996) *Chomsky's Universal Grammar: An Introduction* (2nd ed.). Oxford: Blackwell.

Cowper, Elizabeth (1992) *A Concise Introduction to Syntactic Theory: The Government and Binding Approach*. Chicago: University of Chicago Press.

Haegeman, Liliane (1994) *Introduction to Government and Binding Theory*. Oxford: Blackwell.

Ouhalla, Jamal (1990) *Introducing Transformational Grammar* (2nd ed.). London: Edward Arnold.

Radford, Andrew (1997a) *Syntactic Theory and The Structure of English: A Minimalist Approach*. Cambridge: Cambridge University Press.

Radford, Andrew (2004) *Minimalist Syntax: Exploring the Structure of English*. Cambridge: Cambridge University Press.

Roberts, Ian (1997) *Comparative Syntax*. London: Edward Arnold.

References

Aarts, Bas (1997) *English Syntax and Argumentation*. New York: St. Martin's Press.

Abney, Steven (1987) The English Noun Phrase in its Sentential Aspect. Ph.D. dissertation, MIT.

Adger, David (1996) Aspect, agreement and Measure Phrases in Scottish Gaelic. In Robert Borsley and Ian Roberts (eds.), *The Syntax of the Celtic Languages*. Cambridge: Cambridge University Press. pp. 200–22.

Aikawa, Takako (1994) Logophoric use of the Japanese reflexive *zibun-zisin* 'self-self'. *MIT Working Papers in Linguistics* 24, 1–22.

Aissen, Judith (1987) *Tzotzil Clause Structure*. Dordrecht: Reidel.

Allwood, Jens, Lars-Gunnar Andersson, and Östen Dahl (1977) *Logic in Linguistics*. Oxford: Oxford University Press.

Anderson, Stephen and Paul Kiparsky (eds.) (1973) *A Festschrift for Morris Halle*. New York: Holt, Rinehart and Winston.

Aoun, Joseph (1985) *A Grammar of Anaphora*. Cambridge: MIT Press.

Baker, C. L. and John McCarthy (eds.) (1981) *The Logical Problem of Language Acquisition*. Cambridge: MIT Press.

Baker, Mark (2001) *The Atoms of Language: The Mind's Hidden Rules of Grammar*. New York: Basic Books.

Baker, Mark, Kyle Johnson, and Ian Roberts (1989) Passive arguments raised. *Linguistic Inquiry* 20, 219–51.

Baltin, Mark (1981) Strict bounding. In C. L. Baker and John McCarthy (eds.), *The Logical Problem of Language Acquisition*. Cambridge: MIT Press. pp. 257–95.

Baltin, Mark and Chris Collins (2000) *The Handbook of Contemporary Syntactic Theory*. Oxford: Blackwell.

Baltin, Mark and Anthony Kroch (1989) *Alternative Conceptions of Phrase Structure*. Chicago: University of Chicago Press.

Bard, Ellen G., Dan Robertson, and Antonella Sorace (1996) Magnitude estimation of linguistic acceptability. *Language* 72, 32–68.

Barker, Chris and Geoffrey Pullum (1990) A theory of command relations. *Linguistics and Philosophy* 13, 1–34.

Barsky, Robert (1997) *Noam Chomsky: A Life of Dissent*. Cambridge: MIT Press.

Barss, Andy and Howard Lasnik (1986) A note on anaphora and double objects. *Linguistic Inquiry* 17, 347–54.

Bayer, J. (1984) COMP in Bavarian syntax. *The Linguistics Review* 3, 209–4.

Beck, Sigrid and Kyle Johnson (2004) Double objects again. *Linguistic Inquiry* 35, 97–124.

Belletti, Adriana (1994) Verb positions: Evidence from Italian. In David Lightfoot and Norbert Hornstein (eds.), *Verb Movement*. Cambridge: Cambridge University Press. pp. 19–40.

Borer, Hagit (1999) Deconstructing the construct. In Kyle Johnson and Ian Roberts (eds.), *Beyond Principles and Parameters*. Dordrecht: Kluwer Academic Publishers. pp. 43–89.

Borsley, Robert (1996) *Modern Phrase Structure Grammar*. Oxford: Blackwell.

Bošković, Zeljko (1997) Superiority and economy of derivation: Multiple *wh*-fronting. Paper presented at the 16th West Coast Conference on Formal Linguistics.

Brame, Michael (1976) *Conjectures and Refutations in Syntax and Semantics*. Amsterdam: Elsevier.

Bresnan, Joan (1972) Theory of Complementation in English. Ph.D. dissertation, MIT.

Bresnan, Joan, ed. (1982) *The Mental Representation of Grammatical Relations.* Cambridge: MIT Press.

Bresnan, Joan (2001) *Lexical-Functional Syntax.* Oxford: Blackwell.

Büring, Daniel (2005) *Binding Theory.* Cambridge: Cambridge University Press.

Burzio, Luigi (1986) *Italian Syntax.* Dordrecht: Reidel.

Carnie, Andrew (1995) Head Movement and Non-Verbal Predication. Ph.D. dissertation, MIT.

Carnie, Andrew and Eithne Guilfoyle (2000) *The Syntax of Verb Initial Languages.* Oxford: Oxford University Press.

Chametzky, Robert (1996) *A Theory of Phrase Markers and the Extended Base.* Albany: SUNY Press.

Cheng, Lisa (1997) *On the Typology of Wh-Questions.* New York: Garland Press.

Choe, Hyon Sook (1987) An SVO analysis of VSO languages and parameterization: A study of Berber. In Mohammed Guerssel and Ken Hale (eds.), *Studies in Berber Syntax. Lexicon Project Working Paper* 14, 121–58.

Chomsky, Noam (1957) *Syntactic Structures.* The Hague: Janua Linguarum 4.

Chomsky, Noam (1965) *Aspects of the Theory of Syntax.* Cambridge: MIT Press.

Chomsky, Noam (1970) Remarks on nominalization. In Roderick Jacobs and Peter Rosenbaum (eds.), *Readings in English Transformational Grammar.* Waltham: Ginn. pp. 184–221.

Chomsky, Noam (1973) Conditions on transformations. In Stephen Anderson and Paul Kiparsky (eds.), *A Festschrift for Morris Halle.* New York: Holt, Rinehart and Winston. pp. 232–86.

Chomsky, Noam (1975) *The Logical Structure of Linguistic Theory.* New York: Plenum.

Chomsky, Noam (1977) On *wh*-movement. In Peter Culicover, Thomas Wasow, and Adrian Akmajian (eds.), *Formal Syntax.* New York: Academic Press. pp. 71–132.

Chomsky, Noam (1980) On Binding. *Linguistic Inquiry* 11, 1–46.

Chomsky, Noam (1981) *Lectures on Government and Binding.* Dordrecht: Foris.

Chomsky, Noam (1986a) *Barriers.* Cambridge: MIT Press.

Chomsky, Noam (1986b) *Knowledge of Language: Its Nature, Origins and Use.* New York: Praeger.

Chomsky, Noam (1991) Some notes on economy of derivation and representation. In Robert Friedin (ed.), *Principles and Parameters in Comparative Grammar.* Cambridge: MIT Press. pp. 417–54.

Chomsky, Noam (1993) A Minimalist program for linguistic theory. In Kenneth L. Hale and Samuel J. Keyser (eds.), *The View from Building 20: Essays in Honor of Sylvain Bromberger.* Cambridge: MIT Press. pp. 1–52.

Chomsky, Noam (1995) *The Minimalist Program.* Cambridge: MIT Press.

Chomsky, Noam and Howard Lasnik (1978) A remark on contraction. *Linguistic Inquiry* 9, 268–74.

Chung, Sandra (1976) An object creating rule in Bahasa Indonesia. *Linguistic Inquiry* 7, 1–37.

Cinque, Guglielmo (1981) *Types of A' Dependencies.* Cambridge: MIT Press.

Cole, Peter and S. N. Sridhar (1976) Clause union and relational grammar: Evidence from Hebrew and Kannada. *Studies in the Linguistic Sciences* 6, 216–27.

Collins, Chris and Hoskuldur Thráinsson (1996). VP internal structure and object shift in Icelandic. *Linguistic Inquiry* 27, 391–444.

Cook, V. J. and Mark Newson (1996) *Chomsky's Universal Grammar: An Introduction* (2nd ed.). Oxford: Blackwell.

Cowper, Elizabeth (1992) *A Concise Introduction to Syntactic Theory: The Government and Binding Approach.* Chicago: University of Chicago Press.

Culicover, Peter (1997) *Principles and Parameters: An Introduction to Syntactic Theory.* Oxford: Oxford University Press.

Culicover, Peter, Thomas Wasow, and Adrian Akmajian (eds.) (1977) *Formal Syntax*. New York: Academic Press.

Dalrymple, Mary, Ronald Kaplan, John Maxwell, and Annie Zaenen (eds.) (1995) *Formal Issues in Lexical-Functional Grammar*. Stanford: CSLI Publications.

Dedrick, John and Eugene Casad (1999) *Sonora Yaqui Language Structures*. Tucson: University of Arizona Press.

DeGraff, Michel (2005) Morphology and word order in 'creolization' and beyond. In Guglielmo Cinque and Richard Kayne (eds.), *The Oxford Handbook of Comparative Syntax*. Oxford: Oxford University Press.

Den Dikken, Marcel (1995) *Particles: On the Syntax of Verb-Particle, Triadic, and Causative Constructions*. Oxford: Oxford University Press.

Déprez, Vivienne (1992) Raising constructions in Haitian Creole. *Natural Language and Linguistic Theory* 10, 191–231.

Derbyshire, Desmond (1985) *Hixkaryana and Linguistic Typology*. Dallas: Summer Institute of Linguistics.

Diesing, Molly (1992) *Indefinites*. Cambridge: MIT Press.

Edmondson, Jerold and Donald A. Burquest (1998) *A Survey of Linguistic Theories* (3rd ed.). Dallas: Summer Institute of Linguistics.

Emonds, Joseph (1980) Word order in Generative Grammar. *Journal of Linguistic Research* 1, 33–54.

Escalante, Fernando (1990) Voice and Argument Structure in Yaqui. Ph.D. dissertation, University of Arizona.

Fabb, Nigel (1994) *Sentence Structure*. London: Routledge.

Falk, Yehuda N. (2001) *Lexical-Functional Grammar: An Introduction to Parallel Constraint-Based Syntax*. Stanford: CSLI Publications.

Friedin, Robert (ed.) (1991) *Principles and Parameters in Comparative Grammar*. Cambridge: MIT Press.

Gair, James (1970) *Colloquial Sinhalese Clause Structure*. The Hague: Mouton.

Garrett, Merrill (1967) Syntactic Structures and Judgments of Auditory Events. Ph.D. dissertation, University of Illinois.

Gazdar, Gerald, Geoffrey Pullum, and Ivan Sag (eds.) (1983) *Order Concord and Constituency*. Dordrecht: Foris.

Gazdar, Gerald, Ewan Klein, Geoffrey Pullum, and Ivan Sag (1985) *Generalized Phrase Structure Grammar*. Cambridge: Harvard University Press.

Goodall, Grant (1993) On case and the passive morpheme. *Natural Language and Linguistic Theory* 11, 31–44.

Grimshaw, Jane (1990) *Argument Structure*. Cambridge: MIT Press.

Gruber, Jeffrey (1965) Studies in Lexical Relations. Ph.D. dissertation, MIT.

Haegeman, Liliane (1994) *Introduction to Government and Binding Theory*. Oxford: Blackwell.

Haegeman, Liliane and Jacqueline Guéron (1999) *English Grammar: A Generative Perspective*. Oxford: Blackwell.

Hale, Kenneth L. and Samuel Jay Keyser (eds.) (1993) *The View from Building 20: Essays in Honor of Sylvain Bromberger*. Cambridge: MIT Press.

Halle, Morris and Alec Marantz (1993) Distributed morphology and the pieces of inflection. In Kenneth L. Hale and Samuel Jay Keyser (eds.) *The View from Building 20: Essays in Honor of Sylvain Bromberger*. Cambridge: MIT Press. pp. 111–76.

Harley, Heidi (2002) Possession and the double object construction. *Linguistic Variation Yearbook* 2, 29–68.

Harley, Heidi (2006) *English Words: A Linguistic Introduction.* Oxford. Blackwell.

Heim, Irene and Kratzer, Angelika (1998) *Semantics in Generative Grammar.* Oxford: Blackwell.

Higginbotham, James (1980) Pronouns and bound variables. *Linguistic Inquiry* 11, 697–708.

Higginbotham, James (1985) A note on phrase markers. *MIT Working Papers in Linguistics* 6, 87–101.

Holzman, Mathilda (1997) *The Language of Children* (2nd ed.). Oxford: Blackwell.

Hornstein, Norbert (1994) An argument for Minimalism: the case of antecedent contained deletion. *Linguistic Inquiry* 25, 455–80.

Hornstein, Norbert (1999) Movement and control. *Linguistic Inquiry* 30, 69–96.

Huang, C.-T. James (1982) Logical Relations in Chinese and the Theory of Grammar. Ph.D. dissertation, MIT.

Huang, C.-T. James (1989) PRO-drop in Chinese. In Osvaldo Jaeggli and Kenneth Safir (eds.), *The Null Subject Parameter.* Dordrecht: Kluwer Academic Publishers. pp. 185–214

Hyams, Nina (1986) *Language Acquisition and the Theory of Parameters.* Dordrecht: D. Reidel.

Iatridou, Sabine (1990) About Agr(P). *Linguistic Inquiry* 21, 551–7.

Jackendoff, Ray (1977) *X-bar Syntax: A Theory of Phrase Structure.* Cambridge: MIT Press.

Jackendoff, Ray (1993) *Patterns in the Mind.* London: Harvester-Wheatsheaf.

Jacobs, Roderick and Peter Rosenbaum (eds.) (1970) *Readings in English Transformational Grammar.* Waltham: Ginn.

Jaeggli, Osvaldo (1986) Passive. *Linguistic Inquiry* 17, 587–622.

Jaeggli, Osvaldo and Kenneth Safir (eds.) (1989) *The Null Subject Parameter.* Dordrecht: Kluwer Academic Publishers.

Jelinek, Eloise and Fernando Escalante (2003) Unergative and unaccusative verbs in Yaqui. In Gene Casad and Thomas L. Willett (eds.), *Uto-Aztecan: Structural, Temporal and Geographic Perspectives: Papers in Honor of W. Miller.* Hermosillo: Universidad Autonoma de Sonora.

Johnson, Kyle (1991) Object positions. *Natural Language and Linguistic Theory* 9, 577–636.

Johnson, Kyle and Ian Roberts (eds.) (1991) *Beyond Principles and Parameters.* Dordrecht: Kluwer Academic Publishers.

Kaplan, Ronald (1995) The formal architecture of Lexical-Functional Grammar. In Mary Dalrymple, et al. (eds.), *Formal Issues in Lexical-Functional Grammar.* Stanford: CSLI Publications. pp. 7–27.

Kaplan, Ronald and Joan Bresnan (1982) Lexical-Functional Grammar: A formal system for grammatical representation. In Joan Bresnan (ed.), *The Mental Representation of Grammatical Relations.* Cambridge: MIT Press. pp. 173–281.

Katamba, Francis (2004) *English Words.* New York: Routledge.

Kayne, Richard (1994) *The Antisymmetry of Syntax.* Cambridge: MIT Press.

Koizumi, Masatoshi (1993) Object Agreement Phrases and the split VP hypothesis. *MIT Working Papers in Linguistics* 18, 99–148.

Koopman, Hilda (1984) *The Syntax of Verbs: From Verb Movement Rules in the Kru Languages to Universal Grammar.* Dordrecht: Foris.

Koopman, Hilda (1992) On the absence of case chains in Bambara. *Natural Language and Linguistic Theory* 10, 555–94.

Koopman, Hilda and Dominique Sportiche (1991) The position of subjects. *Lingua* 85, 211–58.

Kratzer, Angelika (1996) Severing the external argument from its verb. In Johan Rooryck and Laurie Zaring (eds.), *Phrase Structure and the Lexicon.* Dordrecht: Kluwer. pp. 109–37.

Kroeger, Paul (1993) *Phrase Structure and Grammatical Relations in Tagalog.* Stanford: CSLI Publications.

Kroskrity, Paul (1985) A holistic understanding of Arizona Tewa passives. *Language* 61, 306–28.

Landau, Idan (1999) Elements of Control. Ph.D. dissertation, MIT.

Larson, Richard (1988) On the double object construction. *Linguistic Inquiry* 19, 335–91.

Lasnik, Howard (1989) *Essays on Anaphora*. Dordrecht: Kluwer Academic Publishers.

Lasnik, Howard (1999a) *Minimalist Analyses*. Oxford: Blackwell.

Lasnik, Howard (1999b) On feature strength. *Linguistic Inquiry* 30, 197–219.

Lasnik, Howard and Mamoru Saito (1984) On the nature of proper government. *Linguistic Inquiry* 15, 235–89.

Lehmann, Winfred (1978) The great underlying ground-plans. In Winfred Lehmann (ed.), *Syntactic Typology*. Austin: University of Texas Press. pp. 3–56.

Levin, Beth (1993) *English Verb Classes and Alternations: A Preliminary Investigation*. Chicago: University of Chicago Press.

Lightfoot, David (1976) Trace theory and twice moved NPs. *Linguistic Inquiry* 7, 559–82.

Lightfoot, David (1991) *How to Set Parameters: Evidence from Language Change*. Cambridge: MIT Press.

Lightfoot, David and Norbert Hornstein (eds.) (1994) *Verb Movement*. Cambridge: Cambridge University Press.

Longobardi, Giuseppi (1994) Reference and proper names: A theory of N-movement in syntax and Logical Form. *Linguistic Inquiry* 25, 609–65.

Manning, Christopher and Ivan Sag (1998) Argument structure, valence and binding. *The Nordic Journal of Linguistics* 21, 107–44.

Manzini, Maria Rita (1983) On control and control theory. *Linguistic Inquiry* 14, 421–46.

Manzini, Maria Rita (1992) *Locality: A Theory and Some of Its Empirical Consequences*. Cambridge: MIT Press.

Marantz, Alec (1984). *On the Nature of Grammatical Relations*. Cambridge: MIT Press.

Marcus, Gary, Steven Pinker, Michael Ullman, Michelle Hollander, T. J. Rosen, and Fei Xu (1992) Overregularization in language acquisition. *Monographs of the Society for Research in Child Development* 57.

May, Robert (1985) *Logical Form*. Cambridge: MIT Press.

McCloskey, James (1979) *Transformational Syntax and Model Theoretic Semantics: A Case Study in Modern Irish*. Dordrecht: Reidel.

McCloskey, James (1980) Is there raising in Modern Irish? *Ériu* 31, 59–99.

McCloskey, James (1983) A VP in a VSO language. In Gerald Gazdar, Geoffrey Pullum, and Ivan Sag (eds.), *Order Concord and Constituency*. Dordrecht: Foris. pp. 9–55.

McCloskey, James (1991) Clause structure, ellipsis and proper government in Irish. *Lingua* 85, 259–302.

Moore, John (1998) Turkish copy raising and A-chain locality. *Natural Language and Linguistic Theory* 16, 149–89.

Ouhalla, Jamal (1990) *Introducing Transformational Grammar* (2nd ed.). London: Edward Arnold.

Perlmutter, David and Paul Postal (1984) The 1-Advancement Exclusiveness Law. In David Perlmutter and Carol Rosen (eds.), *Studies in Relational Grammar*. Chicago: University of Chicago Press. pp. 81–125.

Perlmutter, David and Carol Rosen (eds.) (1984) *Studies in Relational Grammar*. Chicago: University of Chicago Press.

Pesetsky, David (1994) *Zero Syntax: Experiencers and Cascades*. Cambridge: MIT Press.

Petter, Marga (1998) *Getting PRO under Control*. The Hague: Holland Academic Graphics.

Pinker, Steven (1995) *The Language Instinct*. New York: Harper Perennial.

Pollard, Carl and Ivan Sag (1992) Anaphors in English and the scope of Binding Theory. *Linguistic Inquiry* 23, 261–303.

Pollard, Carl and Ivan Sag (1994) *Head-Driven Phrase Structure Grammar*. Stanford: CSLI Publications and Chicago: University of Chicago Press.

Pollock, Jean-Yves (1989) Verb-movement, Universal Grammar, and the structure of IP. *Linguistic Inquiry* 20, 365–424.

Postal, Paul (1974) *On Raising*. Cambridge: MIT Press.

Pullum, Geoffrey (1997) The morpholexical nature of English *to*-contraction. *Language* 73, 79–102.

Pullum, Geoffrey and Barbara Scholz (2005) Contrasting applications of logic in natural language syntactic description. In Petr Hájek, Luis Vladés-Villanueva and Dag Westerstål (eds.), *Logic, Methodology and Philosophy of Science: Proceedings of the Twelfth International Congress*. London: King's College Publications. pp. 481-503.

Radford, Andrew (1988) *Transformational Grammar: A First Course*. Cambridge: Cambridge University Press.

Radford, Andrew (1997a) *Syntactic Theory and The Structure of English: A Minimalist Approach*. Cambridge: Cambridge University Press.

Radford, Andrew (1997b) *Syntax: A Minimalist Introduction*. Cambridge: Cambridge University Press.

Radford, Andrew (2004) *Minimalist Syntax: Exploring the Structure of English*. Cambridge: Cambridge University Press.

Reinhart, Tanya (1976) The Syntactic Domain of Anaphora. Ph.D. dissertation, MIT.

Reinhart, Tanya (1983) *Anaphora and Semantic Interpretation*. London: Croom Helm.

Richards, Norvin (1997) What Moves Where When in Which Language? Ph.D. dissertation, MIT.

Richter, Frank (2000) A Mathematical Formalism for Linguistic Theories with an Application in Head-Driven Phrase Structure Grammar. Ph.D. dissertation, University of Tübingen.

Ritter, Elizabeth (1988) A head movement approach to construct state noun phrases. *Linguistics* 26, 909–29.

Rivero, Maria-Louisa (1991) Long head movement and negation: Serbo-Croatian vs. Slovak and Czech. *The Linguistic Review* 8, 319–51.

Rizzi, Luigi (1982) *Issues in Italian Syntax*. Dordrecht: Foris.

Rizzi, Luigi (1990) *Relativized Minimality*. Cambridge: MIT Press.

Roberts, Ian (1997) *Comparative Syntax*. London: Edward Arnold.

Rosenbaum, Peter (1967) *The Grammar of English Predicate Complement Constructions*. Cambridge: MIT Press.

Ross, J. R. (Haj) (1967) Constraints on Variables in Syntax. Ph.D. dissertation, MIT.

Sag, Ivan and Thomas Wasow (1999) *Syntactic Theory: A Formal Introduction* (1st ed.). Stanford: CSLI Publications.

Sag, Ivan, Thomas Wasow and Emily Bender (2003) *Syntactic Theory: A Formal Introduction* (2nd ed.). Stanford: CSLI Publications.

Saito, Mamoru and Howard Lasnik (1994*) Move Alpha: Conditions on Its Application and Output*. Cambridge: MIT Press.

Sampson, Geoffrey (1997) *Educating Eve: The Language Instinct Debate*. London: Cassell.

Sapir, Edward and Morris Swadesh (1939) *Nootka Texts, Tales, and Ethnological Narratives, with Grammatical Notes and Lexical Materials*. Philadelphia: Linguistic Society of America.

Saxon, Leslie (1984) Disjoint anaphora and the binding theory. *Proceedings of WCCFL* 3, 242–51.

Seiler, Wolf (1978) The modalis case in Iñupiat. *Work Papers of the Summer Institute of Linguistics* 22, 71–85.

Sells, Peter (1985) *Lectures on Contemporary Syntactic Theories*. Stanford: CSLI Publications.

Sigurðsson, Halldór Ármann (1991) Icelandic case-marked PRO and the licensing of lexical arguments. *Natural Language and Linguistic Theory* 9, 327–65.

Simpson, Jane (1991) *Warlpiri Morpho-Syntax: A Lexicalist Approach.* Dordrecht: Kluwer Academic Publishers.

Soames, Scott and David M. Perlmutter (1979) *Syntactic Argumentation and the Structure of English.* Berkeley: University of California Press.

Sobin, Nicholas (1985) Case and agreement in the Ukrainian morphological passive construction. *Linguistic Inquiry* 16, 649–62.

Speas, Margaret (1990) *Phrase Structure in Natural Language.* Dordrecht: Kluwer Academic Publishers.

Sportiche, Dominique (1988) A theory of floating quantifiers and its corollaries for constituent structure. *Linguistic Inquiry* 19, 425–49.

Sproat, Richard (1985) Welsh syntax and VSO structure. *Natural Language and Linguistic Theory* 3, 173–216.

Stechow, Arnim von (1996) The different readings of *wieder* 'again': A structural account. *Journal of Semantics* 13, 87–138.

Stenson, Nancy (1989) Irish autonomous impersonals. *Natural Language and Linguistic Theory* 7, 379–406.

Stowell, Tim (1981) Origins of Phrase Structure. Ph.D. dissertation, MIT.

Szabolcsi, Anna (1994) The noun phrase. In *Syntax and Semantics 27: The Syntax of Hungarian.* New York: Academic Press. pp. 179–279.

Travis, Lisa de Mena (1984) Parameters and Effects of Word Order Derivation. Ph.D. dissertation, MIT.

Uriagereka, Juan (1998) *Rhyme and Reason: An Introduction to Minimalist Syntax.* Cambridge: MIT Press.

Vikner, Sten (1995) *Verb Movement and Expletive Subjects in the Germanic Languages.* Oxford: Oxford University Press.

Webelhuth, Gert (1995) *Government and Binding Theory and the Minimalist Program.* Oxford: Blackwell.

Weerman, Fred (1989) *The V2 Conspiracy.* Dordrecht: Foris.

Williams, Edwin (1980) Predication. *Linguistic Inquiry* 11, 203–38.

Williams, Edwin (1983) Semantic vs. syntactic categories. *Linguistics and Philosophy* 6, 423–46.

Williams, Edwin (1994) *Thematic Structure in Syntax.* Cambridge: MIT Press.

Zaenen, Annie, Joan Maling, and Hoskuldur Thráinsson (1985) Case and grammatical functions: The Icelandic passive. *Natural Language and Linguistic Theory* 3, 441–83.

Index